1513
N
2 PARIS

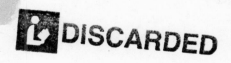

HISTORY OF
THE SECOND WORLD WAR

UNITED KINGDOM MILITARY SERIES

Edited by J. R. M. BUTLER

The authors of the Military Histories have been given full access to official documents. They and the editor are alone responsible for the statements made and the views expressed.

The Prime Minister with President Roosevelt on board the U.S. Cruiser AUGUSTA. The officer with them is Captain Eliott Roosevelt, son of the President. August, 1941.

GRAND STRATEGY

VOLUME III

June 1941–August 1942

by

J. M. A. GWYER
(Part I)

and

J. R. M. BUTLER
(Part II)

LONDON: 1964
HER MAJESTY'S STATIONERY OFFICE

First published 1964

© *Crown copyright* 1964

Published by
HER MAJESTY'S STATIONERY OFFICE

To be purchased from
York House, Kingsway, London W.C.2
423 Oxford Street, London W.1
13A Castle Street, Edinburgh 2
109 St. Mary Street, Cardiff
39 King Street, Manchester 2
50 Fairfax Street, Bristol 1
35 Smallbrook, Ringway, Birmingham 5
80 Chichester Street, Belfast 1
or through any bookseller
Price £4 4s. 0d.
For Parts I and II
(not sold separately)

Printed in England for Her Majesty's Stationery Office
by Cox & Wyman Ltd., London, Fakenham and Reading
Maps by Ordnance Survey

GRAND STRATEGY Volume III

CORRECTIONS

PART I

Page 1 para 2, line 5	*for* '$300,000' *read* '$200,000'
Page 53 footnote	*for* 'Nuremburg' *read* 'Nuremberg'
Page 64 line 13 of quotation	*for* 'rebound' *read* 'redound'
Page 90 footnote, line 3	*for* 'Rooseved' *read* 'Roosevelt'
Page 185 para 3, line 13	*for* 'Germany' *read* 'German'
Page 204 para 2, line 25	*for* 'Harstadt' *read* 'Harstad'†
Page 369 para 2, line 12	*for* 'Commander' *read* 'Commanders'
Page 386 footnote 1 & 2	*for* 'Crutwell' *read* 'Cruttwell'
Page 396 line 2 of quote	*for* 'principal' *read* 'principle'

PART II

Page 449 para 3, line 3	*read* 'three or four divisions'
Page 465 line 11 (and index	*read* 'Lieut.-General T. J. Hutton'
Page 465 last line	*read* 'the Japanese forces advancing through Tenasserim towards Rangoon'
Page 466 para 2, line 12	*delete* 'in Burma and' *
Page 491 line 12	*read* 'Diego Suarez'
Page 523 para 3, line 3	*read* '25th June'
Page 546 footnote 4, line 1	*read* '1957'
Page 574 footnote 2	*read* Chap. XIX p. 472
Page 576 para 3, line 3	*read* 'Boulogne'
Page 579 line 13	*read* '18th April'
Page 636 para 3, line 1	*read* '25th July'
Page 688 under 'Sir S. Cripps'	*read* 'Leader of the House of Commons'

* Note: *There is no evidence that the authorities in Burma expressed any lack of confidence in General Hutton. The author regrets that Burma was mistakenly, and unjustifiably, mentioned in this connexion.*

† *And in Index.*

CABINET OFFICE
January 1966

LONDON: HER MAJESTY'S STATIONERY OFFICE

CONTENTS

Page

APPENDICES

(Printed in Part II)

MAPS

IN PART I

IN PART II

Note. In Map 8 and the End Paper to Part II the Andaman Is. are wrongly shown as the Nicobar Is. and *vice versa.*

PHOTOGRAPHS

PREFACE

THE PERIOD OF the war covered in the present volume is the last in which the enemy powers enjoyed the initiative; it is the first in which the means of victory, in men and materials, were assured to the Allies. The book begins with the German invasion of Russia and includes the entry into the war of Japan and the United States. By its close the Japanese expansion had been checked by the American victories in the Pacific; the Axis attack on Egypt had been held west of the Delta, and an Allied descent on French North Africa was impending; the German armies had failed to secure the oilfields of South Russia and were soon to meet disaster at Stalingrad. But in the meantime vast areas and important cities of the Soviet Union had been overrun; the Western Allies had paid heavy penalties for their unpreparedness in the Far East; in the Atlantic the submarine threat had not been mastered. The British bombing offensive was beginning to show results but was not yet seriously interfering with the German war-effort.

The volume describes the creation of an Anglo-American organization for the central direction of the war and the emergence of an Allied strategy. It shows how this strategy was based on the decision to make the defeat of Germany its first object; how it was affected by the determination to maintain the resistance of Russia, whose early collapse was held to be more than possible; and how the British and Americans at length agreed after protracted controversy on the field of their major effort in 1942.

The present volume was not planned as a composite work. It had been intended that the whole should be written by Mr. Gwyer, and it was only when it became clear that he would not be able to carry his work beyond the end of 1941 that the Editor undertook to write the chapters dealing with events in 1942 which now form Part II of the book. This arrangement inevitably involved differences of style and presentation which both authors regret, while expressing the hope that they will not cause any serious difficulty to the reader.

We have been given unrestricted access to the official records. Besides these our most important source has been the Churchill papers. We are grateful also for the use of private diaries and other material made available to us, as well as for the comments and criticisms of all those who have been good enough to read our chapters in draft. We alone however are responsible for the views expressed in this book; we have received no requests of an official nature for any alterations of substance in our text.

For parts of our story we have been largely dependent on the specialized researches of our colleagues in the military, civil, and diplomatic series of the British official history; we owe much also to the official United States and Commonwealth histories and we are grateful to their authors for reading and commenting on our drafts. The volumes of the official Soviet history began to appear too late for us to use them with profit.

We have also to acknowledge the help freely given us by the British Service Historical Sections both in placing their monographs at our disposal and in answering our exacting questions.

Our treatment of Naval and Air matters owes much to the knowledge which our colleague Captain S. W. Roskill, R.N., and Messrs. J. C. Nerney and L. A. Jackets of the Air Historical Branch generously put at our service.

For information derived from captured documents and other enemy sources, German-Italian and Japanese respectively, we are greatly indebted to Mr. Brian Melland and to Colonel G. T. Wards. Of Mr. Melland's staff we should like in particular to thank Mr. E. M. Robertson for his invaluable monograph on the Eastern Front; Mrs. J. M. Hamilton for a similar paper on German-Italian operations in the Mediterranean; and Dr. G. W. S. Friedrichsen, who has supplied us with information from the captured documents held in the United States.

A study by Mrs. Oakley of the policy governing Bomber Command's expansion and operations has been extremely useful.

Colonel T. M. M. Penney has again superintended the drawing of the maps; we are most grateful for his skilled assistance. For the use of several of the maps, originally prepared under their instructions, we have to thank our colleagues, the authors of the relevant volumes of this history.

We wish further to express our thanks for their advice and criticisms to the members of the Editor's Advisory Panel, namely, Admiral Sir Charles Daniel and Lieut.-General Sir Frederick Morgan (in succession respectively to Vice-Admiral Sir Geoffrey Blake and the late Lieut.-General Sir Henry Pownall), Air Chief Marshal Sir Guy Garrod and Lieut.-General Sir Ian Jacob.

In the Cabinet Office, the late Mr. A. B. Acheson gave constant assistance in the early days of the book; in its later stages it has owed much to Mr. Michael Cary and Mr. A. J. D. Woods. We are greatly indebted also to Mr. A. G. Banks, Mr. F. J. Trigger and Miss A. L. Cooper of the Cabinet Office Staff.

We have left it to the last to acknowledge our debt to Miss P. M. McCallum, who acted as research-assistant to each of us in turn. Without her help in preparing drafts and studies on particular subjects it would not have been possible to bring into focus the very varied material which goes to the making of a strategic history. Much of the narrative is based directly on her work; and we have also to thank her for saving us from many errors and omissions. Her final contribution has been to compile the index. We cannot complete our thanks and acknowledgements without recording that the volume as a whole owes more to her than to anyone.

In conclusion the Editor would like to take this opportunity to express his appreciation of the great services rendered to the military histories by Lord Normanbrook. His interest and support have far exceeded any which might have been reasonably expected from the head of the Government Department under whose auspices the series is being produced.

July,   J. M. A. G.
1963.   J. R. M. B.

PART I

by

J. M. A. GWYER

Chapters I – XV

CHAPTER I

THE OUTLOOK IN JUNE

(i)

Growing Strength of the Allies

THIS VOLUME MAY well begin by reminding the reader of a meeting which took place at St. James's Palace on 12th June, 1941.[1] Its purpose was a formal declaration by the Allies that they would continue to stand together until the war had been won. Apart from Great Britain, the acknowledged leader of the alliance, and the countries of the British Commonwealth, nine nations were represented: Belgium, Czechoslovakia, France (in the persons of General de Gaulle and the Free French Committee), Greece, Luxemburg, the Netherlands, Norway, Poland and Yugo-slavia. This was a much wider combination than the one which had faced Germany in September 1939; it was also much weaker. The nine European nations had already suffered defeat in the field and were represented in London only by governments in exile, which dis-posed of no more than a shadow of their former collective strength.

Nevertheless, they retained certain assets of considerable economic and strategic importance. In the difficult months before the passage of the Lend-Lease Act, for example, the Belgian Government had been able to provide gold-cover for our transactions with the United States to the value of $300 million.[2] The Norwegian, Dutch and Greek Governments still controlled powerful merchant-fleets, in-valuable to an alliance which depended so much on seaborne trade. The Dutch Government also exercised sovereignty over a large colonial empire, including the wealthy and vulnerable Dutch East Indies, later to become the focal point of the war in the Far East. The Belgian Government and the Free French likewise controlled a vast and strategically important area of Central Africa, across part of which ran the air-reinforcement route to the Middle East. Lastly, most of the exiled governments were still in a position to put limited— sometimes very limited—forces into the field. In June 1941, these appeared to be negligible; but the time would come when Dutch forces in the Far East, Polish forces in Europe and French forces in both theatres would play an important part in Allied operations.

---

[1] See Vol. II, p, 560.

[2] Duncan Hall, *North American Supply*, (1955) p. 272.

To speak of an alliance was not therefore an empty or merely symbolic phrase. At this stage in the war the main burden, military, economic and political, necessarily rested on the British Commonwealth; but the nations of Europe still had a contribution to make, and one which would grow with time. That did not mean, however, that the alliance as it then stood was adequately equipped for its task. On the contrary, though it might continue to hold its own, to keep alive the spirit of resistance in Europe and to harass and weaken Germany, it was more than doubtful whether it could ever find the strength to win a decisive victory. But that did not reduce the importance of the alliance or the significance of its task, which was to remain in being, to fight and to provide a rallying-point for the uncommitted nations of the world, when they in turn were drawn into the struggle, whether from motives of idealism or in response to some further threat or aggression by the Axis powers.

With this preamble we may turn to the military situation. At the beginning of June 1941, it still appeared very grave, though no longer so desperate as it had been in the previous year. The fact that the Allies were still in undisputed control of their main base and centre of production in the British Isles was a major victory in itself. Moreover, in the twelve months' grace which had been won since Dunkirk, Great Britain's defensive strength had increased considerably. It could not yet be said that the country was proof against invasion—the threat still remained and would continue to influence Allied strategy for many months to come; but it was no longer so immediate or so apparently overwhelming as it had been in 1940.

The strength of Fighter Command, in this context the country's first line of defence, had risen from 55½ operational squadrons at the beginning of the Battle of Britain to 77 squadrons by June 1941. There was little reason to expect that the mass daylight attacks, which had been the intended prelude to invasion a year before, would be repeated; a second trial of strength on the same terms would even have been welcome. The night-bombardment, to which the enemy had turned when their daylight offensive was failing, had also lost some of its terror. The opening of the attack had found the country's night-defences in a primitive stage of development; and during the first three months the enemy had suffered a negligible rate of loss, of the order of one aircraft for every 200 sorties flown or even less.[1] Yet despite this almost complete immunity the attack had failed to produce the decisive results for which Germany had hoped. There had been much loss of life and extensive damage to property, including industrial damage of some importance; but Great Britain

---

[1] This refers only to losses inflicted by the defence; total losses, including accidents of all kinds, were higher.

had emerged into 1941 with her war-potential intact and even enlarged.

Over the turn of the year the efficiency of the night-defences had been much improved. The inland warning-system had been reorganized and extended and good progress had been made with the application of radar to night-fighter and gunnery control. By the end of May it was beginning to be possible to feel that a significant rate of loss was being imposed on the enemy. No doubt there was some illusion in this; and the calling-off of the night attack, which occurred at about this time, was not in fact the result of a victory but of a change in the enemy's strategy. Nevertheless, there were solid grounds for encouragement. It was clear that, if the attack were renewed on a major scale, it would meet opposition which, though it might not be decisive, would certainly be stronger than any that the *Luftwaffe* had yet encountered.

It thus appeared by June that the command of the air over the British Isles, on which so much depended, had passed or was passing into Allied hands. So long as that position could be held, the danger of invasion was thrust into the background. It was also true that Britain now possessed, apart from her air-shield, something like an adequate land-force with which to meet the threat, if it should develop again. The Chiefs of Staff had estimated that the defence of the United Kingdom required an army of 37⅓ (equivalent) divisions, ten of which should be armoured. By June, if one reckoned in numbers of men only, this garrison was almost up to strength. It is true that the training and equipment of the troops was not uniform and that there was still a grave shortage of armour. In place of the ten armoured divisions of the estimate it had only been possible to form five complete divisions and 2–2/3 Army Tank Brigades; and of these, two divisions and all but four battalions of the brigades were either without tanks or had only a small proportion of their establishment. But despite these obvious deficiencies, which were slowly being filled, Home Forces was already a formidable instrument of war by comparison with the disorganized, unequipped and even partly demoralized army with which we should have faced invasion in 1940.

In all these respects Britain's recovery had been miraculous: her survival, which had seemed impossible a year before, was now a fact. But this did not mean, unfortunately, that the general strategic position had changed. The Allies were still living under the shadow of their earlier disasters. In the spring of 1940 it had been possible to believe that, whatever defeats or setbacks might be met on the way, superiority in manpower and war-potential must ultimately ensure an Allied victory. But now that advantage had passed to the enemy:

'The summer disasters had indeed brought down the balance of manpower in favour of the Axis. Crude comparisons of population were, of course, highly misleading. If all the heads of the British Empire were counted, the balance was still weighted in favour of Britain; the 400 million and more in India and the Colonies were decisive. But the economic and social structure of the Colonial Dependencies could not sustain a ponderous mobilization and the productive effort of India was as yet barely in its initial stages. A more realistic comparison would emphasize rather the combined strength of Britain and the Dominions, pitted against the Europe over which Germany sprawled—some 75 million against more than 200 million. This comparison was also very crude. For example, output per head in many of the agricultural communities of Europe was notoriously low. On the other hand, the United Kingdom was separated from the Dominions by thousands of miles of ocean. For these and similar reasons, there could be little statistical refinement in comparisons of strength. One thing, however, seemed clear. Provided the Germans were sufficiently ruthless, their war effort could not fail for lack of labour. But how could Britain ever hope to arm, and place in the field, forces large enough to conquer?'[1]

For a brief moment in the spring of 1941 it had seemed that an answer to this question might be found in the Middle East. The defeat of the Italians in North Africa and Abyssinia, the sturdy resistance of Greece, Turkey's hesitations and finally the Simovič *coup d'etat* in Yugoslavia, had all combined to open a bright, though fleeting, prospect. If a combined front could be formed in Greece and Yugoslavia, reinforced from the Middle East and supported by Turkey, then the Allies would acquire a new bridgehead on the Continent and with it sufficient resources of manpower to challenge Germany again by land. These were the thoughts which had been in Mr. Churchill's mind at the end of March and which he had confided to Mr. Fadden in a telegram sent immediately after the Yugoslav *coup d'etat*:

'When a month ago we decided on sending an army to Greece, it looked a rather bleak military adventure dictated by *noblesse oblige*. Thursday's events show the far-reaching effect of this and other measures taken on the whole Balkan situation. German plans have been upset and we may cherish new hopes of forming a Balkan Front with Turkey, comprising about 70 Allied Divisions from the four powers concerned. This is, of course, by no means certain yet. But even now it puts "Lustre"[2] in its true setting not as an isolated military act, but as a prime mover in a large design.'

---

[1] W. K. Hancock and M. M. Gowing, *British War Economy* (1949), p. 281.
[2] The Greek operation.

But this was not to be. Before even the semblance of a Balkan front could be created, the German invasion of Greece and Yugoslavia had destroyed the foundations on which it might have rested. At the same time a series of other operations had brought the main Allied position in the Middle East into serious danger. By the end of April, resistance in the Balkans was over and a counter-offensive on the Libyan front, led by Rommel's *Afrika Korps*, had recouped all the Italian losses of the previous January and carried the fighting back to the Egyptian frontier. By the middle of May, Raschid Ali's revolt, inspired and to some extent supported by Germany, was threatening our control of Iraq; the air-borne attack on Crete was about to begin; and there were persistent rumours of German intervention in Syria. Middle East Command, so lately on the crest of the wave, now found itself exposed to attacks and diversionary movements on every side. It was a reversal of fortune as sudden and almost as serious as that which the Allies had suffered in the West in the previous year.

By the middle of June the situation had been partly restored. The Allies had reconciled themselves, as well as they might, to the loss of Greece and Crete and their last foothold on the Continent. The German-Italian attack in the Western Desert, having spent its initial force, had been checked at Sollum. Firmness and vigour had quelled the Iraqi revolt; and the occupation of Syria by combined British and Free French forces was proceeding. For the moment the Middle East was safe; but it was not supposed that the respite would be long. All Germany's recent actions suggested that she was preparing a major offensive, to which her operations in the Balkans and the Western Desert and her political intrigues in Iraq and Syria had been merely the prelude. No one could tell how soon the blow would fall or from which direction it would come, whether from the north through Turkey and Syria or (as now seemed more probable) from the west by a further reinforcement of the Italian thrust on Alexandria. But that it would come was regarded as certain; and it was an open question how far it could be met.

The Chiefs of Staff considered that an adequate defence of the Middle East would require, apart from local forces, a field-army of 19 divisions, including 5 armoured divisions, supported by an air force of not less than 22 fighter and 23 bomber squadrons. By June this total was not even in sight. Reinforcements were flowing out from the United Kingdom as fast as they could be spared and shipped; but the best estimate was that by the beginning of August, if no heavy casualties had been incurred meanwhile, the army in the Middle East would consist of only $11\frac{1}{3}$ infantry divisions, of which five were on a reduced establishment and only partially trained, and $1\frac{1}{2}$ armoured divisions. In the air there would be 35 squadrons—20 fighter and 15 bomber—in place of 45. There was little hope of further reinforcement, at least on a major scale, so long as the United Kingdom itself remained under threat and the garrison there was still below its full strength.

Under these conditions was it worth while to try to hold the Middle East? A withdrawal—or for that matter a defeat—would certainly leave very valuable prizes within the enemy's grasp. The elimination of Allied naval control of the eastern Mediterranean would relieve Germany of any immediate anxiety over her oil supplies by opening the sea-route from Rumania to Italy. From Egypt and Turkey she could expect to draw many commodities, notably foodstuffs, cotton, chrome and wool, of which her economy was greatly in need. The denial to the Allies of the Iraqi oilfields, even if she were unable to exploit them herself, would be an important stroke; and from advanced bases in the same area she would also be able to bring the more important Persian oilfields, and the refinery at Abadan, within range of air-attack. All this was much for Germany to gain. On the other hand, it could be argued that the economic loss to the Allies would not be catastrophic, so long as Abadan itself could be protected and naval control preserved in the Red Sea and the Persian Gulf. And from other military points of view it would come as an immense relief to abandon the Middle East and re-deploy naval forces and shipping, to say nothing of troops and aircraft, which were urgently needed elsewhere.

Against this had to be set the incalculable moral effects of yet another withdrawal. They would be felt not only by public opinion at home, already depressed by a long series of disasters, but also in the remaining neutral countries and especially in the United States. Confidence in the Allies would be further shaken with an immediate effect on the efficiency of the blockade and the extent of the economic and political support which we might expect in the future. There was also another argument, simple but decisive, in favour of continued resistance. The Middle East was the only theatre in which the Allies were fighting Germany by land as well as by sea and in the air, or in which they had any immediate prospect of doing so. Since wars cannot be won without fighting, the only course was to continue, even though it might be at a disadvantage or in vain.

For these reasons the Cabinet had remained firmly resolved to defend the Middle East and had not even brought the alternative into formal discussion. Their confidence was rewarded by events. But there is no doubt that it seemed at the time to imply a dangerous dispersal of force, the more so since an attack on Suez was not the only, or even the most pressing, danger which threatened the Allies in the Mediterranean. There was also the risk—then regarded almost as a certainty—of a German move into Spain with the object of capturing Gibraltar and closing the Straits. By this operation Germany would deny the Allies their only naval base between Plymouth and Freetown, clear the western Mediterranean of hostile forces and herself acquire a series of new bases from which to extend her surface and submarine attacks on Allied shipping in the Atlantic. The consequences in terms of the war at sea would be little short of disastrous; but no completely effective counter-stroke could be devised. We may quote from the strategic review which the Joint Planning Staff circulated in June:

'We do not believe that Spain, though she may procrastinate until Germany's hands are freed elsewhere, will offer any organized resistance once she is faced with an ultimatum capable of immediate enforcement. Even if she did resist, we are unable to give effective military assistance and within three to four weeks Germany would be in a position, if not to capture Gibraltar, at least to deny us the use of the naval base. In the more probable event of Germany acting with the passive acquiescence or active assistance of Spain, she would reach her objective in a matter of days.

At any time that Germany chooses and whatever line Spain may take, the naval base at Gibraltar can, therefore, be denied to us. We believe that sooner or later Germany will take this action.

Subsequently, to maintain any form of blockade, as well as to restrict the egress of Italian or even French naval units into the Atlantic, an alternative naval base must be acquired. Moreover, a refuelling point between the United Kingdom and Freetown is essential. To meet such a threat, we must have the use of the Canaries and, if possible, of the Azores as well.

Realizing the importance of these islands to us, we consider it very possible that Germany will try to occupy the Canaries coincidentally with an ultimatum to Spain, thereby depriving us of any chance of a peaceful occupation even in the unlikely event of Spanish resistance. To recapture the Azores against German opposition may be possible, though costly, but once installed in the Canaries, it is doubtful if we could eject the enemy.

In a matter so vital to our conduct of the war we feel that no chances can be taken. Had it not been that passage through the Straits of Gibraltar is essential to our ability to reinforce the Middle East quickly, we should have recommended immediate action to secure at least the naval base in the Canaries, even if we thereby provoked Spain into open hostility. By such action, though the loss of Gibraltar to the Navy, always inevitable, might have been accelerated, we should at least have made certain of an alternative base which would have enabled us to protect our trade and prosecute our offensive with some measure of success. Although such a postponement may thus be necessary while the situation in the Middle East remains critical, we must at all times be prepared to act instantly, if there are any indications of Germany's attention turning to the Western Mediterranean.'

This was the most that could be done and the Cabinet had already accepted the policy. As early as July 1940 plans had been formed for the occupation of either the Spanish or the Portuguese islands in the event of a German move. Since then a succession of postponements or changes of plan had intervened as the political situation fluctuated; but the project had always remained in being and forces had continued to stand by in England, Gibraltar or Freetown. By June 1941 three separate operations were still on hand: Operation 'Thruster' for the Azores, Operation 'Springboard' for Madeira and Operation 'Puma', the largest of the three, for the Canaries. Troops and shipping had been assembled; but everything was held in suspense by a recent Cabinet decision to postpone action for another month. Germany had not yet moved; and nothing was to be gained by antagonizing Spain, still less our ancient ally Portugal, prematurely or unnecessarily.

The three operations were not, however, dismounted. By a later decision, taken in July, they were combined into a single, enlarged force, for which the code-name Operation 'Pilgrim' was adopted, and in that form continued to stand by at short notice during the rest of the year. The great potential importance of the operation and the need for instant action if the moment came, made this arrangement inevitable; but it imposed an altogether disproportionate strain on the meagre resources of the time. Although the land-forces amounted to less than a division with certain Special Service detachments, or approximately 24,000 men in all, the provision of landing-craft and assault-shipping was a major commitment, absorbing almost the whole of the fleet which then existed. As we shall see in a later chapter, so long as Force 'Pilgrim' remained in being, it was impossible to mount any other amphibious operation of equivalent size.

(ii)

The War at Sea

So far we have spoken only of the war by land and in the air. But in the summer of 1941 by far the most immediate and pressing danger to confront the Allies was by sea. A new and still more threatening phase of that intense struggle, which the Prime Minister named the Battle of the Atlantic, had opened at the end of February or the beginning of March. It had been designed by Hitler as a combined operation in which the German surface and submarine fleets and the *Luftwaffe* would act together to strangle the British Isles. 'In the spring,' he had said in January, 'our U-boat war will begin at sea; the *Luftwaffe* also will play its part and the whole *Wehrmacht* will force a decision by hook or by crook'.[1] Events were to show that he had spoken prematurely and that German naval strength in 1941 was not in fact equal to a decisive campaign. But the margin was very narrow. During the opening months of the offensive appalling losses were inflicted on the Allies; and if the attack had been able to keep its initial impetus for even a short while longer, the results might well have been crippling.

In June the crisis was at its height. The Allies had entered 1941 with a cargo fleet which was already between 1·5 and 2·5 million tons smaller than it had been at the outbreak of war.[2] Moreover, the carrying capacity of the ships had been reduced by the exigencies of war, by longer and sometimes slower voyages in convoy or by evasive routes and by delays and congestion in port. The Allies' shipping capital was declining and they now had to face a heavy increase in the current rate of loss. During March, April and May a total of 473 ships of 1,728,649 tons had been sunk by enemy action or natural causes. This was the equivalent of an annual loss of nearly 7 million tons; and there was no sign in June that the rate was falling. Damaged shipping was also accumulating in port far faster than the dockyards could deal with it. By the end of April something like a million or a million and a half tons had been immobilized from this cause alone. Every effort was being made to accelerate repairs and clear the yards; but there was little hope of any substantial reduction for many months. In the meantime ships put out of service for repair added the equivalent of several million tons to the prospective annual loss.[3]

These strains were clearly reflected in a falling rate of imports. A calculation made in June showed that, in order to feed her population and maintain her war production, Great Britain required to import between 36 and 38·5 million tons of dry cargo in 1941. She also needed, in the eight months between May and December, to bring in not less than 720 tanker-cargoes of oil. But at the rate at which cargo was actually being landed she would only receive 28·5 million tons of dry cargo and 660 tanker-cargoes of oil. By the end of the year there would be a deficit of nearly 7 million tons of supply imports (raw materials and semi-manufactured goods) and 2 million tons of food. Oil stocks, which were already nearing the danger point, would have shrunk by another 318,000 tons; and imports of manufactured goods (at that time mainly American munitions) would also be in arrears.

---

[1] *Reichstag* speech of 30th January, 1941.
[2] This was the estimate made at the time. The difficulty of giving an accurate figure is explained in *British War Economy*, pp. 248–68.
[3] S. W. Roskill, *The War at Sea* (1954), Vol. I, App. R; Hancock and Gowing, p. 251.

For the moment all these shortages, except the last, could be met by withdrawals from stock. This process might tide over 1941; but the outlook thereafter was bleak indeed.

The Navy, already at the utmost strain, could promise little. It was true that by the spring of 1941 we had begun to reassert control over our own coastal waters and that U-boats could no longer operate with impunity close inshore, as they had done with deadly effect in 1940. The battle was being gradually pushed out into the empty waters of the Atlantic. By April new bases in Iceland had made it possible to give convoys some degree of anti-submarine protection as far west as 35°. By June, with the help of the Canadian Navy, arrangements were in train to provide continuous anti-submarine escorts, though still inadequate in strength, over the whole Atlantic route. At the same time the number of independently-routed ships, always the most vulnerable, was drastically reduced; from the end of June onwards all ships of a speed of 15 knots or below sailed in convoy. But these measures had not yet reduced the rate of loss. Since March U-boats alone had accounted for 142 ships of a total of 817,887 tons—an average of over 270,000 tons a month, which was comparable with the worst period of 1940. Moreover, the enemy's strength was increasing almost daily. In April Germany had had only 32 operational U-boats. By July, as the new submarines laid down in 1939 began to come into service, she would have 60 or more and by the end of the year perhaps 100. It seemed, therefore, that each improvement in the defence would be offset, or more than offset, by a proportionate increase in the weight of the attack.[1]

And the submarine war was only one aspect of the offensive. At the end of February a new directive had switched the *Luftwaffe*'s main effort to 'targets the destruction of which will assist or supplement the war at sea.'[2] This had marked the last and potentially most dangerous phase of the night attack, a concentrated bombardment of the west coast ports, through which the bulk of incoming traffic then passed, combined with a great increase in aerial mining and night attacks on coastal shipping. At the same time the creation of the new post of *Fliegerfuehrer Atlantik* had temporarily stilled inter-service jealousies and brought the German submarine command and the long-range bombers of the *Luftwaffe* into effective co-operation. The success of these measures was immediate. During March, April and May losses directly attributable to air-attack had reached the total of 157 ships of 583,070 tons.[3] The bomber had become a naval weapon

---

[1] Roskill, Vol. I, Chap XXI and App. Q and R.

[2] Fuehrer Directive of 28th February, 1941.

[3] This figure includes losses by air-attack in operations off Greece and Crete; but does not include ships sunk by mines laid by aircraft.

as formidable as the U-boat—within its more limited range perhaps even more formidable.

Lastly, there was the threat, at this time still acute, of a major raid by units of the German surface fleet. Earlier in the year one battle-ship and three cruisers—the *Admiral Scheer*, the *Scharnhorst*, the *Gneisenau* and the *Hipper*—in three relatively short cruises had sunk nearly 200,000 tons of shipping and disorganized the cycle of Atlantic convoys to an extent, measured in loss of imports, which was almost as serious as the actual sinkings. In April, after the return of these ships to port, a new and larger incursion had been planned, using the newly-commissioned battleship *Bismarck* and the cruiser *Prinz Eugen* in conjunction with a second raid by the *Scharnhorst* and *Gneisenau*. At the end of May two Allied operations—the continuous bombing of the *Scharnhorst* and *Gneisenau* in Brest and the long sea-chase which ended in the sinking of the *Bismarck*—had temporarily dislocated this plan. But the danger was still there. The two cruisers had only been damaged not sunk and other heavy ships, including the *Tirpitz* and the *Luetzow*, were already coming into service. A new break-out in force, of which it was hard to foresee the consequence, might occur at any time.[1]

In face of these varied dangers, actual and potential, the Allies could not look forward to any early relief from a strain which grew greater with each month that passed. They were obliged to expect, even on the most conservative estimate, that before the end of the year their merchant fleet would have suffered a further loss of at least 4 or 5 million tons. If this process continued, their entire war-effort would be strangled at the source. But how could the losses be made up? The combined output of all Commonwealth yards did not exceed 1 million tons of new shipping a year.[2] Opportunities to aquire additional tonnage by purchase or charter were much restricted; and it was not expected that more than ·5 million tons could be brought in in 1941. Various economies were possible in the use of shipping, in-cluding the acceleration of repairs and of the normal turn-round of ships in port, and, perhaps, some reduction in the 4·2 million tons, which were then allocated to the Services and thus largely withdrawn from the import trade. But it was estimated that all these measures taken together would barely suffice to maintain imports at the level of 28·5 million tons a year, to which they had sunk by June. At the end of 1941 there would be a deficit of at least 7 or 8 million tons and no prospect (with a fleet still further reduced) of making it good in the future.

There was only one other source to which the Allies could apply for

---

[1] Roskill, Vol. I, Chap, XVIII.

[2] These calculations refer only to dry-cargo ships; tankers were a separate problem.

help. Early in March the Prime Minister had sent Sir Arthur Salter to Washington with instructions 'to bring [the facts] home to the United States administration and to convince them that they must act accordingly'. There was no doubt of America's theoretical ability to help. In the First World War she had built up almost from nothing a shipyard capacity which had enabled her by 1918 to turn out 4 million tons of new shipping a year. An equivalent effort would meet, almost exactly, the Allies' annual net loss; but whether America would be willing, or indeed able, to make such an effort while she herself was still at peace, was more than doubtful. Moreover, even if a building programme on this scale were accepted at once, the Allies could not draw benefit from it for at least another eighteen months. In the meanwhile the outlook was very grave.

Such was the shipping position as it appeared in June. It seemed then that disaster was imminent and could only be averted by timely and extensive American help. But even this would not provide a complete solution. In the immediate future the use of American shipping might make it possible to raise imports to what was then believed to be the level of minimum requirements. In following years an enlarged American building programme might keep pace with current sinkings and the Allied merchant fleet at least grow no smaller. But, assuming that the same high rate of loss continued, there would be little or no margin on which to rebuild the fleet which had already been sunk, still less to enlarge it. It followed that, unless some radical improvement could be made in the defence, the shipping shortage in a more or less acute form would become permanent. Allied strategy, especially so far as it concerned any future offensive, would have to conform to this new limitation. On this point the Joint Planners' paper, already quoted, was explicit:

> 'We conclude from the foregoing statement of the position that it is only by a reduction in the rate of loss that a real margin of safety can be acquired. The increment to our escort forces which would result from the entry of America into the war would have an immediate effect on our shipping losses. Apart from the use of the Irish bases, it is the only means by which we can rapidly improve our position at sea.
>
> It also becomes clear that until hopes give place to concrete reality, there is a paramount need for the exercise of the greatest economy in the use of our available shipping. It follows that, during this period, no new large-scale military commitments involving an ocean passage can be justified.

These conclusions, as will be seen, exercised a strong influence on Allied planning at the time. They were held, indeed, to govern the whole basis of future operations. But this, as it proved, was a false view. Inevitable though they appeared at the time, the J.P.S. con-

clusions were not in fact well-founded and had been partially dis-
proved even before the end of the year. It is true that the shipping
shortage continued and even grew worse in 1942—it was not until
well on in 1943 that the Allies were finally relieved of their major
anxieties on this head; but its effects were never so stringent, nor
strategically so crippling, as it had seemed in June that they would be.
There were many reasons for this, some of which lie outside the scope
of this volume; but one important factor must be noted here—the
favourable turn taken by the Battle of the Atlantic in the second half
of 1941.

After the end of June there was a sharp fall in the rate of loss. The
monthly average of sinkings declined from 482,000 tons between
January and June to 237,000 tons between July and December. This
figure, moreover, included the unexpectedly heavy losses incurred in
the Far East in December as the result of Japan's aggression. In the
Atlantic the improvement was even more striking. Many factors, not
all of which could have been foreseen in June, contributed to this
result. The threatened break-out of the German surface fleet did not
take place and there were other unexpected easements. But the main
cause was the success of the defensive measures already referred to,
which began to take effect from midsummer onwards. The reorganization of the convoy system so as to reduce the number of independent sailings, the provision of continuous escorts across the Atlantic,
improved armaments and better air-support all combined to blunt
the edge of the enemy's attack. The last point, that of air-support,
deserves particular attention. By the second half of 1941 it had become possible to provide convoys with an air-escort over a distance of
up to 700 miles from the British Isles, 600 from the Canadian coast
and 400 southward from Iceland. Only during the central section of
their voyage—a three hundred mile gap in mid-Atlantic— were ships
without direct protection from the air. And it was precisely within
this gap, not closed until the summer of 1943, that the great majority
of sinkings now occurred. But the fact that the main battle had been
thrust outwards into mid-ocean was in itself a great advantage. It
reduced the number of active U-boats in proportion to the whole
fleet, since each took longer to reach and return from her operational
area. It also greatly complicated the problem of search; and it was
here that numbers told. A small fleet of 20 or 30 U-boats could be
deadly in the congested waters round the British Isles; but even twice
that number were still too few to cover the whole stretch of the
Atlantic.[1]

This outward drift of the battle, combined with better armament,
including catapult-launched aircraft and the first escort carriers, also

---

[1] Roskill, Vol. I, Chap. XXI and App. R.

went far to break the co-operation between sea and air power on which Hitler had built so much of his hopes. A German account, written later in the war from the point of view of the *Fliegerfuehrer Atlantik*, describes the process:

'Our attack on shipping met (initially) with no opposition either from flak or aircraft; and early successes, especially in the Atlantic, were surprisingly great. Six months later, however, the situation had changed completely. The use of the Kondor as a dive bomber, the only form of attack suited to its armament, had to be discontinued, first against convoys and then against single ships, owing to the introduction of strong defensive armament by the enemy. The continued use of the Kondor on reconnaissance for the submarine fleet would have been to our advantage, if systematic attacks on convoys had been maintained. But as convoys came to be more and more strongly escorted by destroyers and aircraft, our submarines suffered increasingly high losses and their area of operation was shifted to a point on the convoy route to America outside the range of the Kondor . . . By December 1941, almost all combined operations with the submarine fleet had to be broken off, as no more submarines were available for operations in European waters.'

The last sentence of this extract introduces another factor of great, though temporary, importance in easing the strain in the Atlantic. This was the transfer of U-boats to the Mediterranean, which took place in October and November, when the Allies, as will be described in a later chapter, were again able to take the offensive on the Libyan front. Before the end of the year upwards of a third of Germany's submarine strength was employed on this service and, despite the growth of the total fleet, there were actually fewer U-boats at work in the Atlantic than there had been in June. In the meanwhile, the Allies had received an important accession of strength. In September, as we shall also see later, the American 'Hemisphere Defence Plan No. 4' came into operation. This meant that the Neutrality Patrols, which the United States had maintained since the previous year, were enlarged and became for the first time an integral part of the Allied defensive system. American merchantmen joined Allied convoys and, over certain sections of the route, American warships provided the escort. The value of this help in 1941 still lay more, perhaps, in the moral than the practical sphere; but that scarcely diminished its importance. In the words of the naval historian, it brought with it the assurance 'that though the road might yet be arduous and many set-backs be suffered, the Battle of the Atlantic would finally be won'.[1]

On the opposite side of the picture—the acquisition of new shipping

---

[1] Roskill, Vol. I, Chap. XXI.

Map 2

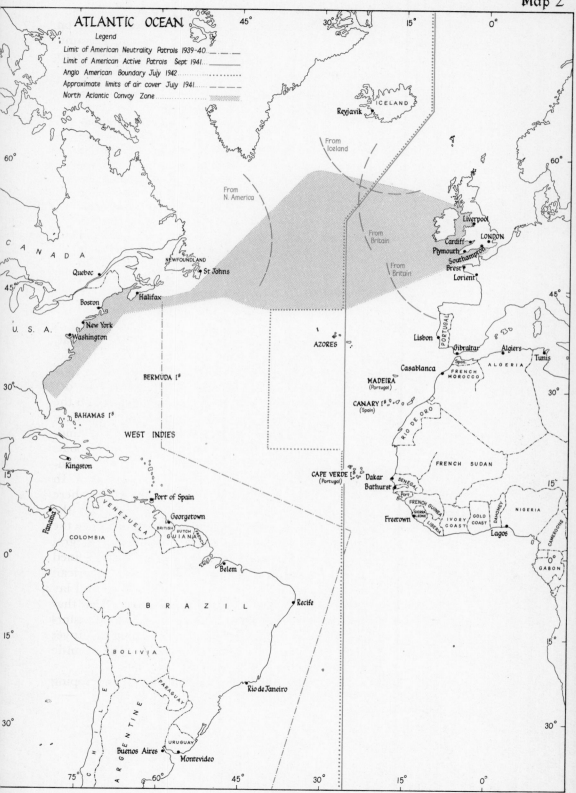

ATLANTIC OCEAN

Legend

Limit of American Neutrality Patrols 1939-40	─ ─ ─
Limit of American Active Patrols Sept 1941	─────
Anglo American Boundary July 1942	··········
Approximate limits of air cover July 1941	─ ─ ─
North Atlantic Convoy Zone	░░░░░

Map 2

—Allied gains were more prospective than actual. The Salter Mission was able to secure the use of enough tanker tonnage to raise oil stocks before the end of the year from the low level of June to the country's maximum storage capacity of about 7 million tons. But dry-cargo tonnage was harder to come by, since America had at that time barely sufficient for her own needs and the programme of new building still hung fire. There was, however, a considerable quantity of shipping, both Allied and enemy, in North or South American ports, part of which the Allies hoped to be able to appropriate to their own use by the intervention or with the help of the United States. In the meanwhile the use of American shipyards for repair helped to clear the block of damaged shipping, which had assumed such dimensions in the spring, or at least to ensure that it grew no worse.

The final effect of these easements was to reduce the Allies' net shipping loss for the year to something under 2 million tons instead of the 3 or 3·5 million which had been expected. The import trade benefited accordingly. By the end of 1941, apart from the building up of oil stocks already mentioned, more than 2 million tons of dry cargo had been landed in excess of the estimate made in June. The final total of a little over 30·5 million tons for the year was still far below what had been calculated as the minimum figure; but here again reality proved to be less alarming than the forecast. In the summer of 1941 import-planning was still in its infancy. Departments lacked the experience or the machinery to estimate their requirements exactly; and the figures given were found to have been uniformly, and in some cases wildly, overstated. Thus the Ministry of Supply, which had put its minimum needs at 21 million tons, had only received 15 million. Nevertheless, by the end of 1941 stocks of raw material had actually risen by 2·5 million tons over their 1940 level. Food stocks had also risen by nearly 1·5 million tons, although the Ministry of Food had received 300,000 tons less than it had asked for.[1]

The year ended, therefore, on a note of confidence in strange contrast to the deep and general pessimism of June. The Allies had demonstrated their ability to keep open the lines of sea-communication on which their survival depended. This was a great deal in itself; but it could not yet be said that they had won the Battle of the Atlantic, nor even that they were within sight of doing so. In the spring the struggle would be resumed against an enemy whose strength was constantly increasing. What the final outcome would be, could not be predicted with any certainty.

---

[1] Hancock and Gowing, pp. 200 and 266–8.

(iii)

The Far East

After this brief excursion into later events, we must return to the situation as it stood in June. Even on the most favourable view, and making every allowance for an upward turn of events, such as actually took place in the Atlantic, the Allies' strategic weakness was obvious. They might continue to hold their own in the British Isles and the Mediterranean, by sea and in the air; they might even be able to force a stalemate; but it did not appear that they could, by themselves, develop the necessary additional strength to attack and defeat Germany. This was the conclusion reached by the Joint Planners in the strategic review circulated in June, from which extracts have already been quoted. Having examined the Allied position from every angle, they could only express the opinion that the immediate entry of the United States into the war had now become essential. 'Without this,' they added, 'it is difficult to see how or when we can pass from a grim defence to a resolute offensive.'

But even an American declaration of war would not mean an easy or a quick victory. On the contrary, the J.P.S. analysis of the results to be expected was extremely cautious:

> 'The practical effect of U.S.A. intervention would be most immediately felt on the sea, where help is most immediately needed. Our naval position, particularly in the North Atlantic, will at once be improved. More adequate convoy escorts would reduce the present crippling rate of losses, the transfer of ships would be assured, and the long term shipbuilding programme would gain in size and intensity by the substitution of war-time for peace-time conditions. Our imports are already short of our requirements and are dropping still further behind. The sooner the U.S.A. come in as belligerents, the less will be the leeway to be made up.
>
> Strategically, the effect of U.S.A. intervention will be most marked in the area of the South Atlantic. It is from there that American security is most directly threatened, and it is there that the U.S.A. have shown the greatest willingness to act. The combined resources of our two countries might make the occupation of the Spanish and Portuguese Atlantic Islands, and the French West African ports a less difficult problem than it would be for ourselves alone.
>
> If we look still further into the future, a time may come when American forces, already established in West Africa, may be able to push northwards. Friendly elements in the French Empire, gaining courage and confidence from active and powerful support,

may be strong enough then to overthrow the authority of Vichy and re-establish their independence. If the enemies of the Axis were once again established on the southern shores of the Mediterranean, new opportunities would be opened out for the growing might of the American forces to close in on German-occupied Europe.

On land, American assistance will be limited, in the first place, by the shortage of trained and equipped troops, and, although more troops will become available, shortage of shipping will prevent more than a comparatively small force being used outside the Americas. Even so, the assumption by the U.S.A. of our responsibility in Iceland and of our potential commitments in the South Atlantic would be of considerable value in releasing our troops for essential duties elsewhere.

The active participation of the American Air Force in the offensive against Germany will be small at the beginning and will grow only slowly. During 1942 it should be big enough to be an appreciable addition to our own offensive effort. Meanwhile, the addition of American fighter and reconnaissance squadrons will increase the security of the United Kingdom and our sea communications.

In the economic sphere, the entry of the U.S.A. into the war, especially if it is followed, as it may well be, by similar action on the part of other South American countries, would lead to a considerable increase in the effectiveness of control at source. Even more important, however, are the additional opportunities which may thus be given to deal with the French Empire, either by helping French territories to withstand German attack, or, if that fails, by actively blockading them even if the hostility of the French Navy is thereby incurred.'

Such was the expected position in Europe; but unfortunately Allied strategy could no longer be discussed in European terms alone. Since the previous September, when Germany, Italy and Japan had signed the Tripartite Pact, the war clouds had also been gathering in the Far East. The impending storm might still be delayed for some months; but it was almost certain to break, if it had not done so before, on the day when the United States joined the Allies. The diplomatic position was all too clear. By the terms of Article 3 of the Pact, Japan had bound herself to give Germany the fullest military support, if the latter were attacked by any Power 'not at present involved in the European conflict'. In other words, if Japan honoured her engagement, an American declaration of war on Germany would be followed automatically by a Japanese attack on Allied possessions in the Far East. So much was clear; the only question of doubt was whether Japan might not anticipate her obligations by launching the attack in any case, without waiting for the formal signal of American intervention.

At the end of January Japan had renewed her pressure on French Indo-China, from whom she had already extorted certain concessions in the previous year. She now demanded the use of the naval base at Camranh Bay and the right to station troops and aircraft in the southern provinces. There could be no military purpose in this manœuvre except that of acquiring a forward base from which to threaten Singapore, Borneo or the Dutch East Indies. In March M. Matsuoka, the Japanese Foreign Minister, had visited Berlin and held long conversations with Hitler and Ribbentrop. Their purpose was uncertain; but it was necessary to assume that they marked a further step in Axis collaboration. They had been followed at the beginning of April by another significant development: Japan had settled her differences with the U.S.S.R. On 13th April the two countries had signed a neutrality agreement, which would have the effect of safeguarding Japan's vulnerable flank in Manchuria, if she decided to commit her main forces to a southward move.

By the first half of June a crisis was felt to be imminent. Japanese forces were still moving southward; and there were already considerable concentrations in Formosa, Hainan, Indo-China and the South China Sea. On 17th June the economic negotiations between Japan and the Dutch authorities in the East Indies, which had been in progress since the previous autumn, finally broke down. The fact was important since it affected Japan's supplies of rubber and oil, two commodities of which she was critically short. Public opinion in Tokyo was known to be excited and perhaps deliberately inflamed. In these circumstances an attack, whether on the East Indies alone or on neighbouring British possessions as well, was possible at any moment.

It will be clear from the map how serious the strategic implications might be, if this attack took place while the Allies were still without American support. Everything would then depend on the defence of Singapore. With this base as the corner-stone, the Allies could expect to hold a defensive line, which covered at any rate the more vital of their Far Eastern interests. From behind its shield, they could draw on the produce of Malaya and at least part of the East Indies; their sea-communications across the Indian Ocean would be protected; and they would be well placed to check any Japanese movement against Australia. But if Singapore fell, the whole defensive system would be unhinged; and it was difficult to see where new positions of any real strength could be found east of India or north of Australia. The vast intervening area, which included Malaya, Burma, Indonesia and the approaches to the Indian Ocean, would be opened to Japanese penetration with results—moral, economic and strategic— which it was impossible to measure.

As matters stood in June, Singapore was already dangerously

exposed. The main defences of the base were admittedly strong; but they had been designed on the assumption, valid when the base was first designed, that the main enemy attack would necessarily come from the sea. Now, with Japan established in Indo-China, an over-land attack through Thailand was equally possible and might prove far more difficult to meet. British land and air forces in Malaya, though recently reinforced, were still inadequate to the size and importance of the territory which they had to defend;[1] but no further reinforcement was possible, on the scale which the new situation demanded, without critically weakening either the United Kingdom or the Middle East. Moreover, the local defence of Singapore and Malaya could never be effective by itself, unless the Allies also held command of the sea. But until the acute strain, under which they were then labouring in Europe, had been relieved, there was no possibility of their being able to build up an effective naval force in the Pacific.

This grim, uncertain situation would be radically altered, if the United States were also belligerent. In the first place, the Allies would then acquire, in the American Pacific fleet, a naval force immediately available with which to challenge Japan's control of the sea. This fact would be a powerful deterrent in itself, since complete security of movement and communication in the China Seas and the eastern Pacific was essential to all Japan's operations. Secondly, the United States controlled a forward base at Manila, which lay directly across the main line of communication between Japan and her objectives in the south. While this remained in Allied hands, a major assault on Singapore or the East Indies would be extremely hazardous. Indeed, the larger the force that Japan committed at any point south of Manila and the farther that it penetrated, the more dangerous her own position would become. She would either have to accept this, and curtail her southern operations accordingly, or stake the issue of the war on a fleet-action with the United States—a risk which she might not be willing to take. In either case a strategic equilibrium would be restored, in which Japan's advantages in the south were offset by the threat of American pressure on her flank.

But this argument was subject to one important qualification: it was only actual strength not theoretical dispositions which would deter Japan. She had already shown, when she signed the Tripartite Pact, that she was not necessarily afraid of war with the United States, if she could be assured in advance that the latter's main force would be committed in Europe. Presumably she calculated, in that event, on being able to mask or neutralize Manila until such time as she had

---

[1] The policy was to rely largely on air-power for the defence of Malaya; but the force available in June numbered only 12 squadrons instead of the accepted minimum of 22.

achieved her primary objectives in the south. It scarcely mattered whether this calculation was correct or not, since the immediate practical result would be the same in either case. A major part of the strictly limited force available to the United States during the early stages of her intervention would have to be deployed in the Pacific in order to hold Japan in check. The extent of her help in Europe would be proportionately reduced; and it was probable, unless Japan changed her attitude, that even the modest offensive programme outlined above would be reduced or retarded in practice.

CHAPTER II

THE DISTANT FUTURE

(i)

Economic Warfare

THE MAIN PROBLEMS of Allied defence, as they appeared in early summer of 1941, were outlined in the last chapter. It was round these immediate problems—the Battle of the Atlantic, the defence of the United Kingdom, the German threat to the Middle East—that strategic discussions of the time largely revolved. That was inevitable, since all these were matters of plain survival. But Allied strategy in its full sense had a wider scope; it was concerned with final victory not less than with present defence. Sooner or later, with or without help from the outside world, the Allies would have to pass to the offensive and find the means, not merely to survive, but actively to impose their will on the enemy. But how could this be done, granted their present and prospective weakness in relation to Germany?

At first sight the problem appeared insoluble. Nevertheless, there were certain elements of hope. However heavily the balance of manpower and immediate war-potential might be tipped in her favour, Germany was not invulnerable. Some obvious weaknesses remained in her position, which the Allies could exploit, though with what effect only time would show. In the first instance, as the reader will remember, they had put their main faith in economic warfare. In a memorandum, written in 1940 in anticipation of the fall of France, the Chiefs of Staff had stated explicitly that 'upon the economic factor depends our only hope of bringing about the downfall of Germany'. They had based this opinion on reports from the Ministry of Economic Warfare, which suggested that Germany was already suffering from certain acute shortages, and might be expected to reach the point of crisis within six or nine months at the outside. These shortages included food (especially fats, animal feeding-stuffs and fertilizer), textiles, rubber, a number of important alloy metals and finally oil. It was expected that they would show themselves in a more or less acute form by the winter of 1940–41 and would reach such a pitch by the summer of the following year as to provoke a general industrial breakdown throughout Europe.

Time was to show, however, that these predictions were unrealistic. Germany did indeed suffer, more or less severely, from all the shortages named; but it did not follow that a general crisis was imminent. Her great technical ingenuity, especially in the use of alloy metals and synthetic substitutes, enabled her to survive for an extended period on supplies of textiles, metal and rubber, which would have been regarded as wholly inadequate in peacetime. Her conquests brought in very considerable stocks of other scarce materials, including oil. Moreover, the economic area, which she controlled from 1940 onwards, was so large and the margin for the internal manipulation of supplies so wide, that essential industry was slow to feel the effects even of a genuine shortage. Allied calculations had also assumed a level of German military activity, and therefore of consumption, which was not immediately attained. The nine months' lull between the Battle of France and the attack on Greece, during which few major operations took place, was enough in itself to upset any forecast of the economic position in 1941.

There was also another point, perhaps of greater importance. The forecasts of 1940 had been based on the assumption that Germany would be cut off from all overseas supplies. But this was not in fact the case. For more than a year after the Battle of France two major leaks remained in the Allied blockade, which it was found impossible to plug. The first was through Soviet Russia. By a series of agreements, signed in August 1939, February 1940 and January 1941, Germany received important supplies of scarce material from the Soviet Union itself; and Russia also acted as Germany's agent for the purchase of other materials from China, Japan and the Far East generally. The nature and value of this traffic is more fully discussed in another volume.[1] Here it is enough to say that the supplies of grain, oil, manganese and other metals, animal and vegetable fats, rubber and cotton, which reached Germany in this way, were regarded by her own experts as 'a very substantial prop' to her war-economy.[2] This was not an overstatement.

There was, however, little that the Allies could do. Direct exchanges between Germany and Russia were clearly outside their control. Some interference was possible, and was attempted, with Russia's purchases on German account; but no complete stoppage could have been achieved without closer American co-operation than was then forthcoming, and a degree of naval control in the Pacific which the Allies, acting alone, were unable to exercise. The Russian leak therefore remained until the time when Germany, by an extraordinary act of aggression, voluntarily closed it herself.

The second leak was through Vichy France. By this channel Germany obtained the produce of the French African territories and,

---

[1] W. N. Medlicott, *The Economic Blockade*, (1959).

[2] See *Nazi-Soviet Relations* (U.S. Department of State 1948), pp. 199–201.

to a lesser extent, of the French colonial empire as a whole. The most important items were vegetable fats and fertilizer; but small quantities of other scarce materials, including rubber from Saigon, were also brought in. Substantially the whole of this traffic entered Europe through the French Mediterranean ports, where in theory it was liable to interception by the Allies. But in fact little or nothing was done to hinder it, for reasons which were explained in June 1941 as follows:

> 'At present, traffic from French North Africa within the Mediterranean passes unmolested, and such few interceptions as have been possible between Dakar and Casablanca have had no deterrent effect. Despite certain difficulties due to Spanish territorial waters, an effective, though not complete, blockade could be maintained, if we were not restrained by the fear of an incident which would precipitate French hostility and the active use of their fleet and ports against us. With our existing naval resources strained to the utmost, this would constitute a danger to the maintenance of our vital lifelines out of proportion to the advantages in the economic offensive which we might hope to gain.'

The combination of all these factors made it more than doubtful whether economic warfare alone could ever defeat Germany. It remained true, of course, despite the defects and disappointments of the blockade, that the German area was not self-sufficient in a number of important products. Continued denial, or even partial denial, of these was bound in time to weaken her economy severely. But how long would it be before weakness reached the point of catastrophe or even the point at which it would seriously hamper military operations? There was no answer to this question. Indeed, if an abstract comparison were made between the Allied blockade of Europe and the German blockade of the British Isles, it was impossible not to feel that here, as elsewhere, the advantage lay with Germany. It was at least a theoretically possible operation to isolate the British Isles completely; and in that event England would starve to death within a few months. But the Allies could not isolate Germany; nor, even if they could, would the results be clear-cut and decisive in the same degree. So long as Germany remained in economic control of the greater part of Europe, she would always have a wide margin of manœuvre.

The force of these and similar arguments was already apparent by the summer of 1941. It would be wrong to say that the Allies had lost faith in the economic war. On the contrary, traces of the optimism of 1940 were still to be found, perhaps more frequently than the facts justified; but the tendency was now towards caution. The economic experts of the Ministry continued to predict a major crisis in Germany; but the date of that event had receded and their new forecasts were hedged with a number of important qualifications. It was expected that Germany's economy would begin to show a marked deterioration during the winter of 1941–42, which would continue and grow worse during the following year. This would not be a result of any single catastrophic shortage but rather of the cumulative effect of a number of associated difficulties and deficiencies, none of which would be decisive in itself. Though the effects would be felt first, and always more severely, by the civilian population, it was probable that certain shortages, as of rubber, leather, textiles and later on various metals, would also impinge on the armed forces. Some loss of efficiency was to be expected during 1942, but it was unlikely to become serious before the following year at the earliest. Even so, the exact extent of the damage could not be predicted with any certainty. The experts were now careful to frame their prophecy only in the most general terms:

> 'We believe that, even if nothing occurs to accelerate German collapse, the strains and shortages of 1943 could not be supported without a drastic reduction in the power of her armed forces, which would leave Germany highly vulnerable to any enemy still retaining power and vigour.'

These conclusions referred to the blockade as a whole. There remained, however, one particular shortage from which more distinct and immediate results were still expected. This was Germany's shortage of oil. On this point, of such importance and so exhaustively discussed, it is of interest to examine the Allied figures in some detail.

The original estimate, made shortly before the outbreak of war, had been that German stocks (reckoned at approximately 3 million tons) would only suffice for a campaign of four and a half to five months. This was very close to the facts; and there had been no lack of nervousness at the time on the German side. Nevertheless, when the plunge was taken, no disaster followed. On the contrary, Germany's campaigns of 1939 and 1940 yielded a handsome profit on the balance of oil spent and oil gained. Exact calculations are difficult; but it is probable that the three campaigns in Poland, Norway and France cost Germany under ·5 million tons of oil, in return for which she received captured stocks amounting, perhaps, to 2 million tons and additional annual production (from the western Polish fields) of about 160,000 tons.

In the light of this, Allied calculations had to be revised. A new estimate, made in July 1940, suggested that Germany, being now in direct or indirect control of the European supply, would be able to postpone the final crisis for another twelve months. By the second half of 1941, however, stocks would be exhausted, and she would face the future with an annual oil production of only 9·7 million tons with which to meet expenditure of not less than 15 million. But this second figure was over-optimistic. It assumed that Germany would not be able to reduce general European consumption by more than 50 per cent. Further calculations, made at the end of the year, indicated that a much more rigorous rationing was possible and was being applied. On this new basis, which allowed for a cut in European consumption of up to 80 per cent, Germany's supplies could be expected to last until the end of 1941 or even, with rigid economy and at some risk to the distribution system, for a few months thereafter.

These broad conclusions were still accepted in the following June; but by then refinements of some importance had been added. It was calculated that, during the six months between April and October, 1941, Germany's position would be at its easiest, since the Danube would be open and she would be able to draw freely on Rumanian supplies. It was likely that her receipts of oil over this period would roughly balance her expenditure. She would therefore enter the winter with stocks at much the same level as they had been in the previous spring, or say about 4 million tons in all. The next four or five months, when winter reduced or halted the river traffic, would be a period of great stringency. But if Germany survived it, she would find her position much improved in the following spring. By then her own synthetic production would have risen by another ·5 million tons a year; and Rumanian production would also have increased, though the full effects of this might not be felt before 1943. It was also probable that Germany would have solved her main distribution problem, either by opening the Mediterranean sea-route to her tankers or by making such improvements in the railway system as would enable her to lift the whole Rumanian surplus by land. In either case her position, though not permanently secure, would be free from immediate anxiety.

These calculations and those of the previous December, though partly based on guess-work, were surprisingly accurate. Figures given by the *Zentrale Planung* show that Germany's actual receipts of oil in 1941 were between 11·2 and 11·5 million tons, against a total expenditure of 12·8 million. By the end of the year, as the Allied experts had foreseen, her stocks were nearly exhausted;[1] and the next twelve months were a period of recurrent crisis, during which even the *Wehrmacht* lived from hand to mouth. In September 1942 the *Luftwaffe* held a bare month's supply of aviation-spirit and by October the Army had run through all its reserves of motor-gasoline. Nevertheless, there was no general breakdown. Certain restrictions

---

[1] No complete figure is available; but stocks of the three major products (aviation-spirit, motor-gasoline and diesel-oil) had sunk to below 800,000 tons by the end of 1941. The distributional minimum for these products was reckoned by the Germans at between 0.8 and 1.3 million tons.

were placed on training, which contributed to a loss of efficiency in the future; but there is little evidence of any adverse effect on operations. Indeed, it appears that, despite local and temporary shortages, a rough balance between receipts and expenditure was achieved for the year 1942 as a whole. This was made possible by the rise in synthetic production already mentioned and a further cut—made, apparently, with no ill effects—of 2·8 million tons in the civil consumption of Germany and German-dominated Europe. By the end of the year the worst of the crisis was over. During 1943 by the exercise of ruthless economy Germany was even able to rebuild a small margin of stock, which she maintained until Allied bombing of her synthetic plants precipitated a final crisis in the autumn of the following year.

We can see in these facts the strategic limitations of the oil-blockade. At the end of June 1941, in circumstances described in the next chapter, Germany launched her attack on Russia, the largest land-operation of the war, to which more than 100 infantry and 30 armoured or motorized divisions were committed. For the next eighteen months her advance into Russian territory was pressed continuously to the accompaniment of heavy fighting, and reached its farthest point over the winter of 1942–43. These immense operations, which the Allied estimates had not foreseen, thus coincided almost exactly with the period when Germany's oil supplies were at their lowest ebb. Nevertheless, the impetus of the German offensive was scarcely affected. It is possible to argue, as we shall see, that the oil shortage exercised a certain influence on the strategic direction of the campaign; but the actual fighting-power of the *Wehrmacht* was never touched except in the minor degree noted above. It was not until 1944, when it became possible to supplement the blockade by the offensive bombing of German synthetic oil plants and other installations, that a degree of famine could be imposed, which had measurable and distinct military consequences.

It will be seen that what was true of the blockade as a whole was equally true of the oil-blockade in particular. It was within the Allies' power to impose certain difficulties on Germany by economic action alone; but these were not insurmountable. They weakened Germany and thus laid a foundation—perhaps the indispensable foundation—for her subsequent defeat by other means; but they were not, and could never have been, decisive in their own right.

(ii)

The Air-Offensive

The second instrument of Allied offensive strategy was the bomber. In their memorandum of 1940, already quoted, the Chiefs of Staff had given 'air-attack on economic objects in Germany and on German morale' an equal place with the blockade as the two principal means of enforcing pressure on Germany. In a paper written in the following September, when the bright prospects of the economic war were beginning to fade, Mr. Churchill had carried the same argument a stage further:

> 'The Navy can lose us the war, but only the Air Force can win it. Therefore our supreme effort must be to gain overwhelming mastery in the air. The Fighters are our salvation, but the Bombers alone provide the means of victory. We must therefore develop the power to carry an ever-increasing volume of explosives to Germany, so as to pulverize the entire industry and scientific structure on which the war-effort and economic life of the enemy depends, while holding him at arm's length in our Island. In no other way at present visible can we hope to overcome the immense military power of Germany, and to nullify the further German victories which may be apprehended as the weight of their force is brought to bear on the African or Oriental theatres.'

The intended policy was thus clear; but in the summer of 1941 the Allies were in no position to carry it out. In the first place, their bomber force was far too small for decisive operations. In June, the order of battle of Bomber Command showed the equivalent of only 51 standard[1] squadrons (8 heavy, 35 medium and 8 light) compared with 55 at the outbreak of war. By the end of the year the total had risen to 62 squadrons, of which 15 were equipped with heavy bombers. But these were only paper figures, subject to many deductions in practice. Some squadrons were short of establishment; the supply of trained air crews was inadequate; and the new heavy bombers—Manchesters, Stirlings and Halifaxes—were still involved in more or less serious technical troubles. During the whole six months between June and December, therefore, the Command could only muster an average of 380 medium and 40 heavy bombers, which were actually available for operations.

How serious a state of affairs this was, may be seen by comparison with the pre-war programme. The original Expansion Scheme M of October 1938, which aimed to build up a striking-force approximately

---

[1] i.e. at 16 aircraft to the squadron.

equal to Germany's, had called for the creation of no less than 82 heavy bomber squadrons by April 1941. And since then require- ments had risen steeply. Germany's victories in 1940, besides greatly increasing the importance of the bomber as a strategic weapon, had altered the balance of air-power. Allied aircraft, deprived of their advanced bases, had nearly twice as far to travel to reach a distant target in Germany, as German aircraft to reach an equivalent target in the British Isles. If only for that reason, a much larger force was now needed to maintain parity, let alone to secure predominance. Moreover, the experience which had been gained by the summer of 1941, whether of German bombing in England or of Allied bombing in Germany, indicated that the total tonnage of bombs required to produce a given result had been gravely underestimated. Earlier calculations about the optimum weight of individual bombs had also been revised. Bombs of 1,000, 2,000 and 4,000 lbs. were now in gen- eral use; and it was agreed that something even heavier would be needed in future. All this implied a further increase in the total strength of Bomber Command and even more complete reliance on the new type of heavy bomber, which alone could carry the necessary weight of bombs over the required distance.

By June, therefore, the Command was working on a new and much enlarged programme: Target Force E. In its original form this called for an expansion to 100 medium or heavy (standard) squadrons by the end of the year, and 250 heavy squadrons by the summer of 1943; but certain modifications were later introduced. The first came when Bomber Command presented its new plan of organization. It was then decided to exchange the standard squadrons for 168 enlarged[1] squadrons with a total of 4,032 aircraft. In July the Target Force was further increased by the addition of 6 (enlarged) medium squadrons and 20 (standard) light squadrons, the latter change being largely the result of the first appearance and great operational promise of the Mosquito bomber.[2] This made the final total, to be achieved in rather less than two years, 194 squadrons of 4,496 aircraft.

Judged in these terms, which were the only ones appropriate to Allied strategy, the position in 1941 was little short of disastrous. With each month that passed the gap between promise and per- formance grew steadily wider, until by the end of the year the pro- gramme might be said to have lost all touch with reality. Thus at the end of November, when the 100 squadron goal should have been in sight, Bomber Command could only muster 54 squadrons of 955 air- craft. Reckoned in terms of bomb-lift, the deficiency was even greater, for only seven squadrons were equipped with the new heavy bombers.

---

[1] i.e. at 24 aircraft to the squadron.

[2] This aircraft had already seen service with Photographic Reconnaissance Units.

And so it continued. Even in the following February, when bombers of the new type should have formed the staple of the force, the Command was still largely dependent, as it had been since 1940, on the older Wellington, already regarded as obsolescent.

There were many reasons for this constant failure to reach, or even approach, the target. Bomber Command had suffered heavy losses in the Battle of France; and it had been necessary since then to divert aircraft and crews both to the Middle East and to Coastal Command. It was also true that in 1941 the general rate of wastage from all causes, including accident, was nearly twice as high as had been anticipated before the war. Aircraft lasted on an average for only 10 to 16 sorties instead of the planned 20 to 25. These facts were enough in themselves to upset the programme. During the four months between April and July 1941, for example, 1,715 new bombers were produced, of which 520 were sent overseas. The total number of aircraft lost during the same period was 776, leaving a balance available in Great Britain of only 419. But even these did not count towards expansion, for metropolitan units, as the result of past set-backs, were already short of establishment by almost exactly the same number.

But too much cannot be set down to heavy losses and diversions, neither of which could be avoided. The root of the trouble lay elsewhere. For reasons which can only be explored briefly here, British aircraft production was not keeping pace with the rising needs of the Command; and American production, on which the Allies should have been drawing heavily by 1941, was lagging still further behind.[1] In England a part of the delay could still be attributed to the events of the previous year. Although the general industrial damage done by enemy bombing had not been severe, certain factories of particular importance to the aircraft industry had been hit. Damage to the B.T.H. magneto factory in Coventry, for example, was reckoned to have delayed the production of aero-engines for nearly a year; and other instances could be cited. The drive for fighter production in the summer of 1940 had also affected the position by depleting stocks and throwing long-term plans out of gear. It is true that normal working was resumed in October; but the after-effects of the emergency, which included a legacy of industrial fatigue, were still traceable for many months thereafter.[2]

In the main, however, these were temporary and superficial difficulties, which were already on the way to be mastered. The real causes of delay, which affected American no less than British production, lay deeper and were less easy to remove, being inherent in the nature of the problem. Of all the weapons of war military aircraft

---

[1] According to the current programme 642 American Bombers should have been delivered in England between April and July 1941; but in fact only 69 were received.

[2] M. M. Postan, *British War Production*, (1952) pp. 123–4, 164–5.

were the least amenable to mass-production. Their design, manufacture and assembly was an immensely complicated task in which little streamlining was possible. New types were constantly being evolved or old types improved; and each modification disturbed the rhythm of production. Factories had to be re-tooled, reorganized or enlarged; there were delays in the production of new components; and in some cases (such as the Vulture engine) new designs proved unsatisfactory in service and had to be discarded even after serial production had begun. Moreover, each new type tended to be heavier and more complicated than its predecessor and thus to make greater demands on the industry in terms both of man-hours and technical ingenuity. This applied particularly to the new heavy bombers. The airframe of a Manchester was 5,000 lbs. heavier than that of a Wellington; that of a Halifax nearly 1,800 lbs. heavier still; and so on in an almost geometrical progression.[1]

Another aspect of the problem should also be mentioned. All the programmes of the Ministry of Aircraft Production, from that of October 1940 to that of June 1943, were deliberately inflated by about 15 per cent in the belief that the aircraft industry would be inspired to great efforts, if the target were always held just out of reach. It was also customary, as a matter of statistical convenience, to assume, when forecasts were made, that a short fall in the early stages of a programme would be made good by increased production in the later stages.[2] But this assumption, for the reasons already given, was rarely valid. Both practices were, of course, known to—and no doubt allowed for by—the Air Ministry and Bomber Command, and did not affect the real problems of production one way or the other. But they added perceptibly to the atmosphere of unreality, which invested the whole bomber programme in 1941 and 1942. Target Force E—the 4,000 bomber programme—remained the official goal; but from the middle of 1941 onwards there can have been few people who still supposed that it could actually be reached within a measurable time.

By the beginning of September, the outlook was so grave as to attract the personal intervention of the Prime Minister. In a minute to the Lord President, he pointed out that, to enable Bomber Command to reach Target Force E by the agreed date, a total production of 22,000 aircraft was required during the two years between July 1941 and July 1943. The latest forecasts showed that British factories would only produce 11,000. To this could be added a prospective 5,500 from American production, leaving a deficit of the same number to be made good. This was wholly unsatisfactory; and he had therefore directed, after discussions with Colonel Moore-

---

[1] Postan, pp. 169–70, 326–45.
[2] Postan, pp. 123–4, 173–4.

Brabazon,[1] that a new plan should be made to raise British production to 14,500. The Lord President was invited to bring the Ministers concerned together and to ensure that the necessary adjustments were made with as little dislocation as possible.

These demands, though fully justified from a strategical view, could not be satisfied in practice. The Lord President was obliged to report in the following month that they could only be met at all by extending the time limit and diluting the quality. By allowing the force a larger proportion of Wellingtons to the new type of bomber, the revised target could be reached by the end of 1943, if production programmes were completed in full, or by June 1944, if they fell short by the accustomed 15 per cent. This was a serious disappointment to Bomber Command; but worse was to follow. In December the Minister of Aircraft Production informed the Defence Committee that shortage of labour would probably make it impossible to carry out the programme in full. The new forecasts, which were received from America at about this time, were even more disquieting. It was now believed, for reasons which will be examined in a later chapter, that not more than 2,100 aircraft would be forthcoming over the period instead of the 5,500 which had been promised. Moreover, the main hold-up in American as in British production was in heavy bombers of the new type; and the few examples which had so far reached England—the early Liberators and the Fortress I— were proving technically even more troublesome than their British counterparts.

At this point we may pause. The story of the bomber programmes has been carried forward so far, only in order to make the position in June fully comprehensible. It can now be seen that the high hopes, which went to the framing of Target Force E, if not misplaced, were at least premature. Before the end of the year it was necessary to take a more cautious and sombre view. A strategic bomber force had, indeed, been planned; and a growing proportion of the country's industrial effort was to be devoted to building it up. But it was already plain that the force could not reach its full strength, or a strength at which it could play a decisive part in the war, in less than two or more probably three years. In the meanwhile, and especially during the first year or eighteen months of the build-up, the role of Bomber Command would be strictly limited. To gain experience, to harass the enemy, to supplement where possible the effects of the blockade —all these were valuable functions; but they were a long way from the air-predominance of which Mr. Churchill had written in September, 1940.

Nor was the retarded growth of their force the only problem which

---

[1] Then Minister of Aircraft Production.

faced the Allies. Many important questions of policy were also un-
resolved. It was agreed that the destruction of German industry and
the breaking of German morale were the two primary objectives; but
there was no settled view how either could be attained. Which objective was the more important? Could both be combined in a single
plan of operations? Should the attack be spread as widely as possible
or concentrated on a limited number of key-points? Which industrial
targets was it most important to destroy and which were the most
vulnerable? All these questions, the fundamentals of bombing policy,
were as yet unanswered.

It must be remembered that, although the tradition of the R.A.F.
had always favoured the use of bombers in an independent strategic
role, there had been little opportunity to test this theory in practice.
Throughout the first eighteen months of the war the main strength
of Bomber Command had been used tactically and defensively. First
there were the leaflet raids, then operations in direct support of the
Allied armies in France and Belgium, and finally attacks on enemy
concentrations in the Channel ports and on the bases in northern
France, Belgium and Holland, from which the German air-offensive
was being directed. Apart from a limited attack on the Ruhr at the
end of May 1940, and some loosely co-ordinated raids on German oil
installations and other industrial targets during the last three months
of the year, there was little which could properly be described as
offensive bombing.

The first real attempt to use Bomber Command in its intended
strategic rôle may be said to have begun in January 1941. This was a
time, as we saw above, of great optimism on the subject of Germany's
oil supplies. A major crisis was thought to be imminent; and it was
believed that a concentrated attack on her synthetic oil plants, which
were said to have suffered some damage already, would force a complete breakdown within a few months. The Prime Minister was dis-
trustful of this calculation, as of all others which attempted to show a
painless and certain method of winning the war, but agreed that the
attempt was at least worth making. Accordingly, Bomber Command
was instructed on 15th January, that 'the sole primary aim of your
bomber force, until further notice, should be the destruction of the
German synthetic oil plants'. These were seventeen in number; but
it was estimated (optimistically perhaps) that the complete destruction of the nine most important would reduce production by more
than 80 per cent.

The attack on oil was pressed for two months, but produced no
significant result. Nevertheless, it had a certain value for the future,
if only for the lessons which it taught or emphasized. The first was the
astonishing extent to which bad weather could nullify, or even reverse, an agreed policy. During January and February Bomber

Command was active on thirty-three nights; but only on three of these was a major attack delivered on the oil installations, which were ostensibly the primary target. On the remaining thirty nights bad weather, or a combination of bad weather and other considerations, diverted the main effort to secondary targets such as German industrial towns or the Channel ports. In all, not more than 10 per cent of the bombs dropped during this period were even aimed at the synthetic oil plants; and it must be supposed that few of these reached their mark. This was the second lesson—the extreme difficulty of identifying, still more hitting, a relatively small and isolated target. Previously, the enthusiastic statements regularly made by bomber crews, supported to some extent by Intelligence reports from Germany, had encouraged the belief that our standard of navigation and bomb aiming was high. Now the introduction of night photography as a check on these reports was beginning to reveal the true position. But more will be said on this subject below.

At the beginning of March, the first major crisis in the Battle of the Atlantic forced Bomber Command to return to its defensive rôle. For the next three months U-boat bases and building yards, the two battle-cruisers in Brest and the Focke-Wulf factories became the principal targets. This pause in strategic operations was not wholly unwelcome, since it gave an opportunity for the bases of policy to be re-examined. At this time there were two more or less sharply opposed schools of thought. The first, which had so far been in the ascendant, advocated the precision bombing of industrial key-points (such as oil installations or coking plants), the destruction of which would shatter German economy at a single blow. The second, which was now gaining strength, found a powerful advocate in Lord Trenchard, who in May submitted a private memorandum on bombing policy to the Prime Minister. This argued with great force that Bomber Command should abandon the 'panacea-system' and devote its whole strength to an onslaught on German morale by the mass-bombing of centres of population, especially those which housed industrial workers.

In fact, the position in 1941 was such that neither policy could be followed in its pure form. Attempts at precision bombing were useless, so long as the standard of accuracy remained as low as it was. On the other hand, Bomber Command was still too small to make any distinct impression by methods of wholesale destruction. Some compromise was necessary; and the lines which it was to take were indicated in a paper prepared for the Chief of the Air Staff in May on the tactical requirements of a target policy:

'(a) The targets selected for attack must be mainly in an area which we can reach within the hours of darkness all the year around.

(b) The task we set ourselves must be commensurate with the
size of the bomber force available. At the moment our bomber
force, even under the most favourable conditions, is only capable
of dropping 200 tons of bombs on Germany on a given night.
Consequently the number of targets selected should be kept low
so as to ensure a concentrated effort upon each.

(c) Owing to the proved difficulty of finding and hitting precise
targets on dark nights, a large number of the targets should be so
situated that the misses and near-misses are of value.

(d) The targets should be in industrial areas, so that 'shorts and
overs' will kill, and if the precise objective cannot be seen there
will be no difficulty in finding a target, whose attack will strike
at the enemy's morale.

(e) The precise targets selected for attack on moonlight nights
should be big enough to ensure that adequate damage can be
inflicted upon them.

(f) The plan should allow for alternative target areas, suitable
for attack when weather conditions over main targets are unsuitable.'

In the meantime, there had also been some shift of opinion among
economic experts. By June, for reasons already examined, they were
no longer so confident as they had been that Germany would succumb to a shortage of oil or, indeed, to a shortage of any one particular commodity. Their tendency was now to rely on the cumulative
effect of a number of associated pressures, which included political
and administrative problems as well as material famine. This line of
argument, combined with the disappointing results of the attack on
oil, led them to offer a new series of targets for attack:

'So far we have dealt only with the difficulties of Germany in
acquiring the commodities she lacks, but equally important are
her problems in distributing the supplies which she already
possesses. The rulers of Germany have been forced to undertake
the most gigantic task of economic management ever attempted.
So complex is the problem of the interchange of goods from un-
accustomed sources by unusual channels to people of varying
degrees of hostility and non-co-operation that it must strain the
German ingenuity and German resources to the breaking point
even under favourable circumstances, and could hardly stand
any degree of dislocation from outside. Distribution and transportation may indeed prove to be the weakest links in the German economic chain.

With long sea communications restricted by our action, available
shipping reduced by heavy losses and road transport limited
by the need for economizing oil and rubber, German transport
is primarily dependent upon its railway system. Although that
system, owing to our blockade, must now carry vast quantities
of bulky traffic, formerly sea-borne, it has, up to the present,

survived these strains without serious deterioration by the commandeering of locomotives and rolling stock in occupied countries, and by the ruthless disregard of civilian needs both in those countries and in Germany itself. Every new extension of the area of German control means new strains on the system and whether or for how long it can continue to bear them will depend on the extent to which we can either force new traffic on to it by the further restriction of alternative routes, or reduce, by means of the bomb or the saboteur, its ability to carry existing traffic.'

All these elements contributed to the new directive, which was issued to Bomber Command on the 9th July. The instructions now were 'subject to essential diversions which might occur from time to time . . . to direct the main effort of the bomber force, until further instructions, towards dislocating the German transportation system and to destroying the morale of the civil population as a whole and of the industrial workers in particular'. To this end nine communication-centres in western Germany, all within relatively easy range, were selected as primary targets, to be attacked with as much accuracy as possible on clear, moonlight nights. The majority were situated in densely populated industrial areas, such as Cologne, Duesseldorf and Duisberg, where, it was hoped, even those bombs which missed the main target would do miscellaneous damage of some value and contribute at least to the lowering of morale. In addition, six major towns—Hamburg, Bremen, Hanover, Frankfurt, Mannheim and Stuttgart—were listed as secondary targets against which area-attacks were to be made, whenever the weather was unsuitable for accurate bombing. This was intended as an 'all-weather' policy, in which raids on secondary targets and near-misses on primary targets would all contribute their quota to the final effect.

On this basis some 10,000 sorties were flown, and between 11,000 and 12,000 tons of bombs dropped during the three months of July, August and September. The results, though superior to any which the Command had yet achieved, were not spectacular. The average bomb load did not exceed 150 tons a night; and with this weight of attack area-raids on large towns could scarcely have more than a harassing effect. And the standard of precision bombing, if it can so be called, remained deplorably low. During the summer and early autumn a series of inquiries based on the new photographic evidence disclosed some disturbing figures.[1] It appeared that under the best conditions of moonlight and clear sky, which did not occur on more than three or four days in the months, only half of the aircraft despatched could be expected to come within five miles of a target on

---

[1] The original inquiry in August, 1941, was undertaken on the initiative of Lord Cherwell's Statistical Section. See also Sir C. K. Webster and N. Frankland, *The Strategic Air Offensive against Germany, 1939–45*, (1960) Vol. I, p. 178.

the Channel coast, and only a third within the same distance of a target in the Ruhr. In bad weather the proportions fell to 15 per cent on the coast and 10 per cent elsewhere; and the general average for all sorties was not higher than 15 per cent. Under these conditions, even area-bombing was uncertain, while the chances of a direct hit on a target less than five miles in extent were so small as to be negligible.

These unwelcome facts gave Allied policy a further impulse towards area-bombing. The movement of opinion was clearly marked in an elaborate paper on the Development and Employment of the Heavy Bomber Force, based on an analysis of the effects of German bombing in England, which the C.A.S. circulated at the end of September. It contained a careful estimate of the effect on an average industrial town of a series of attacks on the same scale as the heavy raid on Coventry in the previous November. On that occasion the weight of bombs dropped had been of the order of one ton to every 800 inhabitants. This had lowered the town's general index of activity[1] by 63 per cent; and recovery had taken about 35 days. If a second attack had been made within a month of the first, when recovery was still incomplete, the same weight of bombs would have brought the index even lower. After a succession of six such attacks, at the same interval of time, the cumulative damage would have reached a point from which recovery was impossible. A further calculation showed that if, in addition to Coventry, twenty-three other industrial towns of the same importance had been similarly reduced to impotence, a complete breakdown of British economy would have followed.

The paper proposed that these methods should now be tried on Germany. Instead of attacking particular industrial or administrative targets, Bomber Command should seek to gain its objective by the methodical wrecking—or, in a later phrase, *emasculation*—of forty-three industrial towns, which normally housed a population of 15 million persons. Six attacks would be made on each, at not more than monthly intervals, using the same weight of bombs in proportion to the population as in the German raid on Coventry. It was assumed that each squadron of heavy bombers would be able to make 100 sorties a month with an average bomb-load of 3 tons an aircraft and that 25 per cent of the total load would fall in the target area. On this basis Target Force E, when it reached its full strength, would be able to drop 75,000 tons of bombs a month on Germany, of which 18,750 would be effective. This was the equivalent of one ton to every 800 persons in a population of 15 million, or the total amount required for one attack on each of the forty-three selected towns. Six months'

---

[1] This was an artificial measurement of air-raid damage which took account of psychological effects and the general dislocation of life as well as material damage.

continuous operations would therefore suffice for the whole cycle of attacks. At the end of that time, if the calculations were correct, German economy would be completely shattered.

Here was the beginning of a new policy, later to find its expression in the thousand-bomber raids on German cities, which Air-Marshal Harris inaugurated in 1942. It cannot be said, however, that the paper was altogether favourably received at the time. The Prime Minister, having studied it, replied in a vein of scepticism closely parallel to his remarks on the precision bombing of synthetic oil plants earlier in the year:

> 'It is very disputable whether bombing by itself will be a decisive factor in the present war. On the contrary, all that we have learnt since the war began shows that its effects, both physical and moral, are greatly exaggerated. There is no doubt the British people have been stimulated and strengthened by the attack made upon them so far. Secondly, it seems very likely that the ground defences and night fighters will overtake the Air attack. Thirdly, in calculating the number of bombers necessary to achieve hypothetical and indefinite tasks, it should be noted that only a quarter of our bombs hit the targets. Consequently an increase in the accuracy of bombing to 100 per cent would in fact raise our bombing force to four times its strength. The most we can say is that it will be a heavy and I trust a seriously increasing annoyance.'

These comments could be taken as implying that Mr. Churchill had temporarily lost confidence in the strategic value of Bomber Command; and it was in this sense that the C.A.S. read them. He replied immediately and at some length, pointing out that a series of Cabinet decisions had allotted a primary rôle to the bomber in our offensive strategy. The expansion programme, to which we were deeply committed, had been conceived on these lines and for this purpose. If it was now thought that the power of the bomber had been over-estimated, it was essential that existing plans, including the proposed size and composition of the force, should at once be reviewed. Nothing could be worse than to continue preparations on the present scale, when we no longer believed that they were capable of producing the results at which we aimed.

But the Prime Minister was not willing, and had not intended, to press his own argument to these lengths. He was at pains to emphasize in his reply that Cabinet policy had not changed. The bomber remained the primary offensive weapon, if only because no other existed. But it was useless to pretend that the exuberant hopes once entertained had not been diminished by contact with reality:

> 'We all hope that the Air Offensive against Germany will realize the expectations of the Air Staff. Everything is being done to

create the bombing force desired on the largest possible scale, and there is no intention of changing this policy. I deprecate, however, placing unbounded confidence in this means of attack, and still more expressing that confidence in terms of arithmetic. It is the most potent method of impairing the enemy's morale we can use at the present time. If the United States enters the war, it would have to be supplemented in 1943 by simultaneous attacks by armoured forces in many of the conquered countries which were ripe for revolt. Only in this way could a decision certainly be achieved. Even if all the towns of Germany were rendered largely uninhabitable, it does not follow that the military control would be weakened or even that war industry could not be carried on . . . It may well be that German morale will crack and that our bombing will play a very important part in bringing the result about. But all things are always on the move simultaneously, and it is quite possible that the Nazi war-making power in 1943 will be so widely spread throughout Europe as to be to a large extent independent of the actual buildings in the homeland.

A different picture would be presented if the enemy's Air Force were so far reduced as to enable heavy accurate daylight bombing of factories to take place. This however cannot be done outside the radius of Fighter protection, according to what I am at present told. One has to do the best one can, but he is an unwise man who thinks there is any *certain* method of winning this war, or indeed any other war between equals in strength. The only plan is to persevere.'

(iii)

Subversion

The only plan, as Mr. Churchill said, was to persevere; but the outlook was not encouraging. It was clear that Germany would never succumb to economic pressure alone. What contribution the air-offensive could make to victory was still uncertain. Time was needed —much more time than had been expected—to build a sufficient force; and it was not until that had been done, and the force tested in action, that Bomber Command's potential could be accurately judged. Meanwhile, the only guide was past experience, which suggested that the power of an unsupported air-offensive was a great deal less than its advocates had hitherto claimed. But if these two weapons, the bomber and the blockade, were both insufficient, what other possibilities remained? There was only one answer: the invasion of Europe and the defeat of the German army in the field.

No one had ever doubted that this was the only certain way of winning the war; but it did not appear to be a practicable operation. In June 1941, Germany was believed to dispose of 250 divisions, of which 90 were ready for immediate service in any theatre. Against this the Allies could only muster a prospective Field Force of just under 60 divisions,[1] which would not reach its full strength until the autumn of 1942. Nor did the discrepancy end there. Germany occupied the central position and could throw the full weight of her force in whichever direction she chose. The Allies, on the other hand, were obliged to divide the greater part of their force between two permanent garrisons, one in the United Kingdom, the other in the Middle East. When the requirements of these two theatres had been satisfied, less than four divisions would remain to cover all other contingencies, including the protection of Allied interests in the Far East.

In these circumstances, and without so much as a foothold on the Continent, the Allies were in no case to challenge Hitler by land. Nor could they expect that their position would alter materially in the future. No doubt the Dominions would be able in time to raise additional forces; but these could never be large enough to turn the balance. The other Allied governments were governments in exile, only able to recruit within a narrow circle of refugees and overseas residents. India, it is true, possessed large reserves of manpower and her mobilization had as yet barely begun. But there were many factors, practical, political and economic, which would always limit the number of Indian divisions which could be raised and equipped for foreign service, especially in the European theatre. It was, therefore, on the manpower of the United Kingdom that the Allies had chiefly to depend; and there were signs even in 1941 that this pool would shortly run dry.

It was calculated that, during the two years between the spring of 1941 and the spring of 1943, the Services and the armaments industry in Great Britain would together require something over 2 million men to complete their programmes. But the natural increase of the male population in the same period would only provide ·32 million. The remainder would have to be found either by withdrawing men from 'non-essential' industry—a process which was already nearing its limit—or by substituting women. If the latter were done to the extent necessary to meet the demand, by the beginning of 1943 nearly 40 per cent of the whole female population would have been drawn into industry or some work depending directly on the Services.[2] This was not impossible—indeed, the figure was only a little

---

[1] This did not include 'forces retained in the Dominions and India for their defence, the garrisons of defended ports abroad and certain local and colonial forces'.

[2] These were the contemporary figures, in which some adjustments were made later, though without affecting the broad principle.

higher than that for women in all forms of employment (including domestic service) before the war; but it was probably a maximum.

It followed that British manpower would already be at full stretch by the time when the Army programme was complete and the Field Force had reached its planned total of 60 divisions. Thereafter no increase in the size of the Army would be possible, except at the expense of one of the other Services or of essential industry. From these facts flowed certain strategic consequences, to which the Prime Minister had already drawn attention. He had noted, in a memorandum written in March, that:

> 'The above considerations and the situation as a whole make it impossible for the Army, except in resisting invasion, to play a primary role in the defeat of the enemy. That task can only be done by the staying power of the Navy and above all, by the effect of air predominance. Very valuable and important services may be rendered overseas by the Army in operations of a secondary order, and it is for these special operations that its organization and character should be adapted.'

There was one sense in which this situation had long been foreseen. Even in 1939 or before the war it had not been intended that Great Britain and the Dominions should attempt to match Germany's strength by land. Their main contribution to the alliance was to be by sea, in the air and through their economic and industrial strength, while the manpower of western Europe, and especially of France, provided the bulk of the land-force. But that pattern, the pattern of England's traditional strategy in a general European war, had now been broken by the German victories of 1940; a new and radically different strategy was required for the future. There was, of course, one obvious basis on which it might rest. If the United States were to join the Allies, the old balance would be restored and more than restored. But this event, however much to be desired, did not appear probable. Moreover, as we saw in the last chapter, contemporary estimates of the immediate results to be expected from American intervention were extremely cautious. No one doubted, it is true, that the manpower and immense industrial strength of the United States would be decisive in the long run. But the difficulty of bringing these resources to bear effectively in Europe was regarded as so great, that no fundamental change in the Allies' strategic position could be expected, at least for some years.

The reason for this will be clear, if we examine the problem in its crudest terms. In order to make a direct assault on the Continent and to defeat the German army in the field the Allies would require at least an equality of force by land—that is to say, an addition to their present strength of the order of 140 or 150 divisions. There was no doubt that the United States could in time raise and equip an army of this size; but there was little probability that shipping would be available to transport it to Europe. Even under the best conditions a movement on this unprecedented scale might be expected to occupy years; and the actual conditions, as we have seen already, were far from the best. In the summer of 1941 an acute shortage of shipping existed, which was expected to continue more or less indefinitely. It was true that an American building programme, on the scale to be anticipated after a declaration of war, together with American naval help in the Atlantic, would greatly ease the position. But it was not likely, even so, that such a surplus of shipping would be created as to make these enormous troop movements easy or even possible.

It was necessary to assume, therefore, that an American expeditionary force would be relatively small. No attempt could be made at this stage to forecast its probable size; but we may suppose that the planners were not thinking in terms of more than 30 or 40 divisions at the most. In that case the odds against the Allies would not shorten appreciably: it would still be 100 divisions or thereabouts against not less than 250. Moreover, the Allies would not be able to use their 100 divisions as a single unit, since they had two theatres to consider—the United Kingdom and the Middle East—both of which were under threat by the enemy. Germany, on the other hand, since she occupied the central position, would be able to keep her forces concentrated.

These calculations are, of course, over simplified. It was rarely possible, least of all in 1941, to consider strategy in such cut-and-dried terms; nor would it have been realistic to do so. Nevertheless, the figures given had a solid base in truth—a truth which was bound to assert itself in some form, however the case were stated and whatever qualifications were allowed. It was plain that even an American declaration of war would not bring about any lightning transformation of the scene. The Allies' defensive position would be much improved; the ring of blockade round Germany would be tightened; and certain local successes were probable. But the general pattern of the war would remain the same. Even with full American help—and how much more without it—the Allies would still be committed to a gradual process of wearing down Germany's strength by a combination of blockade, bombing and limited action by land. But this process could not continue indefinitely. The strain on Allied economy and morale was already great and might well be intensified by future events—by further German victories or a Japanese aggression in the Far East. The Allies had also to consider that their own forces (apart from any American contribution) would reach their peak at some date between the autumn of 1942 and the summer of 1943. Thereafter there would be little to gain, and perhaps much to lose, by delaying the climax.

But what form could the climax take, other than a direct assault on German positions in Europe? In the last section of the strategic review circulated in June, the J.P.S. examined this problem. They reached the conclusion that it could only be solved by calling in the man-power of occupied Europe to support the Allies. The method which they proposed to use requires some explanation. Since the disasters of the previous year 'subversion'—the stirring up of underground re-sistance to Germany—had been recognized as a distinct and poten-tially valuable branch of the Allied war-effort; and a new organiza-tion, the Special Operations Executive, had been created for the purpose. Its origins and early history were described in the previous volume. Here it is only necessary to remind the reader that S.O.E. was not a branch of the Services but a civilian organization under the wing of the Ministry of Economic Warfare, which had an im-portant stake in subversion in the sense that sabotage and the promo-tion of industrial unrest were valuable adjuncts to the blockade.

In their paper of May 1940, the Chiefs of Staff had included sub-version, along with the blockade and the air-offensive, as one of the three potential weapons of victory. It might be thought that the sub-sequent decision in favour of civilian control, which divorced S.O.E.'s operations from those of the Services, implied some reduction in status; but this was not so. On the contrary, it is with the rise of the new department that we first begin to hear of the Fourth Arm and the theory that subversion could play an independent strategic role, comparable in importance with that of the army or the air force. S.O.E., as its founders conceived it, was not simply to be a hand-maid to the regular forces, but to evolve a method and tactic of its own, drawing inspiration less from military history than from the records of political insurrection. The impress of this plausible theory, so well adjusted to the problems and difficulties of the time, is clearly visible in the last section of the J.P.S. paper of June 1941. The out-line plan for the final offensive was there given in the following terms:

'In areas where German power has become sufficiently weak, subjugated peoples must rise against their Nazi overlords. Such rebellions can only occur once. They must not happen until the stage is set, until all preparations are made, and until the situation is ripe. The armed forces at the patriots' disposal must be suffi-cient to destroy the local German forces. The reduction in Ger-man powers must be sufficient to prevent their reinforcing affected areas adequately.

By the time these conditions are obtained, we should have achieved such a degree of air superiority, combined with naval and military strength, as to warrant the dispatch of certain armed forces from the United Kingdom, whether invasion had been attempted or not. We might be able to operate some ten or more divisions (mostly armoured troops), with a considerable air force, particularly if our offensive operations were so directed as to clear the invasion ports area. Smaller forces might be sent from the Middle East to the Balkans.

The German Army, even with its 250 divisions, is very spread out. They cannot be strong everywhere. With every fresh accession of territory they become further stretched. As their mobility is reduced, their difficulties of reinforcement of threatened areas increase. They become more and more vulnerable.

The object of our operations would be the liberation of the area concerned from Nazi rule with a view to enabling an alternative government of its own to assume control locally.

The attack from within will be the basic concept of such operations. The Germans have demonstrated the advantages of the attack in depth, their forward columns receiving help in advance from fifth columnists and airborne troops. We must go one better. Their fifth columnists were traitors and comparatively few in number. Provided we give them the necessary training and make the required preparations, we shall be able to draw on large numbers of patriots of high morale. We should be able overnight to produce the anarchy of Ireland in 1920 or Palestine in 1936 throughout the chosen theatres of operations.

In a German invasion of England, vulnerable points, communications and possibly air landing places are protected by the Home Guard who know every inch of their own areas. On the other hand, when our offensive is carried into German occupied territories, the Home Guard will be there on the side of the invaders. Patriots will, beforehand, have been secretly organized and armed with personal weapons, such as Sten guns, bombs and explosives.

At the chosen moment in each area, these patriots will seize such objectives as headquarters, broadcasting stations, landing grounds and centres of communications. They will attack officers, sentries, guards and alarm posts and, where possible, barracks, camps and aerodromes. They will destroy German communications leading to the theatre of operations.

The patriots will, however, need the support of organized armed forces. For this purpose full use must be made of the "free" allied contingents now in our territories. In addition, in most cases, British armed forces will be required.

The rôles of British armed forces will be to isolate the area from German intervention from outside, to assist the patriots in the capture of important centres and to destroy enemy formed bodies within the area. Powerful air forces will be used to interrupt the German communications and harass their troops. If we have access to the country by the sea, armoured formations will be landed to strike swiftly and deep into the area. Sufficient infantry formations will be required to protect the bases and harbours on which these armoured troops depend.

There will be no methodical advance from one linear objective to another. The only line to be secured is the boundary of the theatre of operations which enemy reinforcements must be prevented from crossing. Within the theatre chosen, we must establish a number of protected areas where our forward aerodromes, dumps and maintenance arrangements will be located. These protected areas will be captured in succession by armoured formations and used as advanced bases for further operations directed to the complete destruction of enemy forces within the theatre of operations.

The role of the "free" allied contingents will be to supply the rebels with specialists using equipment which cannot be put into the country clandestinely beforehand. In this category are, for example, signals, engineers, anti-tank and anti-aircraft artillery. In addition, small, well-armed mobile columns may be required to work in close co-operation with the patriots.

In allocating "free" national troops or British forces to tasks the principle to be observed will be that "free" national troops will be used wherever very close co-operation with patriots is required. British troops will be used for larger operations and, on completion of their tasks, will hand over to local forces.'

These proposals need to be studied carefully if their implications are to be fully understood. At first sight they might be thought to foreshadow an extensive guerilla movement, such as actually developed later in the war in Greece, Yugoslavia and elsewhere. But this would be an error. What was proposed was in effect the antithesis of a guerilla. The essence of the plan, as the J.P.S. stated it, was that the revolt should be as widespread as possible, not that it should be confined to those isolated or mountainous areas, which alone can support partisans. Indeed, the list of targets, with its emphasis on headquarters, broadcasting stations and centres of communication, made it clear that the main scene of action was expected to be in town rather than country. Stress was also laid on another fixture, equally uncharacteristic of a guerilla. The revolt was to be single, sudden and complete; it was to break out everywhere 'at the chosen moment' without warning or rehearsal. But a guerilla movement normally develops slowly, as it did in Greece and Yugoslavia, and only reaches its full intensity after months or even years of continuous fighting.

The aim—and this distinction is important—was not a partisan movement, which could contain and harass enemy troops in certain favourable areas, but a general political insurrection throughout Europe, which would reproduce, as the paper put it, the condition of Ireland in 1920 or Palestine in 1936. This choice of method was partly influenced, no doubt, by S.O.E.'s civilian background; but it could also be supported by other arguments. The Allies expected to make their main thrust in western Europe, where country suitable for a guerilla is difficult to find and of no great strategic significance. On the other hand, the industrial districts of northern France, Belgium and Holland were of prime importance from the point of view of sabotage and the general economic activities of S.O.E. They were accessible from England; the population was thought to be well-disposed; and there was reason to hope that a strong organization could be built up. It was from the same source that the Allies would have to draw the further support, which they would require for their final offensive.

But the task of creating an effective military instrument by the methods proposed was formidable. In the first place, to organize an 'underground army' or series of such armies on a scale appropriate to the situation was to cut across all the accepted canons of conspiracy. Few secret organizations upon such a scale have remained secret for very long; and in fact, all S.O.E.'s organizations in the West suffered much from exposure and penetration by the enemy—a risk which was inherent in the policy. Secondly, any attempt to create an active, nation-wide organization in a defeated country was bound to raise sharp and complex problems of leadership and political allegiance. This aspect of the matter was given all too little thought at the beginning; but it was later to prove one of the main obstacles to success. In almost every country resistance groups were torn by internal jealousies and conflicts of this kind, to a degree that made central control, let alone military planning on a major scale, invariably difficult and sometimes actually impossible.

There were also serious, if not insuperable, logistic problems. The J.P.S. paper made it clear that the initial equipment of the underground armies, to say nothing of their subsequent support, would entail a considerable air effort. No figures were given; but certain preliminary calculations had in fact been made by S.O.E. A draft programme, submitted in May, showed that the equipment of three underground armies in France, Poland, and Czechoslovakia of a total of 130,000 men[1] would require the equivalent of 8,000 bomber sorties. A second and much reduced programme, put forward in June, gave the cost of equipping 45,000 underground fighters in France, Belgium and Holland as rather more than 2,000 sorties. Both estimates were, of course, far below the scale of the J.P.S. plan; and the figures were admittedly tentative. But they were the only figures available; and it was in their light that the position had to be judged. On this basis only one conclusion was possible. Bomber Command was then flying an average of less than 2,000 offensive sorties a month.[2] To equip a force of 200,000 underground fighters throughout

---

[1] They were to be armed on the scale of 500 pistols, 168 sten-guns and 61 light machine-guns to each 'battalion' of 520 men.

[2] This was the average for the nine months between June, 1941 and March, 1942.

Europe would require, if the S.O.E. figures were correct, not less than 12,000 sorties, or six months' effort by the entire Command; and this diversion would have to be made during the next year or eighteen months, while the Command was passing through the most critical phase of its expansion. There was thus a direct incompatibility between the existing bomber policy and subversion on the scale which was now proposed. The Allies could pin their faith to one or the other; but they could not afford, at least in 1941, to support both on an equal scale.

The final problem was at once practical and strategic. The plan depended for its success on a single, instantaneous rising by forces which had lain perdu until that moment. The underground armies were to have no opportunity of exercising themselves in advance, since any premature disclosure of their strength or even their existence would be fatal. This meant that their military potential was impossible to gauge. An uncertainty beyond the ordinary hazards of war would overhang the whole operation; and it would affect both parties equally—the Allied staff on one side and the resistance leaders on the other. The former would be unwilling to commit their regular forces, until after they were satisfied that the rising had already succeeded; the latter would be unwilling—and in any case unwise—to touch off the rising, until they were assured of immediate regular support. The only way out of this impasse was to make the regular forces strong enough to control the situation alone, even on the footing that the rising wholly or partly failed. But once this principle was admitted, the revolt would become a mere ancillary to regular operations instead of being, as the plan required, a prime condition of their success. To this extent the whole theory of the general rising was grounded on a paradox. Since it could only take place once, it was necessary to ensure its success; but the only conditions which could make success certain were also those which would make the rising strategically unnecessary.

These were the main objections to the J.P.S. plan. They were certainly grave and probably decisive; yet it is difficult to see, granted the conditions of the problem, what alternative form the plan could have taken. A differently constituted S.O.E. might have proposed methods which relied more on irregular warfare and less on the indeterminate prospects of political insurrection. But an operation in these terms, whatever local success it gained, would have been strictly circumscribed geographically. Though it might have gained the Allies a foothold somewhere in south-eastern Europe, its further development beyond that area would have been difficult and hazardous, if not impossible. The problem, in short, was one of power rather than technique. Under the conditions which then existed in Europe, subversion was inherently a subsidiary weapon; and it is doubtful whether any method could have been devised, which would have turned it into a valid instrument of major strategy.

This was certainly the view taken by the Chiefs of Staff, when they had studied the proposals. Their collective note to the Prime Minister contained a cautious reference to the need for 'detailed examination' of the plans for the final offensive; but it is clear that this phrase concealed more than a simple lack of enthusiasm. The most outspoken critic was the C.A.S. In a personal minute, which he circulated at the same time, he had no hesitation in condemning the final section of the paper root and branch:

> '. . . I think it would be disastrous' [he wrote] 'if the rather vague possibilities of the distant future, set out in Section IX of the paper, were to be allowed to obscure the need for the clearest possible direction of the whole of our productive programme, during the next two years, towards the breaking of the German will and material ability to continue the war.
>
> 'The Panzer Divisions and the Luftwaffe will be the last of the German forces to be allowed to weaken, and I cannot believe that, so long as these forces are controlled by a resolute German government with the backing or acquiescence of the people, we shall be able to put land-forces on the Continent. I do not think that a patriot "Home Guard" in occupied territory will prevent a Namsos on a grand scale, if we attempt to invade Europe under these conditions.'

By contrast with this plain-speaking the comments of the C.I.G.S. were very cautious and might almost have been read as a qualified approval:

> 'I agree with the general conception of Section IX of the paper. At some period in the future we must intervene with armed forces on the Continent. Long-term plans should be made and equipment ordered.
>
> I entirely agree that subversive action and propaganda are essential features and must form an integral part of such plans and preparations.
>
> Moreover, suitable arrangements must also be made to ensure that adequate air-support will be available for the forces engaged in these operations.'

The force of these remarks was more in the form than the content. By coupling subversive action with propaganda, the C.I.G.S. dismissed it, in effect, from the main battle. He was prepared to make use of it as an ancillary, so far that might be necessary, but he evidently had no faith in it as a principal weapon.

The practical results of this attitude were soon visible. In July, Dr. Dalton, as the Minister responsible, forwarded to Mr. Churchill for the urgent consideration of the Chiefs of Staff the second of S.O.E.'s

5

two estimates of the air-support which they would require. This was the one which provided for an underground army of 45,000 men, distributed between France, Belgium and Holland, and could fairly be described as an absolute minimum, if the plan were to be tested at all. Nevertheless, the estimate was turned down. The Chiefs of Staff took the view that 'it would be unsound to sacrifice the effectiveness of our bombing effort to subversive activities'; and this decision was accepted without protest. S.O.E. was thus deprived, though only for a time, of the means to carry out its policy; but it will be noticed that the policy itself had not been abandoned. The creation of underground armies remained the final goal of S.O.E.'s activities; and in subsequent years, when the supply position was easier, large resources and a considerable air effort were in fact devoted to this object.

The decision in July was not, therefore, so final or so clear-cut as it appeared to be. It arose from a general lack of confidence in the military, or at least the strategic, value of subversion; but it did not amount to a denial that some such method of warfare might, in fact, be necessary. We can see here the essential dilemma which Allied strategy faced at the time. It was admitted that the means proposed were often inadequate to the purpose or mutually conflicting, as bombing then conflicted with subversion; but no other means were available, or could be until the terms of the problem had radically changed.

CHAPTER III

THE ORIGINS OF 'BARBAROSSA'

(i)

Hitler's Dilemma

WHILE THE VARIOUS plans and appreciations, discussed in the last two chapters, were being written and studied in London, a military event was preparing elsewhere, which would presently change the whole nature of the war. The Allies expected, as we have seen, that Germany would make her next move in the Mediterranean, probably by a two-pronged attack, in the east against Suez, in the west against Gibraltar. The strategic advantages of such an operation were obvious and had certainly not been lost on the German General Staff. But they made no appeal to Hitler, whose thoughts had already turned in a different direction. By the spring of 1941 his view of the war had undergone a profound change. He no longer regarded England or the Western Allies in general as his main enemy; to complete the victory in the West, which was already almost within his grasp, seemed comparatively unimportant. His whole attention was concentrated on a totally new adventure—the conquest of the Soviet Union.

The preliminary signs of this metamorphosis had been visible as early as July 1940. In that month, still flushed with his success in the Battle of France, Hitler had found himself confronted by two new problems, which he had some reason to link together. The first was England's stubborn refusal to admit defeat or come to terms, despite the apparent hopelessness of her position. The second was Russia's growing activity on his eastern border. At the end of June she had announced abruptly that her claim on the Rumanian province of Bessarabia must be settled forthwith, if necessary by force. She had followed this with an entirely new claim to the neighbouring province of Bukovina, 'the last missing part of the unified Ukraine'. During July, with an equal lack of ceremony, she had completed the annexation or 'voluntary incorporation' of the three Baltic States, including a strip of Lithuanian territory which previous agreements had allocated to Germany.

These acts were not, of course, unexpected. By the two treaties, which made up the Nazi-Soviet Pact of 1939,[1] Germany had recog-

---

[1] The Non-Aggression Treaty of 23rd August and the Boundary and Friendship Treaty of 28th September.

nized Russia's claim to Bessarabia and had also agreed that, 'in the event of a political and territorial rearrangement' in the Baltic States, the whole of that area (apart from the small strip already mentioned) should fall within Russia's sphere of influence. Nevertheless, their actual execution, its speed and brusqueness and the evidence which it offered of Russia's intention to go beyond the strict letter of the Pact, came as a disagreeable shock to Hitler. It was already plain that his victories in the West had impaired, perhaps even destroyed, the basis of his original agreement with Russia. He had signed in order to free his hands against England and France. Russia had signed in self-protection and in the hope that an arduous campaign in the West would weaken Germany and blunt her appetite for further adventure. But now, with France already prostrate, neither motive had the same force. A new era was beginning in which both parties might wish to revise their policy; and in this context England's continued resistance had a particular importance.

Early in July 1940 Hitler had been obliged to warn Mussolini against any premature adventures in eastern Europe. An attack on Yugoslavia, such as Italy was then contemplating, might well be the signal for a general struggle for power in the Balkans in which Russia would join. Under these conditions, Hitler had added, it was possible that England and Russia 'might discover some community of in-terest'.[1] Exactly what combination of events he had in mind is not clear. He may, perhaps, have feared a bargain by which Russia received a free hand in the Balkans in return for an undertaking to deny Germany the Rumanian oil on which her war-industries de-depended. But there is no doubt that he was serious in expecting some form of *rapprochement* between England and Russia. A week later he reverted to the same subject in conversation with Halder:[2]

> 'The Fuehrer is very much preoccupied with the problem of why England does not wish to come to terms. He sees the answer, as we do, in the fact that England still has some hopes of Russia. He therefore expects that he will have to compel her by force to make peace. But he is reluctant to do this. Reason: if we crush England by force of arms, the British Empire will fall to pieces. But that would be of no advantage to Germany. We should spill German blood only in order that Japan, America and others might benefit.'[3]

Hitler's anxieties had been reinforced by other evidence which came to hand at about this time. In the middle of July the German Foreign Office received, apparently through the Italian intelligence

---

[1] *Ciano Diplomatic Papers* (ed. M. Muggeridge) 1948, pp. 375–9.
[2] Colonel General Franz Halder, Chief of the General Staff from September 1938 to September 1942.
[3] *Halder's Diary* (M.S.), 13th July, 1940.

service, a series of reports or intercepted dispatches, which threw a disturbing light on current diplomatic activity in Moscow. Three in particular described conversations which Sir Stafford Cripps, the newly appointed British Ambassador, had had with his Turkish, Greek and Yugoslav colleagues. He was reported as saying that his reception by President Kalinin and M. Molotov had been most cordial. The former had spoken of England's and Russia's common interests and the need to reach an understanding; the latter had received him twice at a time when he was refusing the German Ambassador on the ground that he was on leave. The general impression was that Russia's dislike and fear of Germany were growing daily. Speaking to the Greek Minister Sir Stafford had added the precise forecast that Russia would be fighting on the Allied side within a year.

The German Ambassador, Count von der Schulenburg, affected to make light of these reports. He maintained that there had been no real change in Russo-German relations. Cripps' remarks were simply the natural language of an energetic diplomat anxious to enhance his country's prestige. Nevertheless, other reports received at the same time offered a certain confirmation. A dispatch, for example, from the Turkish Ambassador to his government gave a startling account of the reorganization and enlargement of the Red Army and stated explicitly that this development was aimed at Germany:

> 'In Moscow it is believed that Hitler has fulfilled his programme in the perfectly logical sequence postulated in *Mein Kampf*. For he has eliminated all States which were potentially dangerous and now Russia alone remains to be reckoned with. War between Russia and Germany will not break out at present; but, as soon as Hitler is resolved to combine all conflicts into one major issue, he will pick a quarrel with Russia.'

We cannot tell what influence these reports had upon Hitler. It may well have been considerable, for he was always more attentive to information from secret or underground sources than to the official dispatches of his Foreign Office. And the reports certainly went far to confirm his belief that new and dangerous combinations might be forming against him. His reaction was immediate. On 21st July he discussed with Brauchitsch[1] the possible implications of a war with Russia and gave instructions that the Army was to study the problem and make preliminary plans:

> 'Stalin is coquetting with Britain in order to keep her in the struggle and tie us down with the object of gaining time and taking what he wants and what he would not be able to get, if peace were to break out. *He has an interest in not letting Germany get*

---

[1] Feldt-Marschall Walter von Brauchitsch, C-in-C Army (Ob.d H.) from February 1938 to December, 1941.

too strong ; but there are no indications of any Russian activity against us.
We must turn our attention to tackling the Russian problem.'[1]

This might have been understood as no more than a prudent pre-caution; but it soon became clear that Hitler had something much more serious in mind. Ten days later, between the 29th and 31st July, he presided at a series of conferences at the Berghof, attended by all his principal advisers, at which the whole military situation was passed in review. There, to the surprise and even consternation of his Staff, he announced a definite intention to attack Russia not later than the following spring.

Unfortunately, no full record of the Berghof Conference has survived. It appears, however, that Hitler's decision was first made known to Jodl,[2] who passed it on to a group of senior staff-officers on the 29th. He was immediately overwhelmed by questions. What about England? Was it assumed that she would have capitulated before the spring or would Russia be attacked first? Jodl replied that the attack would take place independently of developments in the West, but in such a way as to leave the *Luftwaffe* free, if necessary, to resume major operations against England in the autumn of 1941 or the spring of the following year. On the 31st a larger conference took place, which was attended by Brauchitsch and Halder as well as Jodl. Hitler then reaffirmed his decision and explained his reasons. The record in Halder's diary runs as follows:

> '*Something must have happened in London.* The English were down and out; now their spirits have revived again. (We know from) intercepted conversations (that) Russia has been unpleasantly affected by the rapid development of the situation in the West. She need only suggest to England that she does not want to see a strong Germany and the English, like drowning men, will clutch at the hope that within six or eight months the situation will be transformed. *With Russia defeated, England's last hope is blotted out* and then Germany becomes master of Europe and the Balkans.
>
> Decision: *We must settle accounts with Russia and destroy her in the spring of 1941.*
>
> *The quicker Russia is smashed the better. The operation only makes sense if we shatter the Russian state at a single blow.* To gain tracts of territory is not enough. To stand still in winter is dangerous. Therefore it is better to wait, but with the firm resolve to finish Russia off. This is also necessary on account of the situation in the Baltic. Two great States cannot co-exist there side by side. May 1941: operations would take five months to complete. Much better if it were possible this year; but that would not be practicable as a concerted operation.'[3]

---

[1] *Halder's Diary*, 22nd July, 1940.
[2] Lt.-General Alfred Jodl, Chief of the O.K.W. Operations Staff throughout the war.
[3] *Halder's Diary*, 31st July, 1940.

This was the form in which Hitler's decision, the gravest which he was ever to take, was announced to his Staff. The immediate causes of anxiety and irritation which led up to it have been recorded above; but even without them the decision itself was, perhaps, inevitable. No student of Hitler's career can doubt that he had always intended to come to grips with the Soviet Union sooner or later. To do so was the logical outcome of the political and racial theories on which his whole régime was founded. Moreover, his territorial ambitions, vaguely expressed though they often were, certainly included the acquisition of *Lebensraum* in the East, not only in the adjacent areas of Poland but also in the distant Ukraine and perhaps even farther afield. One sentence in an early Nuremberg speech indicates the nature of his dream. 'If only,' he had then exclaimed, 'we had at our disposal the incalculable wealth and stores of the Ural mountains, the endless fertile plains of the Ukraine, then our people would swim in plenty.'[1] And with Hitler to desire and to grasp were two terms almost synonymous.

There was, indeed, nothing surprising in his decision considered in the abstract. What was surprising, and what took his Staff aback, was the particular moment at which it had been made. On the 16th July, barely a fortnight before the Berghof conferences, Hitler had issued his Directive No. 16: 'Preparations for a landing-operation against England.' Thus 'Seeloewe' had been born, the operation which should have crowned his achievement in the West and for which preparations were still in train. Since then Lord Halifax's firm reply to his Reichstag speech of the 19th had removed the last hope that England would capitulate voluntarily; and the proposed invasion had become even more important. Yet here was Hitler already turning his mind to Russia, not apparently in anticipation of England's defeat, but following an argument which presupposed that England would still be fighting in 1941 or even 1942. If that were so, what became of the invasion? Still more, if England were assumed to be fighting when the attack on Russia began, what became of the argument, so strongly stressed in *Mein Kampf*, that a war on two fronts, a war against the East and the West simultaneously, was the fatal error which had cost Germany her defeat in 1914–18?

It is easy to understand a certain bewilderment on the part of Hitler's advisers. But if we examine more carefully his attitude towards the defeat of England and the means by which he hoped to bring this about, much of the seeming confusion disappears. Hitler's original plan had been to proceed from the conquest of France to the slow strangulation of England by means of an intensive sea and air-attack on her supply-routes. For that purpose no actual landing was

---

[1] Speech at Nuremburg, 12th September, 1936.

required; and it had been assumed by all three Services that none would be attempted, except perhaps as a *coup-de-grâce*, 'as the last act in a war against England which had already taken a victorious course'. These assumptions remained in force until the end of June or the beginning of July 1940. Then, in the sudden exhilaration which followed the Battle of France, when all opportunity seemed ripe, the Army conceived the idea that a full-dress invasion with the object of conquering England might, after all, be feasible; and they urged this view on Hitler. The moment was opportune. It was already clear that Germany's success by land had so far outstripped her naval preparations that the original plan of blockade could not be made effective for at least one or more probably two years. Invasion, if it were possible, would eliminate this gap.

In these circumstances Hitler issued Directive No. 16; but he did not do so without certain misgivings. We have already quoted his conversation with Halder early in July—in fact, on the very day when the Army's plan was presented to him—and the reasons which he then gave for not 'crushing England by force of arms'. The argument, as Halder gives it, is condensed; but the outline is clear enough. If Hitler, instead of crushing England, could come to terms with a British Government which still retained its full authority, he could hope to exercise at least some control over the fate of British overseas possessions. But if he were obliged to destroy England, in the sense of eliminating or taking over her Government, then in his own phrase 'the British Empire would fall to pieces' and the spoils would be snapped up by whatever maritime power had the wish and means to do so. This was a strong argument against forcing a military decision too quickly. The methods of blockade, though dangerously slow, would still leave the door open for negotiation.[1]

Apart from these practical arguments, Hitler had another reason, more deeply buried in his consciousness, for preferring settlement to conquest. Towards the end of June, Warlimont had told the Naval Staff in answer to a question, that 'basically the Fuehrer does not intend to destroy the British Empire completely, as the disintegration of Britain would operate to the disadvantage of the white race'. That this or something like it was really Hitler's view is confirmed by Ciano's account of the meeting with Mussolini on 18th June, when the terms of the French armistice were discussed:

> 'Ribbentrop then went on to speak of the possibilities which might arise with regard to England. He said that, in the Fuehrer's opinion, the existence of the British Empire as an element of stability and social order in the world was very useful. In the

---

[1] A parallel exists in Hitler's relatively lenient treatment of France in order to retain, through Vichy, some control of French overseas possessions, especially in North Africa.

present state of affairs it would be impossible to replace it by another similar organization. Therefore the Fuehrer does not desire the destruction of the British Empire'.[1]

These sentiments were not so incongruous as they sound. In Hitler's uneasy temperament strong destructive impulses were allied, not altogether strangely, with a passionate fear and hatred of anarchy. As early as the days of *Mein Kampf*, England had established herself in his mind as a symbol of order. To attack her was possible; but he was, perhaps, genuinely reluctant to destroy what he had once so much admired.

To return to the development of 'Seeloewe': during the latter part of July the Navy raised strenuous objections to the Army's proposal. They made it plain that they could not guarantee to deliver troops across the Channel either at the rate or on the broad frontage which was called for. Their case was so strongly argued as to move Halder to exclaim that, if the facts stated were true, 'we can throw away the whole invasion plan'. In the meanwhile, however, a new element had entered the problem. It had always been conceded that complete air superiority, amounting to the destruction of the R.A.F. as a fighting force, was a necessary prelude to a landing of any kind. Now the hope began to grow, fostered by Goering, that once air superiority had been achieved, intensive and unrestricted bombing might in itself be enough to bring England to her knees. If so, the Navy's objections could be met by reducing the scope of the landing to what it had been originally—an improvised operation against an enemy already defeated.

These problems were reviewed at the Berghof Conference. At the same meeting at which he announced his intention to destroy Russia, Hitler gave his decision in terms which were characteristic of the new mood.

> 'The air war will start now and will determine our ultimate relative strength. If the results of the air war are not satisfactory, invasion preparations will be stopped. But if we gain the impression that the English are being crushed and that the air war is, after a certain time, taking effect, then we shall attack.'[2]

The Navy's objections were thus shelved for the moment; but it is clear that they had had their effect on Hitler. In private conversation with Brauchitsch after the meeting he emphasized that he had grave doubts about the feasibility of a landing.

In fact, when the whole problem was further examined in August, the Navy's case against a full-dress invasion—a landing of conquest rather than occupation—was found to be unanswerable. In its final

---

[1] *Ciano Diplomatic Papers*, p. 373.
[2] *Fuehrer Naval Conferences* (U.S. edition, 1940), Vol. IV, pp. 9–12.

form, therefore, which was reached at the end of the month, the plan laid an almost exclusive emphasis on the air-bombardment. An actual landing was only to be attempted, in Jodl's phrase, 'if it is a question of finishing off an enemy already defeated in the air war'. This was the conclusion which Hitler had, perhaps, foreseen from the beginning and even desired. There is little doubt that the method of air-attack, or air-attack combined with blockade, suited his particular purpose far better than invasion. It avoided the crushing defeat, which he had practical and psychological reasons for not wishing to inflict. At the same time it offered a means of bringing pressure to bear on England and gradually forcing her into a position where she would have no choice but to accept the offers of peace, which she had previously rejected.

Considered in this light, Hitler's decision to attack Russia before he had clinched his victory in the West, was not so rash or so illogical as it appeared. He could not tell how long it would be before England succumbed. If morale were to crack under the stress of bombardment, if Churchill were to fall, a decision might still be reached in 1940. If not, the war might continue for anything up to two years, that is to say, until the time when blockade finally took effect. But he could scarcely afford to wait for so long before addressing his mind to the Russian problem. Russia was growing daily stronger, more active and less friendly; and each increase in her strength was a direct encouragement to England, even if no formal alliance followed. There was also the risk, which time would intensify, of American intervention. If he waited too long, he might well find that the situation had passed beyond his control.

(ii)

Russo-German Relations

The decisions taken at the Berghof were, in form, only planning decisions, which left Hitler free to reverse his policy, if he wished to do so, at any time during the next nine months. Nevertheless, these decisions set off a train of executive consequences. On 5th August, less than a week after the Berghof meeting, the first staff-study for an attack on Russia was circulated by O.K.H. Two days later O.K.W. issued a directive, *Aufbau Ost* (Build-up in the East), which put in motion the transfer of supply-depots, training-centres and other base-installations from Germany's Western to her Eastern frontier. From that date onwards all the administrative preparations for a major campaign in the East were pressed forward vigorously and without a break. Intelligence was collected, stock-piles formed, new airfields built and a considerable programme of road and railway construction taken in hand. As these measures gained momentum, so the limits of Hitler's freedom of choice were insensibly narrowed. It remained open to him to change his mind; but the dislocation which would follow, if he did so, grew greater with each passing month.

These facts certainly influenced events; but it would be wrong to represent Hitler at any stage as their passive victim. Though he may sometimes have wavered in his decision to attack Russia, there is little evidence that he was ever seriously tempted to abandon it. On the contrary, the whole trend of events during the autumn and winter of 1940 seemed to confirm his judgement. It became increasingly clear that Germany and Russia had ceased to have any real community of interest. Their dealings were no longer those of partners, even temporary or unwilling partners, but of active and pertinacious rivals. Let us consider first how the situation developed in the Balkans.

When Russia advanced her own claim to Bessarabia and Bukovina, she also indicated her support of two other claims on Rumanian territory—that of Hungary to Transylvania and that of Bulgaria to the Black Sea province of Dobrudja. The result was to place Hitler in a position of great difficulty. Germany's dependence on Rumanian oil and her economic interests in general suggested that she ought to assume the role of protector and resist these extensive and damaging demands. On the other hand, to support Rumania in rejecting her neighbours' claims was to run the risk, so long as Russia maintained her attitude, of provoking a general war in the Balkans. In that event, whatever the final outcome, Germany's oil supplies would be fatally compromised.[1] There was also the danger, already mentioned, that Russia and the Allies might find some basis of agreement; and this was the more pressing since Germany's own agreement with Russia was far from clear-cut.

In his haste to conclude the Nazi-Soviet Pact in 1939, Hitler had instructed his negotiators to avoid controversial issues and all subjects likely to give rise to prolonged discussion. The Soviet leaders, equally obsessed with the immediate future, had been willing to treat on these terms, so that the final agreements had been dangerously superficial. Their declared object was to draw a line between German and Russian spheres of influence in eastern Europe in such a way as to eliminate future causes of conflict. But in fact they had done nothing of the kind. Except in respect of Poland and the Baltic States, where

---

[1] On 29th May the German Minister in Bucharest had reported that it was the Rumanian Government's intention to fire the oilfields in the event of an attack either by Russia or by Germany.

an exact demarcation was immediately necessary, the two treaties had taken refuge in broad ambiguous phrases, which both parties could interpret at their pleasure. Thus the agreement on spheres of influence in the Balkans had been confined to one clause in a secret protocol annexed to the Treaty of Non-Aggression:

> '13. With regard to South-Eastern Europe, attention is called on the part of the Soviet Union to her interest in Bessarabia. Germany on her part professes her complete political disinterest (*das voellige politische Disinteressement*) in these areas'.[1]

These sentences left everything unexplained. Were Russia's interests confined to Bessarabia or did they extend further and, if so, in what direction? What did 'political disinterest' mean and was it applicable only to Bessarabia or, as the general context might suggest, to south-eastern Europe as a whole? No attempt was made to answer these questions either in the body of the Treaty or in any subsequent document; and Hitler therefore found himself, when the Rumanian crisis broke, with no firm diplomatic platform on which to stand.

His first moves were eminently cautious. The validity of Russia's claim to Bessarabia was not contested; but she was pressed in a strongly worded Note to moderate her further claim to Bukovina. To this she finally agreed, though only to the extent of limiting herself for the moment to the northern part of the province with control of the main railway line. Bulgaria was similarly persuaded to reduce her claim to Dobrudja to the southern half of that province as far as the old 1913 frontier. Pressure was then successfully applied to Rumania to accept these decisions. But the third problem, that of Hungary's claim to Transylvania, was found to be less easily soluble. Direct negotiations between Hungary and Rumania, fostered by Germany, only served to exacerbate feeling on either side. By the end of August a complete deadlock had been reached; both countries had mobilized; and Hungary had already made a formal inquiry as to what Germany's attitude would be, if she were forced 'to seek a military solution'.[2]

This was a moment of particular danger. Russia was reported to be concentrating troops on the Rumanian border and along her Western frontier generally. It was feared that she might seize the opportunity of a Hungarian attack to occupy the whole of eastern Rumania up to the line of the Carpathians. And this might be only the first stage of a general movement directed against Germany. In anticipation of this, orders were given on 27th August to reinforce the German garrison in Poland by 10 infantry and 2 armoured divisions; and plans were formed for an airborne descent on the Rumanian oilfields in the

---

[1] *Nazi-Soviet Relations* p. 78.
[2] Max Beloff, *The Foreign Policy of Soviet Russia*, Vol. II, pp. 352–3, 336–7.

event of a Russian advance. But Hitler was not yet ready to press the conflict to extremes.

On 28th August the announcement was made that the Fuehrer, in response to previous requests from both parties, had decided to arbitrate in the Rumanian-Hungarian dispute. On the following day Ribbentrop, accompanied by Ciano, left for Vienna, where the Foreign Ministers of the two countries were summoned to attend him. On 30th August, after a day of purely nominal discussion, an Award was made, supported by the joint military power of Germany and Italy. It allotted to Hungary an area of Transylvania approximately equal to two-thirds of her original claim and endeavoured to console Rumania by a formal guarantee of the integrity of her remaining territory against all comers. Both countries accepted this act of authority unconditionally. At no point in the whole transaction, however, had Russia, Hitler's supposed partner, even been consulted. She was merely informed after the event of what had been done.

This rough and ready solution of the immediate crisis was regarded by Ribbentrop as a diplomatic triumph. He was later to remark complacently to Ciano that 'the Russian dream vanished for ever in the halls of the Belvedere at Vienna'.[1] Although events were to disprove this judgement, it is true that the temporary and immediate effect of the Award was to demonstrate that, despite Russian intrigues, Germany was still the dominant power in the Balkans. This process was assisted, paradoxically enough, by the strong popular reaction which developed in Rumania against the Award. Within a few weeks King Carol's administration, which had been the unwilling agent of three major cessions of territory in as many months, finally disintegrated. The way was then clear for a *coup d'état*, in which the German Minister played a certain part, by the pro-Nazi General Antonescu and the formal reduction of Rumania to the status of a German dependency.

One of the first acts of the new régime was to renew a request, previously made by King Carol, for a German Military Mission accompanied, if possible, by one or more armoured or motorized divisions. Hitler, who was now fully committed to the support and, if necessary, the defence of Rumania, made haste to comply. The directive subsequently issued to the Mission shows how completely he had abandoned even the pretence of 'political disinterest':

'Following the Rumanian Government's request for German training personnel and demonstration troops, the Fuehrer and Supreme Commander has reached the following decisions:

(1) The Army and *Luftwaffe* will send Military Missions to Rumania. Their ostensible object will be to help Rumania, a friendly country, to organise and train her armed forces.

---

[1] *Ciano Diaries* (ed. M. Muggeridge, 1947), p. 293.

(2) The real objects, which must be concealed both from the Rumanians and our own troops, will be:

(a) to protect the oilfields from attack by a third power and from destruction;

(b) to prepare the Rumanian armed forces to carry out certain tasks in accordance with a definite plan drawn up in Germany's interest;

(c) to prepare for operations by German and Rumanian armed forces from Rumania in the event of our being forced into war with Soviet Russia'.

The terms of this directive indicate the real significance of the Vienna Award. The episode had been a final demonstration of the futility of the Nazi-Soviet Pact as an instrument of long-term policy and its incapacity to forestall or settle any dispute in which a genuine clash of interests was involved. Throughout the crisis Germany and Russia had behaved like two opponents openly manœuvring for position against each other. Apart from the most ordinary diplomatic exchanges—and even these were suspended at the height of the crisis —there had been no consultation, no suggestion of common interest and no attempt at settlement. It is true that the issue had finally been solved without recourse to arms; but this had only been done by a public trial of strength, as if no Non-Aggression Pact and no Treaty of Friendship had ever existed.

Hitler's instructions to his Military Mission reflected this new state of affairs. There is no doubt that he had been badly frightened by the Balkan crisis, which had had all the appearance of a Russian man-œuvre to gain control, or at least to deny Germany control, of Rumania and her indispensable oil fields. Nor was it only in the Balkans that such attempts at encroachment were to be feared. We have seen that in July Hitler was already nervous about the position in the Baltic and the events of the next two months increased his anxiety. The annexation of the three Baltic States was followed by renewed Russian pressure on Finland. A demand that Finland should dismantle her naval base on the Aaland Islands was pressed insistently; there were repeated complaints of the unco-operative attitude of certain members of the Finnish government; and Russian forces on the frontier were reinforced and brought to a state of readiness.

There was one sense in which these activities did not concern Germany, since she had conceded by the terms of the Nazi-Soviet Pact that Finland lay within Russia's sphere of influence. In another sense they touched her closely. She had already suffered a considerable economic loss by the annexation of the Baltic States, from which she had previously imported food, flax, lumber and even a certain quantity of petroleum. The prospective loss of Finland was far more serious. As well as supplying food, timber and copper, she was potentially the richest source of nickel in Europe; and this metal was scarcely less essential to Germany than Rumanian oil. It was known that one of the main objects of Russian pressure was to secure control of the Petsamo mines, which were then being worked, by arrangement with the Finnish Government, on German account. A German Foreign Office memorandum, written later in the year, shows how seriously this threat was taken:

'If the Finnish Government yields to Russian pressure and introduces emergency legislation to cancel the present Canadian nickel concession and transfer it to the Soviet Government, an unpleasant and unfavourable situation will arise for us. Our own nickel interests, which are regulated by an agreement with the Finnish Government will be wiped out as Russia will not acknowledge the validity of the agreement. By the transfer of the nickel concession, Russia will also acquire exclusive territorial rights in the Petsamo area, and will thus be placed in the immediate neighbourhood of Kirkenes, which is occupied by our troops. The Services and the Reichsmarshall in particular have expressed the hope that we shall not lose Petsamo.'[1]

Lastly, there were general strategic considerations of some importance. Russia's new bases in Lithuania were uncomfortably close to East Prussia. From Finland or even from her own territory she could threaten German garrisons in northern Norway. The Red Fleet had acquired important new bases on the Baltic coast and, in the event of war, might seriously hamper German trade with Scandinavia, especially the iron-ore traffic. During August steps were taken to meet certain of these dangers. The German Baltic coast and the northern fjords of Norway were fortified and additional troops were moved to the Narvik area. At the same time negotiations were opened with Finland for way-leave over certain roads and railways in the north, which provided a second and quicker line of communication with the German garrisons. These measures were represented to Russia as a precaution against Allied raids or landings in the Far North. There was some truth in this, since preparations could in fact serve either purpose; but it was hardly enough to satisfy Russia, who was bound to resent this intrusion into her sphere of influence.

---

[1] *Nazi-Soviet Relations*, p. 205.

(iii)

Molotov's Visit

These growing pressures from the Far North to the Danube confirmed Hitler's belief that further collaboration with Russia was
impossible. All his previous arguments in favour of an attack in the
East in the spring had been greatly strengthened. By September
hopes of a rapid decision against England were fading. In the meanwhile Russia grew stronger and there was no lack of evidence that her
intentions were unfriendly. Nevertheless, as so often before his major
decisions, Hitler hesitated. Planning for an Eastern campaign was
allowed to continue; but no final orders were issued. For the next two
months German strategy hung in suspense.

Such periods of hesitation were natural to Hitler's temperament;
but in this case there was a particular reason. Almost to a man his
advisers were opposed to his policy. Not many of them, it is true, felt
able to state this opinion openly and clearly. The atmosphere of
Hitler's court had never been favourable to criticism and this was
especially so in 1940, when his reputation as a strategist stood at its
height. His advisers found themselves doubly afraid to contradict,
both for fear of Hitler as a man and for fear lest he might be right.
Much of their opposition was therefore mute; but there was no doubt
of its reality.

At the end of July, when Hitler's intentions first became known,
Halder and Brauchitsch discussed the future with anxiety. They
agreed that, if no quick decision in the West were possible, Germany
ought to go to great lengths to appease Russia, rather than run the
risk of a war on two fronts:

> 'A visit to Stalin would be desirable. Russia's wish to expand
> towards the Dardenelles and the Persian Gulf need not disturb
> us. In the Balkans, which fall within our zone economically, we
> can manage to keep out of each other's way. There is no risk of a
> collision between Italy and Russia in the Mediterranean. On this
> basis we can strike a decisive blow against England in the Medi-
> terranean, cut her off from Asia and help the Italians to build
> their Mediterranean empire, whilst we with Russian help con-
> solidate the Reich which we have created in northern and
> western Europe.'[1]

To this end they proposed three operations: first, an attack on
Gibraltar through Spain (Operation 'Felix'); secondly, the use of
German armour to support the Italian drive on Suez (Operation

---

[1] *Halder's Diary*, 30th July, 1940.

'Achse'); and thirdly, an independent German attack, directed perhaps through Palestine, on Allied positions in the Middle East. Support should also be given, if necessary, to a Russian move on the Persian Gulf.

Such a policy would have been welcomed by the *Wehrmacht* and equally by the German Foreign Office, who were opposed (largely for economic reasons) to any breach with Russia. Nevertheless, although Halder and Brauchitsch were both present at the Berghof within a day or two of their private discussion, there is no evidence that they argued their case with any warmth or even put it forward at all. They were content to listen to the Fuehrer's voice in silence and to record his words afterwards without the least hint of disagreement. So far had Hitler's reputation imposed itself on his Generals. But if the Army was silent, the Navy was still vocal; and through this channel the views of Halder and Brauchitsch were eventually brought into open discussion.

Towards the end of September, Admiral Raeder sought the first of a series of interviews with Hitler, in which he argued with great force that all Germany's strategic resources should be concentrated on the defeat of England. This was essentially a naval problem; but the Army could also intervene decisively. The prime task was to expel the British from the Mediterranean by simultaneous movements on Gibraltar in the West and Suez in the East. Naval bases would thus be secured from which to press home the attack on England's supply routes; and the whole of the Middle East, with its invaluable re- sources of raw material, would be opened to German conquest. On the other hand, if these actions were neglected, Italy might be unable to hold her position in Libya; and the Allies, supported perhaps by a Gaullist rising in Algeria, might eventually gain control of the whole Northern African coast. This would be a strategic reverse of the first order, for it would open the southern as well as the western coast of Europe to the threat of enemy raids and landings.

Raeder also touched on the question of Russia. She was, he argued, fundamentally frightened of Germany and could therefore be held in check by a threat to her southern frontier such as Germany could exert from the Middle East. The capture of Suez should be followed by a general advance through Palestine and Syria as far as the Turkish frontier. Once these positions had been secured, the Russian problem would assume a very different aspect. 'It is questionable,' he added, 'whether action would be necessary in the north.'[1] These arguments, and perhaps the knowledge that Raeder was expressing the Army's views no less than his own, made a marked impression on Hitler. They obliged him, as he admitted afterwards, to re-examine

---

[1] *Fuehrer Conferences on Naval Affairs* (Admiralty Edition, 1940), pp. 104-5.

his position and consider carefully 'whether he was on the right lines'. That this was more than a form of words became apparent a few days later, when he set in train his last attempt, not indeed to conciliate Russia, but to probe her intentions and feel for himself whether any warmth still remained in the alliance.

A convenient setting was provided by the Tripartite Pact, the agreement between Germany, Italy and Japan, which was signed in Berlin on 27th September. Hitler knew that this treaty was regarded with great suspicion in Moscow, where the spectre of another war on two fronts—a simultaneous attack by Germany from the West and Japan from the East—haunted the minds of the Russian leaders. He was thus in a position at once to tempt and to threaten—to offer Russia protection by inviting her to join the Pact herself and to hint that serious consequences might follow from her refusal. With this in view Ribbentrop addressed a letter to Stalin. Three parts of its length were taken up with an elaborate justification of all Germany's acts since the signing of the agreement with Russia in 1939, which need not concern us. The point came in the closing paragraphs:

> 'As to the attitude of the three partners in this Alliance [the Tripartite Pact] to the Soviet Union, I must say at once that from the very beginning of their exchange of views all three Powers unanimously agreed that the Pact was in no way aimed at the Soviet Union . . . From Germany's point of view the Alliance is the logical outcome of a policy, long followed by the Government of the Reich, which allots an equal place to co-operation between Germany and the Soviet Union on the one hand and co-operation between Germany and Japan on the other. Indeed, friendship between the Axis Powers and Japan. between Germany and the Soviet Union and between the Soviet Union and Japan, form parts of a natural political coalition which, if ably conducted, should rebound to the advantage of all concerned. You will remember that I discussed similar ideas with you most frankly at the time of my first visit to Moscow and offered my help in adjusting the difficulties which then still existed between Soviet Russia and Japan . . .
>
> In conclusion I must add, what is also the Fuehrer's opinion, that it seems to be the historic mission of the Four Powers, the Soviet Union, Italy, Japan and Germany, to adopt a long term policy and to direct the future development of their peoples by defining their respective interests on a world-wide scale.'[1]

The letter ended with an invitation to M. Molotov to visit Berlin in order to discuss these momentous ideas.

M. Stalin's reply, though brief and cautious, was not uncordial; Molotov duly arrived in Berlin on 12th November. The proposals

---

[1] *Nazi-Soviet Relations*, p. 207.

foreshadowed in Ribbentrop's letter were then laid before him. They were based, as Hitler explained, on the assumption that the war in the West had already been won. Either England would succumb to a combination of blockade and air-attack during the winter or she would be invaded in the spring. The possibility of American intervention could now be discounted as the result of Germany's agreement with Japan. It was therefore appropriate to look to the future and to consider how the world, and more especially the 'bankrupt estate of the British Empire', could best be divided between Germany and her allies. The solution seemed to be for each of them to direct her future expansion southward. Germany would seek the *Lebensraum* and raw materials which she needed in Central Africa in the area of her old colonies; Italy would do the same in North and Eastern Africa; and Japan in the direction of Indonesia. Russia, conforming to the same pattern, would expand southward in the general direction of India. Three great zones or spheres of influence would thus be brought into being: a German-Italian African sphere; an East Asian sphere dominated by Japan; and, between the two, an Asian sphere centred on India which would be recognized as belonging to Russia.

These proposals, though more immediately attractive to Germany, Italy and Japan, yet offered much to Russia. There was no obvious reason of principle why she should not have accepted them, at least as a basis for discussion. It is even probable that she would have done so, if her leaders had still preserved even the smallest belief in Hitler's sincerity. But that phase was plainly over. They had made one experiment in dealing with Hitler in terms of loosely defined 'spheres of influence'; and they had no wish to repeat, still less to extend it.

M. Molotov therefore put a series of questions, which were designed to bring these aerial conceptions down to earth. What, he asked, were the exact boundaries proposed for the Japanese sphere in Asia? How would Germany's New Order in Europe affect Soviet relations with Rumania, Bulgaria and other Balkan countries? The Vienna Award had already created a new situation in south-eastern Europe, which appeared to ignore Russia's still unsatisfied claim to southern Bukovina. There was also the question of the Dardenelles, a vital Russian interest. What view would Germany take of a Soviet agreement with Bulgaria on the same lines as Germany's recent agreement with Rumania, which would give Russia the right to establish military bases within range of the Straits? And lastly what of Finland? Was the original agreement on spheres of influence still regarded as valid? If so, how was it that Germany was passing troops through Finland and encouraging the Finnish Government to resist Soviet demands?

None of these questions was easy to answer. The fact that they had been asked at all revealed a fundamental difference of approach between the two negotiators. M. Molotov hoped to pin Hitler down; Hitler hoped to escape from the difficulties and conflicts of the present into the free air of broad resolutions about the future. He was willing, perhaps, to reach a settlement, but not at the sacrifice of any important interest. Accordingly he fell back, incongruously enough in a self-proclaimed victor, on the plea of military necessity. Germany, he said, had no *political* interest in either Finland or the Balkans; but, so long as the war lasted, she was obliged to guard these important sources of raw material against attack or intrusion by the Allies.

All the measures to which M. Molotov took exception should be attributed to this cause. Germany's actions in the Balkans had been designed to protect the oilfields and make it impossible for the Allies to establish a bridgehead, such as they had held in Salonika in 1914-18. In the Baltic Germany's sole desire was to keep the peace and deny the Allies any pretext for intervention. Finland was acknowledged to lie within the Russian sphere. But a Russian attack on Finland would draw in other powers, such as Sweden, and give England and perhaps even America an opportunity to bring their air forces into play. Germany would then be obliged to intervene. But she would do so reluctantly and the necessity would place a heavy strain on her relations with Russia. Russia must therefore wait; she would receive all that was due to her in Finland at the proper time.

On this note, at once ominous and inconclusive, the conversations ended. M. Molotov withdrew to make his report. In Berlin planning for an Eastern campaign, which had not been broken off during the conversations, continued with renewed vigour.

(iv)
The Balkans

Russia did not in fact reject Hitler's proposals. Shortly after M. Molotov's return to Moscow she made a formal offer to join the Tripartite Pact on the following four conditions:

> 1. That all German troops should be withdrawn from Finland, which should be recognized as belonging exclusively to the Russian sphere of influence;
> 2. That Russia should sign a pact of mutual assistance with Bulgaria, giving her the right to establish naval and military bases within range of the Dardenelles;
> 3. That the area lying south of Batum and Baku 'in the general direction of the Persian Gulf' should be recognized as Russia's 'centre of aspiration';

4. That Japan should renounce certain oil and coal concessions which she then held in the Russian half of the island of Sakhalin.[1]

These conditions, except perhaps the last, were unacceptable to Hitler. They would have meant conceding to Russia a dominant position in the Baltic and a position in south-eastern Europe at least equal to Germany's. They would also have involved, once the Allies had been defeated, a complete Russian hegemony in the Middle East. No settlement was worth buying at such a price. It would not only make a future attack on Russia almost impossible, but would place Germany, if she did not attack, in a position of dangerous economic dependence. But it was plain, if only from Molotov's observations in Berlin, that these were the minimum conditions which the Soviet leaders would now regard as consistent with their own security.

No reply was made to the Russian offer. But its effect on Hitler, or that of the preceding conversations, was clearly decisive. On 5th December he presided at a further conference at the Berghof, where the forthcoming campaign in the East was the main subject of discussion. The O.K.H. outline plan, which had received its final revision in November, was examined and subjected to certain alterations by Hitler.[2] A fortnight later the first formal directive for the campaign, to which the title Operation 'Barbarossa' had now been given, was issued by O.K.W.:

'The *Wehrmacht* must be ready to crush Soviet Russia in a rapid campaign even before the conclusion of the war with England (Operation 'Barbarossa').

The Army will assign all available units to this task subject only to the protection of the Occupied Countries against surprise attack.

The *Luftwaffe* will release units for the support of the Army in an Eastern campaign in such strength as will ensure that land-operations are brought to a rapid conclusion and that Eastern Germany suffers as little as possible from enemy air attack. This concentration in the East will be limited only by the need to protect our supply bases and our operational areas as a whole against air attack and to ensure that the offensive against Great Britain and in particular against her supply routes is not brought to a standstill.

The Navy's main effort will continue to be directed against Great Britain even during a campaign in the East.

My orders for a deployment against Soviet Russia will be

---

[1] *Nazi-Soviet Relations*, p. 258.

[2] These mainly concerned the reinforcement of the northern wing of the advance, directed on Leningrad, at the expense of the central thrust on Moscow. A later controversy between Hitler and O.K.H., discussed in Chapter IV below, was thus foreshadowed.

issued, if the occasion arises, eight weeks before the operation is due to start. Preparations requiring a longer period, if they have not started already, will be put in hand at once and completed before 15th May, 1941.

It is, however, of decisive importance that the intention to attack should not become known.'[1]

At the same time a number of adjustments were made in Germany's other operational plans. Earlier in the year, as we have seen, Halder and Brauchitsch had proposed three operations in the Mediterranean in addition or as an alternative to 'Seeloewe'. Hitler had not rejected the idea at the time; but he had shown an increasing reluctance, as his preoccupation with Russia grew, to commit forces to any operation which might conflict with an Eastern campaign. By the end of the year, therefore, a certain simplification had already taken place. Operation 'Seeloewe' was cancelled, or indefinitely postponed, in October. In November the project of a German attack on the Middle East through Palestine or Syria was vetoed, as likely to prove too difficult and costly. In the latter part of December Operation 'Felix' also fell by the way, as Hitler was unwilling either to undertake it without Spanish help (which would have involved a major campaign) or to pay the exaggerated price for that help which General Franco was then demanding.

In the meanwhile, the Italian attack on Greece at the end of October had altered the situation in the Mediterranean. Hitler's first reaction had been to denounce the whole affair as 'a regrettable blunder' for which 'at no time had authorization been given'.[2] But the only course, nevertheless, was to support his partner. The fact that Greece was now a belligerent in active alliance with England had implications which he dared not ignore:

'The British have occupied Crete and Lemnos.[3] As a result Britain's strategic position in the eastern Mediterranean has considerably improved. With Lemnos in her hands she has an advanced position from which to encroach on the mainland, is able to influence and support Turkey and also has the means to launch bomber attacks against Rumania. The Fuehrer considers that the Rumanian oilfields are endangered by the British forces on Lemnos. It is therefore necessary to transfer anti-aircraft reinforcements, fighters and fighter bombers to Rumania immediately'.[4]

Moreover, an Italian failure in Greece, which was only too likely,

---

[1] Fuehrer Directive No. 21 of 18th December, 1940.

[2] *Halder's Diary*, 1st November, 1940.

[3] In fact, Lemnos had not been occupied.

[4] Conference of Chief of Operations, Naval Staff with Chief of Operations Branch, O.K.W., 4th November, 1940.

would provide the Allies with just that bridgehead in the Balkans which Hitler most feared. His main line of communications in south-eastern Europe and the whole right wing of his movement against Russia would be directly menaced.

It was therefore decided in November that Germany should make an independent attack on Greece (Operation 'Marita') in the early spring by a southward thrust from bases in Rumania and Bulgaria. The assembly-order, issued in December, allocated 18 divisions to this task. The striking-force was to assemble in southern Rumania over the winter; and the attack would be opened as early in March as the weather allowed. It was hoped that the whole operation could be completed by the end of April at the latest, after which the troops engaged, less a small number required as an occupation-force, would again be available for 'Barbarossa'.

Over the turn of the year, however, General Wavell's unexpected victories in the Western Desert upset this programme. By the latter part of January they had produced a situation in which the complete collapse of Italian resistance in Libya, with all the dire consequences foretold by Admiral Raeder, might be expected at any moment. In this crisis the plan to reinforce the Italians with German armour, which had been dropped at the end of October, was revived on a new footing under the code-name 'Sonnenblueme'. Immediate arrange-ments were made for the despatch of a *Sperrverband* or containing-force of one motorized division with additional artillery, which was later joined in Libya by another, armoured division. At the same time, or as soon as it became clear that the Allies intended to take advantage of their victory to support the Greek front, the scope of 'Marita' was considerably enlarged, even though this meant that certain forces, previously intended for the attack on Russia, would have to be retained in Greece.

These extensive movements, which had to be dovetailed with the existing preparations for 'Barbarossa', imposed a heavy strain on German staff-work. They also gave rise to what might have been a serious diplomatic problem. The first requirement for carrying out Operation 'Marita' was to secure agreement with Bulgaria about the establishment of bases and the free passage of German troops. Negotiations were taken in hand at once; but it was not long before Russia became aware of what was happening. On 17th January she entered a sharp protest:

> 'According to all reports available in Moscow, large numbers of German troops are in Rumania and are now about to enter Bulgaria with the object of occupying Bulgaria, Greece and the Dardanelles. There is no doubt that England will try to forestall this movement, occupy the Dardanelles and in alliance with Turkey open military operations against Bulgaria, thus making

that country a theatre of war. The Soviet Government has repeatedly informed the German Government that it regards
Bulgaria and the Dardanelles as falling within the Soviet security-
zone, and that it cannot be indifferent to events which threaten
the security of the U.S.S.R. The Soviet Government therefore
considers it a duty to call attention to the fact that the appearance
of any foreign armed forces in the territory of Bulgaria or the
Dardanelles will be regarded as a violation of the security interests of the U.S.S.R.'[1]

There was a distinct note of menace here; but Germany, conscious
that the build-up of her striking-force in southern Rumania was
already well advanced, felt able to brush the protest aside. No
further exchanges of any importance took place until the end of
February when, all arrangements being then complete, Russia was
curtly informed that Bulgaria would announce her adherence to the
Tripartite Pact on 1st March. Immediately afterwards German
troops would move forward into Bulgarian territory 'as a precau-
tionary measure . . . to prevent the British from gaining a firm foothold in Greece'. This news evoked a second and sharper protest,
which was delivered personally to the German ambassador:

> 'Molotov, who received my communication very gravely, said
> first that he knew of the German decision as the Bulgarian
> Minister had already that day informed M. Vishinsky. Molotov
> then expressed his deep concern that the German Government
> in a matter of such importance should have taken decisions
> which were opposed to the Soviet Government's view of the
> security interests of the U.S.S.R. During the Berlin conversations
> and subsequently the Soviet Government had repeatedly em-
> phasized its particular interest in Bulgaria. It was therefore im-
> possible for the Soviet Government to remain indifferent to the
> steps which the German Government had lately taken in Bul-
> garia and it would have to consider what course of action was
> appropriate. It was hoped that the German Government would
> attach a proper significance to this attitude.'[2]

Ominous though M. Molotov's words were, no action followed, a
result for which Hitler had every reason to be thankful. His recent
moves, touching the most sensitive point in his relations with Russia,
might well have provoked a premature crisis, which would have
thrown his whole careful combination into disorder. But nothing
happened; Russia was apparently willing to lie quiet until the
moment when he was ready to attack her. Only a few weeks later,
however, this sense of security was rudely disturbed. On 24th March
Yugoslavia followed Bulgaria into the Tripartite Pact; but three days

---

[1] Dispatch from Schulenburg, 17th January, 1941; *Nazi-Soviet Relations*, p. 270.
[2] Dispatch from Schulenburg, 1st March, 1941; *Nazi-Soviet Relations*, p. 277.

later her government was overthrown in the *coup d'état* organized by General Simović. The new régime did not immediately repudiate the Pact but its sympathies were known, nevertheless, to lie with the Allies. It was thus with a feeling of outrage that Hitler learnt of Russia's next move. She had chosen this moment of all others to sign a Treaty of Friendship with the new Yugoslav Government. Coming at such a time, it was more than a diplomatic rebuff; it had the character of an insult.

It is still uncertain what motive of policy prompted the Soviet leaders. No doubt they welcomed the Simović *coup d'état* as a check, if only a minor one, to Hitler's designs in the Balkans. It is also true that the Treaty was innocuous in the sense that it did not oblige Russia to help Yugoslavia, if the latter were attacked by Germany. But it is difficult to see what advantage Russia hoped to gain, except that of annoying Hitler. In this the Treaty was fully successful. Even a month later he had still not regained his temper, but was angrily inquiring from Schulenburg what devil had possessed the Russians to do such a thing? Were they trying to frighten him off? After such an episode, he added, one was bound to be suspicious for the future.[1]

The real significance of the crisis lay, however, in its effect on German operational planning. Hitler could not afford to risk a hostile Yugoslavia any more than a hostile Greece; and the existence of a link with Russia, however tenuous, made the danger still more pressing. A new operation (Operation '25') was therefore hastily improvised. Its aim was the complete and immediate subjection of Yugoslavia. In order to make this process as rapid as possible—and also, perhaps, as a warning to others—the operation was planned on a considerable scale. Three simultaneous thrusts were to be made into Yugoslavia: one by German and Italian troops from bases in Austria and Trieste; one by German and Hungarian troops southward across the Danube; and one by the right wing of the 'Marita' force westward from Sofia. For this purpose six divisions and two corps headquarters were withdrawn from the second and third echelons of the 'Barbarossa' assembly and a further three divisions from G.H.Q. reserve.

Even German staff-work was unable to cope with this further dislocation of the programme. The orders for Operation '25' were followed almost immediately by another O.K.H. order of far-reaching significance:

'The development of the political situation in Yugoslavia, and the consequent need to deploy larger forces in the south east, make changes necessary in the build up for "Barbarossa" . . . All preliminary plans will be carried out so as to make it possible to

---

[1] *Nazi-Soviet Relations*, pp. 330–2.

launch the attack (B day) on or about 22nd June, as soon as the
transport of the mobile formations earmarked for the first phase
of the attack has been completed.'[1]

The time-table, in other words, had broken down at last; and it had
been decided to postpone 'Barbarossa' for six weeks. The full importance of the decision was not, perhaps, apparent at the time; but
before the year was out this curtailment of the already short campaigning season in the East was to be bitterly felt.

It would, of course, be wrong to attribute this significant postponement solely to Operation '25', though the date and wording of the
order makes it clear that this was the immediate cause. As we have
seen, other pressures were also at work. The enlargement of 'Marita'
and the need to reinforce the Italians in North Africa have already
been mentioned. Equally important was the growing preoccupation
of Hitler and the High Command with the danger of an Allied landing in the West or in Norway. At the beginning of March Halder had
noted impatiently that the requirements put forward for the defence
of the French coast could only be met by sacrificing striking-power in
the East:

> 'The point is not to achieve 100 per cent security everywhere
> but to accept a minimum of safety and then stake all on "Bar-
> barossa".'[2]

Later in the month there had been a similar scare about Norway.
Halder had remained sceptical but had been unable to prevent a
considerable reinforcement of the German garrison. It may be that
the combined effect of all these centrifugal movements would have
forced a postponement of 'Barbarossa' in any case; but to the
Simović *coup d'état* belongs the honour of having made it inevitable.
It was an unintended strategic success of the first order.

(v)

The Last Phase

We have described above the long process of manœuvre and hesitation which followed the decisions taken by Hitler at the Berghof
Conference in July, 1940. By the beginning of April, 1941, all
difficulties had been overcome and the stage was set. Within less than

---

[1] *O.K.H. Directive* of 7th April, 1941.
[2] *Halder's Diary*, 15th March, 1941.

two months Hitler's eastern policy would be put to its final test. It must not be supposed, however, that the opposition among his advisers, which was noted above, had in any way diminished. The High Command were, if anything, less enthusiastic about the campaign than they had been in the previous summer. Raeder had made his last remonstrance at the end of December. 'It is absolutely essential,' he had then told Hitler, 'to recognize that the greatest task of the hour is to concentrate all our resources against England.'[1] Halder and Brauchitsch held the same opinion; and in the New Year Wavell's victories added a fresh argument in their case. After a discussion in January they agreed that the growing strength of the Allies was enough in itself to make 'Barbarossa' inadvisable:

> 'The objectives are not clear. We do not strike at England and our own economic potential will not be improved. We ought not to underestimate the threat from the West. It may be that Italy will collapse, following the loss of her colonies, and that we shall be caught up in a Southern front in Spain, Italy and Greece. If we are then committed to an attack on Russia, our position will become more difficult.'[2]

And again the following day:

> 'Our infantry will be tied down at a time when England disposes of growing forces in every theatre.'[2]

The opposition in the German Foreign Office was also maintained. At the end of April Schulenburg, always a persuasive champion of good relations with Russia, returned to Berlin for consultation and made a last effort in a personal interview to persuade Hitler of the folly, or rather the needlessness, of 'Barbarossa'. He was supported by a strongly worded memorandum which von Weizsaecker, the Secretary of State, addressed to Ribbentrop on the same day:

> 'I can summarize in one sentence my views on a German-Russian conflict. If every Russian city reduced to ashes were as valuable to us as a sunken British warship, I should advocate an attack on Russia this summer. As it is, I believe that our victory in Russia would be purely military; in an economic sense we should come off the losers.
>
> It may perhaps be considered an attractive prospect to give the Communist system its death blow. To rally the whole Eurasian continent against the Anglo Saxons and their following may also seem consistent with the logic of events. But the only decisive factor is whether this plan will hasten the defeat of England. We must distinguish between two possibilities:

---

[1] *F.C.N.A.* 1940, pp. 138–9.
[2] *Halder's Diary*, 28th and 29th January, 1941.

(a) *England is about to collapse.* If we accept this, we shall encourage her by taking on a new opponent. Russia is not a natural
ally of England, who can expect nothing good from her. It is not
belief in Russia which is preserving England from collapse . . .
(b) *We do not believe in the imminent collapse of England.* It may be
argued that we must feed ourselves by force from Soviet territory.
While I take it for granted that we should advance victoriously
to Moscow and beyond, I doubt very much whether we should be
able to exploit what we have gained in face of the notorious
passive resistance of the Slavs. I see in Russia no effective opposition to the Communist system which we could use or with which
we could make common cause. We should therefore have to
reckon, most probably, with a survival of Stalin's system in
Eastern Russia and Siberia and with a renewal of hostilities in
the spring of 1942. Our window on the Pacific would remain
closed.'[1]

These arguments gained added force from certain gestures of
appeasement made by Russia over the turn of the year. The field
selected was that of trade-relations. It will be remembered that
Germany and Russia had signed two major trade-agreements, in
August 1939 and February 1940, both following the same pattern.
Russia had contracted to supply Germany with raw materials, including grain, oil and certain metals, and to act as her agent in the
purchase of other materials, notably rubber, from the Far East.
Germany had contracted to supply Russia in return with manufactured goods; but since these were to be made (in whole or in part)
from the raw materials supplied by Russia, it had been agreed that
German deliveries should start later and be spread over a longer
period than the Russian deliveries which they requited. The total
value to Germany of these exchanges was upwards of RM800
million in the first treaty year, mainly expressed in goods and services
which she could not have obtained from any other source.

Russia had honoured the agreements to the letter; but Germany,
as it presently appeared, had been less scrupulous. She had accepted
orders from Russia, knowing that they were likely to conflict with her
own armaments programme and that, when the time came, she
would be unable or, in certain cases unwilling, to execute them. The
time-lag between the two sets of delivery dates had given her a
margin for manœuvre, of which she had taken full advantage. By the
autumn of 1940, however, it had no longer been possible to disguise
the fact that she was seriously in arrears and likely to fall even
further behind in the future. At this point Russia had threatened, as
she was entitled to do, to suspend her deliveries altogether until the
deficit was made good, and had in fact reduced supplies to a trickle

---

[1] *Nazi-Soviet Relations*, p. 333.

over the next few months. It seemed that collaboration between the two countries was about to break down no less completely in the economic than in the political field.

At the beginning of 1941, however, an abrupt change took place. A new trade-agreement was signed in January and the vexed question of German arrears settled with surprising ease. About half the debt was cleared by an arrangement under which Germany received financial compensation for the strip of Lithuanian territory referred to above; the balance, with Russian consent, was stood over to the future. As soon as the agreement was signed, the trickle of supplies began to grow. A grain-contract, over which there had been months of bargaining, was suddenly closed on favourable terms; and by March, Russian deliveries were again in full flood. At the same time hints were thrown out of further concessions to come. Dr. Schnurre, the principal German negotiator, received the impression that demands could be made, going beyond the January agreement, which would be accepted and even welcomed by the Soviet.[1]

These actions were in strange contrast with Russia's continued intransigence in the diplomatic field; but no doubt the two policies were intended to be complementary. The Soviet leaders hoped to convince Hitler, on the one hand, that any further encroachments would be resisted with all their strength; on the other, that there was no economic advantage, which he could not gain more easily by negotiation than by force. It is possible that they wished to go even further. In the summer of 1939 trade negotiations had paved the way for the diplomatic discussions which culminated in the Nazi-Soviet Pact. Why should not the same pattern be repeated in the spring of 1941? But, if this was their hope, they had grievously miscalculated. Hitler was no longer open to a settlement; and the promise of concessions was meaningless, when all that he could see, or wished to see, was the fact of opposition.

For this reason, while Schurre's report made little impression, the Soviet protests about Bulgaria and the ill-timed agreement with Yugoslavia took on an exaggerated importance. Some German apologists, notably Goering and Ribbentrop at the Nuremburg trial, have even argued that it was the latter episode which finally decided Hitler to launch 'Barbarossa'. 'Before the Simovič incident,' said Goering, 'it is probable that, although preparations had been made, we should have doubted the necessity for an attack on Russia.'[2] There is little evidence to support this view. As we have seen, Hitler took his first decision in July 1940 and his final one shortly after the Berlin conversations in November. Nevertheless, there is another,

---

[1] Memoranda of 5th April and 15th May, 1941: *Nazi-Soviet Relations*, pp. 318, 339.

[2] Nuremburg Documents, Vol. IX, p. 334.

more limited, sense in which Goering's statement had a certain validity. It is noticeable that, during March and April 1941, Hitler's references to Russia assumed a darker tone. Previously he had spoken of 'Barbarossa' in military terms, as an operation comparable in kind, if not in scale, with 'Seeloewe' or even 'Marita'. From March onwards he spoke as a fanatic:

> 'Communism is an immense danger for the future. We must abandon the soldier's normal attitude of comradeship. No Communist can ever be a comrade. This is a war of extermination. If we do not grasp that then, though we shall still beat the enemy, in another thirty years Communism will again bar our path. There is no point in fighting a war in order to preserve the enemy . . .
>
> Formation commanders must know the issue at stake. They must be the leaders in this struggle. The troops must defend themselves by the methods which will be used against them. Commissars and the men of the G.P.U. are criminals and will be treated accordingly. There is no need for the troops to get out of hand; commanders must regulate their orders in accordance with the troops' feelings. But this will be a very different conflict from the one in the West. In the East, harshness now will be tenderness for the future. Commanders must be prepared to sacrifice their personal scruples.'[1]

Once Hitler had adopted language of this kind, it was no longer appropriate to speak of prudence, negotiation or the possibility of further economic concessions. The hesitations of the High Command, the diplomatic arguments of Schulenburg and Weizsaecker, Dr. Schnurre's optimistic reports, were all beside the point. Hitler had ceased to think primarily in terms of strategy or statesmanship and had become once more the anti-Communist agitator of his earlier days. It would, however, be foolish to attribute this change solely, or even mainly, to events in the Balkans. Their function was no more than to bring to the surface emotions and conflicts of mind, which had existed from the beginning and which lay, indeed, at the basis of Hitler's character. To understand what had happened we must turn back to a percipient letter which Mussolini had written more than twelve months before on the subject of the Nazi-Soviet Pact:

> 'I, who was born a revolutionary and have not modified my revolutionary mentality, tell you that you cannot permanently sacrifice the principles of your revolution to the tactical requirements of a particular moment. You cannot abandon the anti-semitic and anti-Bolshevic banners which you have flown for twenty years and under which so many of your comrades died; you cannot abjure the gospel which the German people have blindly believed . . . The solution for your *Lebensraum* is in Russia

---

[1] *Halder's Diary*, 30th March, 1941.

and nowhere else. Russia has twenty one million square kilometres and nine inhabitants for each. It belongs to Asia not
Europe—and that is not just a theory of Spengler's. Four months
ago Russia was Enemy No. 1 ; she cannot now become, she is not,
Friend No. 1. This has profoundly disturbed Fascists in Italy and
perhaps many National Socialists in Germany. On the day when
we demolish Bolshevism we shall have kept faith with our two
revolutions . . .'[1]

---

[1] *Hitler e Mussolini, Lettere e Documenti* (Rizzoli editore, 1944), p. 33.

CHAPTER IV

THE NEW WAR

(i)

Opinion in London

ALTHOUGH THE POSSIBILITY of a German attack on Russia was not seriously considered in the strategic studies which circulated in London in June, it would be wrong to suggest that the event took the British Government wholly by surprise. The general proposition that such a conflict was inevitable sooner or later had long been accepted. In the previous year it had even seemed that the storm might be imminent. On the eve of the Battle of Britain, for example, Mr. Churchill had telegraphed to Field-Marshal Smuts: 'If Hitler fails to beat us here, he will probably recoil eastwards. Indeed, he may do this even without trying invasion.' This opinion had been shared by other members of the Government, notably Sir Stafford Cripps, whose precise forecasts were quoted in the last chapter. During the winter of 1940–41 growing evidence of diplomatic friction between the two countries in the Balkans and elsewhere had seemed to confirm the diagnosis. It had been widely believed that Germany, under the pressure of her economic difficulties, intended to make new and sweeping demands on Russia, which the latter would be compelled to resist. At the time, however, no clear military evidence had been available to support such a thesis, which had rested solely on economic and political arguments. This may seem surprising in view of the massive preparations for 'Barbarossa', which were already in train by January; but several factors had combined to obscure the issue.

During the whole process of planning military secrecy had been strictly, and on the whole successfully, enforced. On Hitler's express instructions no officer, even the most senior, had been told more than the discharge of his immediate duties obliged him to know. The full secret of 'Barbarossa' was thus kept until right at the end within a very small circle. (It is doubtful whether even Hitler's deputy, Rudolf Hess, was fully informed.)[1] The large number of subsidiary operations, mostly in the Mediterranean, which were being planned or discussed over the same period, also helped to distract attention from the main design. This effect was enhanced by deliberate

---

[1] W. S. Churchill, *The Second World War* (1950) Vol. III, pp. 43–9.

measures of deception. At the beginning of February, O.K.W. gave
instructions that ostensible troop-movements and other preparations
for the invasion of England were to be continued and discreetly
publicized. At the same time every opportunity was to be taken to
exaggerate the importance of secondary operations such as 'Marita'
and 'Sonnenblueme'. After the middle of April, when troop concentrations in the East could no longer be disguised, the story was to
be put about (and conveyed to the troops) that these concentrations
were in themselves a gigantic bluff designed to cover a renewed
assault on England. In order to reinforce this fiction the air-attack on
English towns was to continue on a maximum scale until the very eve
of 'Barbarossa'.[1]

It was not until the end of March 1941, that any solid fact could be
discerned through this haze of artificial uncertainty. A report was
then received in London which showed: first, that as soon as Yugoslavia had signed the Tripartite Pact three out of the five German
armoured divisions in Rumania had been ordered north to Cracow;
and secondly, that as soon as the Simovič *coup d'état* had threatened to
change Yugoslavia's allegiance, this movement, which was already in
progress, had been reversed. Mr. Churchill has recorded in his
Memoirs how this single item of information illuminated the European scene like a lightning flash.[2] The transfer of such a considerable
striking-force from Rumania to southern Poland could only portend
an attack on Russia; there was no other opponent in that quarter
against whom it could be used. The abrupt countermanding of the
order as soon as trouble threatened in Yugoslavia indicated an
anxiety about the southern flank, which Hitler was only likely to feel,
if his preparations were already far advanced. The temporary dislocation of his plan, which these movements had made, offered the
Allies an opportunity which they could ill afford to lose.

On 3rd April Mr. Churchill addressed a personal message to M.
Stalin. It was the first item in the long telegraphic correspondence
which the two statesmen were to maintain, not without occasional
acrimony, until the summer of 1945. The text was intentionally short
and even a little cryptic:

'I have sure information from a trusted agent that when the
Germans thought they had got Yugoslavia in the net, that is after
20th March, they began to move three out of five panzer divisions
from Rumania to South Poland. The moment they heard of the
Serbian revolution, this movement was countermanded. Your
Excellency will readily appreciate the significance of these facts.'

The Ambassador was instructed to deliver this message personally,

---

[1] *Nuremburg Documents*, 57–C, Vol. XXXIV.
[2] Churchill, Vol. III, pp. 318–25.

and to add, if he had the opportunity, a commentary on the following lines. The sudden change in German dispositions, which the report revealed, was a clear indication that Hitler had had to postpone his intention of threatening the U.S.S.R. An opportunity thus offered for the Soviet Government to join hands with the Allies in the Balkans and, by doing so, to impose a further and perhaps fatal delay on the working out of Hitler's plans. If the opportunity were neglected, it would not be long before the Soviet Government would again find themselves directly threatened.

Mr. Churchill's design was unhappily frustrated by the egotism of the Ambassador. Sir Stafford Cripps, who had recently addressed a long letter to M. Vishinsky, to which he attached great importance, was unwilling to spoil its effect by delivering the Prime Minister's message to Stalin, which was, as he said, 'shorter and less emphatic in form'. When this was reported to him, Mr. Churchill repeated his instructions; and on 19th April Sir Stafford so far complied as to hand the message to M. Vishinsky for onward transmission to his master. No doubt it finally reached its destination; but by then its effect was gone. The military information on which it depended was stale and the whole political situation had altered. By 19th April Germany had already overwhelmed Yugoslavia and the battle in Greece had entered its final phase. The opportunity of which Mr. Churchill had spoken no longer existed.

The incident was inexcusable; but the results were not, perhaps, so serious as they appeared to be. In the spring of 1941, the Soviet leaders were not yet ready to enter relations with the Allies or even to receive their help. Sir Stafford Cripps had indeed reported earlier in March that the time was ripe for a renewal of political discussions; but his judgement in this case proved to be faulty. When conversations were opened in April between Sir Stafford and M. Vishinsky in Moscow and Mr. Eden and M. Maisky in London, no progress was made. The Russians raised at once the question of the Baltic States in the evident hope of making British recognition of their 'voluntary incorporation' a basis for all further discussion. When Mr. Eden, supported by the Cabinet, refused to yield, the conversations languished. They served no purpose except to give Mr. Eden the opportunity of repeating in more detailed terms our warning of an impending German attack. It was impossible to tell from their reaction whether or not the Russian negotiators believed him.

This aloof and constrained attitude was certainly not the result of any underestimate by the Soviet leaders of the peril in which they stood. While they continued to resist overtures from the West and to pay lip-service to the Nazi-Soviet Pact, they were busy preparing for the worst. Throughout March and April large bodies of troops moved forward to Russia's western provinces and to the Baltic States,

Russian-occupied Poland, Bukovina and Bessarabia. By the beginning of May, more Russian troops were concentrated along the
frontier than at any other period in history. But these precautions did
nothing to relieve the situation. On the contrary, the presence of great
and growing masses of men on either side of the frontier inevitably
gave rise to further incidents which were highly dangerous in themselves. At the end of April the Soviet Government protested that no
less than eighty violations of the frontier by the German reconnais-
sance-aircraft had taken place during the past four weeks; and the
German Government retorted, no doubt with equal truth, that
violations by Soviet aircraft had now become incessant.

But this was not the whole picture. However fiercely the two
governments might bristle at each other across the frontier, one of
them was still determined to avoid a conflict if possible. April and
May saw not only Russian troop-movements but also the various
gestures of conciliation, notably in the economic field, which were
described in the last chapter. Although these demonstrations of
goodwill did nothing to improve the situation, they did produce a
fresh crop of rumours, fostered by the German Intelligence Service,
to the effect that a settlement between Germany and Russia was now
in sight. Since there was still a dearth of accurate military information, these reports gained credence in London, where it was thought
that a general slackening of tension had taken place. An appreciation
circulated by the Director of Military Intelligence at the end of
March stated definitely that 'we have no grounds for believing an
attack on Russia is imminent'; and the same conclusion was repeated
in the C.O.S. weekly résumé for 1st May. Three weeks later the
J.I.C. produced an elaborate paper on Russo-German relations. It
reviewed the economic situation and reached the conclusion (which
was indeed correct) that Germany would have more to gain by
negotiation than war. The Soviet Government would be inclined to
accept any agreement which did not involve an actual loss of
sovereignty; and, though Germany might use a show of force during
the process of bargaining, it was not likely that she would wish or
need to go further.

This opinion, reasonable enough on the facts as they then appeared,
was endorsed in another memorandum, drawing on Polish sources of
information, which General Sikorsky circulated on the same day. He
argued that an attack on Russia would be a reversal of the policy
which Germany had followed since the Rapallo Agreement of 1922
and which Hitler had endorsed. Current political differences between
Germany and Russia were essentially superficial; beneath them lay a
genuine community of interest deriving from the fact that the Soviet
Government was bound to regard Western democracy as its real
enemy. The argument that economic pressure might force Germany,

nevertheless, to attack Russia was overrated. Such a campaign, he pointed out, would not yield food or other materials in large enough quantity or within a short enough time to add materially to Germany's reserves. General Sikorsky added that he did not exclude the possibility of a German attack on Russia in the spring of 1942, if by then Hitler had failed to secure a decisive advantage elsewhere. But for the present such a conflict 'does not seem to enter into consideration'.

When this memorandum was received, the British Government was no better informed than the Polish; but during the course of the following week fresh evidence came to light. It showed that the *Luftwaffe* was constructing an elaborate wireless network along the whole of Germany's eastern frontier from the Baltic to the Black Sea. *Luftwaffe* units from south-eastern Europe were being withdrawn to Eastern Germany for refitting and their groundstaffs assembled in depots in the same area. This was suggestive but not yet final. The *Luftwaffe*'s preparations, though undoubtedly thorough, might be intended only as a demonstration. Accurate reports about the movement of ground-forces, which were regarded as the real test, were still lacking.

No more information of any importance was received until the end of the first week in June. It was then learnt that the headquarters of Field Marshal List's 12th Army had moved from Athens to the Lublin area and that the headquarters of 11th Army had been identified in Bucharest. There was also reliable evidence of the formation of an Army Group headquarters in Rumania. This was felt to be decisive, especially in view of the prominent part which List and his staff had played in earlier German offensives. By 12th June the J.I.C. had revised their previous forecast:

'Fresh evidence is now to hand that Hitler has made up his mind to have done with Soviet obstruction and intends to attack her. Hostilities, therefore, appear highly probable, though it is premature to fix a date for their outbreak. It remains our opinion that matters are likely to come to a head during the second half of June.'

Mr. Eden sent for the Russian Ambassador at once and gave him an outline of this information. He said that the British Government were now convinced that a German attack on Russia was imminent. They intended to reinforce the army in the Middle East, which was now strong enough to hold a German offensive or, if the enemy's main effort were transferred to Russia, to stage an effective diversion. M. Maisky listened politely but without appearing to be convinced. He gave it as his own view that Germany did not intend to fight; the troop movements which Mr. Eden had described were simply part of the war of nerves. Meanwhile the problem of the Baltic States, the main obstacle to improved relations between England and Russia, still remained unsettled. At this point Mr. Eden closed the interview with the remark that he saw no purpose in making concessions which were not reciprocated.

A few days later the Cabinet discussed the situation. By then the evidence of Germany's intentions was clear; but it was agreed that no further diplomatic action was possible, until there had been some response to Mr. Eden's latest overtures. It was suggested that some form of military discussion might produce a better response. Should we offer, for example, to increase our air-effort over Belgium and Northern France? The Chief of the Air Staff, who was present, agreed that this could be done but said that he would prefer to keep any such proposal in reserve until we knew whether or not Russia would fight. This was accepted. At the same time instructions were given to the War Office to assemble a Military Mission which could be dispatched to Russia immediately, if the occasion arose.

The Foreign Secretary summoned M. Maisky again on 13th June. After repeating his previous warning, he added that the Soviet Government were no doubt informed about German troop movements and would interpret them in their own way. But it might be helpful if he were to indicate the British Government's attitude more precisely. They would be prepared, if Russia were attacked, to send a Military Mission to Moscow in order to pass on all the information about German tactics which had been acquired in recent fighting. They would also give attention to Russia's economic needs, which could be made the subject of detailed discussion later. M. Maisky asked whether these facilities would only be accorded when Russia was actually at war? He was told that that was so. He then asked whether the British Government would be willing to communicate their reports on German troop dispositions in detail and perhaps to expand the statement about diversionary operations which Mr. Eden had made at their last meeting? He added that for his own part he did not believe war to be probable. Reports of Germany's intentions had been much exaggerated; and he was doubtful whether any real basis existed for the intimate collaboration which Mr. Eden seemed to be suggesting. 'I replied' wrote Mr. Eden in his subsequent account of the interview:

> 'that we were dealing with a situation which, according to our information, was one of the utmost urgency. There were two courses open to us; either to say nothing to the Soviet Government unless the eventuality we foresaw actually took place and hostilities began; or to show them in advance in all frankness what our attitude would be. We thought that the latter was the fairer course, though we realized that the Soviet Government might not agree with our diagnosis of the danger for them.'

(ii)

Final Manœuvres

This interview was the last official contact of any importance between England and Russia before the German attack began. It owed its negative character to the fact that the Soviet leaders, though in one sense well aware of their danger, still clung to the hope that a last-minute settlement with Hitler was possible. They had decided to make one further gesture and were anxious not to spoil its effect by any premature contact with the West. On 14th June, the day after M. Maisky's meeting with the Foreign Secretary, the Tass Agency in Moscow published the following dispatch, a copy of which was handed personally to the German Ambassador by M. Molotov:

'Even before the return of the English Ambassador Cripps to London, but especially after his return, there have been wide-spread rumours of "an impending war between the U.S.S.R. and Germany" in the English and foreign press. These rumours allege:

1. That Germany supposedly has made various territorial and economic demands on the U.S.S.R. and that at present negotiations are impending between Germany and the U.S.S.R. for the conclusion of a new and closer agreement between them;

2. That the Soviet Union is supposed to have declined these demands and that as the result Germany has begun to concentrate her troops on the frontier of the Soviet Union in order to attack the Soviet Union;

3. That on its side the Soviet Union is supposed to have begun intensive preparations for war with Germany and to have concentrated its troops on the German border.

Despite the obvious absurdity of these rumours, responsible circles in Moscow have thought it necessary, in view of the persistent spread of these rumours, to authorize Tass to state that these rumours are a clumsy propaganda manœuvre of the forces arrayed against the Soviet Union and Germany, which are interested in a spread and intensification of the war.

Tass declares that:

1. Germany has addressed no demands to the Soviet Union and has asked for no new, closer agreement, and that therefore negotiations cannot be taking place;

2. According to the evidence in the possession of the Soviet Union, both Germany and the Soviet Union are fulfilling to the letter the terms of the German Soviet Non-Aggression Pact, so that in the opinion of Soviet circles the rumours of the intention of Germany to break the Pact and to launch an attack on the Soviet Union are completely without foundation, while the recent

movements of German troops, which have completed their operations in the Balkans, to the eastern and northern parts of Germany must be explained by other motives which have no connexion with German-Soviet relations;

3. The Soviet Union, in accordance with its peace policy, has fulfilled and intends to fulfil the terms of the Soviet-German Non-Aggression Pact; as a result, all the rumours according to which the Soviet Union is preparing for a war with Germany are false and provocative;

4. The summer calling up of the reserves of the Red Army which is now taking place and the impending manœuvres mean nothing but a training of the reservists and a check on the operations of the railroad system, which as is well known, takes place every year; consequently, it appears at least nonsensical to interpret these measures of the Red Army as an action hostile to Germany'.[1]

On 21st June, a week after the publication of this document, M. Molotov sent for the German Ambassador. He implored him—no other word is appropriate—to explain 'the reasons for Germany's dissatisfaction'. Rumours of war were still persistent and there had been no reaction to the Tass dispatch which, he observed, had not even been published in Germany. What was the reason? The Yugoslav incident was now closed and the Soviet Government knew of no other episode which could have contributed to the present unhappy situation. Schulenberg, who was now well aware of his Government's intentions, may have found a certain grim humour in these anxious solicitations. He could only reply that he was insufficiently informed on the points at issue to give any answer himself, but would immediately advise Berlin. He did not add that it was already too late.[2]

On the same evening of 21st June, while M. Molotov put his useless questions to Schulenburg, Hitler was dictating a letter to Mussolini:

'Duce:
I am writing this letter to you at a moment when months of anxious thought and nerve-racking suspense are ending in the hardest decision of my life. After seeing the latest Russian situation-map and studying many other reports, I do not believe that I can take the responsibility of waiting any longer. Still more am I convinced that there is no other way of avoiding this danger—unless it were by further waiting which, however, would be certain to produce a disaster either this year or next at latest.'

England, Hitler continued, had undoubtedly lost the war; but she was still sustained by hopes of Russian intervention, which were not entirely unfounded. Since 1939 there had been signs that the Soviet

---

[1] Schulenberg's dispatch of 14th June, 1941, *Nazi-Soviet Relations*, p. 345.
[2] Schulenberg's dispatch of 22nd June, 1941, *N.S.R.* p. 353.

leaders were returning to their traditional policy of expansion and thus had a direct interest in prolonging the war in the West. They were in a position to do so, without fighting themselves, simply by obliging Germany to concentrate forces—especially air forces—on her Eastern frontier on such a scale as to make any decisive blow in the West impossible. That was now happening. Russia was massing all her available troops along the frontier and had also begun to build a defensive line:

> 'If circumstances should compel me to use the *Luftwaffe* against England, the danger exists that Russia would begin her strategy of extortion in the North and South and that I should have to yield silently to it, simply as the result of inferiority in the air. For one thing, without an adequate air force, I could not hope to attack the Russian fortifications with the divisions now in the East. If I decide not to face this danger, the whole of 1941 may go by without any change in the general situation. On the other hand England will be all the less ready for peace since she still pins her faith on a partnership with Russia. Indeed, this hope is bound to grow as the readiness of the Russian forces increases. We must also reckon with the mass delivery of munitions from America which England hopes to get in 1942.'

The United States, Hitler went on, was doing everything in her power to help England and must therefore be counted as an active enemy. There was no way in which Germany or Italy could threaten her directly. On the other hand, by attacking Russia they would encourage Japan and thus contribute to the opening of a new front in the Pacific. By this means pressure could be brought to bear on America indirectly. But if the attack on Russia were postponed, Japan might lose heart and a great opportunity be missed:

> 'Whatever happens now, Duce, this step can make our situation no worse; it can only improve it. Even if I should still be obliged at the end of this year to leave 60 or 70 divisions in Russia, that is no more than a fraction of what I now have to keep permanently on the frontier. If England refuses to draw conclusions from the hard facts which present themselves then once we have secured our rear, we can apply ourselves with increased strength to finishing off our opponent. I can promise you, Duce, that every thing which Germany can do will be done . . .
>
> In conclusion, Duce, let me say one thing more. Since I fought my way to this decision, once more I feel spiritually free. Though my efforts to reach a final settlement were wholly sincere, the partnership with the Soviet Union has often been a heavy burden to me: whichever way I looked at it, it seemed that I was breaking with my whole past, my true beliefs, and my former obligations. I am happy that I am now freed from this mental anguish.'[1]

---

[1] Hitler to Mussolini, 21st June, 1941: *N.S.R.*, pp. 349–53.

Thus Hitler explained his motives, perhaps not insincerely, for Mussolini was the only man in Europe whom he genuinely regarded as a comrade and peer. A few hours later the gigantic war-machine which he controlled was set in motion. By four o'clock on the following morning, when Ribbentrop sent for the Russian Ambassador for the last time, German troops and aircraft were already on the move and, in some cases, already in action. In Moscow at approximately the same time M. Molotov received the German Ambassador from whom he had parted only five or six hours before. Schulenburg handed him in silence a message which had just reached him by wireless. It was a summary of all the complaints which Germany had, or conceived herself to have, against Russia, beginning with the annexation of the Baltic States (now represented as a breach of the Non-Aggression Pact), and ending with the Yugoslav treaty, the concentration of troops along the frontier and the negotiations which were alleged to be taking place with England. The final paragraph ran:

> 'To sum up, the Government of the Reich therefore declares that the Soviet Government, contrary to the obligations which it has assumed:
>
> 1. Has not only continued but even intensified its efforts to undermine Germany and Europe;
> 2. Has adopted an increasingly anti-German foreign policy;
> 3. Has concentrated all its forces in readiness on the German frontier.
>
> The Soviet Government has thereby broken its treaties with Germany and is about to attack Germany from the rear in her struggle for life. The Fuehrer has therefore ordered the armed forces of Germany to oppose this threat by all the means at their disposal.'[1]

No reply was invited or was any longer possible. 'Barbarossa' had already begun.

(iii)

The German Plan

The Prime Minister received the news of the German attack early on the morning of Sunday, 22nd June. There was no opportunity for a formal session of the Cabinet before he broadcast to the nation at nine o'clock that night; but neither he nor his colleagues were in any

---

[1] Ribbentrop to Schulenburg, 21st June, 1941; *N.S.R.* p. 347.

doubt about what he should say. After describing the fact and what was known of the course of Hitler's new aggression, he went on:

'I have to declare the decision of His Majesty's Government—and I feel sure it is a decision in which the great Dominions will in due course concur—for we must speak out now at once, without a day's delay. I have to make the declaration, but can you doubt what our policy will be? We have but one aim and one single, irrevocable purpose. We are resolved to destroy Hitler and every vestige of the Nazi régime. From this purpose nothing will turn us—nothing. We will never parley, we will never negotiate with Hitler or any of his gang. We shall fight him by land, we shall fight him by sea, we shall fight him in the air until, with God's help, we have rid the earth of his shadow and liberated its people from his yoke.

Any man or state who fights on against Nazidom will have our aid. Any man or state who marches with Hitler is our foe. . . . That is our policy and that is our declaration. It follows therefore that we shall give whatever help we can to Russia and the Russian people. We shall appeal to all our friends and allies in every part of the world to take the same course and pursue it, as we shall, faithfully and steadfastly to the end. . . .

This is no time to moralize on the follies of countries and Governments which have allowed themselves to be struck down one by one, when by united action they could have saved themselves and saved the world from this catastrophe. But when I spoke a few minutes ago of Hitler's blood lust and the hateful appetites which have impelled or lured him on his Russian adventure, I said there was one deeper motive behind his outrage. He wishes to destroy the Russian power because he hopes that, if he succeeds in this, he will be able to bring back the main strength of his Army and Air Force from the East and hurl it upon this Island, which he knows he must conquer or suffer the penalty of his crimes. His invasion of Russia is no more than a prelude to an attempted invasion of the British Isles. He hopes, no doubt, that all this can be accomplished before the winter comes, and that he can overwhelm Great Britain before the Fleet and air power of the United States may intervene. He hopes that he may once again repeat, on a greater scale than ever before, that process of destroying his enemies one by one by which he has so long thrived and prospered, and that then the scene will be clear for the final act, without which all his conquests would be in vain—namely, the subjugation of the Western Hemisphere to his will and to his system.'[1]

The Prime Minister was not exaggerating when he spoke of Hitler's hope that it would all be over by the end of the year. Military experts in the West were almost unanimous in reaching the same conclusion.

---

[1] Churchill Vol. III, pp. 332–3.

The J.I.C., though careful not to tie themselves to an exact chronology, clearly expected the war to last only a few months at the outside. From a different point of view Sir Stafford Cripps, an earnest advocate of the Russian cause, had arrived at the same opinion. A week earlier he had reported to the Cabinet that diplomatic circles in Moscow did not expect Russia to be able to hold a German attack for more than three or four weeks. By the end of that time the Germans would have reached Leningrad, Moscow and Kiev; and it was not likely, in view of the shortcomings of Soviet transport, that much of the Red Army would have escaped or would be able to establish positions farther east. These predictions were echoed in the same gloomy key on the other side of the Atlantic. On 23rd June, the American Secretary for War, Mr. Stimson, informed the President that in his opinion and that of the American Chiefs of Staff 'Germany will be fully occupied in beating Russia for a minimum of one month and a possible maximum of three months'.[1]

If these views prevailed among Russia's allies, it is not to be supposed that Germany lagged behind. Hitler himself was exuberantly optimistic. Russia, he constantly asserted, was no more than 'a brainless, clay colossus', an imposing but empty structure which would crumble at a single blow. Four or five months would suffice for the entire campaign. By the end of 1941 the Soviet Union would have ceased to exist and Germany would be in effective control of the whole stretch of territory from Russia's western frontier to the Volga. On the farther side of that river he was content that anarchy should reign. It was possible that elements of the Red Army or the Communist Party might escape and even establish some kind of Soviet rump in Siberia or the Urals. But that could be disregarded. Such an outpost, if it survived at all, would be militarily impotent. Long-range attacks by the *Luftwaffe* would destroy its industrial centres; and a permanent garrison of fifty or sixty German divisions would protect the conquered area against minor raids or incursions.

We may doubt whether this roseate forecast was ever fully endorsed by the German High Command. Their silent but persistent opposition to 'Barbarossa' has already been described. It was not allowed to interfere with the efficient discharge of their duties; but it continued to show itself in recurrent marks of doubt and hesitation. Reliable intelligence was hard to come by and the picture of the enemy's order of battle was sadly incomplete. Even so, the German General Staff knew that they would be outnumbered in Russia and would have to rely heavily on the superior efficiency and fighting power of

---

[1] Robert E. Sherwood, *White House Papers of Harry L. Hopkins* (London 1948), Eyre and Spottiswoode, Vol. I, pp. 303–4. [Copyright in U.S.A. by Robert E. Sherwood as *Rooseved and Hopkins: An Intimate History:* reproduced with permission of Harper and Row Publishers Incorporated.]

their troops.[1] That they had the advantage in this respect no one doubted; but would the margin be great enough? Very little was known of the quality of the Red Army. The old officer-corps was understood to have suffered heavily in the purges of 1937 and 1938 and there was reason to hope that the standard of the new entry was low and their training inadequate. On the other hand, a sudden collapse, such as had overtaken the French army in 1940, was not expected. 'The Russian soldier,' said Brauchitsch, 'will fight to the death'. And beyond the soldier there was Russia herself. 'The endless space in which our forces must assemble for the attack strikes an impression.' So wrote Halder in his diary. The phrase was mild enough; but one can detect behind it a faint note of uneasiness and even of awe.

There was one respect, however, in which the High Command did not challenge Hitler's estimate. All military planning was based on the assumption that the Red Army would be broken before the winter. The campaign would not necessarily be over by then; on any footing a gigantic task of mopping-up would remain. But the main battle would have been fought and won and it would be possible to begin a gradual withdrawal of troops from the East for the benefit of other theatres. This assumption, in apparent contrast to the doubts noted above, derived from the nature of the strategic plan. The General Staff believed, with some though not with entire truth, that Soviet war-potential was based on a relatively small area of western Russia, which included the Ukraine, the Donetz basin and the two industrial centres of Moscow and Leningrad. They also believed—and in this were strongly supported by Hitler—that the Russians would make a tenacious defence of the Baltic States, both for their value as a source of supply and because the loss of the naval bases there and in the Gulf of Finland would cripple the operations of the Red Fleet. It followed that the Russian armies would not be able to use their traditional strategy of withdrawal but would have to make a final stand no farther east than the line of the Dwina and Dnieper rivers. Any retreat beyond that would expose the Donetz basin in the south and the Gulf of Finland in the north.

Everything that was known of Russian dispositions before the attack seemed to confirm this forecast. All her troops were well forward and their placing suggested an intention to give battle in the actual frontier zone. The Germans could have asked for nothing better. They believed that Russian communications both by road and rail were inferior and would not permit any rapid or extensive re-grouping once the offensive had begun. There was thus every chance

---

[1] On 21st June Halder estimated that the Red Army had 213 divisions against Germany's 141.

that the Red Army could be seized and crushed at the very outset of the campaign in a single battle from which it would never recover.

In its final form the 'Barbarossa' plan provided for three powerful and almost simultaneous thrusts into Russian territory. In the north an army group of twenty-nine divisions under von Leeb was to advance from East Prussia on Duenaburg and thence in the direction of Leningrad. Farther to the south a second and stronger army group of fifty divisions under von Bock was to launch two converging attacks on either side of the line Minsk—Smolensk—Moscow. The third army group of forty-two divisions under von Runstedt was to make its main thrust from the Lublin area towards Kiev but would also be supported by a subsidiary movement of the German 11th Army, striking northward from Moldavia.[1] By the end of the first phase, approximately one month after D-day, it was expected that mobile formations from Army Group North would have gained the rising ground near Opochka; the two wings of Army Group Centre would have joined hands somewhere across the main road between Smolensk and Moscow; and Army Group South, having reached Kiev, would have begun to change direction to the south and envelop the rear of the main Russian forces in the Ukraine. At this point a certain regrouping would take place. The armoured spearheads from the Centre would be transferred to the North to enable von Leeb to complete the clearance of the Baltic States and thereafter resume his drive on Leningrad. In the Centre von Bock would pause until his infantry had mopped up the Russian forces, whom the initial pincer movement had trapped. While this operation was in progress, Army Group South, having surrounded and destroyed the Russian forces to the west of Kiev, would cross the Dnieper and continue its advance towards the Donetz basin and the Black Sea coast.

Such was the German plan; and it came within an ace of success. When the attack was launched, for reasons which are still not fully explained,[2] tactical surprise was achieved along the entire front except on the right wing of Army Group South, where the main advance was delayed until 2nd July. In the first day's fighting 10,000 prisoners were taken and 800 aircraft destroyed, the latter mainly on the ground. For the next three weeks the advance continued at extraordinary speed and without a check. It seemed that nothing could stop the Germans. By the second week of July Army Group North had cut its way through the twelve or fifteen divisions in its

---

[1] In the original plan the two wings of Army Group South were of more equal strength; it was on Hitler's insistence that the main force was concentrated on the northern drive to Kiev.

[2] We have already seen that even as late as the evening of 21st June the Soviet leaders were not expecting a German attack. Russian troop dispositions were consistent with this unalert frame of mind. The intention was, perhaps, to make a show of force for political purposes rather than to offer or meet any distinct military threat.

path and was already approaching its first phase objectives near Opochka. Army Group Centre had trapped upwards of thirty Russian divisions in an immense encirclement battle between Bialystok and Minsk and its advanced armoured forces had thrust forward almost to Smolensk. Only in the South, where heavy rain had bogged down the advance on Kiev, was there any delay; but even there the outline of another gigantic encirclement was beginning to show itself in the area south and east of Berdichev.

A wave of justifiable optimism now swept the German High Command. On 3rd July, Halder noted in his diary:

> 'On the whole one can now say that the task of defeating the bulk of the Russian armies in front of the Dwina has already been accomplished. I believe that the statement of a captured Russian General is correct—east of the Dwina and Dnieper only incomplete formations will be met which are not in sufficient strength to hinder German operations. It is thus no exaggeration to claim that the Russian campaign had been won in a fortnight'.

A calculation of Russian losses made by the Intelligence Staff a few days later seemed fully to support this claim. It was estimated that, of the 164 infantry and 29 armoured divisions with which the Red Army had begun the campaign, 89 of the former and 20 of the latter had been put out of action or actually destroyed. Until these shattered formations could be reorganized and refitted, Russia's main army in the West would be reduced to 49 infantry and 9 armoured divisions. Apart from these, she had 18 divisions on other European fronts, of which some had already been committed to action in Finland, and a possible 11 reserve divisions. No formations from her army in the Far East could be transferred to Europe before 20th July at the earliest. It was thus no longer possible—so the appreciation concluded—for Russia to hold a continuous front.

(iv)

Russia and the West

This was the crucial moment of the whole campaign. The final collapse of Russian resistance, the final triumph of German arms, was expected within a matter of weeks. But there was little that Russia's allies could do except wait.

The promised exchange of Military Missions had taken place and there was already a certain flow of military and technical information from London to Moscow. On 12th July a diplomatic agreement was signed between Great Britain and the Soviet Union, by which both parties bound themselves to give aid to the other wherever possible and not to conclude any separate peace or armistice with Germany. Arrangements were also in hand to meet certain of Russia's more pressing economic needs. Supplies of rubber, tin, lead and wool, mostly withdrawn from metropolitan stocks, had been dispatched. A formidable list supplied by the Russian Military Mission of other essential requirements, including such items as 3,000 fighter aircraft and 20,000 A.A. guns, was being studied in the light of our own meagre and inadequate resources. But all these measures, however valuable in themselves, were dwarfed by the scale of events at the front. No raw materials, equipment or technical data which we could send, would be likely to turn the scale; it was not even probable that they would arrive in time to be used at all.

The only thing which could relieve or even mitigate the crisis on the Eastern Front was direct military intervention on a major scale; but in this field we were almost powerless. Mr. Eden had spoken of an 'effective diversion' in the Middle East. No doubt he then had in mind the renewed offensive in the Western Desert (Operation 'Battleaxe') which General Wavell was planning at the beginning of June. But this operation, which was launched a week before the German attack on Russia, only served to disappoint the high and perhaps exaggerated hopes which London had placed in it. It was an affair of three days, effective as a spoiling-attack but without the weight and thrust required for a counter-offensive proper. It proved of great value to the Middle East by forcing a stalemate in the Desert which was to last until the following November; but its repercussions were not on a scale to be felt outside that theatre.

Our capacity for offensive action nearer home was still more limited. On 23rd June the Prime Minister instructed the Chiefs of Staff to examine the possibility of a raid on the Pas de Calais. 'I have in mind,' he wrote, 'something of the scale of 25 to 30 thousand men —perhaps the Commandos plus one of the Canadian divisions'. But even this relatively modest project was found not to be feasible. Our total fleet of landing-craft at that time was only sufficient to lift a balanced force of one Brigade Group or, say, 5–6,000 men at the outside. Whether a suitable target could be found on the heavily de-fended French coast for an attack on this scale was more than doubtful. Moreover, substantially the whole of our assault shipping was already earmarked for the three operations against the Atlantic Islands ('Puma', 'Thruster' and 'Springboard') which had been standing by since the spring. The Cabinet and the Chiefs of Staff were both strongly opposed to dismounting these forces, since a German move into Spain was almost certain to follow within a few weeks of the decisive victory in Russia, which was then expected almost from day to day.[1] But if 'Puma', 'Thruster' and 'Springboard' were to be kept intact, our effort on the Channel coast would be reduced, in the words of the Director of Combined Operations, to 'putting a few hundred men ashore in fast motor boats to do what damage they could'. Such an operation, considered as a method of helping Russia, could have had no effect except to expose our military impotence to ridicule.

There remained the alternative, proposed by the Soviet Military Mission, of some action in the Far North. This was an area in which the Russians had every reason for claiming our help. They had to reckon with two possibilities: a German advance from Petsamo and Kirkenes against Murmansk; or a German-Finnish attack farther to the south with the object of cutting the Murmansk-Leningrad railway. Either operation, if successful, would close the only ice-free route by which our supplies could enter Russia during the winter. A number of projects were discussed, ranging from the provision of British reinforcements for the Murmansk garrison to an amphibious assault on Petsamo or Kirkenes, in which the Russians would supply the troops and we the naval- and air-escorts and the shipping. But the same limitations which prevented a major diversion in the West were equally effective in the North. A combined operation there would also have faced the almost insoluble problem of making a lodgement on a hostile shore under conditions of perpetual daylight with only such air-cover as a small force of carriers could provide.

Operations in the Far North continued under discussion for many months; but for the moment we had no choice but to reject the Russians' more ambitious proposals. The most that we could promise was a possible reinforcement of two R.A.F. squadrons for Murmansk and a limited offensive by submarines and carrier-borne aircraft against German sea communications in the North.

It was not to be supposed that these decisions, arising from problems with which they were barely acquainted, would commend themselves to the Russians. On 19th July, when the crisis on the Eastern Front was at its height, the Prime Minister received a personal message from M. Stalin. After thanking him for two earlier telegrams of goodwill and encouragement, it continued:

'Your messages were the starting point of developments which subsequently resulted in agreement between our two Governments. Now, as you said with full justification, the Soviet Union and Great Britain have become fighting allies in the struggle against Hitlerite Germany. I have no doubt that in spite of the

---

[1] This was correct. Operation 'Felix-Heinrich' (the final form of the Gibraltar plan) was due to take place in the autumn of 1941, immediately after the expected victory in the East.

8

difficulties our two States will be strong enough to crush our common enemy.

Perhaps it is not out of place to mention that the position of the Soviet forces at the front remains tense. The consequences of the unexpected breach of the Non-Aggression Pact by Hitler, as well as the sudden attack against the Soviet Union—both facts bringing advantages to the German troops—still remain to be felt by the Soviet armies.

It is easy to imagine that the position of the German forces would have been many times more favourable had the Soviet troops had to face the attack of the German forces not in the neighbourhood of Kishinev, Lwow, Brest, Kaunas and Viborg, but in the region of Odessa, Kamenets Podolski, Minsk and the environs of Leningrad.

It seems to me, therefore, that the military situation of the Soviet Union, as well as of Great Britain, would be considerably improved if there could be established a front against Hitler in the West—Northern France—and in the North—the Arctic.

A front in Northern France could not only divert Hitler's forces from the East, but at the same time would make it impossible for Hitler to invade Great Britain. The establishment of the front just mentioned would be popular with the British Army as well as with the whole population of Southern England.

I fully realize the difficulties involved in the establishment of such a front. I believe, however, that in spite of the difficulties it should be formed, not only in the interests of our common cause, but also in the interests of Great Britain herself. This is the most propitious moment for the establishment of such a front, because now Hitler's forces are diverted to the East and he has not yet had the chance to consolidate the position occupied by him in the East.

It is still easier to establish a front in the North. Here, on the part of Great Britain, would be necessary only naval and air operations, without the landing of troops or artillery. The Soviet military, naval and air forces would take part in such an operation. We would welcome it if Great Britain could transfer to this theatre of war something like one light division or more of the Norwegian volunteers, who could be used in Northern Norway to organize rebellion against the Germans.'

Nothing could disguise the urgency of the crisis which had produced this message. The reference in one paragraph to the shortness of time and the possibility of Hitler's consolidating his position in Russia suggested that Stalin himself was then thinking in terms, if not of defeat, at least of a wholesale withdrawal across the Volga. It was natural that he should press hardly on his ally for relief; but what he was asking was impossible. In later discussions the Russian General Staff defined a Second Front as an operation which should draw off and contain not less than forty German divisions; and Stalin was evidently thinking in the same terms. But in 1941 or even 1942 we were still far from being able to operate on such a scale in any theatre. Whether the Soviet leaders believed this or not is open to question. They were often to show a strange and seemingly invincible ignorance of all military problems but their own; and they may well have persuaded themselves, even at this date, that it was lack of will rather than lack of means which determined our inaction. The oddly apologetic tone of the first three paragraphs tends to support this view. M. Stalin seems to have been arguing that his earlier actions in Poland, Finland and the Baltic States had been forced on him by military necessity and ought not, therefore, to deter the Allies from coming to Russia's aid.

But Mr. Churchill was unable to reply in any comfortable terms. He could only say that in the West 'we do not see any hope of doing anything on a scale likely to be of the slightest use to you.' The Germans still disposed of forty divisions in France entrenched on a strongly-fortified coast and there was no possibility of our making head against them:

'It is therefore to the North we must look for any speedy help we can give. The Naval Staff have been preparing for three weeks past an operation by sea-borne aircraft upon German shipping in the north of Norway and Finland, hoping thereby to destroy enemy power of transporting troops by sea to attack your Arctic flank. We have asked your Staffs to keep a certain area clear of Russian vessels between 28th July and 2nd August, when we shall hope to strike. Secondly, we are sending forthwith some cruisers and destroyers to Spitzbergen, whence they will be able to raid enemy shipping in concert with your naval forces. Thirdly, we are sending a flotilla of submarines to intercept German traffic on the Arctic coast, although owing to perpetual daylight this service is particularly dangerous. Fourthly, we are sending a minelayer with various supplies to Archangel.

This is the most we can do at the moment. I wish it were more. Pray let the most extreme secrecy be kept until the moment when we tell you publicity will not be harmful.

There is no Norwegian Light Division in existence, and it would be impossible to land troops, either British or Russian, on German occupied territory in perpetual daylight without having first obtained reasonable fighter air cover. We had bitter experiences at Namsos last year, and in Crete this year, of trying such enterprises.

We are also studying as a further development the basing of some British fighter air squadrons on Murmansk. This would require first of all a consignment of anti-aircraft guns, then the arrival of the aircraft, some of which would be flown off carriers and others crated. When these were established, our Spitzbergen squadron could come to Murmansk and act with your naval forces. We have reason to believe that the Germans have sent a strong group of dive bombers, which they are keeping for our benefit should we arrive, and it is therefore necessary to proceed step by step. All this however will take weeks.'

The Prime Minister was able to follow this message with two others announcing the dispatch of 200 Tomahawk aircraft and a further 10,000 tons of rubber withdrawn from our home stocks. The Tomahawks (or Curtiss P.40's) had only just reached this country from America and had been intended partly as reinforcements for the Middle East and partly to equip the new Army Co-operation squadrons which were then forming. It is probable that our loss in parting with them was greater than the Russians' gain in receiving them; but that was true, more or less, of all the limited help which we were able to send in those early days. The only course was to send what we could without attempting to balance the cost and the value of the gift too precisely.

(v)
German Regrouping

Within a few weeks of this exchange of messages a profound change began to take place on the Eastern Front. Its full extent was not immediately apparent to the outside world but may be judged by comparing the statements of the German High Command at the beginning of July with other statements made at the end of that month and the beginning of August. On 3rd July, as we have seen, Halder was jubilant and the events of the next week or ten days seemed fully to justify his optimism. On 11th July came the announcement that the Russian command had been split into three: a northern group under Marshal Voroshilov; a central group, the largest of the three, under Marshal Timoshenko; and a southern group under Marshal Budyonny. This was at first interpreted by the Germans as a favourable sign reflecting the Russians' inability to hold a continuous front. But over the next fortnight other and more disquieting symptoms began to declare themselves.

Halder noted that Russian units, which the Germans had surrounded or by-passed, did not surrender but continued to fight and to exact a heavy toll from their enemies in the back areas and on the lines of communication. He also noted that Russian armoured formations were showing an unexpected skill in extricating themselves and slipping away to the east through the necessarily wide meshes of the German net. Bristling strong-points and pockets of resistance were beginning to form, not only in the path of the German advance, but on its flanks and in the intervals between the Army Groups. The Red Army was now avoiding the open encounter battles, in which the *Wehrmacht* had previously triumphed, and regrouping its strength behind the marshes and natural barriers of the country.

The new pattern, which began to emerge from the fighting in the second half of July, was not wholly favourable to Germany. In the north strong Russian forces still barred the road to Leningrad. A little farther south, on the boundary between Army Group North and Army Group Centre, a group of seven or more Russian divisions had withdrawn into the marshland between Staraya Russa and Veliki Luki, whence they were launching fierce counter-attacks on the flanks of both Army Groups. In the centre Timoshenko's army covering Moscow, to which the main flow of Russian reinforcements was being directed, held a continuous and in parts strongly fortified front, which rested in the north on the Valdai Hills and in the south on the Oka river. Rundstedt's Army Group South was still checked in front of Kiev; and a major concentration of Russian troops, many of which had not yet been committed to battle, was reported east of the Dnieper in the area between Kiev and Konotop. Finally, two further centres of resistance were forming in the Pripet Marshes, which lay like a kind of no-man's island between the boundaries of Army Group Centre and Army Group South. The Russian Fifth Army in unknown strength had withdrawn into the southern fringe of the marshes near Korosten and another, probably smaller, group was collecting on the northern fringe near Gomel. From both these positions the flanks of the two southern Army Groups were being jabbed and harried.

At the same time the German Command began to receive ominous reports of increasing or reviving Russian strength. It became clear that the Red Army had not after all been killed west of the Dnieper-Dwina line; it had only shed limbs which, Hydra-like, it was able to renew. On 27th July the Intelligence Staff reported that twenty-five new Russian divisions were forming. By 4th August fifty Russian armoured divisions had been identified in place of the twenty-nine on which the Germans had reckoned at the outbreak of war. In the following week Halder made a new entry in his diary in strange contrast to his self-congratulation of only a month before:

'The whole situation makes it increasingly plain that we have underestimated the Russian colossus which deliberately prepared itself for war with an outright ruthlessness characteristic of totalitarian States. This conclusion applies as much to its organization as to its economic resources and its system of communications, but above all to its purely military efficiency. At the

beginning of the war we reckoned on about 200 enemy divisions.
We can now already count 360. These divisions are admittedly
not armed or equipped according to our standards and in many
respects the tactical leadership is inadequate. But there they are,
and if we knock out a dozen of them the Russians produce a fresh
dozen. Time is with them in that respect since their resources lie
close to them whilst we draw farther and farther away from ours.
Thus our forces, stretched out along an immensely broad front
without any depth, are subjected again and again to enemy
attacks, which are partly successful just because we have to leave
far too many gaps in our line owing to the stupendous space.'[1]

Faced with this new situation, Hitler and his advisers had to take a
strategic decision of the first importance. They were obliged to recognize that, despite dazzling victories, their original plan had not
succeeded. The Red Army was still in being and three major objectives—Leningrad, Moscow and the Donetz basin—which should
have been within their grasp at the end of the first phase, were still
being obstinately defended. No one could now foretell when the
German armies would reach these objectives or what further fighting
would lie ahead after they had done so. It was not yet true that the
campaign was lost or even seriously endangered. On the contrary, a
frightful mauling had been inflicted on the Red Army, while the
Wehrmacht was still in good heart and able to assert its superiority
in any direct encounter. But there was no disguising the fact that the
war had entered a new and unexpected phase, for which a radically
different strategic plan would have to be evolved.

The immediate question was what to do with von Bock's armour
from the Centre. The moment had been reached when, according to
the original directive, these formations should have been transferred
to Army Group North for the final clearance of the Baltic States. But
the Russians, though they were still holding an enclave on the Eston-
ian coast, had not made the major stand in this area which had been
expected. The wide turning movement of the original plan was no
longer necessary or even desirable. What was to happen instead?
Should the armour be retained in the Centre, transferred to the North
to support the drive on Leningrad or switched to the South, where
operations were still lagging a week or a fortnight behind schedule?
On this decision hung issues which involved the whole future of the
campaign and even, perhaps, though this was far from apparent at
the time, of the Nazi régime itself.

Broadly speaking, there were two solutions. The first, favoured by
O.K.H. and the German commanders in the field, was to use the
whole strength of Army Group Centre in a renewed pincer movement, which should envelop and destroy Timoshenko's army and

---

[1] *Halder's Diary*, 11th August, 1941.

capture Moscow. This followed orthodox military doctrine in concentrating the main effort against the largest fully organized force which the enemy still had in the field. There were also other advantages. Apart from its significance as the capital, Moscow was a major industrial centre and the focal point of the Russian road and railway system. Its loss would unhinge the entire front and make it difficult or impossible for the Russian Command to develop a war of position in the future. Moreover, the defences of Moscow were part of a continuous system running north and south, which also covered part of the eastern Ukraine and the Donetz basin. A thrust through to Moscow would turn this fortified zone and leave the whole of the south open to a subsequent German flanking movement.

These arguments were sound but also bold. The O.K.H. plan would leave the right wing of Army Group North in some danger until the northern arm of the pincer movement had penetrated far enough east to cut off the Russian troops to the south of Leningrad and in the Veliki Luki pocket. Certain risks would also have to be run in the south. The two centres of resistance in the Pripet Marshes would be ignored for the moment; and the growing Russian concentrations east of Kiev, which were in a position to threaten the southern arm of Army Group Centre's advance, would be merely warded off not destroyed.

The alternative plan evolved by Hitler was more cautious, at least in appearance. Army Group Centre, as in the original plan, was to pass temporarily to the defensive. The armoured forces on its two wings were then to turn outwards, one to assist Army Group North in clearing the Veliki Luki pocket and isolating Leningrad, the other to destroy the Russian forces east of the Dnieper by a wide turning movement behind Kiev in the direction Gomel-Konotop-Kremenchug. When these two operations had been completed, Army Group South, the opposition on its left wing having been cleared, would cross the Dnieper at or below Kiev and open a broad advance towards the Black Sea with Rostov as its final objective. While this was in progress, but not before, Army Group Centre would regather its forces for the final offensive against Moscow.

Hitler's first object was to reap all the benefit which he still could from the original strategy. He could no longer hope to destroy the Red Army as a whole; but he could at least make certain of those parts of it which were already within his grasp. He was prepared, in other words, to ignore Timoshenko for the moment, if by doing so he could finally destroy the considerable, though less well organized, Russian forces which were wedged between the flanks of the Army Groups. He had always insisted that it was not enough to surround or isolate Russian formations; they must be hacked to pieces, if necessary unit by unit and man by man. In this he was not without reason, seeing how stubbornly the Russians fought and what heavy losses they were still inflicting on the flanks and even the rear of the German advance. But to his Generals, intent on the larger war of movement in which they knew their troops to excel, this seemed a fatal policy. 'I see in this line of thought,' wrote Halder, 'a beginning of the bogging down of operations which have so far moved rapidly, and a refusal to exploit the momentum of our troops and mobile formations.'[1]

Hitler also believed, again in accordance with the original plan, that the investment of Leningrad, the loss of the Ukraine and the Donetz basin and the cutting of the oil-route from the Caucasus, where it passed north through Rostov, would together be enough to cripple Soviet war-economy. His new plan was designed to secure all three objectives; but he was wrong in supposing that they would be decisive. Much of the information available to German planners before the war had been out of date and there had been a tendency on their part to underestimate Russia's industrial resources farther east. By July, later and better evidence had begun to reveal their error; but its full extent was not known until the autumn, when an appreciation circulated by the *Wirtschaftundruestungsamt* showed that Russia would still be capable of resistance, though not necessarily of an offensive, even if deprived of Moscow, Tula, Kursk, Kharkov and the entire steel, iron and coal resources of the south. If, in addition, she were to lose Gorki, the aircraft manufacturing centre east of Moscow, and the oil of Baku, her position, though gravely impaired, would still not be catastrophic.

There was, however, another motive behind Hitler's plan, which was probably decisive. To a greater extent than his Generals he was preoccupied with the problem of Germany's own economic deficiencies. He took the view that it was more important on balance to acquire resources, especially those which could be exploited immediately, than to concentrate on denying them to the Russians. No doubt this was short-sighted, for in the last analysis nothing could open the resources of Russia to German exploitation except the final overthrow of Soviet power. But Germany's economic position in 1941 did not allow much scope for prudent long-term planning. She had taken a tremendous gamble in cutting herself off from the supplies of grain, oil and metal, which she had been receiving from Russia over the past two years; and it was essential that this gamble should pay off. She had to turn a quick profit or be obliged, sooner or later, to admit her bankruptcy. The pressure of these facts is everywhere detectable in Hitler's plan.

His reluctance to make the main effort in the Centre, though

---

[1] *Halder's Diary*, 26th July, 1941.

supported by certain military arguments, was only really justifiable on the ground of immediate economic necessity. In the North the capture of Leningrad would deprive the Red Fleet of its main base and put an end to the Russian naval threat in the Baltic, which was curtailing Germany's imports of iron-ore from Sweden. A renewed offensive in the South would secure control of the principal food-producing areas of the Ukraine and bring in other valuable prizes, such as the iron-ore and manganese deposits at Krivoi Rog and Nikopol in the bend of the Dnieper. Last and most important of all, in the South lay the direct route to the Caucasus and the oilfields of Maikop, Grozny and Baku. Hitler's plan in its final form made no mention of crossing the Caucasus. But there is no doubt that one of his chief reasons for wishing to press forward in the South, even at the expense of other sectors, was Germany's shortage of oil. This had already reached a point where it threatened to hamper military operations in the near future. The *Wehrmacht* had entered the Russian campaign with reserve stocks sufficient for a full-scale offensive of two to two and a half months. By September these would be exhausted; and the Army would then be dependent on a share of current production, which was considerably less than its stated needs.[1] Since Russian agriculture was largely mechanized, additional supplies of oil were also required for the proper exploitation of the Ukraine. If they were not forthcoming, one of the most important economic objectives of the whole campaign would remain unrealized.

The clash between these contrasting views of the war, between Hitler's applied economics and the General Staff's purely strategic vision, was bitter and prolonged. The controversy raged in one form or another from the end of July until the early weeks of September and was to flare up again after the German reverses of the winter. Its progress was marked by a series of compromises on particular points which need not be examined in detail. Until the beginning of August the General Staff were able to prevent Hitler from introducing any radical change of plan; but, when the controversy finally came to a head in the middle of that month, his views prevailed, as they were bound to do. During the remainder of 1941 German strategy followed, though not without certain fluctuations, the broad policy laid down in a Fuehrer Directive of 21st August:

'The most important aim before the onset of winter is not the capture of Moscow but the seizure of the Crimea and the industrial and coal region of the Donetz, and the interception of

---

[1] During the year 1941 as a whole the Army received a monthly average of only 185,000 tons of oil, instead of 240,000 tons which was accepted as the optimum figure. This, however, was partly due to the difficulties of transport over the immense distances of the Eastern Front.

Russia's oil route from the Caucasus. In the North Leningrad is to be cut off and a junction effected with the Finns. Only after these operations have been completed will forces be available for a renewed offensive on the Central front.'

Hitler was well accustomed to imposing his views on a reluctant Staff and had done so before with triumphant success. But this time there was a difference. He won his usual victory but at the cost of an almost complete rupture of confidence between himself and his Commanders. Halder and Brauchitsch both wished to resign in August and were only deterred from doing so by the knowledge that it would make no difference; their resignations would not even be accepted. Vigorous protests were also made, though not always directly to Hitler, by the commanders in the field. Rundstedt, commanding in the South, was no less insistent than Bock in the Centre on the absolute necessity of breaking Timoshenko's army and capturing Moscow in the next phase. The two commanders of the Panzer groups, Hoth and Guderian, added their own warnings. The German armoured divisions, which had already accomplished so much, were badly in need of refitting. They could no longer be flung across the map with the speed and abandon of the first assault. A decisive concentration could still be achieved in front of Moscow; but the distant objectives in the South, which Hitler proposed, might well be unattainable.

(vi)
Hopkins in Moscow

The effect of these strains and dislocations in the German High Command was not immediately noticeable at the front. July and August were still a period of major victories, despite the stiffening of Russian resistance already referred to. Observers in the West could see only two hopeful signs—a certain slackening of the speed of advance in the North and Centre and a growing German concern over losses of men and material. It was noted from the middle of July onwards that the tendency of German internal broadcasts was to emphasize the difficulties of the campaign and to prepare the public for smaller gains and further sacrifices in the future. But that did not mean that the advance had halted. Rundstedt's great encircling movement west of the Dnieper reached its climax at the beginning of August. In the same week Army Group Centre's southward thrust from Gomel, on which Hitler had insisted, opened with equal success. Deep penetrations were made to the east of Kiev; and it seemed that the Germans were about to tear a gap in the southern sector of the front which would indeed, as Hitler had prophesied, open a clear path to the Donetz basin and beyond. Almost simultaneously with these two operations, however, came the first news of a definite German check. An attempt by Army Group North and part of the left wing of Army Group Centre to clear the Veliki Luki pocket miscarried and the troops engaged were exposed to savage Russian counter-attacks. Meanwhile Timoshenko's forces before Moscow had been given a much-needed breathing-space in which to absorb their reinforcements and tighten their grip on the central front.

There was thus some reason to hope at the end of July and the beginning of August that the German offensive might be losing momentum. The *Wehrmacht* was still able to gather the fruits of victory in the South but only, or so it seemed, at the expense of a flagging effort in the Centre and North. Lines of communication were already stretched over many hundreds of miles of difficult country; and even German formations could scarcely maintain their advance indefinitely without a pause for recuperation and refitting. All this was true and hopeful; but it was only one side of the story. No one in the West at that time had any clear view of Russia's position. She had suffered fearful losses of men, material and territory. What resources still remained to her? Could she withstand a further German offensive even on a reduced scale? These were questions which could not be answered. The trickle of information which reached London through the Military Mission provided no more than the bare facts of the immediate situation. Of Russian reserves, the extent of the war-potential which she still controlled or her future plans almost nothing was known.

Ignorance was no less complete on the other side of the Atlantic. This state of affairs, undesirable in itself, had the added danger of raising a serious, if artificial, obstacle to the organization of aid for Russia. The urgency of the problem was admitted; but supplies were short—hardly less so in the United States than in England— and no one wished to see valuable war-material, which could be put to immediate use elsewhere, lost in the chaos of a collapsing Russian front. The very large demands presented by the Soviet Military Mission could not in any case be met in full. To meet them even partially meant robbing the United Kingdom, the Middle East or America's own expanding forces. Was such a course justified? If so, how far was it prudent to go? Everything depended on an accurate assessment, which no one could make, of Russia's continued powers of resistance.

This central problem, round which so many other problems

revolved, attracted the attention of President Roosevelt's personal representative, Mr. Harry Hopkins, who was in London at the end of July to prepare the ground for the meeting between the President and the Prime Minister, which was to take place in the following month off Newfoundland:

> 'Hopkins realized all too clearly that in one vitally important respect the discussions at the Atlantic Conference would be held in a vacuum without some real knowledge of the situation and prospects of the Russian front. It was obvious that all the prevailing estimates, both British and American, were based on inadequate information and speculation. There was a British military mission in Moscow, but it was gathering no more information than was vouchsafed by Molotov's Foreign Office to the Embassies, which was to say none at all. Since all deliberations on all phases of the war at that time, including American production and Lease-Lend, depended on the question of how long Russia could hold out, Hopkins decided that he should make a quick trip to Moscow and try to get an answer to that question from Stalin himself.'[1]

Mr. Hopkins, though already tired and in indifferent health then as always, lost no time over his journey. On 28th July he left England by flying-boat, preceded by a telegram from the President to M. Stalin. 'I ask you,' wrote Mr. Roosevelt, 'to treat Mr. Hopkins with the identical confidence you would feel if you were talking directly to me. He will communicate directly to me the views that you express and will tell me what you consider are the most pressing individual problems on which we could be of aid.'[2]

On 30th and 31st July Mr. Hopkins had two long and seemingly frank interviews with M. Stalin, which provided the first comprehensive view of Russia's position and military prospects which any Western statesman had received. The substance of these interviews is best given in Mr. Hopkins' own words, for it was one of his merits as a reporter that he interposed nothing, not even a literary style, between the subject and his reader. He was content to put down baldly what he had seen or had been told and to leave it to make its own impression:

> 'I told Mr. Stalin that the President was anxious to have his— Stalin's—appreciation and analysis of the war between Germany and Russia. Mr. Stalin outlined the situation as follows.
>
> He stated that in his opinion the German Army had 175 divisions on Russia's western front at the outbreak of the war, and that since the outbreak of the war this has been increased to 232 divisions; he believes that Germany can mobilize 300 divisions.

---

[1] Sherwood, Vol. I, p. 317.
[2] Sherwood, Vol. I, pp. 321–2.

He stated that Russia had 180 divisions at the outbreak of the war, but many of these were well back of the line of combat, and could not be quickly mobilized, so that when the Germans struck it was impossible to offer adequate resistance. The line which is now held is a far more propitious one than the more advanced line which they might have taken up had their divisions been prepared. Since the war began, however, divisions have been placed in their appropriate positions, and at the present time he believes that Russia has a few more divisions than Germany, and places the number of Russian divisions at 240 in the front with 20 in reserve. Stalin said that about one third of these divisions had not yet been under fire.

Mr. Stalin stated that he can mobilize 350 divisions and will have that many divisions under arms by the time the spring campaign begins in May, 1942.

He is anxious to have as many divisions as possible in contact with the enemy, because then the troops learn that Germans can be killed and are not supermen. This gives his divisions the same kind of confidence that a pilot gets after his first combat in the air. Stalin said that "nothing in warfare can take the place of actual combat", and he wants to have as many seasoned troops as possible for the great campaign which will come next spring. He stated that the German troops seemed to be tired, and the officers and men that they had captured had indicated that they are "sick of war".

The German reserves are as much as 400 km. back of the front and the communications between the reserves and the front line are extremely difficult. These supply lines require many thousands of German troops to guard and protect them from Russian raids.

He said that in the battle now in progress, very many Russian and German troops are fighting far forward of their respective lines, because of the advances made by both sides with their mechanized forces. Stalin said that his soldiers did not consider the battle lost merely because the Germans at one point and another broke through with their mechanized forces. The Russian mechanized forces would attack at another point, often moving many miles behind the German line. . . . This is merely a phase of modern warfare and accounts for the fact that there have been no mass surrenders of troops on either side. The Russians therefore have many "insurgent" troops which operate behind Germany's so called front line. They constantly attack German aerodromes and lines of communications. The Russians are more familiar than the Germans with the terrain and know how to use the natural cover which nature has provided better than the Germans. These "insurgent" troops are proving a great menace to the German offensive.

He believes that Germany underestimated the strength of the Russian Army and have not now enough troops on the whole front to carry on a successful offensive war and at the same time guard their extended lines of communication. He repeatedly emphasized the large number of men Germany was forced to use for this purpose, and believes that the Germans will have to go on the defensive themselves. There is considerable evidence that they are already doing this. They are burying many of their large tanks in the ground for defensive purposes. The Russians have already found fifty such defensive positions.'[1]

There is an interesting contrast between the views attributed to M. Stalin here and those expressed in his earlier telegram to Mr. Churchill. He had then argued that Russia's best defence lay in meeting the enemy as far west as possible on the line Lwow-Brest Litowsk-Kaunas rather than the line Odessa-Minsk-Leningrad. He now maintained that the present fighting-line was in reality the most favourable of all and even congratulated himself on having been unable, when the campaign opened, to send as many divisions westward as he had intended. This was an index of the change, amounting to a complete reversal, which a closer acquaintance with the striking-power of the *Wehrmacht* had effected in Russian strategy. Whatever their original intentions, the Soviet leaders had now reverted to the traditional policy of a fighting retreat. They had realized that the Red Army was no match for the *Wehrmacht* in the full flush of its strength. The only hope was gradually to wear down that strength by stubborn rear-guard actions, by the incessant harassing of 'insurgent' troops in the back areas and above all by relying on the vast distances of Russia and the cumulative strain which they would impose on German movement and communications.

Despite this—indeed, largely because of it—M. Stalin's outlook was far from pessimistic. The figures quoted above show that he was inclined to over-estimate the strength of the German forces opposing him, just as the Germans were beginning at this time to over-estimate Russian strength. Nevertheless, he spoke confidently of the future. Within the past ten days there had been a definite slackening of German pressure, attributable to difficulties of supply which would certainly continue and increase. The Germans were still bringing fresh troops forward and could, if necessary, reinforce the Eastern Front by a further forty divisions withdrawn from Germany and the West. But he did not think that they would attempt to renew the offensive on a major scale before winter closed in. Movement would become difficult after the beginning of September; and bad weather might be expected to halt all operations not later than the middle of October. He was confident that by then the Germans would not have penetrated more than a hundred kilometres east of their present positions and that the Red Army would still be holding Leningrad,

---

[1] Sherwood, Vol. I, pp. 335–6.

Moscow and Kiev. It would then be a case of maintaining the line during the winter, while forces were gathered for a great counter-stroke in the spring.

These opinions, tersely and vigorously expressed, made a strong impression on Mr. Hopkins. He was satisfied that the Soviet leaders had no thought of surrender and little fear of defeat. Although the next few weeks would be critical, there was every chance that the Russian line would hold over the winter; and, when the battle was renewed in 1942, the German armies might well find themselves more evenly matched than military opinion had so far predicted. He was also reassured by the relatively favourable, if far from exact, figures which he was given of Russian industrial potential. M. Stalin admitted that approximately 75 per cent of the Russian armaments industry was concentrated in the areas of which Leningrad, Moscow and Kiev were the centres. If the German army could advance, say, 150 miles east of these points, the loss would be crippling. At present, however, Russia was still producing 1,800 aircraft and 1,000 tanks a month, though she was short of aluminium for the former and of steel for the latter. Of the two aluminium was the greatest need. 'Give us that,' said M. Stalin, 'and we can fight for three or four years.'

This suggested that Russia was planning, and was still able to plan, in terms of a long war. At the last meeting, therefore, Mr. Hopkins made a proposal which he had had in mind from the beginning but had not thought it prudent to bring forward before:

'I told Mr. Stalin at this conference that our Government and the British Government (Churchill having authorized me to say this) were willing to do everything that they possibly could during the succeeding weeks to send material to Russia. This material, however, must obviously be already manufactured and that he—Stalin—must understand that even this material could in all probability not reach his battle lines before the bad weather closes in.

I told him that we believed that plans should be made for a long war; that so far as the United States was concerned we had large supply commitments in relation to our own Army, Navy and Merchant Marine, as well as very substantial responsibilities to England, China and the Republics of South America.

I told him that the decisions relating to the long range supply problem could only be resolved if our Government had complete knowledge, not only of the military situation in Russia, but of type, number and quality of their military weapons, as well as full knowledge of raw materials and factory capacity.

I told him that I knew our Government, and I believed the British Government, would be unwilling to send any heavy munitions, such as tanks, aircraft and anti-aircraft guns, to the Russian front unless and until a conference had been held between our three Governments, at which the relative strategic interests of each front, as well as the interests of our several countries, was fully and jointly explored.

I suggested that, inasmuch as he was so fully engaged with the immediate prosecution of the battle now in hand, he could not give the time and attention to such a conference until after the battle was over.

Stalin had previously indicated that the front would be solidified not later than 1st October.

I was mindful of the importance that no conference be held in Moscow until we knew the outcome of the present battle. I felt it very unwise to hold a conference while this battle was in the balance. Hence my suggestion to him to hold a conference at as late a date as was possible. Then we would know whether or not there was to be a front and approximately the location of the front during the coming winter months.

Stalin said that he would welcome such a conference and that of course it would be impossible for him to go to a conference anywhere other than in Moscow: that he would be glad to make available to our Government all information which was required and he offered to give us the Soviet designs of their airplanes, tanks and guns.

I told him that I was not authorized to make this suggestion of a conference to him officially.

Stalin then stated that in case our Government wished to have such a conference he would receive such a proposal sympathetically and would give the conference his personal attention.'[1]

---

[1] Sherwood, Vol. I, pp. 341–2.

CHAPTER V

THE ATLANTIC MEETING

(i)

Anglo-American Relations

MR. HARRY HOPKINS' visit to London in July 1941 has already been mentioned. It had several important consequences, not least his onward journey to Moscow; but its main purpose was to complete arrangements for the meeting between President Roosevelt and Mr. Churchill, which both had long desired. It was now agreed that they should meet at sea early in the following month. The President would leave Washington by yacht, ostensibly on holiday, tranship secretly to the U.S.S. *Augusta* and proceed in her to the rendezvous at Placentia Bay, Newfoundland. Mr. Churchill would sail to meet him in the battleship *Prince of Wales*, then at the beginning of her tragically short career; and the two ships would lie in company for the two or three days that the Conference was expected to last. No formal agenda was planned; but both statesmen would be accompanied by a full diplomatic and military staff, and their discussions would range over the whole problem of the war.[1]

The origin of this meeting, the first in a momentous series, can be traced back to the previous December. In that month, as readers of the previous Volume will remember, Mr. Churchill addressed a long and grave letter to the President, in which he set out England's prospects and difficulties and asked for American help in three forms:

> (i) Financial aid to enable us to continue our purchases in the United States when our own store of gold and dollars was exhausted;
> (ii) Aid in the Battle of the Atlantic, preferably by American intervention,[2] but failing that, by the loan or transfer of escort vessels and a vast new construction of merchant ships in American yards;
> (iii) Industrial aid, especially in the manufacture of aircraft.

The President read and pondered this letter during a week's

---

[1] Churchill, Vol. III, pp. 380-1.

[2] An American declaration of war was not in question; what the Prime Minister asked for was a 'decisive act of constructive non-belligerency', i.e., a measure of protection by the American fleet for American merchant ships trading with the United Kingdom.

holiday at sea. By the time he returned to Washington he had evolved and discussed with his intimate advisers the basic principles of Lend-Lease, the measure with which he designed to meet the first and most important of the Prime Minister's problems. Before the end of the month he had presented this new policy to the public, first at a Press conference, and later in a broadcast speech in which he defined America's role as the Arsenal of Democracy.[1] The same theme was further developed in his message to Congress at the beginning of the new year. He spoke in the strongest terms of the obligation, which the country must assume, to give 'full support to all those resolute peoples, everywhere, who are resisting aggression and thereby keeping war away from the Western Hemisphere' and ended with a striking passage, which was in effect a definition of America's war aims:

'In future days, which we seek to make secure, we look forward to a world founded on four essential human freedoms.

The first is freedom of speech and expression—everywhere in the world.

The second is freedom of every person to worship God in his own way—everywhere in the world.

The third is freedom from want—which, translated into world terms, means economic understandings which will secure to every nation a healthy peacetime life for its inhabitants—everywhere in the world.

The fourth is freedom from fear—which translated into world terms, means a worldwide reduction of armaments to such a point and in such a thorough fashion that no nation will be in a position to commit an act of physical aggression against any neighbour—anywhere in the world.'[2]

It was during this period that the President, thinking of the second and third points of the Prime Minister's letter, remarked aside to Mr. Hopkins: 'You know, a lot of this could be settled, if Churchill and I could just sit down together for a while.'[3] But the impulse was then premature. Although the response to his early speeches was generally favourable, it was clear that the Lend-Lease Bill would not pass Congress without a struggle; and, while these internal debates were going on, anything in the nature of a formal conference would have been politically unwise. Mr. Hopkins was therefore sent to London as a private emissary to discuss the proposed measures and to make tentative arrangements for a personal meeting in the following April. By that time it was hoped that the Lend-Lease debate would be over and the political position easier.

But when April came, with its tide of disaster in the Middle East,

---

[1] F. D. Roosevelt, *Public Papers and Addresses*, Vol. IX, p. 633.

[2] Roosevelt, Vol. IX, p. 672.

[3] Sherwood, Vol. I, p. 231.

the meeting was tacitly postponed. It was no longer an opportune moment either for the President to propose a Conference or for the Prime Minister to leave the country. The project was not revived until nearly four months later. This long delay was only partly the result of circumstance; one can also detect a certain hesitation on the President's part. From the early part of March onwards he showed a distinct reluctance to take any further public step forward. It was as if he felt that the great exertions, which had seen the Lend-Lease Bill through, had temporarily exhausted his credit both with Congress and the country.

This view was not without substance. The passage of the Lend-Lease Bill was in fact followed by a certain reaction, partly attributable to the success of the arguments used to support the Bill. Lend-Lease had been presented to the country as an alternative to war; America was to take up the rôle of the Arsenal of Democracy precisely in order to make any further intervention unnecessary. If it now appeared that Lend-Lease, so far from providing an ideal middle path between peace and war, was no more than the first in a series of acts, each of which brought America nearer to the conflict, public confidence would be rudely shaken. This was a point on which the Isolationists were quick to seize. They took the stand that the declared objects of Lend-Lease were mere camouflage; the President's real purpose was to lead the country into war by a succession of crablike and seemingly innocent steps. They were alert, inside and outside Congress, for any new development which could be interpreted as supporting this thesis.[1]

Today, when we can see the forces which shaped events more clearly, such an attitude may seem distorted and merely partisan. But contemporary polls of public opinion leave little doubt that it could then command a wide, if confused, support. Public opinion, it is true, had changed much since the outbreak of war. In 1939 the majority of Americans were still thinking in terms of a localized conflict in Europe, from which it was the right and duty of the United States to stand clear. By the spring of 1941 this view was no longer fashionable. It had been replaced by a mood of fatalism, which argued that willy-nilly, sooner or later, America was bound to be involved. But this did not imply any sense of engagement in the issues of the war. Those who believed in supporting the Allies no matter what the risk, were far outnumbered by those who merely believed that war, one way or another, was inevitable. In response to the direct question 'Are you in favour of an immediate declaration of war?' the overwhelming majority still answered, 'No'.[2] It was a puzzling,

---

[1] W. L. Langer and S. E. Gleason, *The Undeclared War* (1953), pp. 441–3.

[2] *Public Opinion Quarterly*, cited by Langer and Gleason.

uncertain picture, which one commentator defined by saying that the American people 'had not yet apparently abandoned their resolution neither to be pushed nor descend into it [the war], if they can safely keep their footing on the rim'.[1]

Under these conditions Roosevelt moved warily. But this did not mean that the last two clauses of the Prime Minister's appeal went wholly unanswered. Progress in the industrial field was necessarily slow, as we shall see in the next chapter; but the situation in the Atlantic called for immediate action, if current American policy were to be sustained. Congress had appropriated $7 billion for the objects of Lend-Lease; but it now appeared, as the tale of losses in the Atlantic rose, that the purpose of the act might be stultified by sheer inability to land the food, the raw materials and the equipment at the place where they were needed. To this challenge the President responded promptly within the limits which he had laid down for himself. During March and April ten coastguard cutters were transferred to the Royal Navy; American yards were opened for the repair of British warships; a modest programme of shipbuilding was initiated; and a number of Danish and Axis merchantmen, then lying idle in American ports, were taken over for the future carriage of Lend-Lease cargoes. But these were all administrative acts, largely unknown to the general public and carefully framed so as not to mark any new development of policy.

On the central issue of American intervention in the Atlantic President Roosevelt continued to hold back. There was, indeed, one moment in April when he seemed about to take the plunge, urged thereto by his naval advisers and a further telegram from the Prime Minister. Instructions were given to reinforce the Atlantic Fleet with warships withdrawn from the Pacific; and operation orders, based on Hemisphere Defence Plan No. 1,[2] were prepared. But these instructions were scarcely given before they were cancelled. The revised plan, put into action later in the month, was far more cautious. It provided that the Neutrality Patrols, which the American fleet had maintained in the Atlantic since the outbreak of war, should be extended as far east as the 26th Meridian and that the position of any U-boat or Axis raider sighted within this area should be reported by wireless in clear. This was an important and unexpected exercise of neutrality; but it still lacked the value of a public gesture. In his telegram to the Prime Minister announcing these arrangements, the President made it clear that he did not wish undue attention to be called to them:

---

[1] Arthur Knock, *New York Times*, 12th January, 1941.

[2] This was the plan, agreed during the Anglo-American Staff conversations in Washington, which outlined America's rôle in the Atlantic in the event of a declaration of war.

'I believe advisable, that when this new policy is adopted here no statement be issued at your end. It is not certain I would make specific announcement. I may decide to issue necessary naval operation orders and let time bring out the existence of the new patrol area.'

This extreme caution was not to the taste of all his advisers. At times even the faithful Hopkins became impatient; and Mr. Stimson, the Secretary of War, uttered the sharp warning that 'without a lead on his part it was useless to expect [that] the people would voluntarily take the initiative in letting him know whether or not they would follow it, if he did take the lead'.[1] This view may have influenced the President; but it did not convert him. He remained throughout May and June in a state of deep inner uncertainty, which found expression in a series of apparently contradictory acts. On 27th May he made an important and widely diffused speech, which called for greater and more active support of the Allies—including, or so it seemed, some measure of intervention in the Atlantic—and ended with the solemn proclamation that an 'unlimited national emergency' now existed.[2] The response was not unfavourable. 'I hope,' said Senator Carter Glass, 'that we will protect every dollar's worth of stuff that we send to Great Britain and that we will shoot the hell out of anyone who interferes.' But at his subsequent Press conference the President was at pains to deprecate any such interpretation. He had no plans, he said, to alter the existing Neutrality Laws, still less to embark on naval action in the Atlantic. Unlimited Emergency was no more than a phase, only to be given substance by the use of executive powers, which he had no intention of invoking.[3]

Yet within a few weeks, these deflationary words notwithstanding, another important step was taken. The President authorized the dispatch of American troops to Iceland, where they were gradually to replace the British garrison.[4] The reinforcement of the Atlantic Fleet, postponed since the beginning of April, was also put in hand; and there was even talk of America's assuming responsibility for the Azores in the event of a German move into Spain. At the same time administrative measures in support of the Allies were increased. Room was found in American flying-schools for British pilots in training; and plans were put in hand to reinforce the British air-ferry across the North Atlantic by a similar service to Bathurst and Freetown. But, although neutrality was thus privately stretched to the limit, the invisible line which divides that state from intervention or

---

[1] H. L. Stimson and Mc. G. Bundy, *On Active Service in Peace and War* (1948), p. 369 et seq.

[2] Roosevelt, Vol. IX, p. 181.

[3] Langer and Gleason, pp. 462–3.

[4] This move, accepted by the Icelandic authorities, had been agreed during the March staff conversations; but no action had been expected before September at the earliest.

even from what the Prime Minister called 'constructive non-belligerency' was never openly passed.

At the beginning of June Mr. Churchill made a new proposal. The meeting of Allied Governments, referred to in Chapter I, was about to take place in London; and it seemed possible that the United States might be willing to make some gesture of support. 'I hope,' wrote the Prime Minister, 'the meeting will provide a convincing demonstration of our common tenacity of purpose, but I need hardly say, Mr. President, what an accession of strength it would be if the United States Government felt it possible to be associated in some form or another with the proceedings.' But Mr. Roosevelt was not to be drawn. Although the terms of the resolutions passed at the meeting differed little in substance from his own pronouncements of December, January and May, he did not feel that he could publicly identify himself or his Government with them. A firm distinction had still to be drawn between the aspirations of the United States and the war-aims of the Allies.[1]

A fortnight later came news of the German attack on Russia. In one sense this added to the difficulties of the President's position. There was no doubt in his own mind that aid should at once be given to the U.S.S.R. on the same terms as to Britain; but he knew that there would be little enthusiasm in the country for this policy and even some opposition, especially from Catholic opinion. The campaign in the East was not then expected to last long, still less to end favourably for the Russians. But it was conceded that there would at least be a breathing space, a slackening of tension in the West, lasting perhaps for three or four months. This seemed a golden opportunity for America to act; and the President was under pressure from many of his advisers to take a further step forward. Not the least vehement was Admiral Stark:

> 'Within forty-eight hours after the Russian situation broke, I went to the President with the Secretary's approval, and stated that on the assumption that the country's decision is not to let England fall, we should immediately seize the psychological opportunity . . . and announce and start escorting immediately, and protecting the Western Atlantic on a large scale; that such a declaration followed by immediate action on our part, would almost certainly involve us in war and that I considered every day of delay in our getting into the war as dangerous, and that much more delay would be fatal to Britain's survival. I reminded him that I had been asking this for months in the State Department and elsewhere . . .[2]

---

[1] Langer and Gleason, p. 521, quote Roosevelt's reply on 11th June, 1941.
[2] Letter from Admiral Stark of 31st July, 1941, quoted in *Congressional Enquiry into Pearl Harbor Attack*, Vol. XVI, p. 2175.

Roosevelt was by no means ready for such drastic counsels. Under the immediate impact of his interview with Stark, he went so far as to agree that plans for Atlantic escorts should be drawn up, to go into action sometime in July. But once more the orders were no sooner given than rescinded, the deciding factor being, no doubt, the Admiral's eager insistence on the risk of war. Nevertheless, some action or gesture was imperative—the more so, since Russia's resistance was expected to be brief and the opportunity fleeting.

These were the circumstances in which it occurred to the President to revive his project for a personal meeting with Mr. Churchill. The propagandist value of such a meeting, both at home and abroad, would be large; but it could be so contrived as not to involve any new major commitment by the United States. On this point Roosevelt was clearly determined, as we can see from the hurried, pencilled notes which Hopkins scribbled down before his departure for London. On the main issue they were categoric:

'Economic and territorial deals—no. No talk about war.'[1]

But this did not exclude some further action at sea, though in less vigorous terms than Admiral Stark had advocated. The President gave Hopkins a map of the Atlantic, torn from a magazine, on which he had marked a line running along the 26th Meridian but bent east at its northern end so as to take in the approaches to Iceland. The significance was in the bend. The United States now had her own base in Iceland, to which regular convoys would have to run; and it was proposed that Allied or neutral ships proceeding in the same direction—i.e. on one leg of their journey to or from the British Isles—should be free to join these convoys under the protection of the American fleet. Hopkins' notes read:

'Merchant ships going all the time [?] in convoy can join up with American flag or Icelandic flag ships. Must be an American ship if conflict comes.'[1]

In other words, this was not to be a general system of patrol or escort in the Western Atlantic but to be confined, at least in theory, to the protection of American ships proceeding on American business. Other ships finding themselves in company would share the benefit, as it were accidentally.

This was the only military measure which the President wished to discuss at the meeting. For the rest, he intended that it should follow a course very similar to that of the recent Allied Conference in London, in which he had been unwilling to participate. It was to be a demonstration, that is to say, of 'our common tenacity of purpose', publicly marking the extent to which America now felt herself

---

[1] Sherwood, Vol. I, pp. 309 and 312.

involved in the war, albeit bloodlessly and at long range. To this
Roosevelt hoped to add some statement of war-aims or of the moral
principles which he believed to underlie the struggle. He had already
approached this matter in his message to Congress in December and
now wished to carry it further. He discussed the project with Mr.
Sumner Welles, who was to act as his diplomatic adviser at the meeting and has left a record of their conversation:

> 'Most important among the political problems which he [Roose-
> velt] desired to discuss with Mr. Churchill was the need for a
> general agreement between the two Governments, while the
> United States was still at peace and the European war was still in
> its early stages, covering the major bases on which a new world
> structure should be set up when peace finally came.
>
> The President felt since the conclusion of the First World War
> that one of the chief factors in the ultimate breakdown of organ-
> ized world society had been the lack of any overall agreement
> between the Allied Powers at the time of the Armistice in Novem-
> ber, 1918. He was foresighted enough to recognize that the
> United States could best prevent a recurrence of these conditions
> by insisting that Great Britain and the United States reach such
> an agreement without further delay. Subsequently, an effort could
> be made to obtain the support of all other nations fighting the
> Axis powers. The President rightly believed that the mere an-
> nouncement of such an agreement would prove invaluable in
> giving encouragement and hope to the peoples now fighting for
> survival.'[1]

(ii)

Atlantic Charter

The Prime Minister's party, including Mr. Hopkins, who had just
returned exhausted from his trip to Moscow, left Scapa Flow in the
Prince of Wales on 4th August. Mr. Churchill, in a buoyant mood,
announced their departure in a circular telegram to the Prime
Ministers of the Dominions, which ended as follows:

> 'I am taking the First Sea Lord, the C.I.G.S. and the V.C.A.S.,[2]
> Sir Alexander Cadogan of the Foreign Office and various techni-
> cal officers. . . . The President is bringing Mr. Sumner Welles,

---

[1] Sumner Welles, *The Time for Decision* (1944), pp. 138–9.

[2] Admiral Sir Dudley Pound, General Sir John Dill and Air Chief Marshal Sir Wilfrid
Freeman.

Admiral Stark and the opposite numbers of the Army and Air Chiefs. We expect the meeting will last about three days, during which time the whole field of future action can be explored. I can return at short notice by air if necessary. I hope you will approve of this action, which may be productive of important benefits and can hardly be harmful. Naturally I hope that the President would not have wished for this meeting unless he contemplated some further forward step. I shall keep you informed of what happens.'

The wording of this telegram suggests that Mr. Churchill was still hopeful of some major practical outcome, over and above the un-doubted political importance of the meeting itself. Precisely what he hoped for is less certain. He knew from Hopkins that there was no question of an American declaration of war and that the forward step planned in the Atlantic was a minor one. He was also aware of the President's plan for a joint declaration and had prepared his mind on this subject. But although Mr. Churchill was the first to acknowledge the necessity for such general statements of principle— and their particular value on occasions like the present—he did not regard them as a substitute for action, in this differing, perhaps, from Mr. Roosevelt, who was not immune from the American belief that manifestoes have an intrinsic value and are themselves to be classed as acts. Since this was not Mr. Churchill's view, there is little doubt that he approached the meeting in the belief that the President was considering, or could be persuaded to consider, some definite stroke of policy. It might be that he had already gone as far as was possible in Europe; but there still remained the darkening scene in the Far East, where the influence of the United States, exerted in time, might yet be decisive.[1]

The President, as we have seen, had other intentions. It would be wrong to say that he planned no more than a propagandist gesture or—in the phrase coined by his opponents in another context—'a tremendous imitation of an act'. On any footing the meeting had great significance and was an act of courage on Roosevelt's part. But for that very reason he could not allow it to involve him in any new commitment which called for more than executive action. He had no mind to lay himself open to the accusation, which would certainly have been raised, of usurping the powers of Congress by making an agreement, or what might pass for an agreement, with a foreign country. Mr. Churchill was, of course, well aware of these difficulties and had modified his hopes accordingly; but there remained, perhaps, some difference between his view and the President's of what was possible.

The two ships reached the rendezvous on the morning of Saturday,

---

[1] See Churchill, Vol. III, p. 380; Sherwood, Vol. I, p. 351.

9th August. That evening the President entertained the Prime Minister to dinner on board the *Augusta* and, in the course of a general conversation, broached his idea of the joint declaration, which he intended to form the centre-piece and main product of the Conference. The Prime Minister responded eagerly and was able to produce a tentative draft by the following morning:

> 'The President of the United States and the Prime Minister, Mr. Churchill, representing His Majesty's Government in the United Kingdom, being met together to resolve and concert the means of providing for the safety of their respective countries in face of Nazi and German aggression and of the dangers to all peoples arising therefrom, deem it right to make known certain principles which they both accept for guidance in the framing of their policy and on which they base their hopes for a better future for the world:
>
> First, their countries seek no aggrandizement, territorial or other.
>
> Second, they desire to see no territorial changes that do not accord with the freely expressed wishes of the people concerned.
>
> Third, they respect the right of all peoples to choose the form of government under which they will live. They are only concerned to defend the rights of freedom of speech and thought, without which such choice must be illusory.
>
> Fourth, they will strive to bring about a fair and equitable distribution of essential produce, not only within their territorial boundaries, but between the nations of the world.
>
> Fifth, they seek a peace which will not only cast down for ever the Nazi tyranny, but by effective international organization will afford to all States and peoples the means of dwelling in security within their own bounds and of traversing the seas and oceans without fear of lawless assault or the need for maintaining burdensome armaments.'[1]

These were unexceptionable sentiments; and we need not look further for their origin than the common stream of Anglo-American political tradition. In so far as the draft had a particular source, it was probably to be found in a combination of two earlier documents: President Roosevelt's speech on the Four Freedoms and the resolutions adopted at the London Conference. If these texts are examined closely, it will be seen with what skill their contents and some hint of their phrasing had been dovetailed together.

The President examined Mr. Churchill's draft on Sunday and, with the help of Mr. Sumner Welles, prepared a revised text which was discussed in detail on the following morning. The first amendment proposed was the addition of two new clauses:

---

[1] Churchill, Vol. III, pp. 385–6.

'Sixth, they desire such a peace to establish for all safety on the high seas and oceans.

'Seventh, they believe that all the nations of the world must be guided in spirit to the abandonment of the use of force. Because no future peace can be maintained if land, sea or air armaments continue to be employed by nations which threaten, or may threaten, to use force outside their frontiers, they believe the disarmament of such nations is essential. They will further the adoption of all other practicable measures which will lighten for peace loving peoples, the crushing burden of armaments'.

There could be no objection to the first, which simply brought into greater prominence an idea already expressed in the original text. Much the same was true of what Mr. Churchill called 'the generalities of Point 7'; but unfortunately the President wished to compensate for this addition by dropping the reference to an 'international organization' in the original Point 5. He evidently felt, with the example of Woodrow Wilson before him, that anything even mildly suggestive of a League of Nations was politically dangerous. But the Prime Minister was equally determined that this part of his text should stand. He pointed out that opinion in England would be shocked, if there were no reference to an international system after the war. It was finally agreed to cover the point by adding the words 'pending the establishment of a wider and more permanent system of general security' after the President's sentence on disarmament.

The next amendment, which seems to have originated with Mr. Sumner Welles, was less happy. Mr. Welles had long been an opponent of Imperial Preference, which he believed to be prejudicial to American trade. It now occurred to him that a slight change in the wording of Mr. Churchill's Point 4 would commit the British Government to some modification of this policy after the war.[1] With this in mind he moved the President to propose a revised text which ran:

'Fourth, they will endeavour to further the enjoyment by all peoples of access without discrimination and on equal terms to the markets and raw materials of the world, which are needed for their economic prosperity.'

This was open to several objections. The Prime Minister, though a Free Trader himself, could not accept a form of words expressly designed to challenge the Ottawa Agreements without consulting the Dominions, who might have withheld their consent. Moreover, as the Cabinet pointed out when the text was referred to them, the clause could also be interpreted as limiting our freedom to continue exchange-control after the war, which the difficulties of our financial position would certainly make necessary.

---

[1] Sumner Welles, pp. 139–40.

During the subsequent discussions the Prime Minister reacted vigorously:

> 'I could not help mentioning the British experience in adhering to Free Trade for eighty years in face of ever mounting American tariffs. We had allowed the fullest importation into all our Colonies. Even our coastwise traffic around Great Britain was open to the competition of the world. All we had got in reciprocation was successive doses of American protection.'[1]

Mr. Welles, who seems not to have considered this aspect of the matter, was silenced; but the sectarian note which he had introduced into the discussion was less easy to dispose of. In the end it was agreed to modify Point 4 by substituting 'trade' for 'markets' and adding the qualifying phrase 'with due respect for their existing obligations'. This covered the main objections but left the clause with an unhappy air of compromise, which was out of place in a Declaration otherwise cast in broad and solemn terms.

In the meantime Mr. Churchill had communicated the whole of the revised text to the Cabinet. He explained in his covering telegram the various amendments for which he was still pressing, including particularly the addition of some words about an international organization, and added:

> 'He [Roosevelt] will not like this very much, but he attaches so much importance to the Joint Declaration, which he believes will affect the whole movement of United States opinion, that I think he will agree.'

The Cabinet, acting with extraordinary dispatch, were able to put a considered reply in the Prime Minister's hands within twelve hours. In the main it welcomed the Declaration as it stood, but suggested a new and perhaps preferable text for the disputed Point 4 and the addition of a further clause on economic advancement and social security. The former Mr. Churchill did not think it wise to press; the latter was accepted without difficulty.

The Declaration was now put into its final shape, the only further change being some modification of the preamble. In his original text Mr. Churchill had described the purpose of the meeting as being 'to resolve and concert the means' of providing against the dangers of German aggression. This, though cautiously worded, was evidently felt by the President to come too close to hinting at an alliance or at least an agreed common purpose. It was therefore dropped from the published version, which the President and the Prime Minister signed at noon on 12 August:

---

[1] Churchill, Vol. III, p. 387.

'Joint Declaration by the President and the Prime Minister: 12th August, 1941.

The President of the United States of America and the Prime Minister, Mr. Churchill, representing His Majesty's Government in the United Kingdom, being met together, deem it right to make known certain common principles in the national policies of their respective countries, on which they base their hopes for a better future for the world:

First, their countries seek no aggrandizement, territorial or other.

Second, they desire to see no territorial changes that do not accord with the freely expressed wishes of the peoples concerned.

Third, they respect the right of all peoples to choose the form of Government under which they will live; and they wish to see sovereign rights and self government restored to those who have been forcibly deprived of them.

Fourth, they will endeavour, with due regard to their existing obligations, to further the enjoyment by all states, great or small, victor or vanquished, of access, on equal terms, to the trade and to the raw materials of the world which are needed for their economic prosperity.

Fifth, they desire to bring about the fullest collaboration between all nations in the economic field, with the object of securing for all improved labour standards, economic advancement and social security.

Sixth, after the final destruction of the Nazi tyranny they hope to see established a peace which will afford to all nations the means of dwelling in safety within their own boundaries, and which will afford assurance that all men in all lands may live out their lives in freedom from fear and want.

Seventh, such a peace should enable all men to traverse the high seas and oceans without hindrance.

Eighth, they believe that all the nations of the world, for realistic as well as spiritual reasons, must come to the abandonment of the use of force. Since no future peace can be maintained if land, sea or air armaments continue to be employed by nations which threaten, or may threaten, aggression outside of their frontiers, they believe, pending the establishment of a wider and more permanent system of general security, that the disarmament of such nations is essential. They will likewise aid and encourage all other practicable measures which will lighten for peace loving peoples the crushing burden of armaments.

It remains to try to assess the value of this Declaration by which the President set so much store. Its primary purpose, as he had indicated, was to influence American opinion; and in this it was probably successful within certain limits. With the publication of the Atlantic Charter, as it was soon called, the American public may well have felt that they had acquired a moral stake in the war and could now identify themselves wholeheartedly with the Allied cause without fear of compromising their own idealism. But beyond this it is difficult to detect any strong movement of opinion. The four months which elapsed between the publication of the Charter and the Japanese attack on Pearl Harbor brought the United States no nearer to actual belligerency. The President preserved his cautious system; there was little or no slackening in the Isolationist campaign; and even in the relatively uncontroversial field of industrial mobilization progress was extremely slow. The American people, however stirred they may have been by the Joint Declaration, were not wrought to the pitch of decisive action.

In England and Europe generally the Charter was received with initial enthusiasm soon fading into disappointment. When news of a meeting between the President and Mr. Churchill first leaked out, exaggerated hopes were founded on the event. To the general public, tenacious but war weary and largely ignorant of the deadweight of Isolationist opinion in America, it seemed inconceivable that some dramatic result—an American declaration of war or a new and decisive form of intervention—should not follow immediately. When it appeared that the only visible result of the meeting was a Declaration which, though perfectly acceptable, was neither new nor startling, the sense of anti-climax was profound. The truth is that people who are fighting for their lives do not attach much importance to a formal statement of war-aims: their position speaks for itself. The temporary warmth engendered by the Charter was therefore difficult to sustain.

This natural disappointment even went some way to disguise the real significance of what had happened. On that point we may quote the Prime Minister:

'The profound and far reaching importance of this Joint Declaration was apparent. The fact alone of the United States, still technically neutral, joining with a belligerent Power in making such a Declaration was astonishing. The inclusion in it of a reference to "the final destruction of Nazi tyranny" . . . amounted to a challenge which in ordinary times would have implied warlike action. Finally, not the least striking feature was the realism of the last paragraph, where there was a plain and bold intimation that after the war the United States would join with us in policing the world until the establishment of a better order.'[1]

---

[1] Churchill, Vol. III, p. 394.

(iii)

Military Discussions

Side by side with these diplomatic conversations, a series of meetings took place between the British and American Chiefs of Staff. The only matter of immediate operational importance to be discussed was the coming extension of American naval patrols in the Atlantic. The plan had already been settled on the American side and its principles communicated by Mr. Hopkins during his visit to London. Certain details, however, remained to be adjusted; and this is a convenient point at which to give a summary of the new system, which went into action in the following month. Its basis was that the Americans, under the guise of protecting their own convoys to Iceland, assumed responsibility for the escort of all fast convoys between the Western Ocean meeting-point south of Newfoundland and the Mid-Ocean meeting-point off Iceland. The Canadian Navy continued to provide the escort between the port of departure (or arrival) on the American seaboard and the Western Ocean meeting-point; and slow convoys were protected throughout by Canadian or British forces as before. Operational control of the whole system remained with the Admiralty. In order to avoid compromising American neutrality still further, there were no mixed escorts; but it seemed inevitable, in view of the intense U-boat activity in the sea area between Iceland and Newfoundland, that the American fleet should see action sooner or later.

These matters apart, the military discussions at Placentia were general and exploratory, though not without value. A number of differences between the British and the American approach to grand strategy were disclosed; and one could already see in dim outline the shape which future controversies were to take. It had been clear at the Staff conversations in March (though the point was not then pressed) that the Americans were more than a little sceptical of our policy of containing Germany, and especially of that aspect of it which involved a heavy commitment in the Middle East. The question had been raised again, in connexion with Lend-Lease shipments, during Hopkins's visit to London; and it will be convenient to quote his remarks on that occasion in full, since they illustrate the American case in its extreme form:

> 'The men in the United States who held the principal positions, and took the big decisions on defence matters, were of the opinion that in the Middle East the British Empire had an indefensible position, in attempting to defend which great sacrifices were being made. They felt that at any moment the Western Mediterranean

might be closed by the Germans, the Canal might be blocked and the position of the Mediterranean Fleet made untenable; at the same time Germany might concentrate a great superiority of air and armoured forces which would overwhelm the armies in the Middle East. In their view, the Battle of the Atlantic would be the final decisive battle of the war and everything should be concentrated on winning it . . .

No one in Britain appreciated the feeling which existed throughout the United States Military Command that the Middle East was a liability from which the British should withdraw. It was difficult to convey this feeling because everyone in authority in Great Britain had made up their minds conclusively on the subject, and found it hard to understand how there could be any doubt. It should be remembered that the problems of the Middle East, the interests of the Moslem World, and the interrelationship of Egypt and India, were not well understood in the United States.

. . . . Everyone in the United States had realized the necessity of helping Greece; they could also understand that the defence of Crete had to be undertaken; but among those men who counted there were grave doubts about the general situation. He did not wish to overstate the case, but it was of great importance that a true understanding should be reached so that the American policy of assistance in the Middle East should be built on a new basis of full confidence in a great joint enterprise.'

These and similar arguments were raised once more at the Atlantic Meeting and provoked some discussion. The British representatives were satisfied that they succeeded in the end in convincing their American colleagues that our policy was sound. They pointed out that for practical reasons, as well as for reasons of prestige, we could scarcely abandon a theatre in which we were already so deeply committed. Merely to transport elsewhere the 600,000 men, who were now concentrated there, with their equipment and very large base-installations would be an immense and complex operation; it was questionable whether it was even within our powers. It was vital to protect our Persian oil supplies; and we did not take at all a gloomy view of the possibilities of defence, whether in the West or against a German southward movement through the Caucasus. Moreover, in accordance with our original strategy, incorporated in A.B.C. 1., of bringing pressure to bear on Italy, we wished to retain and develop the only base in our possession from which such an offensive could be launched.

All this made a strong case; but it is doubtful how far it touched the heart of the American position. Both then and later the United States regarded all British activities in the Middle East with distrust, perhaps because they were felt to be tainted with 'colonialism', perhaps because the outline of a future conflict of interests was already discernible. But there was also a further problem. American military experts had little confidence in the general strategy of 'holding the ring' round Germany and attempting to wear her down by operations on the periphery and an intensive air bombardment. They regarded this as a time-wasting and negative policy. All their instincts, supported by the geopolitical position of the United States with its wealth of manpower and industry, suggested that the correct way to finish any war was by a direct thrust at the centre, and that operations in the Middle East or elsewhere, which did not contribute to this aim, should be dismissed as merely diversionary.

Some hint of these latter objections emerged during the discussions at Placentia, when the British Chiefs of Staff circulated a review of future strategy. This was a digest (with minor alterations) of the J.P.S. paper discussed in the opening chapters; and the argument, based on the familiar triple theme of bombing, blockade and subversion, need not be repeated here. There was no formal debate; but the American Chiefs of Staff took copies of the paper and promised a written statement of their views after their return to Washington. It seemed likely that these would be critical. They were evidently disappointed at the lack of reference in the paper to any major land-campaign in Europe beyond the operations in support of a general rising, which were proposed for the final phase. They also indicated that in their view the paper over-stressed the offensive value of bombing. But, although they were doubtful of our present policy, they had no alternative to offer. Their own planning was still directed almost exclusively to the defence of the Western Hemisphere. Indeed, the extent of their concern with this aspect of the problem came as something of a shock to their British colleagues. They were surprised at General Marshall's statement that it might be necessary to occupy parts of Colombia, Venezuela and Brazil in order to protect the Panama Canal, and at his evident preoccupation with the comparatively remote possibility of a Nazi coup in the last-named country.

Marshall explained that these potential commitments, together with the defence of Hawaii and the Philippines and the provision of garrisons for Iceland and the newly acquired bases on the Atlantic seaboard, would absorb almost the whole force, which the United States planned to raise in the first stage of mobilization. The position was further complicated by the present structure of the army with its high proportion of restricted-service men. In order to find a reinforcement of 5,000 regulars for Iceland, it had recently been necessary to break up one of the newly-formed divisions; and if, as was now proposed, the Marine Brigade were also replaced, another division would have to be treated in the same way. There was also an acute

10

shortage of equipment. Two of the new armoured divisions, for example, had only forty tanks all told, instead of the fifty per cent training scale to which they were entitled. Ammunition, particularly in the smaller calibres, was equally short and would remain so at least until the end of the year. These deficiencies were a matter of growing concern not only to the American Chiefs of Staff but also to the general public. It was well known, since there had been some publicity on the subject, that tanks were now being produced in quantity; and the public would certainly demand that a high proportion were withheld for America's own forces, instead of being distributed under Lend-Lease.

It was clear from this that for many months to come the American Army would be absorbed in its own problems. That was one reason why planning had so far been restricted and local. All questions of policy apart, a new overseas commitment, such as the operations in West Africa tentatively suggested in the Chiefs of Staff paper,[1] was out of the question. The most that could be done was to earmark a garrison for the Azores, and that only because the Azores were now regarded as being technically within the Western Hemisphere. The President had recently received a letter from Dr. Salazar which he had interpreted as meaning that, if the Germans moved against the Peninsula, the Portuguese Government would withdraw after a token resistance to the Azores. Once there, they would be willing to accept American protection, if no British force was available. Arrangements were being put in hand accordingly; but they would apply only to the Azores. The other objectives of Operation 'Pilgrim', the Canaries and the Cape Verde Islands, would have to remain a British commitment.

American strategic plans for the Pacific were equally tentative. It appeared to be their intention to develop their base in the Philippines and to exploit it offensively in the event of a Japanese attack; but the forces available for the purpose were extremely small. The total anti-aircraft protection of Manila Bay, for example, was a single battery of four guns. The local garrison had recently been reinforced by fifteen tanks, fifty fighters and one squadron of nine Flying Fortresses. The latter were intended for offensive operations against the flank of any Japanese movement to the southward; but the American Chiefs of Staff seemed to have an exaggerated view of the results which such a limited striking-force could achieve.[2] They had no plans for any other commitment in the area. An attempt on the British side to interest them in the future of Singapore was wholly unsuccessful. Admiral Stark argued that, as the result of the reserves

---

[1] See p. 16-17 above.
[2] There were, however, tentative plans for building up this force to 200 heavy bombers by the spring of 1942.

which they had built up and the other sources of supply open to them, the United States could, if necessary, do without imports from the Far East. He urged that a careful analysis should be made of the value of Malayan produce to us in order to see whether it could not be dispensed with in the same way. But in this, perhaps, he was speaking for himself, since his views were in direct conflict with those previously expressed by General Chaney in London, who had said that American military opinion rated the value of Singapore far above that of our positions in the Middle East.

This seemingly negative attitude of the American Chiefs of Staff was to be attributed in part to the delicacy of the political situation. Their instructions from the President precluded them from accepting even the shadow of a new commitment. They were also aware that their actions, no less than his, might later be called in question by Congress; and an incident, which occurred while the Conference was sitting, added point to these fears. On 12th August the Bill to extend the period of selective service, without which the whole structure of the army would have been seriously disrupted, passed the House of Representatives by only one vote. It is true that this, as later appeared, was partly due to a miscalculation. A number of Representatives, not themselves opposed to the Bill but judging it to be unpopular, had decided to withhold their votes, each believing that his own abstention would not impair the Administration's majority.[1] Nevertheless, such an extremely narrow vote on a matter which concerned the life or death of the Army, was a potent warning of the continued power of Isolationism. Coming when it did, it impressed the British Chiefs of Staff, as nothing else could have done, with the difficulties and hazards of their colleagues' position.

For this reason they were not unduly depressed by their apparent lack of progress at the meeting. Behind the criticism and the disappointing silence on particular issues, they believed that they could detect a fund of goodwill, which would be exerted on our behalf so far as circumstances allowed. There was only one point on which they recorded a sense of discouragement. This was the Americans' sceptical attitude towards our bombing policy, which promised to have immediate results in the field of supply. At the close of the Staff Conversations in March an informal agreement had been reached between Air Vice-Marshal Slessor and his opposite number on the Air Sub-Committee, by which we were to receive a stated proportion of America's current aircraft production and, until her entry into the war, the whole output of any new production. It now appeared that this agreement would not be ratified. In consequence our expectation of heavy bombers, most of which were to have come from new

---

[1] Langer and Gleason, p. 574.

production, would be sharply curtailed. All that we could definitely count on was some 1,100 over the period up to June 1943. This was less than half of what we had hoped for and barely a quarter of what we needed; but no amelioration was likely. The United States Army Air Corps was short of aircraft—it was said that they had no more than fifty heavy bombers in service—and both Admiral Stark and General Marshall were strongly opposed to any increase in the bomber programme, since they doubted its value and believed that it would conflict with the needs of the other Services.

In all other respects the discussions were cordial and were felt by both sides to have been profitable. The Chiefs of Staff summed up their impressions as follows:

> '. . . . We neither expected nor achieved startling results. The American Chiefs of Staff are quite clearly thinking in terms of the defence of the Western Hemisphere and have so far not formulated any joint strategy for the defeat of Germany in the event of their entry into the War. Nevertheless, the personal contacts with our American colleagues will prove of the greatest value for future collaboration. We have, we think, convinced them of the soundness of our policy in the Middle East. They, in turn, have made us understand their difficulties. A most distressing revelation is the reduction in heavy bomber allocation to us. This we consider a serious matter. We are also concerned at the small numbers of Catalinas[1] allocated to the United Kingdom during the next few months'.

(iv)

Japan

We must now turn to the second phase of the political discussions, in which lay, as the Prime Minister hoped, the real crux of the meeting. The subject was the growing menace of Japan. During July, true to her policy of steady encroachment, Japan had finally extorted permission from the Vichy Government to station troops and occupy bases in southern Indo-China, including the important naval base at Saigon with its adjacent aerodromes. It was known that she had also presented similar demands to Siam. The United States had at first reacted sharply to these moves. On 25th July an executive order, freezing Japanese assets in America, had brought all trade between the two countries to a standstill except by special licence. There had

---

[1] Long-range flying boats of great value to Coastal Command.

been some doubt in London about the wisdom of this move, since it seemed to offer Japan an abrupt choice between the complete reversal of her policy and an immediate advance in search of the raw materials which she was now denied. Nevertheless, we had followed suit. With still greater trepidation, since they had not yet received any firm promise of support from either ourselves or the United States, if they were attacked, the Netherlands East Indies had also come into line. Japan was thus suffering from a severe, though not total, blockade.[1]

Meanwhile desultory negotiations continued between Japan and the United States for a general settlement in the Far East. The particular point on which they turned was the proposal, made earlier by the President, for the 'neutralization' of Siam and Indo-China under the joint guarantee of the United States, Japan, Great Britain and China. It now appeared, perhaps as the result of the economic embargo, that Japan might agree. On 6th August her envoy in Washington, Admiral Nomura, was instructed to advance new proposals. If the United States would resume normal trade-relations, Japan would give an undertaking not to advance farther into south-east Asia and to withdraw her troops from Indo-China at the close of the 'China incident' and on condition that her special status in that country was recognized. In return, she would expect the United States to foster direct negotiations between herself and China; to procure her access to the natural resources of the south-west Pacific which she required; and to refrain, and advise her associates to refrain, from any further military preparations in the area.[2]

Although this was an advance on any previous offer, it could hardly be regarded as acceptable. The Japanese gave nothing away, except a promise not to take more than they had taken already, while America and the Allies conceded everything, including a guarantee not to defend themselves. Nevertheless, the United States, in the persons of the President and Mr. Cordell Hull, were anxious not to abandon the negotiations. They no longer expected that a general settlement would result; but they hoped to obtain a temporary lull, perhaps for a month, perhaps for longer, which they believed to be of value. In the meantime they were reluctant to discuss what their policy would be, if the negotiations finally broke down. Lord Halifax attempted to raise this question with Mr. Hull, but met with little success. The Secretary took the most serious view of Japanese aspirations, which he believed to extend far beyond any immediate objective in the Pacific. He spoke vaguely but alarmingly of Japanese plans to gain control of the Indian Ocean, cut British

---

[1] E. L. Woodward, *British Foreign Policy during the Second World War* (1962), pp. 174–5.
[2] Woodward, pp. 175–6.

communications round the Cape and join hands with Germany somewhere in the neighbourhood of the Persian Gulf. But he would not commit himself to any statement of American policy in such an event. It would all depend, he said, on Great Britain's position at the time: 'circumstances change so rapidly these days, I would not undertake to be very specific.'[1]

In London, on the other hand, attention was concentrated on one definite and immediate issue. There was reason to believe at the beginning of August that Japan's next move would be to occupy the Kra Isthmus, the narrow neck of Siamese territory immediately to the north of Malaya. From this position she would control both the port of Singora and the junction of the two main routes leading southward to Singapore—the west coast route through Kedah and Perak and the central route through Kelantan. She would also separate Malaya from Burma and cut the normal route for air-rein-forcements to the former. Such a movement could only presage one thing—an immediate or almost immediate attack on Singapore. The question arose whether we ought not now to implement a long-considered plan and ourselves occupy Singora in a forestalling action. The Chiefs of Staff[2] were inclined to believe that we should; but the Commander-in-Chief, Far East, when consulted by telegram, was more cautious. Although he had previously been in favour of the operation in just such a contingency as had now arisen, he evidently felt that the weakness of his forces made it extremely risky. He recommended that it should not be carried out unless we had definite information of an impending Japanese movement. In the meanwhile we should content ourselves with political action, which might take the form of a joint warning by ourselves, the United States and the Dutch that any violation of Siamese territory by Japan would be regarded as a *casus belli*.

This was the approximate position when the Prime Minister set out for the Atlantic Meeting. It had long been his policy to try to associate the United States with a definite and clear-cut warning to Japan. Without it war seemed inevitable; but he could not bring himself to believe that Japan would take the risk, if she knew from the outset that she would have to meet the full power of the United States and more especially of the American fleet. Recent events, including the Japanese reaction to the economic embargo, seemed to confirm this view, which was further strengthened by a telegram received from the Cabinet during the voyage:

---

[1] Langer and Gleason, p. 671.

[2] This decision was taken at a meeting of the C.O.S. Committee on 5th August, when the C.N.S. and C.I.G.S. were already on their way to Placentia; the Commander-in-Chief's reply was received on 6th August.

'Defence Committee have had under consideration situation in Siam.

2. It is possible that in consequence of United States and British reactions to move into Indo-China and to present threats to Siam, Japan may now pause to consolidate in Indo-China before taking next step and that during interval she may content herself with economic penetration into Siam. But there is growing feeling here that only hope of preventing Siam from sharing fate of Indo-China is plain warning by ourselves, and *a fortiori* by ourselves and the U.S.A. together, that this will lead to war. Neither United States nor we have yet gone further than to indicate that Japanese move into Siam would be a menace to the security of our respective possessions.

3. Blunt warning that we would regard further Japanese move into Siam as *casus belli* might in itself be too challenging, and obviously goes beyond what United States Government could constitutionally say. Moreover, we ourselves should not necessarily regard Japanese move into north or east Siam as constituting such a direct threat to our own interests as Japanese attempt to occupy Kra Isthmus.

4. Defence Committee are unanimous in the view that situation would best be met by parallel warnings by United States privately to the Japanese Government through the diplomatic channel to the effect that any incursion by the Japanese forces into Siam would produce a situation in which we should be compelled to take counter measures likely to lead to war between our respective countries and Japan.'

Here was the decisive stroke which Mr. Churchill hoped to persuade President Roosevelt to make. A warning to Japan in the terms proposed would not, of course, commit the United States irrevocably; that was in any case beyond the President's power. But it would have the effect, morally speaking, of bringing America's intervention in the Far East to the same level as her intervention in Europe. In other words, it would serve notice to Japan, as notice had already been served to Germany, that the United States did not intend to stand clear or to limit her action to protecting her own interests and territories. This would be an immense step forward, all the more so because the American public, with its inherited distrust of 'colonialism', was apt to take a distorted and partial view of events in the Far East. There was little sense of the unity of the problem and little understanding that an attack on, say, Malaya or the Dutch East Indies might be no less damaging to the cause of democracy than an attack on the Philippines or Hawaii.

On the first day of the Conference there was a preliminary discussion of Far Eastern matters between Sir Alexander Cadogan and Mr. Sumner Welles. The latter described the negotiations which were still going on in Washington and gave details of the latest Japanese

proposals. He added that, although it had been agreed to keep the
negotiations alive, enough had been said both by Mr. Cordell Hull
and himself to make it clear that America's patience was wearing
thin. He doubted whether any further warning would be useful or
desirable. The greatest need at the moment was to gain time. His
own account continues:

> 'I said that I also wished by direction of the President to make it
> clear that the Government of the United States did not believe
> that even should Thailand [Siam] be occupied by Japan, such
> occupation should be made a *casus belli* by Great Britain. I said
> that in the opinion of both the War and Navy Departments of the
> United States the chief objective in the Pacific for the time being
> should be the avoidance of war with Japan inasmuch as a war
> between the United States and Japan at this time would not only
> tie up the major portion, if not the entire American Fleet, but
> would likewise create a very serious strain upon our military
> establishment and upon our production activities, at the very
> moment when these should be concentrated upon the Atlantic.
> This applied, of course, even more strongly in the case of the
> American Fleet.'[1]

Sir Alexander replied with an account of our own difficulties. He
said that the Prime Minister was firmly convinced that nothing but
the most stiffly worded warning from the United States could now
deter Japan. We were also under some pressure from the Dominions
and the Dutch. We had recently gone as far as we could in giving
assurances to the latter; but we were not in a position to make an
unequivocal promise without the support of the United States. The
Australian Government was urging us in the strongest terms to obtain
a definite commitment from the President that, if the Dutch East
Indies were attacked and we supported them, he would seek authority
from Congress to come to our aid. Mr. Welles shied away from this
proposal, saying that the President was most anxious to avoid any
appearance of putting pressure on Congress. Such a move might
react unfavourably on American opinion which, left to itself, was
already showing a mounting opposition to Japanese policy. The
discussion was then broken off, after Sir Alexander had given Mr.
Welles a draft text of the proposed joint or parallel warnings to
Japan:

> 'By the United States Government.
>   1. Any further encroachment by Japan in the South-West
> Pacific would produce a situation in which the United States
> Government would be compelled to take counter measures even
> though these might lead to war between the United States and
> Japan.

---

[1] Langer and Gleason, p. 672.

2. If any third Power becomes the object of aggression by Japan in consequence of such counter measures or of their support of them, the President would have the intention to seek authority from Congress to give aid to such Power.

By the British and Dutch Governments.

1. Any further encroachment by Japan in the South-West Pacific would produce a situation in which His [or Her] Majesty's Government would be compelled to take counter measures even though these might lead to war between Great Britain [or the Netherlands] and Japan.

2. If any third Power becomes the object of aggression by Japan in consequence of such counter measures or of their support of them His [or Her] Majesty's Government would give all possible aid to such Power.'

On the following day Mr. Roosevelt and the Prime Minister took up the discussion. The President explained his policy of spinning out the negotiations in the hope of winning at least a month's respite. He would insist that, during the negotiations, Japan did not extend her occupation of Indo-China and did not use her existing bases for operations against China. He did not think it wise to try to enforce these conditions by the presence of American observers; but he would keep the present economic sanctions in force as a guarantee of Japan's good behaviour. Beyond that he was at first extremely reluctant to go. He discounted, perhaps on Mr. Welles's advice, the value of a further warning and was clear, in any case, that he could not make any statement which involved a contingent promise to seek a declaration of war from Congress. It seemed that a deadlock had been reached. But at last, under strong persuasion from the Prime Minister, Mr. Roosevelt agreed to the principle of a joint warning provided that it was limited on the American side to the first paragraph of the proposed text. He added that he would mark the solemnity of the occasion by interviewing the Japanese envoy himself. At the end of their conversation he would hand him a written statement, which would include the agreed text of the warning. Identical communications could be made simultaneously by the British and Dutch Governments.

The conversation then turned to what part, if any, Russia should play in this *démarche*. Japan still had ambitions in the north and might now be tempted to move in that direction, if she felt herself decisively blocked in the south. The President proposed, therefore, to inform Russia that negotiations with Japan were in progress with the immediate object of securing a delay and the more distant one of reaching a general settlement in the Pacific. It might then be suggested that the Soviet Government should indicate to Japan their hope that these negotiations would succeed and, if so, that the settlement would apply to the North Pacific as well. The point could be further covered by a verbal addition to the warning to the effect that, as the U.S.S.R. was a friendly Power, the United States would be equally interested in any conflict in the north-west Pacific.

Mr. Churchill had every reason to be well pleased with these decisions. It appeared that, after negotiations which had been unexpectedly difficult, he had now secured his main point. Japan would receive a warning in plain terms, which would make it clear that the United States, Great Britain and the Netherlands were acting in concert and that, if she continued her aggressive courses, she would have to meet the united resistance of the three Powers. It was in this sense that he reported to the Cabinet:

> 'At the end of the note which President will hand to Japanese Ambassador, when he returns from his cruise in about a week's time, he will add the following passage, which is taken from my draft:
> "Any further encroachment by Japan in South-West Pacific would produce a situation in which the United States Government would be compelled to take counter measures even though these might lead to war between United States and Japan".
> He would also add something to the effect that it is obvious, the Soviet Union being a friendly power, United States Government would be similarly interested in any similar conflict in the North West Pacific.
> I think this is entirely good and that we should associate ourselves herewith and endeavour to get the Dutch to come in in full agreement, because either the Japanese will refuse the conditions the President prescribes—namely, continuance of the economic sanction and no movements on Japanese part, and no invasion of Siam—or alternatively, they will go on with their military action while lying about it diplomatically.
> In this case conditions indicated by final passage just quoted would come into play with great force, and the full effect of parallel declarations could be realized . . .
> On these grounds I consider that we should endorse proposed course of action, and that the Dominions should be told about it and made to see that it is a very great advance towards gripping of Japanese aggression by united force.'

In a subsequent report, written after his return to London, Mr. Churchill added:

> 'The President said that he would at once telegraph to Mr. Cordell Hull to arrange for the Japanese Ambassador to call upon him on his return to Washington, and to tell his Excellency that he would have an important message to deliver. He would see the Ambassador as soon as possible, and would give him the message in writing.

I later asked for a copy of this message, but I was told, at the time of our departure, that it had not yet been drafted.

The President, however, assured me, on more than one occasion, that he would include in it the final words which I have quoted above. Evidently this is the crucial part of the message, and I am confident that the President will not tone it down. He has a copy of the record of our conversation in which this wording is reproduced . . .

Even taken by itself this warning should have a considerable deterrent effect on Japan. And when we remember that the Japanese will already have suffered the shock of the Anglo-American joint declaration, I think we may hope that they will pause before proceeding to further outrage.'

It is sad to record that on this occasion the Prime Minister's confidence was misplaced. No sooner had the President returned to Washington than his resolution faltered. He yielded to the advice of Mr. Hull, who thought the agreed text of the warning 'dangerously strong', especially in its open use of the word war. This, he felt, was calculated to incite the extremists in Japan at the very moment when, for the reasons already given, the United States were particularly anxious to avoid a conflict. Accordingly the President, without disclosing his intentions to Mr. Churchill, decided to modify the text considerably. In its final form the message, which he handed to Admiral Nomura on 17th August, ended as follows:

'This Government now finds it necessary to say to the Government of Japan that, if the Japanese Government takes any further steps in pursuance of a policy or programme of military domination by force or threat of force of neighbouring countries, the Government of the United States will be compelled to take any and all steps necessary towards safeguarding the legitimate rights and interests of the United States and American nationals and towards ensuring the safety and security of the United States.'[1]

The whole sense of the warning was thus changed, and the impression of a united front and close concert between the Western Powers, which Mr. Churchill had desired to produce, was impaired or even destroyed.

---

[1] Woodward, p. 176.

(v)

Invitation to Stalin

Before the Atlantic Meeting ended on the afternoon of 12th August, one more important piece of business was transacted. The President and the Prime Minister, having heard Mr. Hopkins's account of his Russian visit and discussed his proposal for a Supply Conference, sent the following joint telegram to M. Stalin:

'. . . The needs and demands of your and our own armed services can only be determined in the light of the full knowledge of the many factors which must be taken into consideration in conjectures that we make. In order that all of us may be in a position to arrive at speedy decisions as to apportionment of our joint resources, we suggest that we prepare a meeting to be held at Moscow to which we would send high representatives who would discuss these matters directly with you. If this conference appeals to you, we want you to know that pending decisions of that conference we shall continue to send supplies and material as rapidly as possible.

We must now turn our minds to the consideration of a more long term policy, since there is still a long and hard path to be traversed before there can be won that complete victory without which our efforts and sacrifices would be wasted.

The war goes on upon many fronts and before it is over there may be yet further fighting on fronts that will be developed. Our resources though immense are limited, and it must become a question as to where and when those resources can best be used to further to principal extent our common effort. This applies equally to manufactured war supplies and to raw materials . . .'

CHAPTER VI

SUPPLY, 1941

(i)

America's Position

BY THE MIDDLE of 1941 it was generally agreed that a major change would shortly have to take place in the industrial relations between Great Britain and the United States. During the earlier period of the war it had been possible to assume that, although we should draw heavily on America for food, raw materials and certain types of machine-tool, we should remain largely self-sufficient in the production of finished munitions. The only notable exception was aircraft. Here Lord Beaverbrook had already appealed in December 1940, for all that American industry could supply up to a total of 3,000 a month, or more than twice British production at that date. But in other departments our demands had been deliberately modest. Partly for financial reasons, partly from a preference for British over American designs,[1] we had limited our orders to what was necessary to cover certain specific deficiencies and provide a small margin of insurance against the loss of our own production by bombing. In 1940 and 1941, for example, the Ministry of Supply's American orders accounted for barely 15 per cent of the total programme; and actual deliveries were lower still.[2]

This division of labour could not continue indefinitely. Reserves of industrial manpower in the United Kingdom were running low and home production was nearing its peak; but total output was already only barely sufficient for our needs, which were constantly increasing. And to these had now been added the further burden of supplying arms to Russia. For the future therefore, unless we proposed to limit our already insufficient forces still further, we should have to rely more and more on direct purchase from the United States. We should have to import not only American aircraft but American tanks, guns, rifles and military equipment of every kind.

The first or financial obstacle to this change of policy had been removed by the passage of the Lend-Lease Act in March; but other formidable difficulties remained. Chief among them was the con-

---

[1] Some weapons of purely British design were produced in the United States; but in general American manufacturers were unwilling or unable to deviate from standard American types.

[2] Postan, pp. 228 et seq.

tinuing low level of American production. In 1941 American war
industry was still in its infancy; indeed, its performance during the
first two years of the war had been so disappointing as to raise doubts
about its eventual capacity, which had played their part in deciding
our previous policy:

> 'The "targets" of American production were as yet a matter of
> aspiration or, for some, of faith; in 1940 British supply depart-
> ments had no firm ground for believing that American industry
> would in fact achieve the vast output of which theoretically it was
> capable. The American shipbuilding industry had not yet fully
> emerged from the great inter-war slump and was expanding very
> slowly. In 1940, the second year of war expansion, it was still un-
> able to turn out more than fifty-three ocean-going ships, and in
> 1939 little more than half that number had been built. No
> medium or heavy tanks were produced in the United States in
> 1939 or 1940; and in 1941, with an output of 3,900 medium and
> heavy tanks, American production was still 20 per cent below the
> corresponding figure of British output. The number of guns of
> 2 pounder and above produced in the United States in 1940 was
> 340, and in 1941 6,720—about 30–40 per cent of the correspond-
> ing figure of British output in that year. Until the very end of the
> first quarter of 1942, the volume of American output of munitions
> as a whole was below that of British production.'[1]

This was certainly a meagre record by comparison with the United
States' vast potential; but it could be explained in one sentence—
America was not yet at war. During 1940 and 1941 motor-cars,
refrigerators, washing machines and civilian goods of every kind were
turned out in profusion; and it was this work, not the production of
munitions, which engaged the main strength of American industry.
So long as this was so, the gap between British and American war
production would remain. But to reverse the position, to give war
needs a decisive priority over civil consumption, required an act of
government which the Administration was unwilling to make, or the
public to accept, while the country was still nominally at peace.

In December 1940, in an attempt to bring the position home to the
American authorities, Mr. Purvis, the head of the British Supply
Council in Washington, had drawn up a balance-sheet showing
British requirements for the coming year, estimated British production and the deficit which would remain and could only be met from
American output. The requirement figures given in this paper were
never fully endorsed by departments at home. Still under the spell of
the old policy, they felt that Purvis was asking for too much, even for
impossibilities. Nevertheless, his balance-sheet provided a first sketch
of the position, which was sufficiently authoritative and sufficiently

---

[1] Postan, p. 233.

startling to serve the main purpose. When it was circulated in Washington early in the year, it convinced a number of prominent Americans, including the Secretary of War, Mr. Stimson, that a major revolution would indeed have to take place before their country could become the Arsenal of Democracy in fact as well as political oratory. Whether or not America was actually at war, she would have to adopt the same scale of values as a belligerent and be prepared to accept the privations, the shortages and the dislocation of ordinary life, which that would entail.[1]

In arguing thus Mr. Stimson and his colleagues were ahead of the majority of their countrymen and certainly of the administration as a whole. But they entered vigorously on their task of persuasion. During the next six months the case for increased American production was pressed from both sides of the Atlantic. The method, following Purvis's example, was that of statistical analysis; there were few fervent appeals but many columns of figures, which carried an equally compelling message. At the end of July, judging that the ground had been well prepared, the Prime Minister made a formal proposal to the President for a joint conference on Anglo-American production. Plans were now being matured, he wrote, for operations in 1942 and 1943 and two contingent problems were becoming increasingly urgent:

'(a) framing an agreed estimate as to our joint requirements of the primary weapons of war—e.g., aircraft, tanks, etc.
(b) thereafter considering how these requirements are to be met from our joint production.'

In August Mr. Stimson, acting independently, sent his representative, Mr. Stacey May, to London to explore the same problem. His instructions were to collect material for a joint estimate of Anglo-American production in the coming year together, if possible, with figures for ultimate requirements which could be used, in his own expression, to jolt the American production men. The first point was met without difficulty, much work having been done on this subject since Purvis's estimate of the previous December. The problem of ultimate requirements had also been tackled and certain preliminary figures were available, which Mr. Stacey May was given. But it was impressed on him that these must be regarded as wholly tentative and unofficial. Final figures would have to await the outcome of the proposed Conference. All that we could do beforehand was to give a rough estimate of the maximum quantity of equipment which the British Empire could man and use; but this would not be a true guide to the productive effort required from America, unless it were also

---

[1] Hancock and Gowing, pp. 383–6; Postan, pp. 237–8.

known what proportion of her output she intended to retain for her own use or that of other allies.[1]

This was as much as to say that we could not decide our future strategy—and therefore our requirements—until America had also decided hers. From our point of view that was true, since our sole hope of winning the war now lay in America's active co-operation. But unfortunately American policy had not yet reached a point of development where it could form the basis of a settled strategy. Everything was still vague and uncertain. At the beginning of July President Roosevelt had invited the Secretary of the Navy and the Secretary of War to co-operate 'in exploring at once the overall production requirements required to defeat our potential enemies'. This task was to include 'the making of appropriate assumptions as to our probable friends and enemies and to the conceivable theatres of operation which will be required'.[2] But the President must have known, as he wrote these words, that he was asking for the impossible. He was inviting the two Secretaries to evolve a strategy for the United States and to translate it into industrial terms while the policy of which that strategy was to be the instrument was still undecided. Would America enter the war voluntarily or wait until she was attacked? Was it necessary to assume that she would have to fight Germany and Japan simultaneously? When would her intervention take place and what would be the state of her allies at that time? Would Great Britain already have passed to the offensive or have suffered further set-backs? Would the Russian front still be in being?

These were the vital questions on which future planning depended; but they were all unanswered or unanswerable. It is not surprising, therefore, that some difficulty was found in complying with the President's request. The formal reply did not reach him until the end of September and then consisted not of a single paper but of a dossier containing separate and conflicting opinions from the Army and Navy and a memorandum from the Joint Board, which failed to reconcile them.[3] A full account of the various points of controversy would be outside the scope of this Volume. But something must be said about the strategic dilemma from which the controversy arose, for this bore directly both on the immediate problem of supply and on other problems of Allied co-operation which will be examined later.

A convenient starting point is provided by a paper written by the Joint Board at the same time as their memorandum to the President

---

[1] Postan, pp. 238–9.
[2] M. S. Watson, *Chief of Staff: Pre-War Plans and Preparations (U.S. Army in World War II)* 1950, p. 339.
[3] Watson, p. 351.

and embodying substantially the same argument. This was in the form of a commentary, later forwarded to London, on the review of future strategy circulated by the British Chiefs of Staff at the Atlantic Meeting. That document, as we have seen, outlined a plan for the defeat of Germany which depended, first on a combination of blockade with an ever increasing weight of air-attack, and secondly, on a general uprising of subjugated peoples supported by a small expeditionary force mainly of armoured troops. This was a policy of which the Joint Board were sharply critical. They noted first that:

> '. . . dependence cannot be placed on winning important wars by air action alone. It should be recognized as an almost invariable rule that wars cannot finally be won without the use of land armies.'

And they went on to make it clear that by land armies they meant armies comparable in size with the enemy's. The idea that a substitute might be found in small mobile forces backed by a widespread subversive movement was dismissed even more curtly:

> 'The Joint Board has no comment on these paragraphs, because they appear to lack definition sufficiently clear to form a basis for practical campaign plans.'

So far, the Army and the Navy, both subscribers to the Joint Board's report, were on common ground. Their divergence began in the subsequent working out of these principles. It was implicit in the Joint Board's argument that, sooner or later, America would have to intervene in Europe on a massive scale, for without the support of American manpower the Allies would be unable to launch their final, indispensable land-offensive. The Army, therefore, proposed to base its planning on the assumption that the whole able-bodied manpower of the United States would eventually be mobilized. This would yield, when the needs of the Navy and of industry had been deducted, an approximate total of 8·7 million men, organized according to the original plan in 215 divisions.[1] But at that time—the autumn of 1941—America had barely forty divisions under arms; and these, besides being woefully short of equipment, were manned as to almost 80 per cent either by members of the National Guard, who served under certain restrictions, or by reservists recalled for twelve months only. The effective, freely disposable field-force could not be reckoned at more than two or three divisions.[2]

---

[1] In the final stages of the war, the American Army came very close to this total of men, though its effective strength was only 89 divisions, the difference being accounted for by a large increase in the strength of the supply services and of the Air Corps, then an integral part of the Army.

[2] Watson, pp. 238, 343–5, 358.

11

To expand this minute force into over 200 trained and fully equipped divisions was a gigantic task, which could not be accomplished, even with American industry working at full pressure, in less than a minimum of two years. Moreover, if the army were to be employed in Europe, another limitation had to be considered:

> 'The availability of shipping will be the deciding factor in determining how large a force can be shipped and maintained overseas. In this connexion the following considerations would seem to govern:
>
> By 1st July, 1943, the date assumed . . . to be critical in equipping a force of 10,000,000 men,[1] our proposed shipbuilding programme will provide a total of about 6,000,000 gross tons of shipping, that may be assigned to an overseas effort. Such an amount of shipping would transport and maintain a force overseas of about 3,000,000 men.
>
> Assuming the present planned rate of increased ship construction . . . it would probably be another three years or 1946 before a force of 10,000,000 could be maintained overseas, unless the shipbuilding programme were further accelerated and ship sinkings greatly reduced.'[2]

These calculations suggested that America could not make an effective, still less a decisive, intervention in Europe until some date between 1943 and 1946. But by that time, according to the Army's forecast, Russia would probably have been defeated and Germany would have increased her effective strength to some 400 divisions, of which the greater part would be concentrated in the West. On this basis even 200 American, supporting 100 Allied, divisions would only provide a bare equality of force and would certainly fall short of the two-to-one superiority, which was normally reckoned as necessary for an attack.[3] By the same token a smaller contingent, representing anything less than America's maximum effort, would be useless. The problem, therefore, was to raise, equip and train as large an army as possible in the shortest possible time, which could not in any case be less than two years. It seemed to follow that, during the period of build-up, America should limit her military supplies to other nations to what was necessary to keep them in the fight. On no account should she declare war herself before she was ready or risk what the Joint Board described as 'a piecemeal and indecisive commitment of forces against a superior enemy under unfavourable logistic conditions'.[4]

---

[1] This was a round figure used in the early stages of planning; it can be read as 8.7 million without disturbing the argument.

[2] Watson, p. 346.

[3] Watson, pp. 354–5.

[4] Watson, pp. 406–8.

The Navy did not dissent from these propositions in principle but were appalled at the practical consequences of the Army's vast expansion programme. They feared that their own requirements would be swamped in the pell-mell creation of such an enormous land-force. They were also conscious, more so perhaps than the Army, of the acute danger in which Great Britain then stood in the Atlantic—an area, as the Chiefs of Staff's paper had pointed out, in which American naval support could be immediately effective. For these reasons they were led to urge a policy which was in practice almost directly contrary to the Army's: earlier American intervention, wider material aid to Allied countries and, as the corollary, a smaller eventual commitment by land.[1] Strictly speaking, this was not a logical position, for it implicitly denied the assumptions in the Joint Board paper, which the Navy accepted. But it gained force from another argument not expressly advanced by the Navy and certainly not peculiar to them. This was the argument, accepted by Mr. Stimson and others, that an early declaration of war was essential, since without it the rearmament programme would never attain the scale or vigour which was admitted to be necessary in any case. In the slack, peacetime tempo which then existed, two or three years might pass and America still be unready.[2]

All these were, however, strictly Service views and took little account of public opinion or the political manoeuvres with which President Roosevelt still felt bound to protect himself. His own views on the controversy were never precisely stated; but it appears from his actions that he was unwilling to accept either party's opinion unreservedly. As we have seen in earlier chapters, he was an enthusiastic advocate of the foreign-aid programme and in this certainly went beyond what the Army believed to be wise. He was even prepared in the autumn of 1941, against General Marshall's advice, to carry through an actual reduction in the standing strength of the Army in order to increase the immediate flow of supplies to the Allies.[3] On the other hand, nothing could have been further from the President's thoughts than an early declaration of war. He may sometimes have hoped that events would take the decision out of his hands, as indeed they finally did; but he made it amply clear both at the time of Hopkins's first visit to London and subsequently at the Atlantic Meeting that he had no intention of taking the final plunge himself.

It seems that he still believed, or still hoped, despite the warnings of the Joint Board and the British Chiefs of Staff, that American intervention might be avoided, if only the Allies were given enough moral,

---

[1] Watson, pp. 349–50, 357.
[2] Stimson and Bundy, pp. 366, 380–1.
[3] Watson, pp. 362–6.

material and financial support in good time. The strategic foundations of this belief were slender; but it was an accurate emotional reflection of American public opinion at the time. Although, as the public opinion polls quoted in the last chapter show, an overwhelming majority of American citizens believed that their country would eventually be involved in the war, on the same evidence there was an equally decisive weight of opinion against any step which might precipitate this result.[1] The country was apparently willing to leave its fate to chance and the actions of others. Perhaps these surveys of opinion did less than justice to the true state of feeling by ignoring latent sentiment which a truly vigorous leadership might have evoked. But this view, though held by many statesmen and commentators at the time, was evidently not shared by the President; and no one, least of all a foreign historian, can lightly question his judgement.

(ii)
Preliminary Discussions

Such was the status of Anglo-American relations when the joint proposal for a Supply Conference, which President Roosevelt and Mr. Churchill had made at the Atlantic meeting, was received in Moscow. Although the idea was warmly welcomed by the Russians, it was some time before a convenient date could be fixed. There was strong pressure from the Russian side for as early a meeting as possible; but the Americans, acting on Hopkins's advice, wished to wait at least until the middle of October, by which time, it was hoped, the position on the Eastern Front would have stabilised. While these discussions were still proceeding, Mr. Churchill, anxious not to lose the impetus of events, sent a further, personal telegram to M. Stalin:

'I have been searching for any way to give you help in your splendid resistance pending the long term arrangements which we are discussing with the United States and which will form the subject of the Moscow Conference. Maisky has represented that fighter aircraft are much needed in view of heavy losses. We are expediting the 200 Tomahawks about which I telegraphed in my last. Our two squadrons should reach Murmansk about the 6th of September, comprising 40 aircraft. You will, I am sure, realize that fighter aircraft are the foundation of our home defence, besides which we are trying to obtain air superiority in Libya, and

---

[1] *Public Opinion Quarterly*, cited by Langer and Gleason, p. 442.

also to provide for Turkey, so as to bring her in on our side. Nevertheless, I could send 200 more Hurricanes, making 440 in all, if your pilots could use them effectively.'

The reply, received on 3rd September, was sharp and gloomy. After thanking the Prime Minister for his offer,[1] M. Stalin added that such a small number of aircraft, brought piecemeal into action along the enormous front, could scarcely affect the position one way or the other. The temporary lull in the fighting, which had been noted in August, was now over. The Germans, reinforced by 30–40 fresh divisions from the West, had resumed the offensive all along the front. In the south they had overrun the greater part of the Ukraine; in the north they were already at the gates of Leningrad:

'These circumstances have resulted in our losing Krivoi Rog iron ore basin and a number of metallurgical works in the Ukraine; we have evacuated one aluminium works on Dnieper river and a further aluminium works at Tikhvin, one motor and two aircraft works in the Ukraine, two motor and two aircraft works at Leningrad; and these works cannot be put into operation in the new localities in less than from seven to eight months.

This has weakened our power of defence and faced the Soviet Union with a mortal menace. The question arises how to emerge from this more than unfavourable situation.

I think there is only one means of egress from this situation— to establish in the present year a second front somewhere in the Balkans or France, capable of drawing away from the Eastern Front 30 to 40 divisions, and at the same time of ensuring to the Soviet Union 30,000 tons of aluminium by the beginning of October next and a monthly minimum of aid amounting to 400 aircraft and 500 tanks (of small or medium size).

Without these two forms of help the Soviet Union will either suffer defeat or be weakened to such an extent that it will lose for a long period any capacity to render assistance to its Allies by its actual operations on the fronts of the struggle against Hitlerism.'

Mr. Churchill's first impulse was to reply to this ominous telegram in kind. He drafted an answer stating in plain terms that military operations on the scale proposed were out of the question; as to supplies, we should do our best, but there was little likelihood that anything substantial could reach Russia in time to influence current operations. The only resource was to look forward to 1942, when the flow of supplies would have increased and it might also be possible to initiate joint operations either in the Far North or the Caucasus.

When this draft was discussed in Cabinet on 5th September it was

---

[1] Stalin referred to 'your promise . . . to sell to the Soviet Union'; in fact, by an agreement of 27th June, 1941, military equipments were supplied to Russia on terms roughly equivalent to those of Lend-Lease.

generally felt to be too bleak and depressing. Russia's position was evidently so desperate and the value of her continued resistance so enormous, that some encouragement must be given, if that could be done without raising false hopes. Lord Beaverbrook, the champion of this point of view, proposed the immediate gesture of offering Stalin one half of his stated requirements of tanks and aircraft. To honour such a promise would be a heavy sacrifice; but he believed it to be possible and was convinced in the circumstances that it was necessary. After further discussion and consultation with the Chiefs of Staff this proposal was accepted and the following passage incorporated in the Prime Minister's reply:

> 'About supplies. We are well aware of the grievous losses which Russian industry has sustained, and every effort has been and will be made by us to help you. I am cabling President Roosevelt to expedite the arrival here of Mr. Harriman's mission and we shall try even before the Moscow Conference to tell you the numbers of aircraft and tanks we can jointly promise to send each month, together with supplies of aluminium, cloth etc. For our part we are now prepared to send you, from British production, one half of the monthly total for which you ask in aircraft and tanks. We hope the United States will supply the other half of your requirements. We shall use every endeavour to start the flow of equipment to you immediately.'

A later telegram added the promise that five thousand tons of aluminium would be despatched from Canada as soon as possible, followed by two thousand tons a month thereafter.

A week after these exchanges the Prime Minister received a letter from Mr. Hopkins, which outlined the final American proposals for the Moscow Conference. It was now suggested that Mr. Harriman and the American team, which he was to lead, should arrive in London about 15th September and confer with their British colleagues for four or five days before both parties left together for Moscow, where the main Conference would open at the end of the month. The preliminary meeting in London was to serve a double purpose. First, the American delegates would put forward a statement showing the total quantity of military equipment, including that already earmarked for Britain, which would be available for export during the coming year, and would seek agreement as to the proportion to be allotted to Russia. Secondly, they would invite the British Government to make a comprehensive statement of its ultimate needs, a 'complete estimate of what British requirements for material and [equipment] from this country will be in order to accomplish a victory over the Axis powers'. President Roosevelt had already instructed his Chiefs of Staff to prepare a similar statement of America's needs; and these two statements, together with what was learnt in Moscow of Russia's needs, would form the basis of future production plans.

The second part of this letter was in fact a belated answer to the Prime Minister's earlier proposal for an Anglo-American conference on supply. As such it fell short of what he and his advisers had hoped. It appeared from this letter that there was not to be a formal conference—no doubt because of the uncertainties which still beset American strategy—but only a presentation of needs by Britain and Russia, which would later provide material for purely American planning. But even this, different though it was from the intimate collaboration which the Prime Minister had suggested, was better than nothing. It offered at least some hope that American production would be raised in future to the level of actuality.

The proposal in the first part of the letter was also welcome. Since Russia's entry into the war, and especially since she had established her own Supply Mission in Washington, there had been a recurrent danger that her demands for American material would dislocate deliveries on which we were relying. Much of the trouble lay in the American machinery, or rather lack of machinery, for the allocation of supplies. There was no ultimate authority except the President and he was besieged by conflicting requests from every quarter, not least from his own Service departments. Some degree of confusion had already resulted. On his return from America after the Atlantic Meeting, Lord Beaverbrook had drawn the Cabinet's attention to a number of cases in which supplies, ordered by us before Lend-Lease, had since been diverted to other recipients. He thought, and the Ambassador agreed, that this was likely to be a growing problem in the future.

Unfortunately, the only step so far taken to co-ordinate British and Russian demands was open to strong objections. At the end of July, on the proposal of Sir Stafford Cripps, a three-man committee had been set up in Washington, consisting of Mr. Hopkins as the President's representative, the Russian Ambassador and Mr. Purvis of the British Supply Council. Lord Halifax, reporting this arrangement to the Cabinet, had commented:

'I think the setting up of the Committee was inevitable, and indeed desirable, if only to prevent decisions being taken here by the United States Government entirely over our heads. But decisions to be taken on the allocation of United States production involve on our side major strategical and political issues, which can only be properly reviewed in London.'

The Cabinet took the same view. They were not prepared to delegate such complex and important decisions to the judgement of a single man acting at a distance; and in face of their opposition the Committee's work had lapsed. Now Mr. Hopkins's letter offered an opportunity to reopen the question and arrive, perhaps, at a more satisfactory solution.

There was, however, one point on which the American proposals gave rise to a certain nervousness. President Roosevelt had already decided that the Moscow Conference should confine itself to the immediate future, that is to the question of supplies to Russia up to July 1942 only. But the preliminary talks in London were also to cover the wider problem of the supplies needed for ultimate victory. There was an obvious danger in thus bringing together the short and the long-term, the general and the particular. Russian demands were certain to be large and insistent; and the Americans might well be tempted to meet them at our expense, or rather to barter the future against the present by holding out promises of increased production in subsequent years, if we would agree to Russia's receiving the lion's share over the next twelve months.

These doubts found expression at a meeting of representatives from the Service and Supply Ministries on 13th September, at which Lord Beaverbrook outlined his plan of campaign for the forthcoming talks. He said that he would concentrate first on pressing the Americans to fulfil the allocations which they had already promised. He would not approach the question of what should be offered to Russia until that point had been settled. On the question of aircraft he proposed to stand firmly on the Slessor Agreement, which would give us all that we could reasonably hope for over the next nine months. He would deal similarly with Army and Navy requirements, concerning himself in each case to secure delivery of the substance rather than to chase the shadow of larger future requirements. Finally, when agreement had been reached on the short-term position, he would associate himself with the paper, which he understood was being prepared, on our long-term or victory requirements.

In laying down this uncompromising procedure Lord Beaverbrook was reflecting the views of the Chiefs of Staff as well as his own. They had circulated an aide-mémoire to the meeting, which emphasized the same points that he made implicitly. First, it was essential to make it clear to the Americans that anything which they intended to offer the Russians, should not come out of supplies already promised to us. Secondly, shortage of shipping and other difficulties of transport would in any case limit the amount which could be delivered to Russia by the following July. It might be thought expedient for this reason to make large promises, knowing that their fulfilment would be limited in practice; but care should be taken not to promise undue quantities of small or mobile equipment, such as certain types of ammunition which were already scarce, or heavy bombers which the Russians might expect to be flown direct.

(iii)

The London Conference

These fears were not unjustified; but the actual point of contention, when the London talks opened on 15th September, proved to be slightly different from what had been anticipated. It was not that the Americans wished to make particularly lavish promises to Russia; on the contrary, our proposal for a joint promise of 400 aircraft and 500 tanks a month went rather beyond their intentions. But there was another and more important distinction dividing their attitude from ours. We assumed that a close partnership already existed between our two countries and were steadily pressing for still more intimate collaboration, especially in the field of supply. We were now brusquely reminded that the Americans did not yet regard themselves as our allies. They took the view that their country occupied a more isolated and more important position, that of a general dispenser of supplies to a number of recipients, including the United Kingdom, Russia, China and certain South American states. They were unwilling to admit that any of these had a prior, still less an exclusive, claim on their bounty.

This attitude was made clear at the first meeting, when Lord Beaverbrook's proposed procedure was firmly and even roughly rejected by Mr. Harriman. He would allow no separate discussion of the allocations already promised to Britain nor even of those which were offered now. The American delegation, he said, would state the total quantity of supplies which was available for export over the next nine months; and the sole question before the meeting was what proportion of this total should be allocated to Russia. This should be discussed as an isolated issue in purely strategic terms and without reference to other considerations. He proposed that Sub-Committees should be formed at once to consider the American proposals for naval, military and air force supplies and to discuss such related matters as transport.

The only course was to accept this revised procedure; but the American figures, as disclosed to the Sub-Committees, came as a profound shock. The two critical items were aircraft and tanks. As to the latter, we had previously been led to expect that American production over the next nine months would yield between 5,000 and 5,500 medium tanks, the type most needed, of which we should receive 1,485 from our own contracts and a further 1,233 from Defence Aid and United States Army contracts or 2,718 in all. It now appeared that total production would be less than 4,000, of which we should receive the 1,485 from British contracts and only 611 from

Defence Aid, a net loss of 622. Russia would receive 795, all from Defence Aid. In addition, 2,529 light tanks would be available for export, of which we should get 1,800 and the Russians 729. This meant, however, that the total Russian share of American tanks over the whole period would be only 1,524. In order to bring this up to the level of 250 a month, at which it would match the offer that we were making, Lord Beaverbrook felt obliged to suggest that a further 726 light tanks should be allotted to Russia from the British share.

The final effect of these allocations, taking our own promises to Russia into account, was to leave us 1,613 tanks short of our minimum requirements, even if no allowance were made for wastage except in the Middle East. This meant that we should have to delay at least until the late autumn the formation of one armoured division and one Army Tank Brigade in the United Kingdom and two armoured divisions, one Australian and one Indian, in the Middle East. But there was no way of making good the deficit except by substantially increasing American production or cutting into the 926 medium tanks which the United States Army proposed to retain for their own use.

The aircraft position was still more serious. Under the terms of the Slessor agreement we had expected to receive between 9,000 and 9,500 aircraft from the United States over the next nine months, of which rather more than 6,000 would be from British contracts, 3,000 from Defence Aid and the remainder from a share of United States Army production. Under the new allocations we should receive a total of only 8,234 aircraft, of which less than 2,000 would be from Defence Aid. The position was particularly grave in respect of the much needed heavy bombers. It appeared that American production over the period would be approximately 700; and even under the terms of the proposals tentatively discussed at the Atlantic Meeting we had expected to receive at least 350 of these. We were now offered less than 200, of which all but forty-nine were due under British contracts. Similarly, of the 1,720 medium bombers which would be produced in the United States over the period, we should receive only 831, of which all but seventy-six were due under British contracts. There was also a heavy reduction in our expectation of fighters and light bombers.

All in all we should receive approximately 1,800 aircraft less than we had counted on. Expressed in squadrons, the loss could be tabulated as follows:

600 Heavy and medium bombers	= 20 squadrons
600 Light bombers	= 15 squadrons
600 Fighters	= 15 squadrons[1]

---

[1] The loss would have been smaller in this case, if our own promise of 1,800 aircraft to Russia had not largely extinguished our reserves.

There would thus be a heavy reduction in the strength of Bomber Command during precisely the period when it was agreed on all sides that the bombing of Germany was likely to be most important. Fighter Command would also fall short of expectation by some ten squadrons; and in addition we should be unable to find the fighter reinforcements which had been planned for the Middle and Far East. It was a situation which the Chiefs of Staff could only regard with dismay.

It was true that nearly 1,200 of the 1,800 aircraft lost to us would go to Russia, whose need was certainly no less. But, however fully this was admitted, there remained two grounds on which the American proposal could be criticized. In the first place, the allocations had been planned not in relation to any known or stated strategic need but on a flat percentage basis. We were to receive the produce of our own contracts, 50 per cent of Defence Aid and 7·5 per cent of United States Army contracts; Russia 30 per cent of Defence Aid and 4·5 per cent of United States Army contracts; and China and others 20 per cent of Defence Aid and 3 per cent of United States Army contract. This method of calculation produced some striking anomalies. Russia, for example, received thirty heavy bombers and China ten, though neither of these small parcels was likely to be of the slightest military value. With the exception of the Rumanian oilfields there was no strategic target in Germany, which was still within range of the Russian air attack; nor could China do anything with her bombers unless, as a member of the American delegation suggested, they might come in useful later for long-range attacks on Japan. On the other hand, it was agreed by the American no less than the British Chiefs of Staff that intensive air-attack on Germany from the United Kingdom was an indispensable prelude to victory.

The second criticism was of the quantity of aircraft which the United States were withholding for their own use. Once more heavy bombers provided the most striking example, for there the United States proposed to retain 500 out of 700, a decision difficult to justify on any strategic ground. And the same was true, though in a lesser degree, over the whole field. In fact, we had reached almost exactly the position which Lord Beaverbrook and the Chiefs of Staff had feared: American allocations to Russia were being carved out of allocations already promised to Britain, so that the sacrifice fell almost entirely on us and not on the American armed forces. At the same time it had to be admitted that, whatever promises might have been made before Russia entered the war, the aircraft in question were still the property of the United States and at their free disposal; it was for them to decide to whom they should go. This was the view advanced, a little bluntly perhaps, by the American delegation; and it was one, however unwelcome, which we were finally obliged to accept.

The concluding work of the conference was to give some consideration to ultimate or victory requirements; but here, for the reasons already suggested, little real progress was possible. A Planning Sub-Committee examined the strategic background of these requirements and reported that they found British and American views to be much the same. But this agreement was more in the realm of appearance than fact; and it is doubtful whether it extended much beyond the harmless generalities of ABC I, paragraph 11,[1] to which the Sub-Committee referred. The sharp comments of the American Chiefs of Staff on certain aspects of British strategy, which were quoted above, had not yet reached London; nor was the full statement of the American Army's requirements, which might have revealed these differences, available to the meeting. There was consequently little argument; and the Sub-Committee's report consisted only of a statement of Britain's theoretical needs, prefaced by a short introduction, which did little more than reiterate the views already expressed by the Chiefs of Staff at the Atlantic Meeting.

The British estimates, set out in three appendices, need not be examined in detail. They were an amplification of the unofficial figures already handed to Mr. Stacey May and did not differ materially from the various estimates of future strength and requirements, which have been discussed in earlier chapters. Their main significance was the emphasis which they laid on the need for American help even within the framework of existing strategy. The naval estimates showed, for example, that over the next eighteen months we should require twelve auxiliary aircraft carriers, ten destroyers, twenty submarines, 150 escort vessels and a very large number of smaller craft in excess of our own capacity to build. These could only come from the United States. From the same source we should also require some five million gross tons of merchant shipping, over and above the tonnage for which orders had already been placed in American yards.

The Army estimates were based on the creation of a Field Force of approximately 100 divisions, backed by suitable reserves; but a warning was added that 'the forces which the British can man from their own resources will not suffice to cover the total estimated'. Nor should we be able to supply full equipment even for that proportion of the force which we could man. There would be a deficiency of 12,000 tanks, 5,700 A.A. and 7,000 A.T. guns, 1,043 medium and heavy field-guns and over one million rifles, and of ammunition and other supplies in proportion.

---

[1] This stated that the 'paramount territorial interests' of the United States were in the Western Hemisphere and of the United Kingdom in the British Isles, the Dominions, India and British possessions in the Far East. Both countries also agreed on the importance of keeping sea communications open.

The Air Force estimates were on a slightly different basis, since here it was possible to include some indication of America's requirements, or rather of what America's requirements would be, if she entered the war. These included two substantial forces of heavy bombers to be stationed within the British area: 1,844 based on the United Kingdom and 880 based on the Middle East. But it is significant of the general atmosphere of strategic uncertainty, in which these conversations took place, that this intention was not held to justify any reduction in British requirements of heavy bombers, which were still calculated in terms of Target Force E. On this basis our total needs over the next eighteen months, making allowance for wastage but not for building up a reserve or for non-operational aircraft, were given as 13,770 heavy bombers, 12,440 medium and light bombers, 20,610 fighters and 2,565 other types or 49,385 aircraft in all. Over the same period our own production was expected to yield 35,832 aircraft, leaving a deficit of 13,353 mainly in heavy and medium bombers, for which we should have to draw on the United States.

(iv)

The Moscow Conference

Lord Beaverbrook's report on these discussions was considered by the Defence Committee in the presence of the Chiefs of Staff on 19th September. It was agreed that we had no option but to accept the American proposals as they stood, despite the adverse and even dangerous effect that they would have on our own programmes. We were already being pressed by the Russians to open military operations in their support; but the size of our forces and the shortage of manpower made it impossible to do so on the scale proposed. The alternative was to supply the Russians, who had no lack of men, with the arms and equipment which they needed. Evidently this could only be done by retarding the growth of British and Commonwealth forces; but that was a sacrifice which we should have to accept. The final remedy, both for ourselves and the Russians, was a great increase in American production. No doubt this would come, though it was still hampered by the delays and disappointments to be expected in a country which was not yet at war. In the meantime we must accommodate ourselves as best we could to the existing programme.

Two days later, on the eve of the Missions' departure for Moscow, the Prime Minister issued the following directive to the British delegation:

'The position reached as the result of the Beaverbrook—Harriman conversations is set out in Lord Beaverbrook's report of today's date. We must consider ourselves pledged to fulfil our share of the tanks and aircraft which had been promised to Russia, and Lord Beaverbrook must have a considerable measure of discretion as to what quantities of other equipment and of material should be offered at the conversations in Moscow.

Assurance must be given to Russia of increased quotas from the 1st July, 1942 to the 30th June, 1943. During this period British war production will be at its height and American ditto in its third year of development. It would be wiser not to be committed to precise figures based on optimistic forecasts of Anglo-American production. There are dangers also in promising the Russians a percentage of British and American output which they may immediately ask should be increased. We should not disclose speculative figures of our joint production when none are given of theirs by the Russians. They should, however, be invited to set forth their remaining resources in accordance with the various rearward lines they may hope to hold. Lord Beaverbrook should be free to encourage the prolonged resistance of Russia by taking a justifiably hopeful view of these more distant prospects.

Russian attention should be directed to the limitations of shipping, and still more of transportation from the various ports of access. The rapid destruction of world shipping, the effort required to make it good, and the vital needs of this country, now cut to the bone, should be stressed.

Encouragement should be offered, with American approval, to the keeping open of the Vladivostok route and overawing Japan for that purpose. Special emphasis should be laid upon the development on the largest possible scale and with the utmost energy of the route from the Persian Gulf to the Caspian, both by rail and road. The practical limitations which time enforces both upon working up the traffic on the Trans-Persian Railway and upon the motor road construction should be explained. The conflict between the movement of supplies and of troops and their maintenance at any given period along this route must be pointed out. The Russians will no doubt give their own estimate of the capacity and facilities of Archangel and of its railway connection with Central Russia, having regard both to winter ice and probable enemy action.

The Conference must proceed upon the basis that the United States is not a belligerent . . .'

The remaining paragraphs of the directive contained an analysis of British manpower, resources and commitments, designed to show that 'all ideas of 20 or 30 divisions being launched by Great Britain against the western shores of the Continent . . . have no foundation in reality on which to rest.' When we had provided for the garrison of the United Kingdom, the army in the Middle East and some addition to our defensive forces elsewhere, we should be able to find an expeditionary force for other operations of only six or seven divisions at the outside, including two armoured divisions. Nevertheless, we had every intention of intervening by land in the spring of 1942, if that were possible. Three projects were being considered:

(1) An operation in Northern Norway which, if it succeeded, might also bring Sweden into the Allied camp;

(2) An operation in French North Africa in the event of a further German encroachment, which the French were prepared to resist;

(3) Further operations in the Middle East after the Western flank had been cleared, which might take the form either of direct support of the Russians in the Caucasus or east of the Caspian, or of the encouragement and support of Turkey, if she could be induced to enter the war.[1]

The third of these courses would involve a difficult choice, on which Russian views were invited. If British troops were to operate in the Caucasus or on the Caspian, they would have to be supplied across Persia; and this would diminish or even halt the normal flow of supplies along one of the three main routes into Russia. Similarly, if Turkey were to be persuaded to join the Allies, it would be necessary to offer her modern arms and equipment, which would have to be subtracted from the totals promised or about to be promised to Russia.

All this was set out in detail in the directive because it was assumed, in view of M. Stalin's recent telegrams, that the Conference would touch on questions of strategy as well as supply. For the same reason General Ismay, Mr. Churchill's Chief of Staff, had been named a member of the British delegation with authority to discuss any plans which the Russians might put forward. It was hoped that a full explanation of our own plans and capabilities would destroy the ill-considerered proposals for major operations 'somewhere in Europe or the Balkans' which the Russians were still pressing on us. But in the event the extreme brevity of the Conference ruled out any possibility of military discussion. This was the more unfortunate, since General Ismay's one conversation with Stalin showed how little the latter had grasped the realities of the British position. Their talk, which lasted ten minutes, occurred during an entertainment at the Kremlin. M. Stalin began by saying that Great Britain ought to maintain a large army as well as her navy. When it was explained that limitations of manpower made this impossible, he brushed the argument aside, saying that the whole situation had now changed. England could never again rely on France and must therefore have

---

[1] For a further discussion of these projects see Chapter VIII below.

conscription and a large army even in peacetime. If Japan could
man both an army and a navy, why could England not do the
same?

This brief conversation was typical of the whole Conference, which
stood in marked contrast to the earlier talks in London. The proceedings were curt and businesslike; but there was little real contact
and certainly no intimacy between the participants. For the same
reason there was less argument. The Russians volunteered no information and initiated no discussion; and the whole business of the
Conference was concluded within two working days. But instead of
the full picture of Russian production and future requirements which
it had been hoped to obtain, the British and American delegations
had to be content with Stalin's bare statement that Germany now
had 320 divisions in the field to Russia's 280 with a fifty per cent
superiority in the air; and that Russian tank production, which had
been 2,000 a month at the outbreak of war, had now declined to
1,400 a month. No information on other aspects of the Russian
position was obtained nor anything from any source but Stalin himself. It was noticed, however, that the Russians showed little interest
in the conventional weapons of war, such as field artillery and
machine-guns. Their demands were almost exclusively for raw
materials or for the modern weapons which had come into their own
since 1939—aircraft, tanks, A.A. and A.T. guns. From this it could be
inferred both that the Russians were limiting their demands to what
they really needed, and that the Red Army, though in some respects
out of date, was essentially well equipped.

The consolidated list of requirements, which the Russians presented, followed much the lines already indicated separately to Great
Britain and the United States, except that the demand for tanks had
now more than doubled. In general it was only possible to satisfy a
proportion of the requests for finished equipment, though most of the
raw materials could be supplied in full. After a minimum of discussion, agreement was reached on the following main items:

Equipment	Monthly Requirements	Decision
Aircraft		
Light Bombers	300	100 a month from U.S.
Fighters	100	200 ,, ,, ,, U.K.
		100 ,, ,, ,, U.S.
Tanks		
Medium and Light	1,100	500 a month from U.S. and U.K.
Bren-gun carriers	—	250 a month from U.K.
Scout Cars	2,000	5,000 from U.S. over nine months

Equipment	*Monthly Requirements*	*Decision*
Lorries		
3, 2 and 1½ ton	10,000	To be investigated in U.S.
A.A. Guns		
37 mm. and over	300	152, 90 mm. from U.S. over nine months
A.T. Guns		
37 mm. and over	300	756, 37 mm. from U.S. over nine months
		500, 40 mm. from U.K. over nine months
Raw Materials		
Tin	1,500 tons	from U.K.
Lead	7,000 ,,	,, ,,
Cobalt	10 ,,	,, ,,
Copper	3,000 ,,	,, ,,
Zinc	1,500 ,,	,, ,,
Aluminium	4,000 ,,	half from Canada; possible further supplies from U.S.
Armour Plate	10,000 ,,	1,000 tons from U.S.
Molybdenum	300 ,,	from U.S.
Rolled Brass	5,000 ,,	part from U.S.
Nickel Chrome Wire	70 ,,	from U.S.
Barbed Wire	4,000 ,,	,, ,,
Toluol	4,000 ,,	1,250 tons from U.S.
Phosphorus	100 ,,	from U.S.
Graphitized Electrodes	400 ,,	from U.S.
Diamonds	£150,000 ,,	from U.K.
Rubber	6,000 ,,	,, ,,
Jute	4,000 ,,	,, ,,
Wool	2,000 ,,	,, ,,
Wheat	200,000 ,,	available in Canada
Sugar	70,000 ,,	available in Philippines and N.E.I.
Cocoa Beans	1,500 ,,	from U.K.

In addition to this, two considerable lists of naval and medical requirements and a number of demands for other raw materials, ranging from shoe leather and cloth to high-grade steel, were reserved for further consideration in London or Washington. Extensive Russian demands for machine-tools and factory equipment were also held in suspense, pending the production of more exact specifications. It was clear that Russian requirements in this respect were related to her plans, much accelerated by the German advance, for transferring war industry to the east. This made it very desirable that they should be satisfied; but the extreme secrecy of the Russian negotiators

12

stood in the way. Machine-tools and the type of equipment for which they were asking, were equally short both in Britain and the United States; and, if the limited supply were to be used to the best advantage, it was essential to have a full exchange of information about the potential value of particular items to each of the three claimants. But the Russians were not prepared for such close collaboration; what they wanted was an agreement to supply a fixed quota of machine-tools irrespective of any conflicting claims. This was impossible to grant; but for the moment, while exact specifications were awaited, the point was not pressed unduly.

The quantities, both of equipment and materials, which were finally promised to the Russians, corresponded closely to the proposals previously discussed in London. The most significant changes were the addition of 250 Bren-gun carriers a month to the total of light tanks and an important alteration in the aircraft figures. It will be seen from the table above that the Russians agreed to accept their quota of aircraft in the proportion of 300 fighters to 100 bombers, instead of the reversed proportions for which they had originally asked. This was advantageous to us, since it had the effect of cancelling the proposed American allocation of heavy and light bombers, which had been such a bone of contention during the London talks. The Russian agreement did not, of course, imply a definite promise on the American side to allocate the bombers to us instead; but it gave some hope that the grave situation revealed in London might yet be partly retrieved.

The final question discussed was that of transport. The Russian delegates informed the Conference that they would require an average total import of 500,000 tons a month, made up as to three-fifths of food-stuffs, which they were buying in the open market in North America or the East Indies. To maintain imports at this rate would require, according to the British calculation, about 1·5 million tons of shipping, of which the Russians could only supply a small proportion. For the rest they would be obliged to look to Great Britain and the United States, although the formal agreement only provided for aid in transport and did not include any guarantee of delivery on our side.

Three possible routes were open: by Vladivostok and the trans-Siberian railway; by Archangel or Murmansk; and across Persia. The first could handle some 220,000 tons a month by the Russian estimate or rather less than half that by ours; but the Russians were anxious to confine its use to supplies, mainly of food, for their Far Eastern provinces. For equipment and war-like stores they looked almost entirely to the northern ports and especially to Archangel, since the only route inland from Murmansk was along the Murmansk-Leningrad railway, which was exposed to enemy attack almost throughout its length. They estimated, in our view optimistically, that Archangel could handle an average of 270,000 tons a month and could be kept open by ice-breakers throughout the winter. They were confident of being able to clear the whole of this load inland by rail and river. The remaining route through Persia attracted them less. Indeed, they seemed to view our plans for raising its capacity with surprise and even alarm, apparently because they wished, even at this crisis in their fortunes, to keep foreign influence as far away from the Caspian as possible. For this reason they insisted, though it was plainly uneconomic to do so, that all traffic north of Kasvin should remain in their hands. Subject to this, they saw no difficulty in clearing the 60,000 tons a month, which we hoped eventually to pass over this route.

To the closing session on 1st October, M. Molotov contributed a cordial, valedictory speech. He expressed his Government's great satisfaction at the speedy and outstanding success of the Conference and their conviction that the great partnership, which had now been formed, would be successful in bringing victory and the downfall of the common enemy. There was, perhaps, a gleam here of more than formal sentiment. Although the Conference had not dissipated the atmosphere of frigid secrecy, so familiar to foreign negotiators in Moscow, the fact that it had taken place at all, and the practical results which it had achieved, had perhaps lessened Russia's suspicions of the West.

CHAPTER VII

THE MIDDLE EAST

(i)

Reorganization

AT THE BEGINNING of July General Auchinleck took over command in the Middle East from General Wavell, who in turn replaced him as Commander-in-Chief in India. This exchange was a natural, and perhaps inevitable, consequence of the events of the spring and early summer. The succession of disasters in the Western Desert, Greece and Crete had dimmed the lustre of Wavell's earlier victories; and subsequent events—his reluctance to move at the time of the Iraqi revolt, his apparent hesitations over Syria and the relative failure of 'Battleaxe', his last desert offensive—had created the impression in London that his vigour was temporarily exhausted. 'It might well be said,' wrote Mr. Churchill afterwards, 'that we had ridden a willing horse to a standstill.'[1] That may have been true; but there were also other reasons which made this an appropriate moment to appoint a new commander.

It was already apparent that the whole character of the war in the Middle East was changing. The initial phase, in which Italy had been the main enemy and the consolidation of the theatre our first objective, was almost over. Some operations remained to be completed in Abyssinia; the Syrian campaign had still a few weeks to run; and the possibility of action in Persia was already on the horizon. But these were residual problems, which did not affect the substance of what had been accomplished over the past twelve months. During that period, starting from an insecure position in Egypt and Palestine, we had gradually extended and confirmed our control over the whole area from Kenya to the Turkish frontier, from the Western Desert to the Persian Gulf. This feat of arms, carried out with small and improvised forces, had been Wavell's achievement. The new task, radically different in kind, was to defend the enormous theatre which he had created against the coming German onslaught.

In parallel with these strategic developments important changes were taking place in the organization and internal structure of the Command. Since the beginning of the year a continuous stream of reinforcements had reached the theatre. The Army's share had included two complete divisions (the 50th and the 2nd Armoured),

---

[1] Churchill, Vol. III, p. 308.

parts of four others (the New Zealand division, the 7th and 9th Australian and the 2nd South African) and many artillery, technical and administrative units. This had made a total of more than 200,000 men, a figure approximately equal to two-thirds of the whole ration strength of the Army in January. During the same period the Air Force had received an equivalent reinforcement of 13,000 men, mostly ground-staff, and more than 1,300 aircraft, the latter including 724 fighters (Hurricanes and Tomahawks), 421 light bombers (Blenheims and Marylands) and 104 heavy bombers (Wellingtons). These were enormous figures by comparison with the round total of 250 aircraft with which the Middle East had entered the war against Italy.[1] In the air, no less than on the ground, the increased scale of our forces amounted almost to a revolution.

It must not be supposed, however, that there was an immediate increase in the fighting-strength of the Command to the extent which these figures may suggest. Even under the most favourable conditions so large a reinforcement would have been difficult to absorb; and there were many factors, peculiar to the Middle East, which tended to prolong and complicate the process. In the first place, the period of reinforcement had also been a period of continuous and widely-dispersed fighting during which all arms had suffered heavily. The Army, for example, had lost nearly 30,000 men in Greece and Crete alone, together with the entire equipment, apart from personal arms, of the equivalent of at least four divisions. Not all these material losses had since been made good, despite a greatly increased flow of supplies. In July there was still an acute shortage of vehicles, of which over 8,000 had been lost in Greece; and the American replacements, on which the Command was largely relying, were only just beginning to come forward in the promised number. The bewildering succession of overlapping operations in Abyssinia, the Western Desert, Greece, Iraq, Crete and Syria had also played havoc with the order of battle. No smooth deployment had been possible; troops had had to be used as they came to hand, with the result that units had been separated from their parent formations and the normal chain of command confused or broken. By July, when General Auchinleck took over, an extensive programme of regrouping was already in train; but it was clear that some time must pass before the Command could regain its full coherence and efficiency.[2]

These were, however, only minor and passing troubles on the surface of a deeper problem. From the point of view of supply and administration, the Middle East was, and would always remain, an

---

[1] I. S. O. Playfair, *The Mediterranean and the Middle East* (1954), Vol. II, Chap. 11, and App. 7.

[2] Dispatches by Gen. Sir A. Wavell and Gen. Sir C. Auchinleck, *Middle East,* 7th February, 1941 to 15th July, 1941, and *Middle East,* 5th July, 1941 to 31st October, 1941.

exceptionally awkward theatre. It covered an immense area of un-developed territory, in which communications were poor or non-existent, industrial resources meagre and the local labour force inadequate. Almost everything that the three Services required had to be brought into the theatre from outside. The nearest source of supply of any importance was India, 3,000 miles away; but the great bulk of stores and equipment of all kinds had to come either from England, a distance of 12,000 miles by the long sea-route round the Cape, or from the United States. Distances within the theatre were also great and were made more formidable by bad communications and the fact that the main base in Egypt had to supply three distinct operational areas: Cyrenaica in the west, Palestine and Syria in the north-east, the Sudan and Abyssinia in the south. It is 230 miles by sea (the shortest route) from Port Said to Beirut, 450 to Tobruk and over 700 to Port Sudan. A unit, transferred from one operational area to another, might easily have 1,000 to 1,500 miles to travel and in some cases much more.

The anomalous position of Egypt added a further complication. Although in appearance an occupied country, she preserved in fact the status of an independent state with rights which she was able to assert. Her Government, for example, retained control of the posts and telegraphs, the railway system and the greater part of the port facilities; and certain restrictions were also placed on the use of Egyptian labour for military purposes. It is true that Egyptian de-partments were generally co-operative; but their interests did not always coincide with ours; nor was the loyalty of their Government to the Allied cause ever more than doubtful.

One consequence of this delicate political situation was that little had been done to develop the Egyptian base either before the war or during the period when Italy was still neutral. The first adminis-trative instruction on the subject, for the establishment of a main base for nine divisions in Egypt and Palestine, did not receive final approval until May 1940, though some work had been put in hand in advance. In October of the same year further instructions were given to expand the base for the reception of fourteen divisions by June 1941, and twenty-three divisions by March 1942; but by then the Command was already deeply involved in operations, and all sup-plies were delayed by the lengthening of the sea-route and the shortage of shipping. Moreover, the new plan had scarcely been initiated before the first German air-attacks on the Suez Canal raised a further problem. Although almost all supplies were now reaching the theatre by the Cape and the Red Sea, two of the main ports of discharge, Alexandria and Port Said, were within the Medi-terranean. The threatened interruption of traffic through the Canal made it urgently necessary to increase the unloading capacity at

Suez and to develop other ports farther to the south. This in turn involved extensive work in improving, or in some cases creating, communications between these ports and the main base area.[1]

All these were central problems which affected the three Services about equally; in addition the Royal Air Force had certain special problems. Only a limited number of aircraft could be flown direct to the Middle East. The majority were dismantled and shipped in crates either to Port Sudan and Suez[2] or to Takoradi on the west coast, where they were reassembled. The aircraft from Takoradi were then flown along the arduous route across central Africa to Khartoum and often required a further complete overhaul before they were fit for operations. The whole system, the best that could be devised in the circumstances, was extremely expensive in man-power—the assembly depot at Port Sudan alone absorbed 1,000 men —and subject to endless difficulties and delays. Convoys from the United Kingdom to Port Sudan or Suez might be three months at sea; and aircraft on the Takoradi route were held up by bad weather, lack of spare parts or the shortage of ferry pilots. Some aircraft arrived in the theatre without their full equipment; and others, like the American Tomahawk, required extensive modification before they could be put into service. A heavy additional burden was thus thrown on the Command and specially on the repair and main-tenance organization, which was already overstrained by operational casualties in Greece, Crete and Cyrenaica.

By May a crisis had been reached. Despite a heavy reinforcement during the first four months of the year, returns from the Middle East showed fewer than 400 modern aircraft as actually serviceable or expected to be so within fourteen days. This was absurdly dispropor-tionate to the total strength of the Command and gave the impres-sion, not perhaps entirely unjustified, that the whole Middle East was littered with aircraft awaiting repair, modification or some minor re-equipment. At this point the Cabinet, strongly urged by Lord Beaverbrook, decided to send out Air Vice-Marshal Dawson of the Ministry of Aircraft Production to review the whole maintenance organization and introduce 'methods which have been proved successful in the United Kingdom'. This intervention, combined with measures already taken by the Command, was effective; and the proportion of serviceable aircraft rose steadily from June onwards. Details of the reorganization would be out of place here; but one point may be noted because of its probable influence on other events. The final scheme provided for the appointment of a Chief Main-tenance and Supply Officer, responsible only to the Commander-in-

---

[1] Playfair, Vol. II, Chap. 11.

[2] A further depot was later developed at Basra.

Chief, who thus became the head of what was in effect an independent organization. The Air Ministry objected to this arrangement at the time as unorthodox; but it was held to be justified by the size and complexity of the problem, the length of the supply line and the lack of local resources.

These arguments may well have influenced the Prime Minister in his next step. Although there had been no such obvious block in Army administration as in R.A.F. maintenance, there had been difficulties nevertheless. In particular, complaints had been made about the number of men who were being drawn into the rearward services at the expense—or so it often seemed—of the front line.[1] This controversy came to a head in June. It was then the eve of our advance into Syria; and Mr. Churchill complained bitterly that Wavell, although he had more than 500,000 men under command, was apparently hard put to it to find an active brigade or even battalion. This seemed to argue a great want of management. He was not satisfied with the explanations which he had so far received, and proposed to deal drastically with the situation by appointing a senior officer to take entire charge of the Army's rearward services and control the use of manpower behind the front. The officer selected—General Haining, until then the V.C.I.G.S.—would assume the title of Intendant-General of the Army of the Middle East and, while acting under the general direction of the Commander-in-Chief, would enjoy a largely independent status:

'General Haining's duties, in the first place, will be to examine on the spot and to discuss with you the implementing and precise definition of the general directive and policy set forth in the preceding paragraphs which must be accepted as a decision of His Majesty's Government. After not more than a fortnight from the date of his arrival, the report must be telegraphed home. I hope it may be agreed, but any points of difference will be settled promptly by me. Moreover, I shall not allow the scheme to lose any of its force in the detailed application which must now be given to it'.

This wording might be taken to suggest that the Prime Minister expected General Haining to encounter obstruction as well as confusion in the Middle East; but this was not an accurate picture. Indeed, the basis of Mr. Churchill's argument was partly unsound. Of the 530,000 men then drawing rations in the Middle East, 132,000 were African or Sudanese troops, who were not employable in the north; and the front-line strength of the remainder was limited far more by the shortage of transport and the problems of regrouping than by any administrative failure. That this was so became clear

---

[1] Playfair, Vol. II, Chap. 11.

from the Intendant-General's first report, received in London on 24th June, which contained little to support a charge of muddle or mismanagement. On the contrary, while admitting the existence of serious problems arising from the natural difficulties of the theatre, it expressly exonerated the military authorities:

'The root of the administrative problem is not within the Army or peculiar to it. It lies in the relationship between the Royal Navy, the Army and Royal Air Force and representative Government Departments, both with each other and the Egyptian Government. For these reasons it is clear to me that the solution of the present difficulties and the development of a long term policy cannot be confined to the Army alone, but must be expanded to cover those administrative activities of the Royal Navy, the Royal Air Force and the Civil Authorities which are common to two or more of them. . . . In order to carry out the directive policy set forth in the Prime Minister's telegram, the Intendant-General must be given powers to set up and control a system of administrative co-ordination of all the elements concerned, which, while leaving the execution of day to day administration in the hands of the Commanders-in-Chief, will control their administrative relationships with each other and with the external authorities with whom they now deal individually . . .'

This and other passages in the report pointed the way to a superior solution, which was in fact already under discussion. It was clear that, if General Haining were given the powers for which he asked, he would become in effect a local War Minister, nominally responsible to one of the three Commanders-in-Chief, but actually in authority over all of them. This would not be a tenable position. On the other hand, the need for someone to exercise the local powers of a Minister had long been recognized and not only in the field of supply. Nearly a year before Wavell had suggested the formation of a Ministerial body, acting under the War Cabinet but situated in or near the Middle East, to which major questions of policy could be referred. Nine months later he had joined with the two other Commanders-in-Chief in repeating this proposal. More recently, the Prime Minister had received a further impulse in the same direction in the form of a telegram sent by his son, Major Randolph Churchill, through and with the warm approval of the Ambassador in Cairo.

This chimed exactly with the proposals in General Haining's report, and, as Mr. Churchill wrote afterwards, clinched the matter in his mind.[1] Three weeks later, on 28th June, Captain Oliver Lyttelton, who had entered the Government in 1940 as President of the Board of Trade, was given a seat in the War Cabinet as Minister of State with special responsibility for the Middle East. He left at

---

[1] Churchill, Vol. III, p. 312.

once to take up his duties in Cairo, where his instructions gave him the fullest powers:

'The Minister of State will represent the War Cabinet on the spot and will carry out its policy and use its authority for that purpose.

To enable him to discharge these functions he will be fully informed of the approved policy of His Majesty's Government on all major issues. If any question should arise on which he requires special guidance, he will, provided that there is time, refer the matter home. He will in any case report constantly to His Majesty's Government. His official channel of communication with His Majesty's Government will be the Secretary of the War Cabinet through the medium of the office of His Majesty's Ambassador in Cairo and the Foreign Office. He will also communicate directly with the Prime Minister and Minister of Defence by personal telegrams whenever convenient.

The principal task of the Minister of State will be to ensure a successful conduct of the operations in the Middle East by:
(a) relieving the Commanders-in-Chief as far as possible of those extraneous responsibilities with which they have hitherto been burdened; and
(b) giving Commanders-in-Chief that political guidance which has not hitherto been available locally;
(c) settling promptly matters within the policy of His Majesty's Government but involving several local authorities.

Examples of the above are:
(i) Relations with the Free French.
(ii) Relations with the Emperor of Abyssinia.
(iii) The administration of occupied enemy territory.
(iv) Propaganda and subversive warfare.
(v) Finance and economic warfare.
(vi) General supervision over the activities of the Intendant-General, including all matters locally connected with supplies from the United States of America.
(vii) Disposal of prisoners of war.

On these matters the Minister of State will of course refer home where necessary on important issues and will receive from time to time directives from His Majesty's Government.

To enable him to discharge the functions in (b) above he will preside over meetings of the Commanders-in-Chief whenever they so desire or he has any point to raise.

On the diplomatic and political side he will concert so far as is necessary the policy of His Majesty's Government representatives in Egypt and the Sudan, Palestine and Trans-Jordan, Iraq (which will however remain for operational purposes under the Government of India), Abyssinia, British Somaliland, occupied enemy territories (Eritrea and Italian Somaliland),

Syria (when occupied) and Cyprus.[1] This instruction in no way detracts from the existing individual responsibilities of His Majesty's representatives in the above territories, or their official relationships with their respective departments at home.'

The appointment of a detached Minister, acting with the full authority of the War Cabinet but physically separated from his colleagues, was a bold experiment. The nearest recent precedent was the appointment of Lord Halifax, who still retained his seat in the War Cabinet, as Ambassador in Washington; but the two cases were not parallel. Captain Lyttelton was to be more than an Ambassador; he was to act as the executive head of what was then our only active theatre of war. At any earlier date such a delegation of authority would probably have been regarded as impossible. What made it feasible now was partly the extraordinary development of modern communications, and partly the smoothness with which the central machine was then operating in London. The Minister could be kept daily and even hourly informed of Cabinet decisions and the progress of current business and could communicate his own views with the same ease. If necessary, he could return home for consultation at very short notice. Even so, his position might have been difficult, if there had been a major division in the Cabinet or a sharp cleavage, such as existed in the First World War, between civilian and military opinion. As it was, the experiment was wholly successful. The Cabinet's central control of the war was extended rather than impaired; and the Middle East gained immensely from the decentralization of executive authority, which the new system made possible.

One effect of Captain Lyttelton's appointment, though this was not apparently intended at the time, was to make the post of Intendant-General superfluous. General Haining might have remained as Quartermaster-General of the Army in the Middle East; but the inter-service authority, for which he had asked, was now vested in the Minister of State. Though he remained for some months a member of the War Council, set up by Captain Lyttelton on his arrival, his executive functions dwindled and finally disappeared. In October he was relieved of all his strictly military duties and attached to the Minister of State's staff in a general advisory capacity. By the end of the year his appointment had lapsed altogether; and he returned home, having failed by no fault of his own to play the major part in Middle Eastern affairs, to which he must have looked forward in July.

---

[1] The territories of Aden and the Yemen were later added to this list.

(ii)
Strategic Problems

It is against this elaborate background of reorganization that we must consider the strategic problems facing General Auchinleck, when he took up his command. His first task was defensive; he had to prepare the Middle East to resist a major German attack, which was then expected from either of two directions, the north or the west, or from both simultaneously.

The more immediate danger was in the west. There General Rommel, who had already shown his quality as a desert tactician, commanded a mixed force of two German and six Italian divisions, including two armoured divisions. His successful offensive in April had carried his advanced troops to the Egyptian frontier, where they occupied positions in the area round Sollum, from which Wavell's last operation, 'Battleaxe', had failed to dislodge them. In their rear, however, the fortress of Tobruk was still holding out; and Rommel could not risk a further advance until this threat to his communications had been cleared. It was unlikely, as his forces had suffered heavily in 'Battleaxe', that he would be able to mount a full-scale attack on Tobruk before September at the earliest. The Allies were also held in temporary check, partly by their losses in 'Battleaxe', and partly by the need to detach troops for the Syrian campaign. A pause of two or three months was therefore to be expected, during which both sides would endeavour to refit and recruit their strength for the coming battle.

The outcome of this logistic struggle was not easy to predict. Difficulties of supply were acute on both sides, but so evenly matched that either army was inclined to concede a slight advantage to the other. The complexities of the Allied problem, arising from the length of their supply-line and the size of the theatre, have already been described. By comparison the enemy's problem, which was concentrated on the defence of the short sea-route between Italy and North Africa, seemed delusively simple. But this route was exposed to attack almost throughout its length; and the task of guarding it had proved to be beyond the strength, or at least the capabilities, of the Italian Navy and Air Force. It had not been until January 1941, when the Germans transferred *Fliegerkorps X* to Sicily, that Allied naval ascendancy in the central Mediterranean had been seriously challenged. Since then the German conquest of Greece and Crete and the recapture of Cyrenaica had again altered the strategic balance. From these new bases the *Luftwaffe* had been able to extend their area of operations and to impose severe restrictions on Allied fleet movements outside the corner of the eastern basin, over which air cover could still be provided from Egypt or Palestine. The supply-route was thus secured against a major attack by surface forces. On the other hand, since *Fliegerkorps X* was not reinforced, this eastward shift of German air-power reduced the direct protection which could be given to convoys in passage. From the middle of July onwards, this was again left to the Italians.

It was here that the full strategic importance of Malta became apparent. From this exposed but still undaunted base British aircraft and submarines could continue to prey on enemy communications even in the absence of the Fleet. It was true that, without surface support, they could no longer hope to cut the supply-route; but they could and did make its working increasingly costly and uncertain. So long as Malta remained in Allied hands, the enemy's advantage in supply was largely negatived. It was reasonable to expect, therefore, that a renewed German offensive in the west would be accompanied or preceded by an attempt to eliminate Malta, perhaps by an air-borne operation such as had captured Crete. It remains one of the surprises of the war that no such attempt was made.[1] On the contrary, after May, when the greater part of *Fliegerkorps X* was trans-ferred to Greece, the attack was allowed to fall off. A gallant but wholly unsuccessful assault on shipping in the Grand Harbour was made by Italian E-boats and midget submarines at the end of July; but there was no serious attempt to put the base itself out of action.[2]

Nevertheless, the supply and reinforcement of the two outposts, Malta and Tobruk, imposed a heavy burden on the Allies. The task of supplying Tobruk fell on the Mediterranean Fleet operating from Alexandria, and was maintained without a check until the relief of the fortress in December; but the cost to the Navy was twenty-five ships sunk and eleven, including two hospital ships, seriously damaged.[3] Although losses in the Malta convoys were propor-tionately less, in every other respect these operations involved an even greater strain. During the summer and early autumn of 1941 virtually all supplies had to be brought in from the west; and a major fleet movement was entailed on each occasion. Apart from a number of isolated operations, in which aircraft were flown to the island from the carriers of Force H,[4] three main convoys were passed

---

[1] The Allies could not then know that German losses in Crete had been so heavy that no airborne operations on the same scale would ever be attempted again. General Frey-berg and his troops, though they lost the battle of Crete, may well have won the more important battle of Malta.

[2] Roskill, Vol. I, pp. 518 and 523.

[3] Roskill, Vol. I, pp. 519–20.

[4] Admiral Somerville's detached squadron at Gibraltar.

from Gibraltar in 1941, each consisting of twelve to fourteen merchantmen. The smallest escort and covering force required for any one comprised two battleships, one aircraft carrier, five cruisers, eighteen destroyers and eight submarines. Owing to the Italian Navy's unwillingness to accept battle, losses were confined to one cruiser and one destroyer sunk and two cruisers and two destroyers damaged. But it was clear that the Allies, already at the fullest stretch in the Atlantic, could not long afford this constant diversion of capital ships to the Mediterranean.[1]

Enough has been said to show why Auchinleck could not be certain of forestalling Rommel in the desert. Yet the importance of clearing this flank as soon as possible was only too evident. For the moment the main German armies were tied down in Russia; but their campaign there was expected to be short and decisive. By August or September the Red Army might have sustained a crushing defeat; and Hitler would be able to release forces for the next stage in his programme, an attack on our Middle Eastern positions from the north. This could be developed in far greater strength than the Germans could profitably use on the narrow desert front. It will be seen from the map that there were two possible lines of advance: through Anatolia and Syria on the Suez Canal; and through the Caucasus on the Persian oilfields and our position at the head of the Gulf. These routes could be used singly or in conjunction; but Germany's interest in Syria earlier in the year, and her recent Treaty of Friendship with Turkey,[2] were some indication that she might prefer the former, at least in the first instance. It was true that we had since been assured by Turkey that the Treaty did not affect her relations with the Allies; but this statement, however true at the moment, would tend to lose its validity once Russia had been defeated. Turkey would then be exposed to the full weight of German attack and might well find it prudent to do as she was told.

It was estimated that Germany, if she could disengage troops from Russia by mid-August and had secured Turkish acquiescence, would be able to concentrate up to nine divisions on the Anatolian frontier before the end of the year. They would be backed by an air force of some 110 long-range bombers and a proportionate number of fighters and close-support aircraft. Bad weather and poor communications through Anatolia would probably hold up land operations during the winter; but we should have to expect a fairly heavy scale of air attack on aerodromes and other key points in northern Syria and Iraq. By the spring Germany would have increased her land forces to fourteen

---

[1] Roskill, Vol. I, p. 531 (Table).

[2] Signed on 18th June, 1941.

or more divisions[1] and would be ready to open the main offensive. This might well be combined with a sea or air-borne operation against Cyprus. Indeed, the importance of Cyprus, as a base immediately on the flank of the advance, was so great that the attempt might be made much earlier, especially if any opportunity offered for a *coup-de-main*, while the island was still only lightly held.

These potential dangers, which might soon become actual, underlined the extreme importance of current operations in Syria. If any pocket of Vichy resistance remained in that country when the German attack began, the Allies would find themselves in a difficult and even precarious position. But by the first week of July this risk could be largely discounted. Damascus was in Allied hands; the 10th Indian Division from Iraq was already threatening Homs and Aleppo; and preparations were in train for a renewed attack in the coastal sector, which was expected to result in the fall of Beirut. The Vichy forces, though still resolute, were tiring; and their single attempt to bring in reinforcements had failed. The campaign was evidently approaching a climax. In fact, General Dentz, the Vichy commander, made his first proposals for an armistice only a few days later, on 11th July; and the formal capitulation followed, inappropriately enough, on 14th July.[2] But even so, the situation was not entirely easy. Although we should now have time to establish a firm military control before any German attack could develop, Syria would remain a disturbed and partly disaffected country. Nor could we hope to hold more than a small part of it in face of a determined German attack. If we were outmatched in armour, as was almost certain, we should have to abandon the open country in the north and concentrate our main defence in the mountainous area of the Lebanon.

This, however, would open Iraq to a German attack along the line of the Euphrates. Here again, as in Syria, we should feel our lack of armour; and it was doubtful whether we could establish any effective defence north of Baghdad. We should also have to reckon on the possibility, even the certainty, of a supplementary German thrust through the Caucasus. The scale of attack would always be smaller there than in the main operations through Anatolia; but it was estimated that the Germans could, if necessary, bring forward up to five divisions in northern Persia by the spring. The supporting air force would be of approximately the same size as that covering the Syrian front. These forces would be used in the first instance to assist in clearing northern Iraq and subsequently for a southward drive

---

[1] These figures are taken from the estimate made in London, which was disputed by both the Middle East and India, who thought 9–10 divisions the maximum that the enemy could support through Anatolia.

[2] Auchinleck's dispatch.

against our main base in the Basra-Abadan area. Strategically, such a movement would be even more dangerous than a direct advance on Suez, for, without the produce of the Iraqi and Persian fields and the output of the Abadan refinery, the whole Allied war-effort in the Middle East would wither for lack of oil. There could be no question, with the shortage of tankers as acute as it then was, of supplying the theatre from outside. Moreover, even without land operations, a German bomber force based on northern Persia and Iraq could bring a scale of attack to bear on the ports at the head of the Persian Gulf, which would seriously hamper, if it did not prohibit, the movement of oil from Abadan.

This forecast was admittedly founded on the worst case, which assumed an early and complete German victory in Russia with all the advantages to the enemy that that would entail. To this extent it was speculative and was not, in fact, borne out by events. Nevertheless, it was on calculations of this kind, modified and adjusted as the situation developed, that the Middle East's plan of defence had to be based. It was not a promising outlook. It is true that General Auchinleck had a total force of between 550,000 and 600,000 men under command; but this included, as we have seen, a high proportion of second-line troops, so that his effective Field Force did not exceed the equivalent of sixteen divisions. Even from this certain deductions had to be made. Three equivalent divisions of African troops, on a reduced scale of equipment, were still tied down in Abyssinia, where fighting continued in the Gondar and Galla-Sidamo areas until the end of the year. After September, when the new East Africa Command was formed, these troops passed out of Auchinleck's control.[1] The troops in Iraq, though included in the total given above, had reverted to the Commander-in-Chief, India, at the end of June, but on the understanding that they would return to Middle East, if major operations developed in the north. In the meantime there was a free exchange between the two commands. The 10th Indian Division had taken part in the Syrian campaign; and Middle East was later to lend India some of the troops required for operations in Persia.

All in all, only $11\frac{1}{2}$ divisions could be counted as immediately available; and these included many units in need of rest and refitting. There was also a conspicuous shortage of armour, which Auchinleck rightly judged would be the deciding arm both in the desert and in any operations in the north. In July the Middle East had only one complete armoured formation, the 7th Armoured Division, Wavell's other formation, the 2nd Armoured, having been almost completely destroyed in earlier operations. The 7th Armoured, moreover, was still partly equipped with heavy Infantry tanks, which were unsuited

---

[1] Playfair, Vol. II, p. 304.

to the terrain and restricted the division's range and power of manœuvre. There was no prospect of re-equipping with cruiser tanks before October; and the division would then require a further period of training to fit it for battle.[1]

It was only in the air that the position could be regarded as at all satisfactory. The problems of R.A.F. supply and maintenance, described earlier in the chapter, were gradually being solved; and the steady flow of reinforcements was beginning to take effect. By the second half of June there were thirty-five formed squadrons in the Middle East, including Malta—sixteen fighter, thirteen medium and five heavy bomber, and one flying-boat squadron—with a total initial establishment of 605 aircraft. To equip them the Command could now find 725 serviceable aircraft, of which 600 were modern types. By August these figures, still low in relation to the rate of reinforcement, had increased to $52\frac{1}{2}$ squadrons formed or forming—including thirty fighter and twenty-two bomber squadrons—with a total paper strength of 853 aircraft. Just over 1,000 serviceable aircraft were available, of which 833 were modern types. This did not compare unfavourably with the current enemy strength in the Mediterranean of 170 German and 650 Italian aircraft, the latter including a large number of obsolete or semi-obsolete types. But if aircraft were now fairly plentiful in the Mediterranean, there was still a serious shortage of pilots, especially of fighter-pilots; and the output of the Middle East's understaffed training schools was very small. Many squadrons had to remain under strength; and there was almost no reserve. Until this deficit had been made good, the Command would not be able to support heavy or continuous operations.

(iii)

Timing the Offensive

It is not surprising that the new Commander-in-Chief was cautious and inclined, at first, to speak less of operations than of the need for regrouping, reorganization and further reinforcement. Nevertheless, his first signal to London, giving an outline of his plans, came as something of a shock:

'Subject to further investigation and consideration my views are as follows:

---

[1] Playfair, Vol. II, Chap. I.

1. No further offensive Western Desert should be contemplated until base is secure.

2. Security of base implies completion occupation and consolidation Syria.

3. Consolidation Syria includes making Cyprus secure against attack.

4. Immediate action required is therefore eliminating Vichy French from Syria earliest possible moment and completion defence measures in Cyprus.

5. Offensive in Syria being prosecuted already with all vigour but hampered by shortage M.T. Iraqi force is giving all possible aid.

6. Reconnaissance shows at least one division required ensure reasonable possibility successful defence Cyprus and plans are being made accordingly.

7. Once Syria is secure, and this implies consolidation our position in Iraq, offensive in Western Desert can be considered, but for this adequate and properly trained armoured forces, say at least two, and preferably three, armoured divisions, with a motor division, will be required to ensure success; this is first essential.

8. Final object should be complete elimination enemy from Northern Africa, but administrative considerations would entail advance by stages, so that first objective would probably be re-occupation Cyrenaica, which itself would have to be effected by stages for same reason.

9. It is quite clear to me that Infantry divisions, however well trained and equipped, are not good enough for offensive operations in this terrain against enemy armoured forces. Infantry divisions are, and will be, needed to hold defended localities after enemy armoured forces have been neutralized or destroyed, but the main offensive must be carried out by armoured formations supported by motorized formations.

10. Second essential to successful offensive is adequate and suitably trained air component at disposal Army for all its needs, including fighters, medium bombers, tactical reconnaissance and close support on the battlefield. This is non-existent at present.

11. In my opinion there can be no question of carrying out simultaneous offensive operations in Western Desert and Syria. To do so is to invite failure on both fronts.

12. Third essential to success in any offensive operation in this theatre is close and constant co-operation fleet, both in close support of Army and in harrying enemy sea communications. This co-operation is taken for granted, but itself entails constant close support by air forces which must be at disposal of the Navy and additional to those required for close support of Army and for long range strategic air operations'.[1]

---

[1] Signal of 4th July, 1941.

The Prime Minister replied at once that the need to complete operations in Syria and to garrison Cyprus was accepted. But the Western Desert remained the dominant theatre, because it was only by recapturing the airfields of Cyrenaica that freedom of movement could be restored to the Fleet. It seemed to him that a renewed offensive in the desert ought to be possible in the near future. Earlier signals had shown that there were six trained regiments in the Middle East awaiting tanks, besides three others which were now approaching round the Cape. It was also estimated that by the end of July the Middle East should have 500 Infantry and Cruiser tanks, if the workshops were properly organized. No large reinforcement of armour could be expected during the next two months; and from September onwards the renewed risk of invasion would make the Chiefs of Staff extremely reluctant to spare anything from England. In the air we could expect to have superiority over the enemy during July, August and part of September; but the future thereafter was uncertain. Lastly, there was Tobruk, which seemed equally important both as a check on the enemy's advance and as a base from which to support our own offensive. But what would be Tobruk's position in two months' time? Would the garrison still be capable of effective action? All this seemed to point to early September as the most favourable time for an offensive. This view was supported by what was known of the enemy's position. So far, though there were reports of Italian reinforcement, no German troops appeared to be reaching Libya; but this might soon be altered to our disadvantage by a German victory in Russia:

'From all these points of view it is difficult to see how your situation is going to be better after the middle of September than it is now, and it may well be worsened. I have no doubt you will maturely but swiftly consider the whole problem'.

This telegram indicated clearly enough what line the Cabinet wished to take; but Auchinleck was not to be drawn. He replied with a careful message rebutting certain of the Prime Minister's arguments point by point. It was true that he had six regiments of trained tank personnel; but they were only trained in the tanks which they had previously used, not in those, such as the American Stuart, with which it was now proposed to equip them. Indeed, the whole standard of individual and collective training in the armoured formations was too low and must be raised, if they were to meet the Germans on level terms. It was also true that he had 500 Infantry and Cruiser tanks; but this was the total number. When allowance had been made for reserves and for tanks temporarily under repair, he could not expect to bring more than 350 into action at any one time. As for Tobruk:

'Consider there is every indication that enemy would like to be free of commitment of containing Tobruk and while I do not intend to alter our present policy of holding Tobruk, I cannot be confident that Tobruk can be maintained after September. Everything possible is being done but enemy air activity against ships at sea and in harbour is taking its toll. Furthermore, should enemy secure Sidi Barrani (which he could do at any time) it will not be possible to provide the present scale of fighter protection for supply ships to and from Tobruk.

I agree that with possible threat from the north, our position may well be worsened. North may become the decisive front'.

Two points here are worth remarking. First, Auchinleck's comments on Tobruk, though they appeared to support the Prime Minister's argument, were clearly not intended to do so. He seemed to wish to say, on the contrary, that the offensive value of the fortress had been over-stressed in London, and that it was in fact immaterial whether or not it was still holding, when the main operation took place. Secondly, the Prime Minister's telegram had not mentioned the threat from the north; his reference to the situation's worsening after September had applied only to German land and air reinforcement in Libya. Mr. Churchill had based himself on the forecast quoted above, which showed that a German offensive through Anatolia or the Caucasus was unlikely to develop before the spring. But it is clear from his response that Auchinleck did not agree. He was expecting to have to defend his northern flank in the near future—at any time, perhaps, from September onwards.

These arguments, stated and implied, were far from satisfying the Defence Committee. While admitting Auchinleck's difficulties, they could not agree to allow our forces in the Middle East, the only theatre in which we could come to grips with the enemy, to stand idle during the crucial period when the main German army was committed on the Eastern Front. Such inaction seemed no less intolerable strategically than politically. The conditions stated by Auchinleck for a successful offensive could not be fulfilled before the end of the year at the earliest. But by that time Rommel would almost certainly have attacked; and we should have suffered losses in the ensuing battle, whatever its result, which would put off the date of our own offensive still further. In the meantime, if events followed their expected course, the Germans would have opened a new front in the north. This would oblige us to divide our forces, so that we should no longer be able to operate in strength on either front. It seemed, therefore, that the only opportunity open to us was to snatch a quick victory in the desert before Rommel was reinforced and while his supply position, as Intelligence reports were beginning to show, was even more precarious than our own.

It is at this point that one can feel the impact on the argument of a question which was never formally posed. What precisely was meant by snatching a victory in the desert; what kind of victory? It is clear from his original telegram that Auchinleck was thinking in terms of a methodical—and necessarily prolonged—operation to recapture Cyrenaica as a prelude to driving the enemy out of North Africa altogether. But was this the only form of operation conceivable? The earlier 'Battleaxe', on which Mr. Churchill had now begun to look back with more understanding and less regret, had certainly not been an entire failure. It had halted Rommel and inflicted enough casualties to immobilize him, as it now appeared, for at least three and possibly four or five months. Might not another such stroke, applied while he was still off balance, cripple the enemy and secure the desert flank before a major attack could develop from the north?

There is no doubt, though the full facts were not then known to the Allies, that Rommel's position in midsummer was extremely bad. His Italian divisions, never vigorous at best, were worn out; they were down to half their normal strength in men and material and had lost almost all their transport. His two German divisions were in better case, but also desperately short of transport and living from hand to mouth for fuel, ammunition and even rations. Nor did these difficulties show any sign of easing. Shipping losses were still rising, and negotiations with the French for the use of the relatively safe port of Bizerta had broken down. By August the outlook was so unpromising that Rommel had difficulty in persuading the Italian High Command against an immediate withdrawal to Gazala or even to the line Derna-Mechili.

It was with considerations such as these in mind that the Defence Committee decided to make one further effort to stir Auchinleck to early action. On 19th July he received the following telegram from the Chiefs of Staff:

'In [yours] of 4th July, paragraph 7, you said that an offensive in Western Desert could not be contemplated until you had at least two and preferably three properly trained armoured divisions. Until Germany attacked Russia it was impossible for us to contemplate sending any considerable reinforcements of cruiser tanks from here since we had to regard invasion in August or September as a distinct probability. We cannot say this probability has disappeared altogether, since Russia might crack quite soon, but we are prepared to take a chance, if by doing so we can regain Cyrenaica with all the benefits that this implies.

In [yours] of 15th July, paragraph (H), you expressed a doubt whether you can maintain Tobruk after September. We therefore assume that any offensive to regain Cyrenaica cannot be postponed beyond that month. In our estimation there is every chance of our relative air strength improving up to September, and possibly even continuing to improve after that date, but this of course depends on the outcome of the Russian campaign.

Having regard to the above considerations, it looks from here that the best, if not the only, chance of retaking Cyrenaica is to launch an offensive by the end of September at the latest. Would you feel like doing this if we were to send you an additional 150 cruiser tanks at once? We reckon they could reach Suez by September 13–20. We would also be prepared to send you up to 40,000 men in W.S.11, leaving it to you to decide what you most need from what we can make available.

If on the other hand, you do not feel that you could undertake an offensive in the Western Desert by the end of September, we would not feel justified in taking ships from food imports, breaking up the first armoured division, and sending you 150 cruisers before it is practically certain that invasion cannot take place this year'.

Auchinleck, though he accepted this bait, declined to swallow the hook. He replied to the Chiefs of Staff that by the end of September he would not have even one armoured division equipped and trained. By the middle of October he hoped to have one division and one Army Tank brigade. If he received 150 extra tanks, he would be able to form an additional Brigade Group, which would be ready for action by 15th November or by 1st November, if the tanks were accompanied by trained crews. He would then be willing, provided that Rommel had not been reinforced and that no serious danger threatened from the north, to undertake a limited offensive to relieve Tobruk. If, in addition, he received 150 American tanks, he would be prepared by the same date and on the same conditions to attempt a full-dress offensive; but for this purpose he would also require 'large numbers 10-ten lorries and considerable transport aircraft'. He would communicate the details later.

This reply was supported and to some extent qualified by a telegram in more general terms to the Prime Minister:

'We think here that German offensive against Syria through Anatolia might develop in first half September . . .

I entirely agree as to desirability of using present German preoccupation in Russia to hit enemy in Libya, but I must repeat that to launch an offensive with the inadequate means at present at our disposal is not in my opinion a justifiable operation of war . . .

My immediate intentions are: first, to consolidate our positions in Cyprus and Syria as soon as possible and to maintain our positions in latter. Second, to press on with the sadly needed regrouping, reorganization and re-equipment of divisions and brigades which have not only suffered casualties and losses of equipment in Greece, Crete, Libya, Eritrea and Syria, but which had to be [used] in most instances not as formations but piece-meal. Third, with the Intendant-General, to expedite the re-organization and modernization of the rearward service of supply, movement and repairs. Fourth, to safeguard the training and equipment of our armoured formations without which no offen-sive is possible. Fifth, to reconnoitre and plan intensively for an offensive in Libya as foreshadowed in telegram . . . As the result of this planning I shall, I am sure, be asking you in near future for further means necessary to success.'

As it was now clear that a deadlock had been reached, Auchinleck was summoned home for consultation. He arrived in London, accom-panied by Air-Marshal Tedder, on 29th July and plunged at once into a series of meetings with the Defence Committee and the Chiefs of Staff at which the whole problem was exhaustively re-examined. No new arguments were advanced on either side—there were none to use—but in the end what Mr. Churchill has called 'General Auchin-leck's . . . high dignified and commanding personality' carried the day. His attitude throughout was entirely uncompromising. He must be allowed to carry out the task entrusted to him by his own methods and in his own time; and his military judgement did not permit him to attempt any operation in the desert before November. To do so would mean committing his only brigade of cruiser tanks to an action in which, in his view, it might well be destroyed. His utmost con-cession was to say that, if there were signs of a voluntary withdrawal or a spontaneous disintegration of Rommel's army, he would attack at once. Otherwise he could not allow any alteration in his pro-gramme. The Cabinet, who had no choice but to accept these condi-tions or find another commander, yielded with great reluctance, and the date of the offensive was provisionally fixed for 1st November.

There is no doubt that, in taking this rigid stand, Auchinleck was strongly influenced by his fear of an early German attack in the north. At the time of his visit to London, he can scarcely have expected that this blow would fall as early as September, since it was already August and hard fighting was still in progress in Russia. But he may well have feared an attack later in the year. His main pre-occupation was evidently to have his Field Army well in hand by then, re-equipped, re-trained and, above all, not prematurely com-mitted to operations in the desert, from which it might not be possible to extricate it in time to meet an alternative threat.

(iv)
Turkey and Persia

Two other matters of great importance were discussed during Auchinleck's visit to London. The first concerned Turkey. There had recently been a scare, based on reports of Bulgarian mobilization, that Germany was planning an immediate move against Turkey. In fact, these reports were ill-founded, all the troop movements in question being linked with Germany's operations in Russia; but they served the useful purpose of obliging or encouraging Turkey to clarify her attitude to the Allies. As the result, on 24th July, she had made a formal request for staff conversations. This approach was welcomed wholeheartedly by the Chiefs of Staff. They felt that the talks should cover as wide a field as possible. We might not be able to promise all that the Turks needed; but we should assure them that our supply of arms would be maintained and increased. We should also point out that, since our occupation of Syria, we had a common frontier with them, which would greatly facilitate troop movements in an emergency:

> 'The advantages of Turkish resistance to German aggression are so great that, subject to the security of our Western flank in Egypt, all possible measures should be concerted to meet the German attack as far from our bases as possible'.

Preliminary arrangements for the talks were put in hand at once. After some discussion Cyprus was selected as a convenient and inconspicuous meeting-place. It was hoped at first that the Turkish delegation would be led by General Chakmak, the Chief of Staff, and the British by Auchinleck, probably accompanied by either Cunningham or Tedder; but it later appeared that the Turks wished to begin with exploratory conversations on a lower level. The agenda was to include a general statement of British strategy and intentions, a discussion of the probable scale and timing of an enemy attack, and an exposition of the Turkish defence plan with special reference to their requirements from us and the capacity of their lines of communication. Further discussions would then follow on possible joint action and the help which we could provide in various contingencies.

The Allied attitude on these points was defined at a meeting at Chequers on 2nd August, which Auchinleck attended. It was agreed that we should give all possible help to Turkey, if she resisted a German attack. The clearing of the desert flank would still remain our first strategic commitment; but, once that had been completed, we could and should put our whole weight behind Turkey. All the information available in London suggested that no attack was likely to develop before 1st November at the earliest or, more probably, not before the spring. By November we could, if necessary, offer Turkey four divisions and one armoured brigade. The extent of our help in the air would depend on the current position in the Western Desert; but we should inform the Turks that we expected to have 1,000 front line aircraft in the Middle East by the end of the year and 1,250 by 1942. But before we could bring any considerable part of this force to their aid, we should require facilities to reconnoitre and improve aerodromes and to lay the foundations of a ground-organization. We could also provide A.A. defence, if the need arose, for Turkish aerodromes and other key-points and should be prepared—though this offer was to be held back as a bargaining counter—to make 100 3·7″ A.A. guns available immediately.

At this point an unfortunate hitch occurred. The Turks reported that, as the Germans had now got wind of the proposed conversations, they thought it unwise to send a delegation out of the country. It was proposed instead that discussions should begin in Ankara between our Military and Air Attachés and the General Staff. This reduction in the scale and importance of the talks, implying some hesitation on the Turkish side, was regrettable but could not be helped. However, when the talks opened on the new basis on 15th August, progress was not unsatisfactory. It appeared that the Turks, relying on their own army, attached far more importance to air support than to the infantry divisions which we had offered. Our proposal was therefore amended to include a substantial air component of twenty squadrons —nine bomber, eight fighter and three A/C—of which four fighter squadrons were, if necessary, to be made available in November, regardless of the situation elsewhere. The Turks raised no objection to our proposed reconnaissance of their aerodromes. A party set out for this purpose on 15th September; and work was put in hand on a number of sites two months later. On the other hand, all our proposals for the improvement of road and rail communications between Turkey and Syria were, if not rejected, at least set aside. The offer of four divisions therefore remained in suspense, as the Turks perhaps intended, for it was very doubtful whether more than two Allied divisions at most could be maintained over existing communications.

It will be seen that we obtained much from these conversations, though not all that had been hoped for. On the credit side we now had a reasonable assurance that Turkey would resist a German attack and, at least to some extent, concert her plans with us in advance. On the debit side we had failed to negotiate any arrangement, which would enable us to base our future defence of Syria on a line inside the Turkish frontier. But the door was open for further discussion; and it was reasonable to hope that before the spring, if all went well in the desert, we should have larger forces to offer and, in particular, more armour, in which the Turks were deficient. It ought then to be possible to reach a final agreement.

The second and, as it proved, far more important subject of discussion during Auchinleck's visit was Persia. For some time past the Allies had been gravely disturbed by the extent of German influence in Persia and the size of the German community, which by 1941 numbered some 5,000 persons. They were mainly technicians, employed in accordance with the Shah's policy of modernization in developing the industry and communications of the country. But this, though it gave a valid reason for their presence, made them all the more dangerous. The Shah's Government was itself none too stable; and there was a constant risk of a German-inspired *coup d'état* on the same lines as Raschid Ali's revolt in Iraq. After the German attack on Russia at the end of June, this danger was felt to have become acute. Representations were made in Teheran by the British Minister but produced no result. To all inquiries about the German community the Persian Government replied, in effect, that they were performing an essential service and could not be dispensed with.

On 10th July, Mr. Eden informed the Cabinet that the Russian Ambassador had called to discuss the Persian situation. He had said that his Government was anxious to clear the matter up at once and proposed a Joint Note demanding the expulsion of the German colony, to be followed, if the Persian Government did not comply, by military action. This course was accepted; and inquiries were made from India and the Middle East as to what troops could be made available. It should be noted, however, that the military action proposed at this stage was strictly limited. It was to be confined on our side to the occupation of Abadan Island and the neighbouring oilfield. Even this was to be in the nature of a gesture, designed to show the Persian Government, if they seemed unwilling to satisfy us in the matter of the Germany colony, that we had both the means and the will to protect our essential interest. This was the British view; but the Russians, as presently appeared, understood the position differently and perhaps more clearly.

At the end of July Mr. Eden brought the Persian question before the Cabinet again. In the meantime he had discussed the terms of the Joint Note with the Russians. They now wished to extend its demands to include the right of free passage for troops and war material across Persia; and it was implied that, if the Note were rejected, they would extend their military operations so as to secure control of Persian communications. But the Cabinet would not accept this on the ground that it was inconsistent with earlier approaches to Persia, which had been confined entirely to the future of the German colony. They admitted that the question of transit rights might arise later;

but, if so, it should be dealt with as a separate issue. This hanging back may seem curious in view of the great importance which later attached to Persia as the only land-bridge between Russia and the West and one of the main routes for Allied supplies. The Cabinet's decision was, however, supported by a number of arguments, which seemed valid at the time.

In the first place, we had few, if any, troops to spare in the Middle East and were anxious not to tie down more than an absolute minimum in preventive action in Persia. We wished to secure the co-operation of the Persian Government, if only under protest, but to avoid any action, which might commit us to a general occupation of the country. Secondly, at the end of July, Russia's military position was at its most precarious. It was by no means clear how long it would be necessary or prudent for us to go on sending supplies. Existing routes were more than adequate for all the supplies that we could afford to send for the moment; and the development of a new over-land route across Persia was a long-term project, which would make a heavy call on equipment of precisely the kind already needed for the development of the Middle Eastern base.

In the meanwhile military preparations were going ahead. On 28th July the Foreign Secretary presided at a meeting of the Chiefs of Staff, at which it was agreed that our Note to Persia should be presented on or about 12th August. By that time a force of 1½ divisions with a small armoured contingent would be available in Iraq and could be supported by a small air force of six or seven squadrons, including four bomber squadrons. If our Note were rejected, this force would advance and occupy Abadan and the adjacent oilfield, while the Russians took similar action in the north. These movements could be supported, if necessary, by a threat to bomb Teheran. If, in face of these pressures, the Persian Government agreed to expel the German colony, we should then consider whether or not to raise the further question of transit-rights. But it was of great importance that all demands should be made jointly and that the Russians should be persuaded not to act ahead or independently of us either diplomatic-ally or in any subsequent military action.

All this was strictly conformable with the Cabinet decision recorded above; but doubts seem already to have developed in the Prime Minister's mind about the efficacy of what was, in fact, a policy of half measures. Three days later he presided in person at a meeting of the Chiefs of Staff, at which the Foreign Secretary and Auchinleck, who had just reached London, were also present. Mr. Eden explained the measures which had so far been taken. The Prime Minister approved but added that a number of points, diplomatic and military, still seemed to require clarification. What did we propose to do, for example, if the Persians offered strong resistance, seized British subjects as hostages or attempted to damage the oil-wells? Was it wise to persist in the threat of bombing Teheran, which might be regarded as an atrocity? How far north did we propose to go and what plans were there for keeping the railway in action if the Persians refused to help?

The last of these questions suggests that the Prime Minister, despite the recent Cabinet decision, was now thinking of Persia largely in terms of a through-route to Russia. But this was not yet a general view. Only a few days later, the special Cabinet Committee, appointed on Mr. Churchill's proposal to co-ordinate the whole operation, again repudiated the idea of including a demand for transit rights in our Note to Persia. The reason given was that our forces were not large enough to occupy the whole country, though they could, if necessary, take possession of the oilfields as far north as Dizful. But we did not wish to lock up any troops in the country for longer than was necessary. We should therefore adopt a firm but friendly attitude and limit our demands to the essential minimum. We should insist on the removal of all Germans in potentially dangerous positions and the strict surveillance of the remainder. But we should not press for the immediate expulsion of the German colony as a whole, which might be impracticable. We should also consider the offer of some form of financial compensation, which might be accompanied by a personal gift to the Shah. It was also decided that the question of bombing Teheran should be shelved for the moment. Aircraft were to act only in support of our own troops or against Persian aerodromes.

During the following week a new argument was found in favour of a policy of strict moderation. The Chiefs of Staff were alarmed by reports of Turkey's probable reaction. She was known to be sensitive to any exercise of foreign influence in Persia and especially to the possibility of Russian encroachment in the northern provinces. Since the staff conversations, already referred to, were now about to open, it was important that nothing should be done to disturb or annoy Turkey needlessly. On 8th August Mr. Eden discussed this point with the Russian Ambassador. It was agreed that a reassuring joint statement should be made to Turkey a few days before our Note was delivered to Persia. This was done and in fact, when the time came, Turkish reactions were less severe than had been expected. The use of force against Persia was deplored on principle; but its necessity was generally admitted; and the main criticism of our action was that it lacked speed and vigour.

These preliminaries over, the Anglo-Russian Note was presented in Teheran on 17th August. In deference to our wishes nothing was said about transit-rights; but a formal demand was made for the expulsion of the German colony. As many as possible were to leave at once; and lists of any key-technicians remaining were to be supplied and a strict surveillance exercised over them. This control was also to be extended to the refugees from Iraq, who had entered the country at the time of the collapse of Raschid Ali's revolt. In their reply the Persians made a show of agreeing but hedged their compliance with so many conditions and qualifications as to make the whole unacceptable. It was therefore decided to proceed to military action.

After a few days' delay, requested by the Russians for operational reasons, troop movements began on 25th August. By an extension of the original plan there were now two columns, the first directed from Basra on Abadan and the Ahwaz oilfield, the second from Baghdad on the Khaniqin oilfield farther north. A naval force with a small landing-party was also dispatched to the port of Bandar Shahpur on the Persian Gulf. These operations were entirely successful and met with only trifling opposition. By 28th August, when the Shah ordered a cease-fire, Bandar Shahpur had been occupied, the northern column had reached its main position at Kermanshah and the southern column was only a few miles short of Ahwaz. In the meantime the Russians had also moved in the north; and advanced parties from the two armies made contact with each other at Senna on the 29th and a few miles south of Kasvin two days later.[1]

After the cease-fire, armistice terms were imposed which went a little further than our original demands. Persian troops were to withdraw from specified areas in the north and south-west, which would then be occupied by British or Russian forces. All Germans, apart from the Legation staff and a strictly limited number of technicians, were to leave the country within one week. In addition, the question of transit-rights for British and Russian troops and war material was raised for the first time. But at this point the limitations of a cautious policy became apparent. Although the Persian Government accepted the Anglo-Russian terms, they gave few signs of active co-operation, still less of what Mr. Churchill called 'proper alacrity' in carrying them out. Even the rounding-up of the German colony was attended by delay and prevarication. This was not perhaps entirely the Persians' fault. The whole course of recent events, culminating in the almost unopposed entry of British and Russian troops, had weakened the authority of the Government. There was a recrudescence of tribal unrest; desertions from the army were frequent; and considerable quantities of arms and ammunition were finding their way into the wrong hands. But this incipient disorder, though it might serve as an excuse for the Persian Government, also emphasized the difficulty of our own position. It was now clear that we could not get what was needed without a more extensive physical control of the country.

---

[1] Wavell's *Persian Dispatch.*

This was all the more important because the question of the through-route to Russia, hitherto passed over or kept in the background, was now emerging into an acknowledged prominence. On 25th August Lord Hankey's Committee for the Co-ordination of Allied Supplies raised the matter with the Chiefs of Staff:

'At the present time the only route of access to Russia being used on any considerable scale is that to Vladivostok, but this route may be closed at any moment by the Japanese. The northern routes are exposed to enemy action and to seasonal limitation. It follows that the Persian routes alone hold out a certain prospect in providing for large volumes of supplies to Russia in the coming months. At the moment, however, the quantity of goods they can carry . . . is negligible. The East Persian lorry route could be developed to a limited extent by the provision of motor transport etc., which the Government of India would be prepared to undertake. The Government of India point out however that a limited improvement of this route, such as has been proposed, would probably lead to heavy pressure to develop it more fully, and that this would involve strategic considerations of the highest importance. It is on this strategic issue, namely on the advisability of departing from the traditional policy of providing for the defence of India's north-western frontiers by maintaining a vacuum beyond them, so far as communications are concerned, that the Government of India desire guidance from the highest military authority before agreeing to the proposals. . . .'

'The Government of India have raised no objection to the development of the railway through Western Persia. Efforts are now being made to provide a small number of locomotives and waggons and to improve the capacity of the railway from Bandar Shahpur to Bandar Shah on the Caspian, but action on a more considerable scale will be required, if the railway is to be fully developed. Provision of the additional equipment required would raise questions of priority which in the event of an affirmative answer, Lord Hankey would propose to the Chiefs of Staff Committee in due course. . . .'

The Chiefs of Staff replied that they saw no objection to the development of the east Persian route to its maximum capacity of 2,000 tons a month. Work on the ports and railways of west Persia should also begin as soon as possible. But such a programme could not be executed without physical control of at least the main junctions of the railway system, including Teheran, and a degree of co-operation from the Persian Government, which had not so far been forthcoming. These questions were discussed at meetings of the Defence Committee and the War Cabinet on 3rd and 4th September. The Prime Minister said that the time had come to take a firm line with the Persians and make it plain that we and the Russians were now in

military control of their country. We should have to extend the scope
of our original demands and could not permit any haggling over
terms. It was important that we should exercise complete control
over Persia for the duration of the war and especially over the road
and railway communications to Russia. He had already held discussions with the Ministries of Supply and War Transport; and
arrangements were in hand to supply the necessary locomotives and
rolling-stock. On the same day Mr. Churchill telegraphed to M.
Stalin in similar terms:

> 'We have already given the orders for supplying the Persian rail-
> way with rolling stock to raise it from its present capacity of two
> trains a day each way up to its fullest capacity, namely, twelve
> trains a day each way. This should be reached by the spring of
> 1942 and meanwhile will be steadily improving. Locomotives and
> rolling stock have to be sent round the Cape from this country
> after being converted to oil burners and a water supply along the
> railway has to be developed. The first forty-eight locomotives
> and 400 steel trucks are about to start . . .'

Meanwhile it had been decided that British and Russian troops
should advance and occupy Teheran. While preparations for this
move were still in progress, Mr. Eden reported to the Cabinet that the
Persian Government had now offered to close the German and Italian
Legations and to intern all German nationals. The question was
whether our advance should continue in face of this apparent willingness to meet our wishes. There were many things that we did not like
about the present Persian administration. Apart from the particular
questions so far raised, there was an obvious need for reform throughout the country which would be greatly facilitated by the removal of
the Shah. Propaganda in this sense was already having some effect;
and there were signs that the Persian Prime Minister might be willing
to co-operate. The best solution, perhaps, would be to couple a
rigorous enforcement of our demands with proposals for an alliance
with Persia. This policy was accepted. As the Prime Minister pointed
out, we only required concessions for the duration of the war;
thereafter, it would be much in our interest to have a strong and
independent Persia.

From this point onwards events moved swiftly. On the 10th Sep-
tember the Persian Government closed the German and Italian
Legations but received, on the same day, a further Note requiring the
execution of our other terms, which now included the control of
Persian communications, within the next forty-eight hours. On 15th
September British and Russian troops began to move on Teheran.
No resistance was offered; and on the following day the Shah
announced his abdication. He was succeeded by his son, the Crown
Prince, who informed our Legation with mild irony that he would be

delighted to co-operate fully with the Allies, as soon as it could be indicated to him precisely what was required. The British Minister replied, on instructions from London, that we intended to occupy Teheran temporarily in order to bring the German colony under final control and take necessary measures to protect and improve Persian communications. When that had been done, we should withdraw from the capital and reduce our military commitments in Persia to a minimum. We hoped that at this stage a formal alliance might be concluded between the Soviet Union, Persia and ourselves.

Everything was now in train for a final settlement. Before the end of September all the members of the German colony, who had not already left the country, were interned at Basra. In the following month British and Russian troops withdrew from Teheran to their original zones of occupation, leaving a small force behind to guard the key-points on the railway. At the same time negotiations were opened for an alliance between the three countries for the duration of the war, which was signed at the end of January 1942.

14

CHAPTER VIII

THE TWO FLANKS

(i)

'Barbarossa'—Phase II

ALTHOUGH HITLER'S DECISION, taken at the first crisis on the Eastern front, to reinforce the south at the expense of the centre was ultimately fatal, its immediate dividends were impressive. In the fourteen weeks between the middle of August and the end of November Russia suffered losses of men and territory almost as great and almost as crippling as those she had endured in the first shock of the campaign. Once more the whole issue of the war seemed to hang in the balance.

Rundstedt's great encircling movement to the west of Kiev, which reached its climax early in August, has already been mentioned. The effect of this battle, the last major stroke of the original strategy, was to break the back of organized resistance in the western Ukraine. Within the next three weeks the whole province was overrun up to the line of the Dnieper. The naval base at Nikolaiev on the Black Sea and the metallurgic centres of Krivoi Rog and Nikopol were all in German hands by 18th August. Ten days later Dnyepropetrovsk on the east bank of the Dnieper had also fallen. By the end of the month the only remaining pocket of Russian resistance was a small enclave round Odessa, which kept up a spirited defence for another six weeks against the Rumanian forces on the right wing of the advance.[1]

In the meantime Army Group Centre's thrust on Gomel had been developed, in accordance with Hitler's directive of 21st August, into a major turning movement to the south with the object of trapping Budyonny's concentrations on the farther side of the Dnieper to the east of Kiev. Here again success was rapid and, in one sense, complete. By the second week of September the spearhead of the advance had reached Lokhvitsa, seventy-five miles south of Konotop, where contact was made with advanced elements of Army Group South, who had forced the crossing of the Dnieper above Kremenchug. Kiev was now completely isolated and fell four days later.[2] But, as in earlier operations, the 'encirclement' of Budyonny's army was little more than a technical expression. Despite the vast number of

---

[1] Russian communiqués of 18th and 28th August and 16th October, 1941.

[2] Russian communiqué of 30th September, 1941.

prisoners captured or claimed by the Germans, a substantial part of his force was able to withdraw to the south and east before the jaws of the pincers closed. He thus retained a considerable mass of troops under command, though their value as a formed body—the largest, apart from Timoshenko's army group, with which the Germans were then in contact—had been temporarily destroyed. For the moment the Russian defence in the south was off balance. Withdrawals were reported in the Kharkov area and the Donetz Basin; and the way was open for Army Group South to resume its advance on a broad front against opposition, which was not expected to be more than local and sporadic.

This much accomplished, Hitler's attention turned again to the centre. At the beginning of October the delayed offensive against Moscow, for which O.K.H. and the Field Commanders had pleaded six weeks before, was finally launched. It prospered well at the outset. Local surprise was achieved with penetrations of up to forty miles on the first day; and throughout the next week or so Halder's diary continued to record 'classic victories'.[1] By the middle of the month the southern arm of the attack had reached Briansk and Orel; in the north Vyasma had fallen and fighting was in progress round Rzhev. But this pace was not maintained. As the Germans approached Moscow, resistance stiffened; and the autumn rains, coming earlier than had been expected, bogged down the armour. Nevertheless, by 20th October German advanced forces were reported at Mozhaisk within 65 miles of their goal. This was a time of crisis and even, according to some reports, of panic in Moscow. Women and children had already left the city; now a state of siege was proclaimed, followed by a general evacuation of civilians. The official seat of government was transferred to Kuibyshev on the Volga; and only Stalin himself and part of the central executive remained in the Kremlin.[2]

This episode was a minor triumph for Hitler; but it was to be the last. By the end of October the German offensive was losing impetus. Some further progress was made by the southern arm in heavy infantry fighting round Tula; and the Germans were also able to extend their hold on the north-western approaches to Moscow in the direction of Kalinin. But these were minor gains. From the swift battle of movement planned by O.K.H., the operation now degenerated into a mere slogging match, compared by von Bock to the Battle of the Marne, in which the last battalion would turn the balance.[3] It was at this point that the full extent of Hitler's miscalculation began to be apparent. His staff had warned him early in August that good campaigning weather could not be expected in the

[1] *Halder's Diary*, 30th September to 8th October, 1941.
[2] Russian communiqués of 8th, 12th, 13th, 16th, 19th and 20th October, 1941.
Halder's Diary, 18th and 22nd November, 1941.

central sector after the middle of October. They had also warned him of the growing strength of Russian concentrations before Moscow and the war-worn condition of German armour, which could no longer exert the same easy dominance as before. He had ignored them and was now about to lose the prize, if only by the narrowest margin.

This was the High Command's view; but Hitler himself was still largely unconscious of failure. It is true that, once the battle for Moscow was joined and he felt his prestige to be involved, he pressed the operation to the utmost, regardless of stiffening resistance, bad weather and the exhaustion of his own troops. When success was still denied him, he blamed the Field Commanders, of whose shortcomings he was constantly and bitterly critical. But this did not prevent him from repeating his previous argument that Moscow, so far from being the crux of the Eastern front, was a 'mere geographical expression' of little or no military value. An offensive in the centre might have its uses and, once launched, must be forced to succeed; but it was on other sectors of the front, especially in the south, that the real prizes were to be gained. On this view, despite the temporary setback before Moscow, the general situation was not unfavourable.

By the beginning of November Hitler could fairly claim that all the more important objectives specified in his August directive had either been gained or were within the Germans' grasp. In the northern sector, admittedly, there had been little progress since September. Leningrad had not fallen nor had the intended junction with the Finns taken place. But the city was closely invested, as the directive required; and the capture of Tikhvin on 10th November cut the last railway-link with the interior.[1] In the centre—the least important sector according to the directive—the issue was not yet decided. It was still possible to believe that a final effort would capture Moscow before the end of the year. In any case, whether Moscow fell or not, the offensive drew Russian troops away from the all-important south, where Rundstedt was making enormous strides. By the first week of November Army Group South had already reached the line Kursk-Kharkov-Stalino-Taganrog. On the extreme right of the advance 12th Army had forced the passage of the Perekop Isthmus and was fanning out into the Crimea.[2] Only a few more weeks were needed to complete the whole programme—the occupation of the rest of the Donetz Basin and the Crimea, the capture of Rostov and the interception of Russian oil supplies from the Caucasus.

The value of these immense gains could not be disputed. Indeed, if pre-war calculations had been correct, the loss of the Ukraine and the Donetz should have gone far towards crippling Soviet war-economy.

---

[1] From the end of November onwards the Russians supplied Leningrad by a temporary railway laid across the frozen surface of Lake Ladoga.

[2] German communiqués of 29th October and 10th November, 1941.

Even on the basis of the later and more accurate information, which the Germans had acquired by the autumn, it could be counted as a very serious blow. From a strictly military point of view the outlook seemed equally promising. There was reason to hope, at least in the early stages of the advance, that Rundstedt's offensive would finally dislocate the Russian defensive system in the south. Optimistic notes in Halder's diary spoke of the possibility of a general withdrawal. It was thought that the Russians might have to give up territory as far as the line of the Don, thus breaking their front in two and exposing the southern flank or even the rear of their positions in the centre. In that event the Caucasus would be isolated. Whatever local defence the Russians were able to organize would presumably be based on the line of the Caucasus mountains. But the oilfields of Maikop and Grozny (though not the major field of Baku) lie to the north of this natural barrier and might, therefore, fall to the Germans by the winter or at worst in the spring.[1]

There were two factors in the situation which this analysis ignored or underrated. The first was the inherent weakness of Rundstedt's position despite its imposing appearance on the map. His Army Group was already stretched to the limit. It had overrun far more territory than it could occupy in any but a nominal sense; and its communications were extended through nearly a thousand miles of hostile country on which the winter was closing in. Under these conditions it was still possible to advance; but there could no longer be any weight in the attack. The second factor was the unexpected tenacity and recuperative power of the Red Army. The Russians had never had any intention of withdrawing voluntarily in the south, still less of allowing their front to be broken without a struggle. At the end of October, as soon as the pressure on Moscow slackened, Timoshenko had been sent to the south to reorganize Budyonny's shattered army, now withdrawn somewhere to the east of Kharkov.[2] During the next three weeks he was able to concentrate a sizeable and well-equipped force in the Voroshilovgrad area and was making preparations for a local counter-offensive.

The German advance in the south now came almost to a standstill, partly as the result of bad weather but mainly from sheer exhaustion. In the Crimea 12th Army was decisively checked before the defences of Sevastopol. There was little further progress in the Donetz Basin; and the drive on Rostov, though it still crept forward, had lost pace and weight. By 22nd November German advanced forces were fighting in the streets of the city; but a brisk Russian counter-attack ejected them a few days later. At the same time Timoshenko opened

---

[1] *Halder's Diary*, 23rd September, 10th October and 7th November, 1941.

[2] Russian communiqué of 24th October, 1941.

his offensive from the north-west against German positions in the Donetz. Within the next fortnight the forward elements of Army Group South were in general retreat towards the old line Stalino-Mariupol, which they had first reached nearly a month before.[1] This was no more than a local set-back of the kind to which any army is exposed at the end of a long advance; but it was enough to show that the offensive had reached, or slightly overpassed, the limit of its strength. And the same was evidently true, not only in the south, but along the whole length of the front. In the north the Russians were still counter-attacking fiercely in the area between Lake Ladoga and Lake Ilmen. In the centre a renewed and final effort by the Germans at the end of November to break the deadlock before Moscow was completely unsuccessful.[2]

The second phase of 'Barbarossa' thus ended in the same relative failure as the first. By the beginning of December the Germans were no nearer to a final decision than they had been at the beginning of August. They had won remarkable victories and taken possession of vast tracts of territory; but they had neither broken the Red Army in the field nor destroyed, though they had certainly injured, the industrial foundations on which Soviet resistance rested.

(ii)
How to help Russia ?

At the end of August, shortly after the Germans had opened their renewed offensive, the Russian Ambassador called on Mr. Eden. He wished, he said, to ask a most serious question: what had Great Britain so far done to help her new ally? It appeared to his Government that she had done very little. They understood from the Prime Minister's earlier telegrams that their plan for an immediate attack in the West had been rejected; but they were still waiting to hear what alternative was proposed. In their view England should either agree to stage some appropriate diversion or, if that were impossible, increase the supply of arms to Russia so as to enable her to intensify the fighting on her own front. He had now to ask which course had been selected. Could he say, for example, that we had agreed to attack across the Channel in the spring? Or must he report that nothing whatever would be done?

---

[1] German communiqué of 22nd November 1941; Russian communiqués of 24th and 28th November and 2nd December, 1941.

[2] German communiqué of 25th November, 1941.

It was not easy to find an answer to these questions, which was at once diplomatic and convincing. It was true that we had done our best and had wished to do more; but the fact remained that our total effort had so far been meagre. The aircraft-carriers *Furious* and *Victorious* had made two strikes against German shipping and port installations in the Far North; and further operations of the same type were being planned. Two Hurricane squadrons had been established at Murmansk and had made some contribution to the defence, though hampered by bad flying weather and the inadequacy of the local warning system. An unopposed raid had been carried out at Spitzbergen with the object of putting the coal-mines out of action and withdrawing the Russian and Norwegian miners, who still remained on the island.[1] Finally, our air-offensive in the West had been enlarged by a series of daylight attacks on industrial targets in occupied France, which were later extended to the unoccupied zone and parts of western Germany.

Of all these operations it was only the last for which any distinct importance could be claimed. The daylight raids had inflicted considerable damage; but this was subsidiary to the main purpose of holding back the *Luftwaffe* from the Eastern front. We could show that, since the attack on Russia began, Germany's fighter strength in the West had been maintained and even slightly increased. This was not a spectacular success; but it was fair to say that each squadron thus withheld had diminished, if only by a little, the *Wehrmacht*'s striking power in Russia during the first and crucial months of the campaign. To this extent we could claim to have influenced the main battle. But unhappily, our contribution was not of a kind which it was easy to measure exactly; and we could not expect the Russians to rest content with the statement, however well supported by facts and figures, that this was the most that we could do. Further pressure for operations more on the scale of their own endeavours was only to be expected.

This was not long in coming. M. Maisky's interview with Mr. Eden was followed by M. Stalin's telegram of 3rd September, quoted in an earlier chapter, with its urgent plea for the establishment 'already this year [of] a second front somewhere in France or the Balkans,' which would be able to draw off thirty to forty German divisions from the Eastern front. The ominous impression made by this message was more than confirmed at a subsequent interview between Mr. Churchill and the Russian Ambassador. The latter made it clear, though the thought was never put into words, that his country was now at the breaking-point. The possibility of a collapse, followed by a

---

[1] In peacetime Russia and Norway had each drawn some 500,000 tons of coal a year from Spitzbergen. It was held to be important to deny Germany the Norwegian share, though it does not appear that she made any serious attempt to exploit it.

truce or armistice with Germany, could not be excluded. On the same day came a dispatch from Sir Stafford Cripps in a similar vein. He had seen Stalin's message—'a document of the gravest importance'—and was satisfied that it gave a true and even moderate picture of the situation:

> 'It demonstrates the result of our not being able to do anything to create a diversion, and shows that unless we can now at the last moment make a superhuman effort we shall lose the whole value of any Russian front, at any rate for a long time and possibly for good.
>
> We have unfortunately considered the war here as no direct responsibility of ours, but merely as a war which we desired to assist in any way that we could, without unduly endangering our own position. I have tried to emphasize how vital it was that we should do our utmost if we wanted to keep this front effectively in being but I fear it is now almost too late unless we are prepared to throw everything in, in an effort to save this front. I beg that you will consider this point of view with the great seriousness that it deserves, and even now take some action to save a collapse here'.

No one will blame the Ambassador for this appeal on behalf of the country to which he was accredited; but the reproaches in the second paragraph were unjust. Since the first day of the attack on Russia, Mr. Churchill, supported by the Cabinet, had pressed the Chiefs of Staff to explore every possible type of diversionary operation. They had reported that nothing could be done on a scale which was likely to be of the slightest value; and their military argument was unanswerable. Germany was believed to have 30 divisions, half of them of good quality, in the West and a reserve of 24 divisions in the Reich.[1] She could therefore put into the field, without disturbing her Russian concentrations, a larger force than we possessed either in the United Kingdom or the Middle East. But the discrepancy did not stop there. Since we had no port of entry, an attack on the Continent would have to take the form of an opposed landing on open beaches; and we had only enough landing-craft to put one Brigade Group ashore at a time. An attack on this scale would offer no problem to the Germans, who could contain or destroy our bridgehead without moving so much as one battalion from Russia.

Mr. Churchill communicated these facts to Sir Stafford Cripps in a sharply worded telegram which ended:

> 'When you speak . . . of "a superhuman effort", you mean I presume, an effort rising superior to space, time and geography. Unfortunately, such attributes are denied us.'

---

[1] The German order of battle for September 1941, shows 37 infantry and 1 Panzer division under OB. West and 1 Panzer and 31 Ersatz divisions in Germany.

His answer to M. Stalin, though more diplomatically phrased, was equally final. It held out no hope of a major diversion at least in the current year:

> 'I reply at once in the spirit of your message. Although we should shrink from no exertion, there is, in fact, no possibility of any British action in the West except air action, which could draw the German forces from the East before the winter sets in. There is no chance whatever of a second front being formed in the Balkans without Turkey. I will, if your Excellency desires, give all the reasons which have led our Chiefs of Staff to these conclusions. They have already been discussed with your Ambassador in conference with the Foreign Secretary and the Chiefs of Staff. Action, however well meant, leading only to costly fiascos, would be no help to anyone but Hitler . . .'

[Here followed the passage about supply, which has already been quoted.]

> '. . . We are ready to make joint plans with you now. Whether British armies will be strong enough to invade the mainland of Europe in 1942 must depend on unforeseeable events. It may be possible, however, to assist you in the extreme North when there is more darkness. We are hoping to raise our armies in the Middle East to a strength of three quarters of a million before the end of the present year and thereafter to a million by the summer of 1942. Once the German-Italian forces in Libya have been destroyed, all these forces will be available to come into line on your southern flank, and it is hoped to encourage Turkey to maintain at least a faithful neutrality. Meanwhile, we shall continue to batter Germany from the air with increasing severity and to keep the seas open and ourselves alive.'

M. Stalin did not respond to this offer of further discussion. No doubt, in the bleak and ruthless atmosphere in which he lived, discussions and explanations appeared equally otiose. The issue was simple: either the British Government could be persuaded or compelled to do as he wished, or they could not. The reasons, or the reasons given, for their attitude were relatively unimportant. Nevertheless, he seems to have pondered the Prime Minister's message; and his reply, received on 15th September, outlined a new proposal, which may well have been based on his reading of the last paragraph quoted:

> 'In my last message I stated the viewpoint of the Soviet Government that the establishment of a second front is the most fundamental remedy for the improvement of the situation with regard to our common cause. In reply to your message, in which you stress once more the impossibility of a second front at the present moment, I can only reiterate that the absence of a second front simply favours the designs of our common enemy.

I have no doubt that the British Government desires to see the Soviet Government victorious and is looking for ways and means to attain this end. If, as they think, the establishment of a second front in the West is at present impossible, perhaps another method could be found to render the Soviet Union an active military help?

It seems to me that Great Britain could without any risk land in Archangel 25 to 30 divisions or transport them across Iran to the southern regions of the U.S.S.R. In this way there could be established military co-operation between the Soviet and British troops on the territory of the U.S.S.R. A similar situation existed during the last war in France. The arrangement mentioned would constitute a great help. It would be a serious blow against the Hitler aggression.'

The impracticability of this plan needs no emphasis. We were being invited, in effect, to transfer to Russia all the field-divisions which we then had in the United Kingdom or twice the number that we had in the Middle East. Even if transport had been available, no Government could have considered such a proposition for a moment. It is even difficult to believe that Stalin himself meant the plan seriously. One might suppose that his message was a mere retort, made with some object of capitalizing on our inevitable refusal. But apparently this was not so. The vigour with which it was pressed subsequently, suggests that the plan was put forward in earnest and in the belief that it was operationally feasible. Such a complete misconception on the part of a Government, to whom normal sources of information were open, is almost impossible to explain; but some speculation may be allowed.

M. Stalin's message was sent at a moment of acute crisis. The battle for Kiev was ending; Budyonny's army group had been thrown back in disorder; and withdrawals were already beginning in the eastern Ukraine and the Donetz Basin. Within a week or ten days Halder would be making jubilant notes about the possibility of a general breakdown in the south, which would split the Russian front in two. In the meanwhile German pressure in the centre had only slackened temporarily; and a renewed drive on Moscow was expected at any moment. It was an open question whether the Red Army would be able to meet this double threat. There can have been few reserves left, apart from the divisions in the Far East, and none of the first quality. The prodigious losses of the past three months had almost destroyed the military organization with which Russia had entered the war. For the moment, despite her immense reserves of man-power, she was woefully short of formed bodies of troops to fill the line. It is not surprising that the Soviet leaders should have looked enviously at the intact and well-equipped divisions, not yet committed to battle, which they knew to exist in the West. To call them in from

two thousand miles away to support the front was a desperate expedient; but at the time it may have seemed, not merely a possible
course, but the only one. It may be added that there is some evidence
from German sources that the plan originated with Marshal Timoshenko, then the Red Army's senior field-commander.[1] If so, it is
unnecessary to look further for the motive than plain operational
necessity.

One further conjecture may be added. It is not impossible that
Stalin had arrived at a false estimate of British strength by misinter-
preting such round figures as were available to him. He knew from
the Prime Minister's telegram that we hoped soon to have 750,000
men in the Middle East; and he was probably also aware that there
were upwards of two million men on the ration-strength of Home
Forces. Arguing from his own experience and the relatively sparse
organization of the Red Army, he may have believed, or chosen to
assume, that these figures could be translated into a total of, say, 100
equivalent divisions. We know, if only from his remarks to General
Ismay at the Moscow Conference, that his notions of British military
capacity were vague; and, to one accustomed to think in Russian
terms, a wartime army of 100 divisions may well have seemed the
bare minimum of probability. Considered in this light, his plan was
less fantastic than it appeared. True, it ignored completely the almost
insuperable problems of transport and subsequent supply. But if
these points had been raised, M. Stalin would perhaps have answered
that sea transport should present no difficulty to a maritime power; or
alternatively, that the movement of 25 divisions across Persia was no
worse a logistic problem than many which the Red Army had had to
face in its current operations.

If these were indeed the arguments which the Soviet leaders used
in their own minds, no short answer was possible. The fallacy in their
reasoning could only have been made clear by a long dissertation on
the defence of the British Isles, the Battle of the Atlantic and its
effect on the shipping position, the nature of the Middle Eastern
theatre with its insatiable demand for second-line and administrative
units, even the relative standards of equipment and mobility of the
British and Russian armies. All these were problems with which
Stalin and his advisers were only dimly acquainted; and it is doubtful
how far they really wished to be enlightened. Nothing would have
moved them, in any case, from their primary position, that the duty
of an ally was to contribute to the defence of the U.S.S.R. at the time
and in the way that the Soviet Government indicated. The idea of an
alliance based on discussion, mutual understanding and the adjustment of conflicting interests was foreign to their whole way of

[1] *Fremde Heer West*, report of 15th November, 1941.

thought. The centralized and supremely egotistic régime in the Kremlin had no procedure to meet such a case and little wish to evolve one.

Mr. Churchill did not reply to Stalin's message at length; it would have been useless to do so. The military facts had already been laid before the ambassador; and if they had not been understood or believed, nothing was to be gained by repeating them. He therefore confined himself to saying:

'All possible theatres in which we might effect military co-operation with you have been examined by the Staffs. The two flanks, north and south, certainly present the most favourable opportunities. If we could act successfully in Norway the attitude of Sweden would be powerfully affected, but at the moment we have neither the forces nor the shipping available for this project. Again, in the south the great prize is Turkey; if Turkey can be gained another powerful army will be available. Turkey would like to come with us, but is afraid, not without reason. It may be that the promise of considerable British forces and supplies of technical material, in which the Turks are deficient, will exercise a decisive influence upon them. We will study with you any other form of useful aid, the sole object being to bring the maximum force against the common enemy.'

(iii)

Norway and Sweden

The reference to Norway in this telegram needs some elaboration. It will be remembered that an attack on German positions in the Kirkenes area had been discussed at the very beginning of the Russian campaign, but rejected for the same reasons as made a landing in the West impracticable. The Prime Minister had never been wholly satisfied with this decision. The importance of the northern theatre was obvious; and it seemed to him to offer certain advantages from the attacker's point of view. Neither side could deploy large forces in that difficult terrain, so that the German advantage in numbers would be largely offset. In the winter the long Arctic nights would reduce air-activity to a minimum. If we succeeded in gaining a foothold in northern Norway and were able later to develop our operations to the south, we could count on the vigorous and effective support of local patriots. Their attitude, in turn, would affect that of Sweden, whose armed forces, though not large, were serviceable and well-equipped.

It was also in the Prime Minister's mind that Finland was not irrevocably tied to the Nazi cause, with which, indeed, she had little sympathy beyond a shared dislike of Russia.

For these reasons Mr. Churchill continued to press for action in the North. At the end of August, when reports of an impending German offensive against Murmansk provided a suitable occasion, he instructed the Chiefs of Staff to re-examine the whole problem. He suggested that an operation on the scale of four divisions might be considered for the following January or February. But this project, though superficially attractive, could be shown to have many flaws and difficulties. The first was the size and composition of the force. We could only muster three Brigades and one Mountain regiment suitably trained and equipped for winter warfare in the Arctic; and even this force could not be complete before March. The Germans, on the other hand, had six divisions divided between northern Norway and the Murmansk front. They were well equipped and acclimatized and could be rapidly reinforced either from the rest of the German garrison in Norway or by Finnish troops. The second problem was air-cover. Though it was true that during the winter months from November to April flying weather would be at its worst, three of the German aerodromes in northern Norway were equipped for winter flying and could probably mount a scale of attack, which we should not be able to meet from carriers. Lastly, there was the choice of an objective. In winter a landing on open beaches would be impossible; and we should be confined to an attack on one of the five ports in the area with sufficient wharfage to disembark the force. Three of these— Narvik, Tromsoe and Kirkenes—were known to be well defended and a direct assault was considered impracticable; one, Harstadt, was on an island, so that its capture would not open the way to further operations. This left Petsamo, the least suitable of the five from the point of view of port accommodation. Little was known of its defences; but it was not thought likely that a sea-borne attack would succeed unless combined with an overland offensive from Murmansk. But in that event the operation would become a predominantly Russian affair, in which we should play only a small supporting rôle.

These negative conclusions were not to the Prime Minister's taste, who would certainly have pressed the matter further but for an unexpected intervention, which changed the whole character of the problem. For some months past Sweden had been involved in a legal and diplomatic wrangle with Germany over the possession of some Norwegian ships, then lying in Swedish ports, which were claimed by Germany as the Occupying Power and by us on behalf of the lawful Norwegian Government. By the middle of September this dispute was coming to a head; and there was a growing suspicion on the Swedish side that Germany was deliberately exploiting it as a pretext to justify invasion. The Swedish Secretary-General therefore approached the British Minister to inquire, in veiled and tentative terms, what our attitude would be and what help we could give in such a case. It was understood that the Swedish General Staff had a plan to seize Trondheim as a port of entry for aid from the West; but no details were available and, in the circumstances, consultation or even informal contact was out of the question.

It seemed at first as if this development might open a new and hopeful field of action. Considered simply as a tactical exercise, the capture of Trondheim by an Anglo-Swedish operation was certainly possible. The Swedes, it was assumed, would use a force of approximately two divisions, directing one half by the northern route through Grong and Levanger with the secondary task of blocking German reinforcements from northern Norway, and the other by the southern route through Röros with the task of blocking reinforcements from the Oslo area. The whole operation would be covered by long-range aircraft based on Östersund. While these movements were in progress, a British Brigade Group, supported by carrier-based aircraft, would attack Namsos from the sea. As soon as that town had fallen, a second Brigade Group would land and the whole force would then join hands with the right wing of the Swedish advance. It was expected that Trondheim itself would be captured a fortnight later; but a further allowance of time would be required to clear the approaches and bring the port back into action.

Unfortunately this plan—the only feasible one from the military point of view—ignored the political realities of the case. The Swedes had already indicated that they could not concert plans with us in advance. It was equally unlikely that they would be willing to take the initiative to the extent of beginning their movement on Trondheim before they had actually been attacked by Germany. But any delay would enable the Germans to raise the existing garrison to a strength of at least three divisions with a proportionate air force; and in that event the attack would certainly fail. The only alternative was for us to take the initiative and open our own attack on Trondheim before either the Germans or the Swedes had moved. For that purpose we should have to put not less than three Brigades ashore at Namsos. The overland movement on Trondheim could begin as soon as the second Brigade had landed; but, owing to the shortage of landing-craft, that would not be until at least D+5. A further fifteen to eighteen days would elapse before we could expect to capture the Trondheim airfields. During this period we should be dependent for air-support on 120 aircraft of the Fleet Air Arm, the maximum force which we could operate from carriers. This would be wholly insufficient in face of the expected scale of German attack. Moreover, with no Swedish force in the field, the Germans would be able to use these three weeks to reinforce Trondheim with one, or more probably two, divisions. If so, an assault with three Brigades was unlikely to succeed.

When a report in this sense was made to the Prime Minister, he was at first inclined to dismiss it as 'a mere catalogue of difficulties'. This was unfair. The essential flaw in the whole operation was the time needed for an overland advance from Namsos to Trondheim; but this was imposed by the nature of the ground and the impossibility of operating carriers in the enclosed waters round Trondheim itself. Although every possible expedient was examined, including diversionary landings and the use of parachute troops,[1] no satisfactory solution could be found. The plain fact was that the capture of Trondheim, an operation which we had attempted in vain in 1940, was still beyond our means without a degree of co-operation from Sweden which would certainly not be forthcoming.

By the time this conclusion was reached, the urgency of the problem had faded. During October, perhaps as the result of growing difficulties in Russia, Germany slackened her pressure on Sweden. The dispute over the Norwegian ships was transferred to the law-courts, where a learned but peaceful argument dragged on for many months. When the Supreme Court finally gave judgement against Germany in March of the following year, no military consequences followed or were expected.

(iv)

The Caucasus

We must now return to the main story. Mr. Churchill's telegram about the two flanks was received with keen disappointment in Moscow, where it was taken to mean that the British Government had dismissed out of hand any idea of sending a force to Russia. This, though a natural inference from the text, was not entirely true. As we saw in an earlier chapter, the dispatch of a small British force to the Caucasus was already under discussion. This was one of the projects which it was hoped to examine with the Russians when the Supply Conference met in Moscow at the end of the month. If the Prime Minister had not referred to it in his telegram, that was largely because further argument at long range seemed futile; the gap between what Stalin proposed and we could perform was too wide to be bridged by such methods. The delegation to the Supply Conference

---

[1] Only one battalion of parachute troops then existed; it had not yet completed its training.

was, however, provided with an elaborate brief setting out the true facts of our military position and indicating the scale and type of operation which we could carry out. In this way the Prime Minister hoped both to soften the impact of his telegram and to inject some measure of reality into future discussions.

In the end, as we have seen, no military conversations took place in Moscow. This was much to be regretted. Our relations with the Russians would have run more smoothly over the next few months, if they had not denied themselves this opportunity of learning what we could do and what we could not. Why they did so must remain obscure. Perhaps it was only natural intransigence; or perhaps a deeper misunderstanding clouded the issue. It will be remembered that one passage in the Prime Minister's telegram referred to the promise made to Turkey of 'considerable British forces and supplies'. It is conceivable that M. Stalin, ignoring the context, saw in this phrase a confirmation of his worst suspicions. Did he understand it to mean that, although a force such as he was asking for existed, we preferred to use it to support a neutral Turkey, rather than commit it to action alongside the Red Army? If so, his resentment and certain brutal comments, made then and later, about our desire to put troops where there was no fighting, are more easily explained. But this is speculation. We can only record that the Russians, from whatever motive, avoided conversations at the very moment when they were pressing us most strongly to undertake operations in their support.

Nevertheless, planning for the Caucasus project continued. At the end of September and the beginning of October a German break-through at the southern end of the Russian front appeared only too probable. If it occurred, the defence of the Caucasus would become a matter of vital importance to us no less than the Russians. Our two interests were, however, slightly divergent. To the Russians the Caucasus was the southern anchor of their main front, which then extended in a slanting, irregular line from Leningrad to Rostov. It was their purpose to bring the defence as far forward as possible and to fight, if not at Rostov itself, then in the area between Rostov and Astrakhan. To us the Caucasus had another significance; in the event of a Russian collapse it would become the first line of defence against an attack on our Middle East positions from the north. Under these conditions it would suit us best to keep the defence as far south as possible and make the main stand on the mountain-barrier itself.

These differences were not irreconcilable; but other factors in the problem served to stress their importance. The capacity of the Persian road and railway system was very limited and already fully taken up with the carriage of supplies to Russia. If the whole system were turned over instead to the transport and supply of troops, it would only suffice to maintain a maximum of three British divisions

15

or forty-five R.A.F. squadrons in the Caucasus.[1] Alternatively, if the railways were kept free for Russian supplies and only the roads used for troop movement, a force of one Brigade or five squadrons could be maintained in winter, rising to a maximum of two divisions or thirty squadrons in summer. A force of this size would have little value in the open country to the north of the Caucasus, though it might make an important contribution to the defence of the mountain barrier. In either case, its usefulness to the Russians would be partly offset by the stoppage of supplies along the Persian route, which might become of great importance during the winter, if Archangel and the northern ports were icebound.

The problem was complex and nicely balanced. On the whole the Chiefs of Staff were inclined to favour limited action in the sense of putting a force of two or three divisions on the mountain-line but not beyond. If the German advances continued as expected, this would bring British troops into action with the Red Army and go some way to satisfy Russia's demands. A successful defence on this line would cover not only our own positions in the Middle East but also the main Russian oilfield at Baku, which it was of great importance to deny to the enemy. On the other hand, it would not be easy to find the necessary force at once. The Indian Army divisions in Iraq and Persia were not considered suitable for the purpose; and almost all the divisions in the Middle East were already involved in the preparations for 'Crusader'.[2] Even divisions not scheduled to take part in that operation had been largely stripped of their transport and rearward services. The first step, therefore, was to consult the two Commanders-in-Chief as to what troops they could spare by what date. On the basis of their reply we could decide whether or not to make a formal offer to Russia.

The Prime Minister took a different view. He was not convinced that the Germans would penetrate into the Caucasus that winter. If they did not, and we already had a force in motion, the Russians would certainly press us to send it forward to Astrakhan or wherever fighting was still in progress. Once there, its position would be precarious and its lines of communication awkward and exposed. He also found it difficult to accept the argument that the Russians really needed troops on any sector of their front. A reinforcement of two or three divisions would mean little or nothing to them by comparison with the loss of supplies through Persia. He therefore favoured another expedient. On 12th October he telegraphed to M. Stalin suggesting that we should assume responsibility for the occupation of

---

[1] i.e., with communications as they were; when planned improvements had been carried out, the total would rise to seven divisions.

[2] The proposed offensive in the Western Desert.

the whole of Persia, thus releasing five or six Russian divisions for service at the front without interrupting the flow of supplies. He offered a guarantee that we would protect Russia's interests equally with our own.

No formal reply was ever made to this proposal, though we were left in no doubt about Russia's attitude. Sir Stafford Cripps reported that M. Molotov had protested bitterly when the telegram was handed to him. Why, he had asked, could British troops not go to the front instead of to Persia, where there was no fighting? A few days later the Russian Ambassador repeated almost the same phrases to Mr. Eden. During the next fortnight further dispatches arrived from Sir Stafford Cripps, which emphasized the growing atmosphere of suspicion and distrust in Moscow. M. Molotov had complained that his Government were still without a reply to their request for twenty-five or thirty divisions to be transferred to the Russian front. This was not strictly true; but it was useless to deny that strong feeling existed in official circles, in the Red Army and, so far as he could judge, in the country as a whole about our continued failure to help Russia. It was his considered opinion that, if we wished to preserve good relations, we ought to make an immediate offer to bring at least one Corps with appropriate air-support into action on either the northern or the southern flank of the Russian line.

Simultaneously with these disturbing reports the J.I.C. circulated an up-to-date estimate of the military position. Germany, it was thought, would make a major effort to reach the Caucasus before the end of the year, mainly because of her need for oil but also partly in order to secure positions for a subsequent attack on the Middle East. She had three armoured and three motorized divisions in the Rostov area, which could be rapidly reinforced from other sectors of the front. Although most of her troops had been in continuous action since the beginning of September and were therefore in need of rest, it was judged that she could still produce a powerful striking force. The country beyond Rostov was ideally adapted to armoured warfare; and a rapid advance could easily maintain itself on local supplies of food and fuel. The weather was extremely variable, but on the whole less unfavourable to a winter campaign than in other parts of Russia. Distances, however, were immense; it was 1,300 miles from Rostov to Baku by the shortest route.

The Russians were believed to have a total of twenty four divisions on the Caucasus front, including their divisions in northern Persia. Of these, seven had already been drawn into the battle for Rostov, where they had suffered heavy losses, and nine were reserve divisions of doubtful quality. There thus remained only eight first-line divisions, as yet uncommitted, for the defence of the whole area. This force might be joined by units extricated from the fighting round

Rostov or evacuated from the Crimea; but it could be assumed that these would be exhausted and would have lost a great part of their equipment. The Russians were therefore unlikely to be able to maintain their defence for very long. Under the worst conditions, if there were a general collapse in the south, the Germans might reach the line of the Caucasus Mountains by the end of November; at best, if Russian resistance stiffened, they might do so by the end of January. It was at this point, however, that their real difficulties would begin. The subsequent advance on Baku would be confined to a narrow coastal strip, no more than fifteen or twenty miles wide, between the mountains and the Caspian. There were many good defensive positions; and almost any degree of resistance would impose a delay of at least a month or six weeks. Under no conditions would the Germans be able to cross the mountain barrier in force before the spring.

The Cabinet had this document before them as well as Sir Stafford Cripps' dispatches, when they met to consider the position in the last week of October. To some extent the Ambassador's conclusions and those of the J.I.C. pulled in opposite directions. It was the essence of Sir Stafford's proposal that our force should join the main battle in south Russia; but if the J.I.C. were right, that battle would almost certainly be over before the force could reach the scene of action. On the other hand, the local defence of the mountain line was a less urgent problem, since the Russians would probably be able to meet from their own resources any scale of attack which the Germans could mount before the spring. But there was no guarantee that the J.I.C. were right; in fact, as we have seen, they had greatly over-estimated Germany's offensive capacity. Thus all the original uncertainties remained and had even been slightly aggravated. There were stronger reasons than ever for sending a force to Russia, but equally strong reasons for supposing that it would be useless to do so, at any rate for the moment. From the military point of view our wisest course was to wait and see.

The Cabinet finally decided to make no immediate offer to Russia but to invite the views of the Commander-in-Chief, India, and the Commander-in-Chief, Middle East, on a new and detailed proposal. It was suggested that the 50th Division, then in Cyprus, and the 18th Division, then *en route* to the Middle East, should form the nucleus of a small expeditionary force to be based on Baku. They might be joined later by one of the British-Indian divisions from Persia or Iraq. Air support would be provided by four Hurricane squadrons from the United Kingdom, reinforced either by four squadrons from Middle East or by two squadrons from Middle East and the two Hurricane squadrons then at Murmansk. It was intended that the two leading divisions should be in place by the end of January. By that time the Germans would probably have reached the Caucasus range; but if they had not, the force must be prepared to operate farther north. The whole operation would be under the control of the Commander-in-Chief, India, and would take priority immediately below 'Crusader' but above normal supplies to Russia.

(v)

Misunderstandings

While comments on this plan were being awaited, a further dispatch was received from Sir Stafford Cripps which enlarged the scope of his previous argument:

> 'You will recall that it was thought worth while to send the Foreign Secretary and the C.I.G.S. for some weeks to the Middle East in order to try and organize the defence of the Balkans when conditions there became serious, and yet so far as this country is concerned, where conditions are no less serious from our point of view, not only is His Majesty's Government unwilling to enter into consultations with the Soviet Government as to the best method of employing our combined forces against the common enemy but they are apparently not prepared to give the Soviet Government a reasoned statement through the mouth of someone fully qualified by status and knowledge to explain the situation to Stalin. . . .
>
> Hitherto the Soviet Staff have displayed a marked lack of co-operation and communicativeness in their dealings with the Military Mission, but they led the Mission to understand some time ago that as soon as we could do something on land to relieve the German pressure, they would be prepared to take the head of the Mission into their confidence. I have, as you know, had the same impression conveyed to me on more than one occasion.
>
> This is the reason why I associate the two matters of consultation and some form of assistance on the land front, since I feel if we were to initiate consultations solely for the purpose of explaining we could do nothing, we should not materially improve the situation though it might help to prevent a deterioration.'

Here the Ambassador was overstating his case. So far from being unwilling to hold military discussions, we had felt ourselves rebuffed on this very point at the Supply Conference. Nor was it reasonable that Russian 'co-operation and communicativeness' should depend on our accepting in advance plans which we were unable, or did not think it wise, to carry out. It was clear that Sir Stafford had so far absorbed the atmosphere of the country as to interpret words like 'discussion' and 'co-operation' in a strictly Soviet sense. Nevertheless, there was force in his argument. It was true, no matter by whose fault, that the Soviet Government had not received a full account of our military position, any more than we had received one of theirs; and there was no doubt that they harboured a number of gross misconceptions. The sooner these were removed the better. If the normal channels did not suffice, as they readily could have done, extraordinary measures would have to be taken.

On 4th November the Prime Minister sent a further telegram to Marshal Stalin:

> 'In order to clear things up and plan for the future, I am ready to send General Wavell, Commander-in-Chief in India, Persia and Iraq, to meet you in Moscow, Kuibyshev, Tiflis or wherever you will. Besides this, General Paget, our new Commander-in-Chief secretly designated for the Far East, will come with General Wavell. General Paget has been at the centre of things here and will have with him the latest and best opinions of our High Command. These two officers will be able to tell you exactly how we stand, what is possible and what we think is wise. They can reach you in about a fortnight. Do you want them?'

This choice of emissaries was a natural one. General Wavell spoke Russian and operations in the Caucasus would be under his jurisdiction. General Paget, the former Chief of Staff, Home Forces, was as well placed as anyone to explain why we could neither attack across the Channel nor spare twenty-five divisions for the Russian front. But it may have been unwise, nevertheless, to plan the mission on a purely military footing. The quarrel over the second front, though the most urgent, was only one of several issues, which then divided us from Russia. Important political questions were also involved, ranging from the future of the Baltic States to the minor but vexatious problem of Finland. This last point was already in active discussion. Immediately after the German attack, the Soviet Government had pressed us to declare war on Finland; but we had demurred, hoping that with the help of the United States means might be found to persuade Finland to withdraw voluntarily. This had failed to satisfy the Russians; and the Prime Minister now reverted to the subject in the second paragraph of the telegram just quoted:

> 'We told you in my message of 6th September that we were willing to declare war on Finland. Will you however, consider whether it is really good business that Great Britain should declare war on Finland, Hungary and Rumania at this moment? It is only a formality, because our extreme blockade is already in force against them. My judgement is against it, because first, Finland has many friends in the United States and it is prudent to take account of this fact, secondly, Rumania and Hungary: these

countries are full of our friends, they have been overpowered by Hitler and used as a cat's paw, but if fortune turns against that ruffian, they might easily come back to our side. A British declaration of war would only freeze them all and make it look as if Hitler was the head of a grand European alliance solid against us. Do not, pray, suppose it is any lack of zeal or comradeship that makes us doubt the advantages of this step. Our Dominions, except Australia, are reluctant. Nevertheless, if you think it will be a real help to you and worth while, I will put it to the Cabinet again'.

The conjunction between this message and the proposal that Generall Wavell and General Paget should visit Moscow proved unhappy, though for a reason which could not have been foreseen. Before writing to Stalin, Mr. Churchill had communicated with President Roosevelt to ask his advice and the help of the United States. An unfortunate leakage of information followed on the American side, with the result that the whole question of Finland's status *vis-à-vis* the Western Allies became a matter of public discussion in the Press. Nothing could have incensed the Soviet Government more. They took the episode as a deliberate affront; and their sense of resentment and injured pride was everywhere apparent in Stalin's reply:

'Your message received on 7th November. I fully agree with you that clarity should be established in the relations between the U.S.S.R. and Great Britain. Such clarity does not exist at present. The lack of clarity is the consequence of two circumstances:

(a) There is no definite understanding between our two countries on war aims and plans for the post-war organization of peace;

(b) There is no agreement between the U.S.S.R. and Great Britain on mutual military assistance against Hitler in Europe.

As long as there is no accord on both these questions there can be no clarity in the Anglo-Soviet relations. More than that: to be frank, as long as the present situation exists there will be difficulty in securing mutual confidence. Of course the agreement on military supplies to the U.S.S.R. had great positive value, but it does not settle, neither does it exhaust, the whole problem of relations between our two countries. If the General Wavell and the General Paget whom you mention in your message will come to Moscow with a view to concluding agreement on the two fundamental questions referred to above, I naturally would be happy to meet them and to discuss with them these questions. If, however, the mission of the Generals is confined to questions of information, and to the consideration of secondary matters, it would not be, I think, worth while to intrude upon the Generals. In such a case it would also be very difficult for me to find time for the conversations.

It seems to me that an intolerable situation has been created in the declaration of war by Great Britain on Finland, Hungary and Rumania. The Soviet Government raised this question with the British Government through the secret diplomatic channels. Quite unexpectedly for the U.S.S.R. the whole problem, beginning with the request of the Soviet Government to the British Government and ending with the consideration of this question by the United States Government, received wide publicity. The whole problem is now being discussed at random in the Press— friendly as well as enemy. And after all that the British Government informs us of its negative attitude to our proposal. Why is all this being done? To demonstrate the lack of unity between the U.S.S.R. and Great Britain?'

Mr. Churchill did not answer this message. Indeed, no answer was possible; the only course was to wait and hope that M. Stalin would recover his equanimity. In the meanwhile the replies from India and the Middle East had been received, and did not suggest that either Commander was wholly in favour of the Caucasus operation. They pointed out that a German attack from this quarter was not the only threat that Middle East might have to face in the following year. There was also the danger of an alternative or supplementary thrust through Anatolia, an operation which the Germans were known to have planned. In order to meet this and give Turkey the help which she had been promised in the event of an attack, Middle East would require replacements for the 18th and 50th divisions and any other major formations sent to the Caucasus. It was also considered essential that the Caucasus force should include an armoured element, which Middle East could not provide. Subject to these conditions, a build-up was proposed in five stages:

   (i) Air forces and troops for their defence;
  (ii) Equipment and munitions, including supplies for Russian land or air forces operating in the Caucasus;
 (iii) Engineers and other specialized units;
 (iv) Armoured formations;
  (v) Infantry.

It was assumed that there would be a considerable gap in time between the third stage and the fourth and fifth. Since transport would be the main problem, it might even be better to send no infantry divisions or, if they were sent, to hold them back near the base ports in Persia, so as to free the lines of communication for supplies.

These comments seemed to indicate that the two Commanders had a different view of the whole operation from that prevailing in London. They assumed that our intervention in the Caucasus would be little more than a reconnaissance. Even the defence of the mountain-line was to be left almost entirely to the Russians; and nothing was said about operations farther north. This attitude was partly explained by their reference to Anatolia, where they clearly expected a major threat to develop in the spring. Further justification could be found in the forecast time-table of our own and the enemy's movements. It was now estimated that, if the Germans crossed the Don by 15th November, they would reach Baku even in the face of strong Russian resistance not later than the end of February. But it was not expected that we could place either the 18th or the 50th division in Trans-Caucasia before 15th March at the earliest.

If these assumptions were correct, the Commanders-in-Chief had a strong case. But they were on less certain ground in arguing, as they seemed to do, that an operation in the Caucasus would conflict with our obligations to Turkey. All our promises to Turkey, so far as they concerned ground-forces, had been made conditional on the state of our reserves at the time. In any case, until the Turks improved communications, we could not maintain more than one or two divisions in Anatolia; and the Chiefs of Staff considered that Middle East could, if necessary, find a force of this size as well as the two divisions for the Caucasus. The only real problem was air-support. Any squadrons sent to the Caucasus would have to be subtracted from the number promised to Turkey; but this could probably be done by agreement, since the defence of the Caucasus, which covered her eastern flank, was as much in Turkey's interests as ours. On balance, therefore, the Chiefs of Staff were in favour of adhering to the original plan; and the Commanders-in-Chief were informed accordingly:

> 'Although Russians are still being sticky about telling us their intentions and dispositions, and have not reacted to our offer of Staff Conversations, we must be in a position to give them a firm offer of assistance the moment they show signs of being more forthcoming. We consider offer should be a corps of two divisions, 18th and 50th, one A/C Squadron, six fighter and one Bomber squadron, to be available for operations by the end of March'.

Planning for the move was to begin at once.

By this time, however, an alternative was under discussion. On 5th November the Prime Minister had sent the following minute to the Chiefs of Staff:

> 'We do not know when the Germans will arrive in the Caucasus, nor how long it will be before they came up against the mountain barrier. We do not know what the Russians will do, how many troops they will use or how long they will resist. It is quite certain that if the Germans press hard neither the 18th nor the 50th British divisions could be on the spot in time, and the British-Indian divisions in Persia and Iraq would not be good enough to send. We are held in a grip by the delay in 'Crusader' and it is not possible to see beyond that at the present moment. I cannot feel any confidence that the Germans will be prevented from occupy-

ing the Baku oilfields or that the Russians will effectively destroy these fields. The Russians tell us nothing and view with great suspicion any inquiries we make on this subject.

The only thing we have it in our power to do is to base four or five heavy bombing squadrons in Northern Persia to aid the Russians in the defence of the Caucasus, if that be possible, and if the worst happens, to bomb the Baku oilfields effectively and try to set the ground alight. These squadrons will of course require fighter protection. Neither bombers nor fighters can be provided till after 'Crusader' and its consequences can be judged. A plan should, however, be made, based on a large transference of Air from Libya to Persia, so as to achieve the denial of the oilfields to the enemy as long as possible. Pray let this be done during the next week, so that we can see what is involved. One cannot tell how long the Russians will retain command of the Black Sea, although with their forces it is inexcusable they should lose it.'

Although this minute gave an accurate picture of the situation, it did not solve the problem. The new plan offered almost as many difficulties as the old. Since the Russians had so far refused all facilities for reconnaissance, we had little detailed knowledge of the aerodromes in northern Persia. It was understood, however, that none was suitable for the operation of heavy bombers without extensive improvements, which could only be put in hand with Russian co-operation. A force of medium bombers could be sent but would probably not be equal to the task of destroying the oilfields.

(vi)

Invitation to Eden

When matters had reached this point, some welcome signs of ease-ment began to appear in Russia's attitude. On 20th November M. Maisky called on the Foreign Secretary with a small olive-branch in his hand. He said that M. Stalin's object in sending his recent tele-gram had been purely practical and business-like. He had had no intention of giving offence to any member of the Government, least of all to the Prime Minister. The truth was that Stalin was concen-trating his whole attention on military affairs. He had, however, felt the difficulties and embarrassments of the recent Finnish dispute most acutely, but despite that was still pursuing the same goal—to secure agreement on combined operations against Hitler and on the post-war organization of peace.[1] This partial apology was followed by other gestures. The Russian Chief of Staff at Tiflis suddenly became ready

---

[1] Churchill, Vol. III, pp. 470-1.

to answer questions about roads, railways and aerodromes in the Caucasus; and it was even indicated that a party of demolition experts would be received at Baku.

It is difficult to assign any reason for this sudden lightening of the atmosphere. By late November the German threat to the Caucasus, though not yet over, was considerably less than it had been a month before. The speed of the advance had slackened, and Timoshenko's counterstroke was about to be launched. The immediate crisis, in which the Russians had originally invoked our help, might be said to have passed. It may have been this release of tension which made them more accommodating and enabled them to see the uselessness of quarrelling with their only ally. Or perhaps, since it was no longer necessary to press their demand for troops so insistently, they were the more hopeful of reaching an agreement.

Whatever its motive, this sudden comparative friendliness called for a response. This could no longer be made in purely military terms. The extended discussions recorded above had made it clear that we should find it very difficult to put an adequate force, whether a ground-force or an air force, into the Caucasus for another three or four months at least. By that time the whole situation might have changed; it might become necessary to explore an entirely different field of action. Moreover, the tone of M. Stalin's recent telegram had suggested that broader and more important questions were at issue than whether we did or did not undertake a particular operation. The Prime Minister therefore reverted to the proposal which Sir Stafford Cripps had made, or rather implied, a month earlier. On 21st November he telegraphed to Stalin:

'Many thanks for your message just received. At the very beginning of the war I began a personal correspondence with President Roosevelt, which led to a very solid understanding being established between us and has often helped in getting things done quickly. My only desire is to work on equal terms of comradeship and confidence with you.

About Finland. I was quite ready to advise the Cabinet to declare war upon Finland when I sent you my telegram of 5th September. Later information has made me think that it will be more helpful to Russia and the common cause if the Finns can be got to stop fighting and stand still or go home, than if we put them in the dock with the guilty Axis powers by a formal declaration of war and make them fight it out to the end. However, if they do not stop in the next fortnight and you still wish us to declare war on them, we will certainly do so . . .

Should our offensive in Libya result, as we hope, in the destruction of the German-Italian armies there, it will be possible to take a broad survey of the war as a whole, with more freedom than has hitherto been open to His Majesty's Government.

For this purpose we are willing in the near future to send the Foreign Secretary, Mr. Eden, whom you know, via the Mediterranean to meet you at Moscow or elsewhere. He would be accompanied by high military and other experts, and would be able to discuss every question relating to the war, including the sending of troops not only into the Caucasus but into the fighting line of your army in the South. Neither our resources nor the communications will allow large numbers to be employed and even so you will have to choose between troops and supplies across Persia'.

M. Stalin's reply was almost cordial:

'I support by all means your proposal of an early visit to the U.S.S.R. by the Foreign Secretary, Mr. Eden. I believe our joint consideration and acceptance of an agreement concerning the common military operations of the Soviet and British forces at our front, as well as speedy realization of such an agreement, would have a great positive value'.

After further discussion the date of the meeting was fixed for the second week of December.

CHAPTER IX

CRUSADER

(i)

The Build-up

THE FOUR MONTHS' DELAY in the Middle East, on which Auchinleck had insisted, served many purposes. It gave time for the new organization under the Minister of State to establish itself and to make important progress in developing the base and improving the rearward services. It also enabled Auchinleck to complete an extensive regrouping of his forces. In September, as we have seen, the formation of East Africa Command relieved him of responsibility for the fighting in Abyssinia and the administration of a vast stretch of territory south of the Sudan. The next step was to create two Army Headquarters to replace the improvised staffs, which had hitherto controlled operations in the rest of the theatre. At the beginning of October the old Western Desert Force was reconstituted as Eighth Army with two Corps, the 13th and the 30th, under command. In the following month the same headquarters also took control of the Tobruk garrison, then at the strength of one augmented division. The forces in Syria and Palestine were similarly grouped into Ninth Army, also of two Corps, the 1st Australian, of which more will be said later, and 10th Corps, a miscellaneous formation partly composed of Free French and other Allied troops. Outside these two main commands there was one division in Cyprus and a small improvised armoured force and a number of unbrigaded battalions in the Delta.[1]

Within this general reorganization Auchinleck's other and most urgent task was the reconstitution of his armour. In July, when he took up his command, the only complete armoured formation in the theatre was the 7th Division in the desert, badly in need of refitting. In addition there was the 1st Armoured Brigade in the Delta, which hardly existed except in name, some scattered units of Infantry Tanks and a number of light tanks and armoured cars, with which the Cavalry Division in Palestine, then in process of mechanization, was temporarily equipped. To bring this force to the minimum strength required for an offensive Auchinleck was relying on the punctual arrival of the 22nd Armoured Brigade from England, promised for

---

[1] Auchinleck's Dispatch.

the middle of September, and on supplies of American Stuart tanks with which to re-equip one brigade of the 7th Division. The 22nd Brigade was, however, delayed in transit and did not reach Egypt until the second week of October. Even then, by an error for which all parties disclaimed responsibility, the axles of its tanks were found to need an important modification to fit them for desert service. It was not therefore until the beginning of November that this brigade, after a minimum of desert training, could be regarded as ready for operations.

By that time the order of battle of the armoured forces presented a more hopeful appearance. The 7th Division had been re-equipped and could now be supported by the 22nd Brigade, acting as an independent formation. An Army Tank Brigade had been formed in Tobruk and another, attached to 13th Corps, was in process of forming. In Egypt the 1st Armoured Brigade was beginning to take on substance; and in Palestine the two Cavalry brigades were re-forming as the 10th Armoured Division. All in all, Auchinleck could now boast some 850 infantry and cruiser tanks in addition to his light tanks and armoured cars.

The regrouping of the Army was matched by a reorganization of local R.A.F. commands. This was a longer process as Tedder's command covered a wider area than Auchinleck's. It included Malta and Iraq and still retained the whole area in the south which had passed, on the Army side, to East Africa Command. By September air-operations in this part of the theatre were almost over; but two Groups, No. 203 in the Sudan and No. 207 in Kenya, remained in being and were turned over to maintenance and training respectively. Early in October No. 204 Group in the desert under Air Vice-Marshal Coningham was reinforced and raised to the status of an Air Headquarters, thus beginning the long and fruitful collaboration between 8th Army and the Desert Air Force. Two months later, after the desert offensive had started, a parallel headquarters, A.H.Q. Levant, was formed in Jerusalem to stand in the same relation to 9th Army. At the same time another Air Headquarters was brought into being in Egypt with responsibility for the air defence of the Delta. As subordinate commands already existed in Malta, Iraq and Aden, this left only two operational groups under the direct control of H.Q. Middle East: No. 205 Group comprising the long-range bomber force, and No. 201 (Naval Co-operation) Group, which formed a miniature Coastal Command.

This bringing into line of Army and Air Force headquarters was a first step towards closer co-operation between the two Services. It will be remembered that this was a point on which Auchinleck had laid great stress in one of his earliest telegrams to the Prime Minister.[1]

---

[1] See page 177 above.

He had then appeared to favour a form of co-operation which, carried to its logical conclusion, would have split the Air Force into three, one part serving the Army, one the Navy and one concentrating on long-range strategic operations. In his reply Mr. Churchill had made it clear that any system which encroached on the independence of the R.A.F. was out of the question. He agreed that in general the employment of the Air Force in a theatre of war should be governed by the Army's operational plans; but the proportion of the whole force to be used in direct support of the Army or the Navy or in strategic operations should be settled by consultation between the three Commanders. He later elaborated these remarks in a detailed directive:

'Nevermore must the Army expect, as a matter of course, to be protected against the air by aircraft. If this can be done, it must only be as a happy makeweight and a piece of good luck. Above all, the idea of keeping standing patrols of aircraft above moving columns should be abandoned. It is unsound to distribute aircraft in this way, and no air superiority will stand any large application of such a mischievous practice. Upon the military Commander-in-Chief in the Middle East announcing that a battle is in prospect, the Air Officer Commanding-in-Chief will give him all possible aid irrespective of other targets, however attractive. The Army Commander-in-Chief will specify to the Air Officer Commanding-in-Chief the targets and tasks which he requires to be performed, both in the preparatory attack on the rearward installations of the enemy and for air action during the progress of the battle.

'It will be for the Air Officer Commanding-in-Chief to use his maximum force on these objects in the manner most effective. This applies not only to any squadrons assigned to army co-operation permanently, but also to the whole Air Force available in the theatre. Bombers may, if required, be used as transport or supply machines to far-ranging or outlying columns of troops, the sole object being the success of the military operation. As the interests of the two Commanders-in-Chief are identical, it is not thought any difficulty should arise. The Air Officer Commanding-in-Chief would naturally lay aside all routine programmes and concentrate on bombing the rearward services of the enemy in the preparatory period. This he would do not only by night, but by day attacks with fighter protection. In this process he will bring about a trial of strength with the enemy fighters and has the best chance of obtaining local command of the air. What is true of the preparatory period applies with even greater force during the battle. All assembly or refuelling points for marching columns of the enemy should be attacked by bombing during daylight with strong fighter protection, thus bringing about air conflicts not only of the highest importance in themselves but directly contributing to the general result.'

This directive may be regarded as having settled the pattern of Army-Air co-operation on the higher level; but it left unsolved the technical problem of close support in the field. In one sense it even made it worse, for the system of standing patrols, though inherently wasteful, had been adopted in response to the Army's legitimate demand for better support and protection. It was now necessary to evolve an alternative by which, without the use of patrols, the Army could nevertheless have aircraft on call throughout the battle. For this purpose there were two main requirements—a new and more rapid system of communication, and greater experience and understanding by both Services of each other's needs and limitations. It was to these aspects of the problem that the authorities in the Middle East now addressed themselves.

From July onwards a series of joint exercises were carried out by 8th Army and No. 253 Wing controlling the army-co-operation squadrons of the Desert Air Force. An Inter-Service Committee was also formed to study the problem and was able by September to agree on certain recommendations. In its original form the new system provided for the establishment at each Corps or Armoured Division of an Air Support Control, jointly staffed by the Army and the R.A.F. It was to have its own wireless-net linking it both with the airfields in the rear and with forward tentacles at each brigade, the latter being also equipped with another wireless-link for direct communication between the ground and the air. A request for air-support or tactical reconnaissance would normally originate with a forward brigade, who would pass it back to the parent A.S.C. for approval. If aircraft were available and the target was judged to be suitable, the A.S.C. would then issue orders to the airfield. The aircraft thus called up, when they reached the forward area, would be directed to their precise target by the brigade concerned over the air-ground link.

After further experiment it was found that this system, designed primarily for speed, was too decentralized. During October a modification was introduced by which all requests for air-support passed through, and received their final approval from, Air Vice-Marshal Coningham's headquarters, the A.S.C.'s at Corps or Division acting only as preliminary filters. This, though it imposed a slightly longer delay, ensured the unified control of air-operations and made it possible to switch the whole available air force, if necessary, on to one particular target or series of targets. With this amendment the system was given its first operational trial in the 'Crusader' offensive. It was found to be a clear advance on any previous arrangement, though both sides had still much to learn. Delays in the calling up of aircraft were too long; many problems of recognition, including the recognition of our own troops, remained unsolved; and there were errors and misunderstanding in the selection of targets. But these were problems which time and experience would solve. The system itself had been shown to be workable and formed, in fact, the basis of later practice throughout the war. Whatever imperfections remained, it could no longer be said, in the words of Auchinleck's complaint in July, that Army-Air co-operation was non-existent.

(ii)
Commonwealth Problems

These urgent problems of reorganization were not Auchinleck's only preoccupation during the waiting period. He also had to deal with another range of issues, of some constitutional importance, which arose from the mixed nature of his command. Apart from British and British-Indian troops, he had one New Zealand, two South African and three Australian divisions under command, as well as small contingents of Free French, Polish, Belgian and Greek troops. He thus occupied, though in respect of one Service only, a position analogous to that of a Supreme Allied Commander. But, unlike the Allied Commanders later in the war, who were responsible to the Combined Chiefs of Staff in Washington, he had no single body interposed between himself and the various Governments with jurisdiction over the forces in his command. It is true that the great majority of his troops were drawn from the Commonwealth and thus owed, apart from their particular allegiance to their own Governments, a general and common allegiance to the Crown. But despite this—in part, perhaps, because of it—Auchinleck was not immune from the normal troubles of an Allied Commander, though he lacked the machinery to deal with them.

Within the Commonwealth there was no formal system, such as was later developed with the Americans, of joint decision on military matters. On two or three occasions during the war Commonwealth Conferences met in London to consider strategic as well as political and economic questions. Between these meetings individual Prime Ministers visited London and, while there, took part in the daily business of the War Cabinet. There was also a frequent correspondence throughout the war between Mr. Churchill and his fellow Prime Ministers, as between him and President Roosevelt or M. Stalin, which served as a channel for strategic discussion and decision. On a lower level the High Commissioners and the Dominions Office maintained a constant liaison between the various Govern-

16

ments of the Crown. But there was no point at which these threads were brought together into a single knot.

It may be argued that an extensive network of personal intercourse was enough and that any more formal system would have been a mistake. This was certainly Mr. Churchill's view, and was shared by many of his colleagues and most, though not all, of the Commonwealth Prime Ministers. There was, however, one dissentient. In May 1941, Mr. Menzies, the Prime Minister of Australia, had returned home after a prolonged visit to England. As his visit had coincided with the disasters of the spring, it is not surprising that he should have been dissatisfied with much that he had seen. In particular, he had formed the impression that the War Cabinet in London and Mr. Churchill personally were attempting too autocratic a control of the war. He had therefore made a formal proposal for the development of the existing War Cabinet in London into an Imperial War Cabinet by the addition of representatives from Canada, Australia, New Zealand and South Africa. This scheme, which did not command much enthusiasm from the other Dominions and was even strongly opposed by Canada, had been rejected by Mr. Churchill on two grounds. He did not wish to swell the War Cabinet, already criticized as over-large, by adding four new members; and he felt doubtful about the status of the Dominions' representatives. If they were to attend regularly in London, they could clearly not be the Prime Ministers of their respective countries; but if they were only delegates, their need to refer home on any important issue would hamper the dispatch of business intolerably.[1]

These practical arguments were strong and, no doubt, decisive against Mr. Menzies's proposal in its original form; but they did not answer the general problem which he had raised. As the sequel was to show, situations could arise with which the existing machinery was not adequate to deal, largely because it lacked any central organ of joint responsibility. Such a case now occurred in the Middle East, where it marred, to an extent which might have been more serious than it was, Auchinleck's preparations for the November offensive.

Towards the end of July, shortly before Auchinleck's visit to London, the Australian Government repeated an earlier request that its three divisions in the Middle East should be aggregated into a single formation, the 1st Australian Corps. Although this proposal was accepted in principle, the practical difficulties of carrying it out were considerable. Two of the divisions concerned, the 6th and 7th, were already with Ninth Army in Syria; but the third, the 9th Division, then formed the Tobruk garrison. Enough has been said about the

---

[1] Churchill, Vol. III, pp. 365–6.

difficulties of supplying Tobruk to make it clear that the relief of the entire garrison would entail a major sea and air operation of precisely the kind that Auchinleck was most anxious to avoid on the eve of his offensive. Moreover, it was implicit in the arrangement that the Australian Corps, once formed, should be kept intact. It would not be possible, therefore, to use any of its component divisions in 'Crusader', whether as part of the initial order of battle or as subsequent reinforcements. The three divisions would have to remain in Syria, since that was the only place where they could be used together as a single formation. For these reasons Auchinleck wished to put off forming the new Corps until after the battle and proposed a compromise. He agreed to relieve one of the four brigades in Tobruk, which would then join the 7th Division in Syria and bring that formation up to its full strength. The remaining three brigades of the 9th Division would stay where they were, until automatically relieved in the course of the November offensive. Subsequently, the whole Corps could be brought together in Syria.

This solution did not appeal to the Australian Government, who now introduced a new element into the argument. They represented that the 9th Division, having been in Tobruk since the spring, had suffered a decline in health to the point where it was no longer capable of resisting a determined attack. If it were not relieved at once, a catastrophe might follow. This opinion, derived from General Blamey, the senior Australian officer in the Middle East, was not without substance. No one denied that the conditions of the siege had been hard on the troops; but it did not follow that a breaking-point had been reached or was even in sight. On the contrary, the Australian brigade relieved under Auchinleck's original scheme arrived in the Delta in August in good health; and an Indian cavalry unit brought out with them, which had been in Tobruk for the same length of time, was reported to be fit for immediate action.

In these circumstances Auchinleck decided to stand firm. In a telegram of 10th September he set out in detail his reasons for postponing the relief. It would throw an additional burden on the Navy and the R.A.F. to the detriment of more important operations. It could only be carried out during a moonless period and would therefore have to be split into two operations, one in September, the other in the third week of October, on the very eve of the offensive, when a maximum air-effort would be required in the desert. It would also be difficult for him, without jeopardizing his other plans, to find a replacement for the 9th Division. He did not fully accept the account of the Australians' physical condition but was prepared to allow for some decline in their resistance by reinforcing the garrison with a battalion of Infantry Tanks.

He concluded:

'The matter has today been placed before the Minister of State and the other two Commanders-in-Chief, at a meeting of the Defence Committee, and they agree with my opinion that to attempt any further relief of the Tobruk garrison, however desirable it may be politically, is not a justifiable military operation in the circumstances, and would definitely prejudice the chances of success of our projected offensive in the Western Desert.'

When these views were communicated to Australia, Mr. Fadden, who had meanwhile succeeded Mr. Menzies as the head of the Government,[1] replied with a long telegram, in which he attempted to refute the Commander-in-Chief's argument point by point on purely military and professional grounds. On any view of the case this was an error. Each participating government in an allied command must necessarily remain responsible, in the last resort, for the use made of its troops. It can withhold them from operations which it does not approve; and it can press for the resignation of a Commander-in-Chief in whom it has lost confidence. What it cannot do, without disrupting the whole system, is to try to substitute itself for the Commander-in-Chief by regulating the details of the campaign from a distance. Yet that was, in effect, what Mr. Fadden was doing. From Auchinleck's point of view there was also another, more personal difficulty. He was only too well aware that Mr. Fadden's military arguments were those of General Blamey, who was his own Deputy and immediate subordinate as well as being the senior Australian officer. To Auchinleck, already restive under the strong pressure exercised from Whitehall, it seemed that there was a want of confidence on every side. He felt that he had no choice but to offer his resignation and was only dissuaded from this course with great difficulty by the Minister of State.

Meanwhile, though further appeals were addressed to Mr. Fadden and later to his successor, Mr. Curtin, the Australian Government remained obdurate. It was therefore necessary to proceed with the relief. The second part of the operation was carried out in September, fortunately without loss or incident. During the last phase in October, however, the destroyer *Hero* was damaged and two store-ships and the new fast minelayer *Latona* were sunk. It became necessary to call off the operation prematurely while some 1,200 Australian troops still remained in Tobruk.

Thus ended an unfortunate episode. Many factors, political, military and even personal, had gone to its making; but in essence the problem was constitutional. The Australian Government had received contradictory advice from two different sources, Auchinleck

---

[1] Mr. Menzies remained in the new Government as Minister for the Co-ordination of Defence.

and his Deputy, who should have spoken with the same voice. Yet each had acted within his rights. General Blamey was entitled, and even required, to correspond directly with his Government on matters affecting the welfare of Australian troops; to press for the formation of an Australian Corps and to communicate his anxieties about the 9th Division. General Auchinleck, on the other hand, so long as he remained in command, was entitled to have his military judgement respected, not less by his subordinates than by the various Governments with whom he had to deal. That there should sometimes have been differences of opinion was inevitable. With a certain minimum of goodwill all round, most of them could be settled by normal processes of discussion. But if, as in the present case, the conflict became acute, who was to arbitrate? This was a question to which the existing system provided no answer. Perhaps a solution could have been found in Mr. Menzies's Imperial War Cabinet; or perhaps what was needed was a reorganization on the military level, which would have interposed some joint body, some collective authority, between the Commander-in-Chief and the Governments whom he served. We shall return to this problem later in another context, when Anglo-American relations and the formation of the Combined Chiefs of Staff are discussed.

It must be added that the Australian Government were not alone in feeling anxiety about the position of their troops in the Middle East. On 13th October, while the question of Tobruk was still under discussion, Mr. Churchill received a long telegram from Mr. Fraser, the Prime Minister of New Zealand. Its courteous language did not disguise the strong feeling which underlay it:

'In the light of our experience in Greece and particularly in Crete you will understand that we are naturally apprehensive lest our troops should again and for the third time be committed to battle without adequate air support and in circumstances in which they are unable to defend themselves against unrestricted air attacks. We fully realize the exigencies of the present situation and the necessity for striking an early blow in the Desert not only to improve our own position while the enemy is heavily engaged elsewhere but also by such a diversion to ease by some degree the pressure upon Russia. Nothing could be further from our intention than to add unnecessarily to your burdens at such a time as this but we would, if this is at all possible, be glad to be advised of the best appreciation possible of prospective air, tank and A.F.V. strengths of the enemy and ourselves in the Middle East with such details as may be possible as to the types of machines available on both sides and the degree to which and the time within which the enemy air, tank and A.F.V. forces respectively could be reinforced from Europe. We should greatly welcome an assurance also that the question of air support, which we, having regard to our experiences in the past, regard as a vital factor, has been fully considered and appreciated by those responsible, and that a situation in which our men are called upon to fight without the necessary means of defence and offence, particularly in aircraft, tanks and A.F.Vs., will not recur'.

Mr. Churchill replied at once with a general assurance that 'ample air and tank strength' would be available and promised detailed figures within a week. But the problem was not so easily solved. On the very same day the C.A.S. received a signal from Tedder, implying that he expected to be outnumbered in the air. He estimated that the enemy would be able, in any case, to concentrate 300 German and 350 Italian aircraft against us. If, as he appeared to expect, fighting were to die down on the Russian front during October, the figure would rise to a total of 790 aircraft, 420 German and 370 Italian. Against this, we should only be able to muster 500 aircraft for 'Crusader', including the heavy bombers operating from Malta. More aircraft were indeed available; but the shortage of trained fighter pilots and the lack of mobile equipment for certain squadrons made it impossible to bring forward any greater strength in the desert. This did not mean, of course, that we might not obtain tactical air-superiority over the battlefield, although outnumbered; but on this point Tedder's forecast was cautious:

> 'Exact nature of action once land battle is joined must depend on air and land situation, but principle clearly established that main army requirement is freedom from air interference, which can only be given by air superiority. Complete immunity from air impossible until enemy air [is] knocked out, but reasonable degree of freedom from air attack should be obtainable provided enemy does not send substantial air reinforcements during next three weeks'.

The C.A.S. replied sharply that Tedder's figures did not agree with the information available in London. They seemed to include a number of enemy aircraft which, though present in the Mediterranean, were unlikely to be able to intervene in the battle; and they took no account of the enemy's low state of serviceability. He did not himself believe that there were more than 100 serviceable German aircraft in Libya. He added that, so far as our own forces were concerned, all other fronts must be stripped in favour of the desert:

> 'Nothing must be held back for insurance in Syria, Iraq and Persia or to enable our promises to Turkey to be kept. It is the responsibility of the Air Ministry to ensure that your losses are replaced to enable you to meet these later commitments'.

Seventy-five fighter-pilots were due at Takoradi on the following day and should arrive in Egypt in time to take part in the battle. He was arranging to send another hundred pilots, of whom half would have done at least a hundred hours with operational squadrons at home. They would arrive by the end of November at the latest and would be available as a reserve for future operations.

There remained the problem of framing a detailed telegram to Mr. Fraser. Evidently it could not be based on the air figures so far presented, which could scarcely be said to provide the promised reassurance. But did they give a true picture of the situation? Mr. Churchill was disinclined to think so and decided, after consulting the Defence Committee, to send a senior officer to the Middle East to make an independent report. Air Chief Marshal Freeman, then the V.C.A.S., was selected. On the eve of his departure the Prime Minister wrote to Auchinleck to assure him of his conviction and that of the Air Staff, 'that you will have a substantial numerical superiority in the battlezone'. The estimates given by Air Headquarters, Middle East, seemed to him highly misleading, especially in their reference to the Eastern Front, which would certainly not be stabilized as early as October. He added that, for the purposes of 'Crusader', Auchinleck should regard the Air Force as being, in effect, a subordinate arm. If he felt that his operations would be assisted by a change of command, he was at full liberty to retain Air Chief Marshal Freeman in Cairo for that purpose. The telegram ended:

> 'Upon "Crusader" and the use made of it, issues affecting the whole immediate future of the war depend. Turkey, French North Africa and Spain will pick their steps accordingly. The struggling Russian armies will feel that our long period of inaction has been at last broken and that they are not the only people engaging the enemy. Feeling here has risen very high against what is thought to be our supine incapacity for action. I am however fully in control of public opinion and of the House of Commons. Nevertheless it seems to me, on military grounds alone, that everything should be thrown into this battle that can be made to play its part. This is also the view of the Defence Committee, both political and expert members. God has granted us this long breathing space and I feel sure that if all is risked all may be won . . .'

This telegram must be understood in the light of its closing paragraph. Many weeks before, during Auchinleck's visit to London, the Prime Minister had said that he was 'ready to authorize quite exceptional measures' to ensure the success of the offensive. Since then the period of waiting had increased the importance of 'Crusader' both strategically and politically; even the most drastic action was now justified so long as it contributed to its punctual launching and success. But we may doubt whether Mr. Churchill would have written in such terms to Auchinleck, or included his remarkable suggestion about the Air Command, if he had not received Mr. Fraser's message, or if that message had not followed so close upon the Tobruk controversy. For the second time what was essentially a problem of military organization within the Commonwealth had entered the field of strategy and had disturbed the relations between the Cabinet and a Commander in the field.

But too much should not be made of this second incident. There was no real question of a change in the Air Command. Tedder retained the confidence both of Auchinleck and the C.A.S.; and the controversy about relative air-strengths was settled with surprising ease. Within a day or two of his arrival Freeman was able to agree on a new set of figures which, without upsetting the basis of the original calculation, presented a new and much more favourable picture. It was now estimated that the enemy would have a total of 642 aircraft in Cyrenaica itself, of which 385 would be immediately serviceable. There would also be a further 156 German aircraft in Greece and Crete, which might intervene in the battle to the extent of attacking our lines of communication. We should thus be opposed by a grand total of 798 aircraft, 363 German, 435 Italian. This differed very little from Tedder's original estimate. On the other hand, largely as the result of measures taken before Freeman's arrival, it was now expected that initial British strength in the desert would amount to 660 aircraft, of which 528 would be immediately serviceable. This would provide a clear numerical superiority over the actual battlefield, even if the Germans and the Italians were counted as equal opponents. Making due allowance for low Italian efficiency it was reasonable to claim an approximate equality over the area of operations as a whole. Moreover, we should have the advantage, denied to the enemy, of substantial reserves amounting to almost 50 per cent behind the front line.

On the basis of this new estimate, which differed from Tedder's more in form than fact, there was no difficulty in giving Mr. Fraser the assurance that he needed. But the Prime Minister was perhaps justified, when it was pointed out to him how closely the two estimates tallied, in minuting crossly:

> 'The only difference was that the first version stated that we should be inferior and the revised version that we should be superior. It is only the kind of difference between plus and minus or black and white'.

(iii)
Enemy Supply Routes

In one of his later telegrams about Tobruk the Prime Minister expressed the hope that the relief of the garrison would not mean any delay in 'Crusader'. Auchinleck replied on 17th October that the relief would not affect the issue, as he had already decided for other reasons to postpone the offensive for about a fortnight, from 1st to 15th November. This news, the first hint of a new delay, alarmed and angered the Prime Minister, who telegraphed at once:

'Your [signal] confirms my apprehensions. Date [i.e., 1st November] was mentioned by you to Defence Committee and though we felt the delay most dangerous we accepted it and have worked towards it in our general plans. It is impossible to explain to Parliament and the nation how it is our Middle East armies have had to stand for four and half months without engaging the enemy while all the time Russia is being battered to pieces. I have hitherto managed to prevent public discussion but at any time it may break out. Moreover the few precious weeks that remain for us for the exploitation of any success are passing. No warning has been given to me of your further delay and no reasons. . . Of course if it is only a matter of two or three days the fact could be endured. It is not however possible for me to concert the general movement of the war if important changes are made in plans agreed upon, without warning or reason. Pray therefore telegraph in time'.

Auchinleck's reply, in an explanatory letter written on the same day, left no doubt that the delay was inevitable and could not, in fact, be blamed on the Middle East. All calculations had been upset by the late arrival of the 22nd Armoured Brigade and the need to put its tanks through the workshops for modification. As upwards of six weeks had been lost in this way, a delay of only a fortnight in starting the offensive seemed modest. But this was a point at which any delay might be critical. Apart from the political dangers, which Mr. Churchill had mentioned, Rommel's movements and intentions had to be considered. He was known to be preparing an attack on Tobruk as the prelude to a general advance into Egypt. It had always been an open question which army held the advantages in supply or would be ready to take the offensive first. By November even a fortnight either way might make the difference between Auchinleck's forestalling his opponent and being forestalled himself.

To understand how narrow this issue was we must follow the course of events from the German point of view. At the beginning of August, as we saw above, Rommel's supply position was extremely bad; but it gradually improved during the course of the month. His immediate requirements of fuel and ammunition were met and he began to receive reinforcements. One of his German divisions, the 5th Light, started to re-form as a full-scale Panzer division and the first elements of a new division, later known as the 90th Light, arrived in the theatre. On 25th August it was agreed at a meeting in Rome that, provided future supply convoys arrived punctually, the German contingent would be ready for the Tobruk operation by the middle of September and the Italians by the end of the month. But everything depended on the qualification: provided future transports arrived punctually.

At that time the main route for supplies to Libya was by sea-convoy from Naples to Tripoli and thence by road or coasting vessel to the forward base at Benghazi. It was a route exposed to many hazards and delays. The first section from Naples to Tripoli brought the convoys within range of air-attack from Malta; and there was a chronic shortage of coasters and still more of road-transport for the second leg from Tripoli to Benghazi. Even when supplies had crossed the Mediterranean safely, there were often serious delays in their onward movement to the front. The only alternative was to route convoys or single ships direct to Benghazi. This would avoid the long coastal haul from Tripoli. It would also mean that convoys could start from one of the eastern Italian ports, such as Brindisi or Taranto, or even from Greece, thus keeping clear of Malta and also benefiting from the air-cover provided by *Fliegerkorps X*. But the capacity of Benghazi was limited and the harbour too shallow for the large ships normally used on the Tripoli run. The Italian Navy, then held in the grip of a severe fuel shortage, also made difficulties about providing escorts for the longer voyage and pointed out that the Benghazi route, though largely safe from Malta, was within range of submarines and aircraft operating from Alexandria.

The Allies were in fact well placed to keep the greater part of the central Mediterranean under observation or attack. Air-reconnaissance from Malta could cover the whole triangle Naples-Tripoli-Benghazi and was supplemented by flying boat and long range fighter patrols from Alexandria and Cyprus. A detailed picture of Axis ship movements was thus built up, which provided the basis for a systematic sea- and air-offensive. The operation fell into three parts. First came the submarine campaign, directed from either end of the Mediterranean. Boats of the 8th Flotilla from Gibraltar operated mainly in the Tyrrhenian Sea and off the Italian coast, and boats of the 1st Flotilla from Alexandria in the Ionian Sea and on the approaches to Benghazi. They were supported by a detached group of submarines at Malta, later formed into the 10th Flotilla, whose main hunting-grounds were in the Straits of Messina and off the African coast. Shipping which escaped this net, had next to run the hazard of short-range air-attack from Malta. This was pressed round the clock, by Blenheims and Marylands by day and by torpedo-carrying Alba-cores at night, so that a convoy, once sighted, could be kept under continuous attack so long as it was within range of the island. Lastly, there was a regular bombardment of the ports of discharge in Africa, and to a lesser extent of the embarkation ports in Italy and Sicily, by Wellington squadrons from Malta and Egypt. These raids were not heavy—the average was only five or six aircraft a night; but they were frequent enough, at least on Tripoli and Benghazi, to do steady and accumulative damage.[1]

German and Italian losses in these operations were severe. Supply convoys were disorganized and the hopes of an early offensive faded. At the beginning of September, only a week or so after the Rome meeting, Rommel was obliged to report that, unless the transport position were radically improved, the attack on Tobruk would have to be postponed until the end of the year. He would thus miss the opportunity of attacking Egypt, while the main British forces in the Middle East were still tied down elsewhere by the threat of a German move through the Caucasus, by Turkey's uncertain attitude and by political difficulties in Syria and Palestine. Rommel, who did not expect this favourable situation to last for more than another two months, appealed urgently to the Italian authorities to take the necessary steps to ensure that the attack on Tobruk could be opened not later than October or November. This was the first of a series of protests. On 12th September he drew O.K.W.'s attention to the fact that, within the past month, eight German cargo ships had been sunk with a loss of 12,000 tons of stores, 352 vehicles and a quantity of arms. He had already requested the transfer of German submarines and M.T.B. to the Mediterranean and the opening of a new supply route through Greece. He must now point out that, unless these or similar measures were taken, the offensive would have to be post-poned indefinitely.

This complaint was followed by a detailed memorandum on the same theme by the German Military Attaché in Rome, which was vigorously backed by the Naval Staff:

> 'The situation described is untenable. Italian air and naval forces are incapable of providing adequate escort. Italian measures are quite insufficient and will continue to be so. The Naval Staff considers that radical changes and the acceleration of relief measures are urgently necessary, if the whole German-Italian position in North Africa—to say nothing of the offensive—is not

---

[1] Roskill, Vol. I, Chap. 24; Playfair, Vol. II, Chap. 14.

to be lost. The loss of the North African position would be tantamount to the loss of the entire Mediterranean. The catastrophic effects of this would be incalculable . . . Besides meeting the demands of the German General, the Naval Staff considers it necessary to arrange immediately for the quickest possible transfer of M.T.B. and motor minesweepers to the Mediterranean and for the return of the *Luftwaffe* to Sicily . . . It is requested that the Fuehrer be informed of the views held by the Naval Staff. If necessary, the Commander-in-Chief, Navy, will request a special conference with the Fuehrer'.[1]

Here was a repetition of Raeder's earlier warning to Hitler which could not be entirely ignored. But the possible range of action had narrowed since the previous December. Germany was now so deeply committed in Russia that she could not spare more than minor forces for the Mediterranean. Halder had stated the position exactly only a few weeks before: 'Safeguarding transports to Africa is an Italian affair. In the present situation it would be criminal to allot German aircraft for this purpose.'[2] The O.K.W.'s reponse to Rommel's appeal was therefore tentative and inadequate. Six submarines were ordered to the Mediterranean from the Atlantic; arrangements were put in hand for the transfer of M.T.B. and minesweepers as soon as current operations in the Baltic should be completed; and *Fliegerkorps X* was instructed to devote its main effort in future to convoy protection rather than the offensive bombing of Alexandria and Suez.[3] It appears, however, that this last order was only partly obeyed. According to Admiral Weichold, the German naval liaison-officer in Rome, *Fliegerkorps X* consistently refused to operate west of Benghazi so that the Naples-Tripoli and Tripoli-Benghazi routes remained as before an Italian responsibility.

These half-measures were not effective. In September and October Axis shipping losses in the Mediterranean rose to a total of 147,000 tons, of which two-thirds—eighteen ships of 98,000 tons—were sunk on the African route. Only one convoy of the October cycle succeeded in reaching Tripoli and, after the middle of the month, the route was temporarily abandoned as too dangerous. This meant that Rommel's build-up was brought to a standstill, for the Benghazi route, as then organized, was barely adequate even for current requirements. It seemed that the date for the attack on Tobruk, now tentatively fixed for 20th November, would have to be set back even further. This was the more serious as reports were now reaching both the O.K.W. and the *Commando Supremo*, which suggested that an Allied offensive was imminent. British action in Persia was being

[1] *Fuehrer Naval Conferences* 17th September 1941, Annex III.
[2] *Halder's Diary*, 29th July, 1941.
[3] *F.N.C.*, 22nd August and 17th September, 1941.

limited to the delivery of supplies to Russia; and troops were reported
to be leaving Iraq for Palestine and Egypt. Both Rommel and the
Italian Commander, General Bastico, were inclined to discount this
information on the ground that British dispositions at the front were
not consistent with an immediate attack. But they admitted that the
offensive might well start, if not before 20th November, then while
the attack on Tobruk was in progress. Indeed, it seemed likely that
the Allies would regard this as a favourable opportunity.

Towards the end of October came a new and, from the German
point of view, most sinister development. For the first time since the
spring a British surface-force (Force K) of two light cruisers and two
destroyers appeared at Malta. The effect was immediate. On 8th
November a convoy of seven ships of a total of 40,000 tons left
Naples escorted by two heavy cruisers and ten destroyers. Force K
attacked and in a brief but crushing night-action sank the entire
convoy and two of the escorting destroyers and damaged a third.[1]
But Hitler had already taken warning. As soon as the existence of a
surface-force at Malta was reported to him, he decided that German
intervention had at last become inevitable. On 29th October a series
of emergency measures were taken. A further twenty-one submarines
—twelve for the western basin and nine for the eastern—were ordered
to the Mediterranean with additional minesweepers and M.T.B. It
was also decided to reinforce the *Luftwaffe* in the Mediterranean
with another *Fliegerkorps* and an air-headquarters, *Luftflotte* 2,
withdrawn from the Eastern Front. The whole operation was to be
under the command of Field Marshal Kesselring as *Oberbefehlshaber
Sud* with his headquarters in Sicily. His instructions were to safeguard
supplies to Libya by establishing sea and air supremacy in the central
Mediterranean, to neutralize Malta and to act generally in support of
Rommel's forces.

These decisions were taken without consulting Mussolini; but as
Kesselring's headquarters were to be on Italian soil, it was necessary
to go through the form of securing his consent *ex post facto*. This proved
unexpectedly difficult and time was also needed for the transfer of
Luftflotte 2 from Russia. The new command was not finally set up
until December, so that its subsequent operations, which again
altered the strategic balance in the Mediterranean, belong to a later
part of the story. But the significance of Hitler's decision in relation to
'Crusader' will be apparent at once. It showed on what a fragile
tenure the Allies had held their temporary command, or partial
command, of the central Mediterranean during the summer. They
were in the curious position of only being able to succeed up to a certain point. Once that point had been passed and complete success

---

[1] Roskill, Vol. I, Chap. 24.

was in sight, Germany was bound to intervene and, despite her commitments in Russia, still had the power to do so effectively. That was the real danger in Auchinleck's four months' delay. If Hitler had yielded even a little sooner to Rommel's protests or the Naval Staff's advice, the Allies would not have won the battle of supply.

Another point must also be noticed: the Allies' victory was only partial. There was no actual breakdown on the African supply-route until November. During the whole of the earlier period, from the beginning of July to the end of October, the net loss did not amount, on the best calculation, to more than 20 per cent of the supplies shipped.[1] This was enough to delay and in the end to frustrate Rommel's offensive plans; but it left a margin, nevertheless, for reinforcement and the building-up of stocks. The German-Italian position was substantially better by the end of October than it had been in July or August. Losses suffered in 'Battleaxe' had been made good; and there were adequate supplies of fuel and ammunition. On the German side, the 5th Light had re-formed as the 21st Panzer Division, part of the Afrika Division had arrived, and Rommel had also received artillery and other reinforcements. On the Italian side, the Sabratha Division, almost destroyed in earlier operations, had been re-formed and the greater part of the Trieste Division brought over.

Rommel's plans, though delayed and reduced in scope, were not abandoned. At the end of October he still hoped to be able to capture Tobruk in the following month and reported that his troops would be ready for action from the 15th November onwards. He believed that the chances were good, for the Allies, given their current dispositions, would not be able to intervene in strength before the third day of the attack, by which time the operation would be virtually over. But he added the warning that this favourable situation would not last beyond November; thereafter the balance of advantage would drop in the Allies' favour. Rommel seems to have held to this opinion even after the loss of the November convoy, which temporarily brought the flow of supplies almost to a stop; but his Italian colleague, General Bastico, was far more cautious. On 11th November he informed the *Commando Supremo* that recent changes in Allied dispositions suggested an intention to take the offensive, probably as soon as German-Italian forces had been decisively committed to an attack on Tobruk. In that event the position would be extremely dangerous. He did not see how the German-Italian army, hampered as it was by difficulties of supply, could hope to emerge intact from a major battle. This report, though dismissed by Rommel as an example of

---

[1] Playfair, Vol. II, Chap. 14.

'excessive Latin nervousness', was not without its effect. On 14th November Rommel was obliged to fly to Rome for a conference on future plans with General Cavallero, the Italian Chief of Staff. He was still there when Bastico's prediction was fulfilled and the Allied attack began.

(iv)
The Battle

'Crusader' was finally launched at dawn on 18th November, three days late by Auchinleck's reckoning of the previous month.[1] The ensuing operations, which lasted well into the following January, are not easy to describe succinctly. Any short account of a complex and long drawn-out operation, in which little went according to plan, is bound to be over-simplified and to that extent inaccurate. But the intrinsic importance of 'Crusader,' as the main offensive effort in the West in 1941, was so great, and its impact on the strategic discussions of the time so considerable, that some narrative must be given. What follows is not intended to do more than indicate the main turns of fortune on the battlefield and some of the reasons why the operation proved more costly, and the victory less complete, than had been expected. For a full account of the battle, or rather the series of engagements that made up the battle, the reader is referred to the official history of the Mediterranean campaigns.[2]

The start of 'Crusader' found Rommel on his way back to North Africa from the conference in Rome. During his absence preparations had continued for the attack on Tobruk; and his army was disposed accordingly. Four Italian divisions (Bologna, Brescia, Pavia and Trento) and one German (the 90th Light) held the ring round the fortress. They were protected to the south by the Italian 20th Corps, consisting of the Ariete (armoured) and the Trieste (motorized) divisions, which occupied a position between Bir Hacheim and Bir el Gubi. The frontier defences and the two strongholds of Bardia and Sollum were relatively lightly held by the Savona Division and some Italian militia, stiffened by German infantry. Between these two wings of the army, in positions astride and to the south of the Capuzzo track, lay the German armour. The 15th Panzer Division was on the west, ready to take part in the operations against Tobruk; the 21st

---

[1] The delay was to enable the 1st South African Division to complete its training and make an issue of additional vehicles.

[2] Playfair, Vol. III, Chaps. 1–3.

Panzer Division on the east, ready to move, if necessary, to the support of the frontier garrisons.[1]

General Cunningham, commanding 8th Army, had a force approximately equal in size to his opponent's; the equivalent, that is to say, of some nine divisions or between 100,000 and 120,000 men in all. He appeared, however, to enjoy a distinct superiority in armour. His main striking-force, consisting of the 7th Armoured Division and the 4th Armoured Brigade Group, would bring into the field nearly 480 cruiser-tanks, backed by a substantial reserve. Against this Rommel's three armoured divisions (two German and one Italian) could only muster some 390 cruisers with few or no reserves. In addition, 8th Army's infantry was supported by two Army Tank Brigades, for which the enemy had no equivalent. But the actual balance was less favourable than these figures may suggest. It was partly a question of design; in general, and with certain reservations, the English- or American-built cruisers, with which 8th Army was equipped, were less well-armed and mechanically less reliable than their German counterparts. It was also partly a question of training. At this stage in the war the German handling of armoured forces in the field was still markedly superior to the British; so much so, that one observer described the difference as that between the amateur and the professional.[2]

These comparisons had a particular significance in relation to the 'Crusader' plan. In the opening phase of the battle 30th Corps (7th Armoured Division, 4th Armoured Brigade Group, 1st South African Division and 22nd Guards Brigade) was to cross the undefended frontier south of Sidi Omar and then strike north-west with the double object of bringing the enemy's armour to battle and threatening Rommel's main communications south of Tobruk. But in the event this thrust miscarried. When the general tank-action, which it was designed to provoke, finally began at Sidi Rezegh on 21st November, the British armour was dispersed and out of balance. In a battle lasting three days 30th Corps suffered a severe defeat.

Meanwhile, however, some progress had been made on other parts of the front. On 21st November, while the enemy armour was absorbed in the struggle round Sidi Rezegh, 13th Corps began a subsidiary movement. Leaving the 4th Indian Division to hold down the enemy troops on the frontier, the New Zealand Division and the 1st Army Tank Brigade passed round the flank of the defences and advanced towards the coast with the intention of isolating Sollum and Bardia and then moving west along the Capuzzo track. By the 23rd the leading brigades, having overrun the airfield at Gambut,

---

[1] Playfair, Vol. III, p. 392 and Map 3.

[2] Playfair, Vol. III, pp. 26–31.

were approaching Sidi Rezegh from the east. At the same time the Tobruk garrison (70th Division, Polish Brigade Group and 32nd Army Tank Brigade) had made a strong sortie to the south and gained ground towards El Duda. A threat was thus developing to Rommel's communications, though not in the way originally intended.[1]

There was no disguising the fact that the main thrust had failed. On the morning of the 23rd November Cunningham estimated that 30th Corps had only 44 tanks still fit to fight, whereas the two German Panzer divisions retained 120. The superiority in armour, which was the basis of his whole plan, had disappeared.[2] When Auchinleck visited him at his headquarters that afternoon, he felt obliged to raise the question of calling off the offensive. If losses continued at the present rate, there would soon be no serviceable tanks left; and nothing could then save Egypt from an enemy counterstroke. But Auchinleck rejected this argument. The successful advance of 13th Corps convinced him that Rommel was also fully extended and that victory was still possible, if pressure were relentlessly maintained. He therefore instructed Cunningham to continue the offensive, even though he might in the process immobilise the whole of his remaining armour. Two days later, when the trend of events seemed to confirm Cunningham's worst apprehensions, the Commander-in-Chief took a further decision. On 25th November he telegraphed to the Prime Minister:

'I have decided to replace General Cunningham temporarily by General Ritchie, my present Deputy Chief of Staff. This is not on account of any misgivings as to the present situation in my mind, but because I have reluctantly concluded that Cunningham, admirable though he has been up to date, has now begun to think defensively, mainly because of our large tank losses.'[3]

After the action at Sidi Rezegh Rommel took a bold and characteristic decision. On 24th November, ignoring the disorganized 30th Corps, he led his entire armoured force, including the Ariete Division, eastward along the El Abd track with the intention of surrounding and destroying the Allied troops on the frontier. This move, if successful, would have left 8th Army in a very precarious position; but Rommel was asking more of his armour than it could perform. The two Panzer divisions had just emerged from three days' heavy fighting; they were hampered throughout the action by difficulties of supply; and their attacks seem to have been less well co-ordinated than usual.

---

[1] Playfair, Vol. III, pp. 6–8 and 38–49.

[2] The conclusion was broadly correct, though later figures showed a less unfavourable balance.

[3] Playfair, Vol. III, pp. 52 and 60–1.

17

Although some alarm and dislocation was caused in the back areas, all the main positions on the frontier held firm. Meanwhile, the temporary absence of the enemy's armour transformed the situation on the main battle front. 30th Corps was given a welcome opportunity to reorganize and refit;[1] and 13th Corps' advance continued. In four days' hard fighting the New Zealand Division, supported by the 1st Army Tank Brigade, recaptured Sidi Rezegh, secured positions on the northern escarpment at Zaafran and Belhamed and cleared the valley between. The 70th Division also resumed the attack and took firm possession of El Duda. By the 27th November the whole of this area, lying directly across Rommel's communications, had passed into Allied hands.[2]

But the position was far from secure. 13th Corps had no reserve strength; and 30th Corps, now concentrated in the area south and west of Gabr Saleh, was almost as far from the main battle as the German armour. On 27th November an unsuccessful attempt was made to pass the remaining brigade of the 1st South African Division to the support of the New Zealanders. But by that time Rommel's armoured divisions, having broken off the action on the frontier, were once more moving west along the Capuzzo track. The remaining armour of 30th Corps, now reduced to two brigades with about 70 tanks between them, made a series of flank attacks from the south but did not succeed in halting the enemy. The New Zealand Division was thus exposed on the 29th and 30th November to a formidable assault, which it was unable to withstand. By 1st December Rommel had recovered all the lost ground except El Duda; and the two armies had returned to almost the same positions as they had held in the previous week after the first action at Sidi Rezegh.[3]

But there was this important difference, that Rommel was now beginning to feel the pinch of supply. After their exertions of the past fortnight his two Panzer divisions were in urgent need of refitting; they had, perhaps, some 40 tanks between them. Other replacements, of artillery, signals equipment and vehicles, were equally necessary; and a general shortage of fuel and ammunition was beginning to develop. But the Allies still throttled his main supply-route across the Mediterranean. A signal from Rome on 4th December informed him that he could expect to receive nothing during the rest of the month beyond small quantities of fuel, food and medical supplies. Thereafter, as Hitler's emergency measures began to take effect, it might become possible to run regular convoys again; but they would evidently come too late to influence the current battle. Rommel

---

[1] The 7th Armoured Brigade was withdrawn from the battle; one brigade of the 1st South African Division had, in effect, ceased to exist.

[2] Playfair, Vol. III, pp. 61–2.

[3] Playfair, Vol. III, pp. 62–9.

therefore took the first steps towards a general withdrawal. Under cover of some demonstrations along the Capuzzo track and towards El Gubi, he withdrew his troops from the east side of Tobruk and begin to re-align his army on a new front along the line Acroma-El Adem-El Gubi. The frontier garrisons were left to withdraw into Bardia whence it was hoped to extricate them later by sea.[1]

After the second failure at Sidi Rezegh, Ritchie regrouped his army. The gallant remnants of the New Zealand Division and the 1st Army Tank Brigade were withdrawn from the battle; and the 2nd South African Division, until then in general reserve, took over the positions on the frontier from the 4th Indian Division, which moved forward to join 30th Corps. Certain reinforcements were also made available. Auchinleck sent up the armoured cars and divisional artillery of the 1st Armoured Division which had arrived in Egypt towards the end of November. One brigade of the 50th Division was brought from Iraq as an Army reserve; and another brigade was formed from three Indian battalions in the Delta to serve on the lines of communication.[2]

Thus refreshed 8th Army prepared to resume the offensive. The new plan turned on the capture of El Adem by two simultaneous thrusts, by 30th Corps northward from El Gubi and by the 70th Division westward from El Duda. But in fact this operation was never fully developed. The main attack opened on the 7th December; by the following morning it was clear that Rommel was withdrawing his whole force to the Gazala line, a prepared position of some strength though recently neglected, from which he might hope to cover Western Cyrenaica. The next week saw something of a lull in this obstinate battle. Rommel's disengagement was smoothly managed; and the mobile columns sent in pursuit could make little impression on his well-organized rearguard. Since the supplies accumulated in Tobruk before the offensive were now largely exhausted, some days elapsed before sufficient stocks could be built up to allow 8th Army to make a general advance. Ritchie used this interval for a further regrouping. Control in the forward area passed to 13th Corps; and the headquarters of 30th Corps were withdrawn to the frontier to take charge of operations against the remaining enemy garrisons, whose reduction had now become a matter of some urgency, if only to eliminate the long and wasteful detour to the south which supply-columns still had to make.[3]

It is doubtful whether Rommel, as distinct from his Italian allies, ever intended to fight more than a delaying-action at Gazala. Nevertheless, a serious effort was required to eject him. By 13th December

---

[1] Playfair, Vol. III, pp. 69–70, 74–5.
[2] Playfair, Vol. III, pp. 73–4.
[3] Playfair, Vol. III, pp. 77–8, 81.

8th Army was in front of the new position in strength. Two days later an attack was launched by the Polish Brigade Group and the 5th New Zealand Brigade in the coastal sector and the 4th Indian Division, supported by infantry-tanks, farther to the south. By the evening of 16th December, after an initial failure in the south and some heavy casualties, this attack was successful. But an attempt to pass the 7th Armoured Division, now reduced to one brigade, round the flank of the enemy's position so as to cut off his retreat, ended in complete failure. Rommel, though forced to abandon the Gazala line, was able to withdraw in good order with his diminished army substantially intact. But he had now lost the last position on which he could hope to stand east of Agedabia and with it the honours of the campaign. It was only a question of time before the Allies reoccupied the whole of Cyrenaica.[1]

To this extent the action at Gazala was decisive, though operations continued in western Cyrenaica and on the Egyptian frontier for another three or four weeks. The weather was exceptionally bad; and 8th Army began to experience acute difficulties of supply. Middle East's always inadequate equipment of M.T. had already been stretched to the limit to sustain the battle in its first phase, 100 to 150 miles west of the rail-head; but now troops were operating, often over waterlogged roads or tracks, at twice or three times that distance from the new forward base at Tobruk. Although the pursuit was maintained, there was little weight behind it; and it was as much as Ritchie could do to keep his mobile forces in more or less constant touch with Rommel's rearguard. Armoured cars of the 7th Armoured Division entered Benghazi, already evacuated by the enemy, on Christmas Eve; and by the end of the year all the hill country between Benghazi and Gazala had been cleared and much material captured, though few prisoners. Rommel meanwhile had temporarily occupied a strong position farther to the west at Agedabia, where he was able to delay our advanced troops for nearly a fortnight. On 7th January, anticipating an attack in strength, he withdrew to his final position at El Agheila on the western border of Cyrenaica. A few days later, at the opposite end of the Allies' now enormously extended line, 30th Corps captured Sollum and the last remaining enemy strongholds on the Egyptian frontier were overrun.[2]

'Crusader' thus ended in a substantial victory. In fighting extended over nearly two months Rommel had lost, killed, wounded and captured, nearly a third of his total force and had retreated more than 500 miles to precisely the point from which he had started a year before. The Allies had lost barely one man to Rommel's two; and

[1] Playfair, Vol. III, pp. 81–4.
[2] Playfair, Vol. III, pp. 84–91, 94–6.

the haul of material, strewn over the vast battlefield, promised to be enormous. Nevertheless, the offensive had not achieved its final object of clearing the western flank. However much reduced in strength, Rommel's army was still in being and occupied a strong position from which it could debouch again on Cyrenaica as soon as supply and reinforcement allowed. The Allied front, on the other hand, still hung in the air:

'If by any chance [wrote Auchinleck to the Prime Minister] we have to break off the offensive on the borders of Cyrenaica, we must at all costs secure a position which can be held, and held indefinitely, against a possible counter-offensive by the enemy. Such a position was not secured last year when Rommel hustled us back to Tobruk and the frontier. It is not necessary for me to presume to explain to you that such a position must cover the routes leading across the desert from Sollum and Siwa towards it, and for these reasons it must be well "round the corner". The best defensive position is that on the line of the marshes west of Agheila, where there is plenty of water. It will be necessary also to secure Marada, a small oasis 70 miles south of Agheila, so as to secure our southern flank and prevent its use by the enemy.'

In other words, the gains already made could only be consolidated at the cost of a further offensive effort. But the Agheila position, whether approached from the east or the west, is of great natural strength; and a serious operation would be required to eject even Rommel's depleted army. The armoured forces already on the frontier, in the last stage of mechanical exhaustion after their long pursuit, were not capable of more than a demonstration. The bringing up of fresh troops and the maintenance of any substantial force before Agheila was hampered by difficulties of supply and in particular by the delay, mainly occasioned by bad weather, in opening Benghazi as a forward base. For these reasons Auchinleck did not expect to be able to renew the attack before the middle of February. But while he paused, held in the grip of local problems and the difficulties to be expected at the end of a long advance, the general current of the war, which had hitherto set in his favour, turned decisively against him.[1]

By the end of 1941 control of the central Mediterranean, the key to all Libyan operations, was passing or had already passed out of Allied hands. The first sign of the changed situation was the increased and deadly activity of German submarines and light naval forces during the last two months of the year. Their successes had begun on 13th November, when two U-boats attacked and sank the carrier *Ark Royal* on her return to Gibraltar after the last of many operations,

---

[1] Auchinleck's Dispatch.

in which she had ferried aircraft to Malta. Less than a fortnight later *Barham*, the flagship of the 1st Battle Squadron, was lost in the same way. December saw the loss of the cruiser *Galatea*, again to a U-boat, and the end of Force K's brief but brilliant career, when the whole Squadron ran foul of a newly-laid minefield off Tripoli. On the same day an even worse disaster overtook the main Fleet in Alexandria. Three Italian 'human torpedoes', launched from a submarine, penetrated the harbour defences and planted delayed-action mines on the hulls of the battleships *Queen Elizabeth* and *Valiant*. Both ships were badly holed and were out of commission for many months. Before the end of the year, therefore, the Mediterranean Fleet had been temporarily reduced to a handful of destroyers and the three cruisers of Admiral Vian's squadron.[1]

These naval losses were accentuated by the great increase in German air-power in the Mediterranean, which followed the setting up of Kesselring's new command at the beginning of December. By the middle of that month the *Luftwaffe*'s total establishment had risen from 464 to 798 aircraft and actual strength, which was still growing, from 400 to 637. The greater part of this reinforcement was concentrated in Sicily. Italian convoys on the Tripoli route began once more to receive adequate protection from the air; and the systematic bombardment of Malta was resumed. The results were almost immediately apparent in a sharp fall in Axis shipping losses. Whereas in November only 30,000 tons of military stores were landed in North Africa, representing barely 40 per cent of the total tonnage shipped, in December nearly 40,000 tons were landed with a loss of less than 20 per cent. In January the figure was 60,000 tons and the loss negligible. By the beginning of 1942 it was the Axis not the Allies who were winning the battle of supply. The repercussion of these events on Auchinleck's position in Cyrenaica was bound to be severe. The crippling of the Fleet, which hampered his own forward movement, and the re-emergence of German air-power in Sicily, which released the pent-up flow of Rommel's supplies, were two factors which might well have been decisive in themselves. But they had already been overshadowed by another and far more potent influence—the entry of Japan into the war.[2]

---

[1] Roskill, Vol. I, Chap. 24.
[2] Playfair, Vol. III, p. 107 (Table).

CHAPTER X

TOWARDS PEARL HARBOR

(i)

The Japanese Constitution

AFTER COMPLETING HER occupation of Indo-China in the latter part of July, Japan took no further open step forward. The attack on Siam, so freely predicted at the beginning of August, was not carried out; and a pause followed, which almost suggested that Japan had recovered her caution or temporarily outrun her strength. Negotiations with the United States for a general settlement in the Far East were resumed. True, they produced little or nothing in the way of concessions by Japan; but their mere continuance could be regarded as hopeful. President Roosevelt, it will be remembered, had only set himself the limited objective of gaining time. At the Atlantic Meeting he had spoken of a possible month's respite; and it seemed that he was succeeding beyond expectation, when August passed into September and September into October with the negotiation still alive.

But these hopeful signs were in fact illusory. Other forces, over which the negotiations had little influence, were driving Japan steadily towards war. She was caught in a dilemma, from which neither her unstable economy nor her clumsy political system would allow her to escape. Its outlines were simple enough. Japan was an overcrowded country, poor in natural resources, whose whole livelihood depended on a specialized export trade, largely in manufactured goods for which the raw materials were imported. To this extent her position was parallel with that of Great Britain; but her population was over twice as large, her merchant fleet a great deal smaller and her foreign investments negligible. She had also been a comparative late-comer in the markets of the world and, in consequence, had often found what seemed to her an unreasonable and unfair discrimination against her products.

The traditional remedy for a country in this position is to found an overseas empire so as to secure both access to raw materials and an assured market for her own products. Here again Japan had been hampered by a late start. Over the past fifty years, she had, in fact, acquired a considerable holding of overseas territory in Formosa, Korea, Manchuria and latterly in China; but she was still far from the security and economic stability which she sought. At the outbreak of the Second World War the Japanese Empire was barely self-supporting even in food and wholly dependent on the outside world for most of the other necessities of life. She imported 90 per cent of her oil, between 50 and 75 per cent of all her requirements of metal, more than half her cotton and all her wool, rubber and jute. She was also entirely dependent on foreign sources (mainly the United States) for her supply of machine-tools.

It is not surprising that Japan should have turned her eyes towards the rich colonial territories in the south, which could supply so many of her needs. From Indo-China, Malaya and the Dutch East Indies—to take only the nearest and most important—she could draw rice and other foodstuffs, rubber, iron-ore, tin, manganese, bauxite and all the oil that she required. She was already a large importer of their produce, but had not so far included them in her plans for conquest, except perhaps as a distant goal. In 1939, however, and more especially after the German victories of 1940, it seemed that her chance had come. The road to the south lay open, though one major obstacle remained. The Philippines were not economically important to Japan; but it was impossible to ignore their awkward geographical position, directly athwart the main line of communication with the south.[1] This was the main reason for Japan's caution during the first year of her opportunity. She was willing to risk a conflict with defeated France, with the Dutch or even with Great Britain; but it was another matter to try conclusions with the unimpaired strength of the United States.[2]

This mood continued until the end of July 1941, when the economic sanctions imposed on Japan after her occupation of southern Indo-China changed the whole situation. These sanctions, as we have seen, rapidly developed into a complete embargo. Something like three-quarters of Japan's foreign trade was cut off—a blow which her economy could not hope to survive. Even on a short view the outlook was critical, for the loss of certain imports would make itself felt in a matter of months. It is only necessary to consider one item here. Japan imported rather over 5 million tons of oil a year, substantially the whole of which came from sources under Dutch or American control. Her home production was negligible; and her stocks in 1941 did not amount to more than 7 million tons. Even with the most rigid economy this would not suffice for more than two years' consumption in peacetime or between a year and eighteen months in war.[3] The last point was the vital one. The reserves shrank

---

[1] This was largely independent of the question of American intervention. Manila would still have been a potential menace to Japan after the conquest, even if America had not intervened during the course of it.

[2] S. W. Kirby, *The War Against Japan* (1958), Vol. I, Chap. 5.

[3] Kirby, Vol. I, Chap. 4 and App. II.

by a little each month; and the moment could be exactly forecast when major operations—any major operations—would become impossible. Japan would then have no choice. Since she could not fight, she would have to capitulate on whatever terms her opponents were willing to offer.

That was the position as it appeared in Japan; but the Western world saw it differently. The three Powers mainly concerned did not wish to humiliate Japan or to deny her access to the raw materials which she needed. If they had imposed certain restrictions on her purchases even before July, that was because they could not allow her to build up excessive stocks or to act as a channel of supply to Germany. They had not intended to interfere with her normal trade and in general had not done so. The more recent embargo was admittedly a punitive measure, but one which Japan could be said to have brought upon herself by her close association with Germany, her consistently aggressive attitude and her actions in Indo-China. It was, moreover, of a nature more to invite than to exclude negotiation. The grand object of the three Powers was to secure a settlement in the Pacific on terms which would allow them to deploy their full strength in other theatres. It was not in their interest to drive Japan to extremities or to impose conditions which she might subsequently be tempted to break. On the contrary, they could only obtain what they wanted by reaching a settlement which left Japan visibly content.

Japan's position was not therefore as painful as it seemed. But if negotiations were opened, two very difficult problems were bound to arise. The first concerned Japan's relations with Germany and the extent of her obligations under the Tripartite Pact; the second her war with China, to whose support the three Powers in general and the United States in particular were already deeply committed. Neither problem was necessarily insoluble. There was already a school of thought in Japan which believed that the Pact had outlived its usefulness. Germany's attack on Russia, it was argued, had altered the whole position by destroying any hope of an early victory in Europe and creating a far stronger hostile coalition than had been anticipated.[1] Doubts about the wisdom of pressing on with the 'China Incident' were also widespread. Indeed, questions of prestige apart, Japan desired nothing better than an end to this obstinate war, in which she could no longer hope for a decisive military result. That did not mean that she was willing to abandon the fruits of conquest, such as they were; but it did mean that she was willing and even anxious to open negotiations for a settlement of some kind.

But there was one further obstacle. It was to be found not in the

---

[1] Langer and Gleason, p. 626.

situation itself, nor in any aspect of policy, but in the Japanese political system. This was a complex and anomalous structure. In theory the Emperor was supreme and exercised a direct authority over the whole executive field which was comparable with, and in some respects greater than, that of an American President. He nominated the Prime Minister and the Cabinet, who did not necessarily require the support of the Diet; and he also controlled the Army and Navy through their Chiefs of Staff, who were answerable only to him. But this was only appearance. In practice and by tradition the Emperor did nothing except on the advice of his officers of state. Even in the selection of the Prime Minister he was regularly guided by a body of *Genro* or elder statesmen, which became in time no more than a committee of ex-Prime Ministers. And so with other appointments; the tendency was for all office-holders to be nominated either by their predecessors or by the general sense of the departments which they nominally controlled.

The result was a government without a head. The Prime Minister, its nominal chief, had little of the independent authority and prestige, which popular support gives to his European counterparts. Even his formal powers were strictly limited. The constitution obliged him, for example, to include two serving officers in the Cabinet, holding the portfolios of the Army and the Navy. These Ministers were, of course, the nominees of their respective Services, who were thus able to overturn the Government at any time by threatening their withdrawal. Moreover, the Service Ministers, and through them the Cabinet, only exercised a partial authority in their own departments. They were responsible for the supply and to some extent the administration of the Army and Navy; but all questions of strategy and operations were reserved to the General Staffs, who were under no obligation to keep the Cabinet informed of their plans. It followed that, whereas the Chiefs of Staff could exert a strong and often decisive influence on Cabinet policy, the Prime Minister had no means to retaliate. Indeed, if the two Chiefs of Staff had been willing to act together, they would soon have dominated the Government. But the Army and Navy were often at loggerheads, so that an astute Prime Minister, by playing one off against the other, could sometimes secure a measure of independence for himself.

Such a government could only be carried on by an endless process of bargaining between its component parts. This was hardly favourable to quick or decisive action; and an attempt was made, under the stress of the war in China, to simplify and formalize the procedure. The system finally adopted provided for discussion at four levels. First, there were consultations between the War Ministry and the Army General Staff, and between the Admiralty and the Naval Staff, in order to settle the policy of each Service. Secondly, the two

Services met together at Imperial General Headquarters and endeavoured to arrive at a common policy or at least at agreement on certain main points. The next step was a series of meetings or Liaison Conferences between Imperial General Headquarters on the one hand and the Cabinet of the day on the other, at which an attempt was made to harmonize civil with military policy. Finally, the agreements reached at the Liaison Conferences were ratified at formal Imperial Conferences, over which the Emperor himself presided, normally in silence.

At best it was a clumsy method of doing business. It will be noticed among its many defects, that considerations of civil, as opposed to military, policy were not allowed to enter until the final stage, when the views of the Services had already been fixed and could not easily be modified without loss of prestige. Moreover, whether because of the actual difficulty of reaching agreement or owing to some defect in the Japanese language, statements of policy were normally cast in imprecise and even cryptic terms, which lent themselves to a wide variety of subsequent interpretation. Thus, the important statement of policy agreed by the Liaison Conference in July 1940, which led to the signing of the Tripartite Pact, opened with the following preamble:

> 'The Japanese Empire will strive for the immediate settlement of the China incident by improving internal and external conditions in accordance with changes in the world situation and at the same time will solve the problem of the southern area by taking advantage of opportunities.
>
> Changes in policy, placing the emphasis on measures for the southern area, will be decided on consideration of various conditions, internal and external.
>
> Various preparations for the measures described above will be put in hand as soon as possible.'[1]

All this may seem strangely inconsistent with the appearance, which Japan often gave, of acting methodically in accordance with a master plan. But the paradox can be simply explained. Japanese policy at its highest level—the general trend of her aspirations—was not open to argument; it was the natural product of her economic difficulties and her strong militaristic tradition. Its basic assumption, that Japan needed to expand and had a moral right and even duty to do so, was never seriously questioned, but provided a uniform, almost unnoticed, background to all discussions. At the lower or executive level, especially when only one Service or department was concerned, planning was thorough and usually effective. Operations such as the move into Indo-China—or, indeed, the later attack on

---

[1] Quoted in Japanese Monograph, No. 146, *The Army Forces, Far East*, App. II.

Pearl Harbor—were well timed and smoothly executed. But between these levels of thought and action lay a void. Japan had no machinery, or only the clumsiest, for reducing her aspirations to a clear-cut national policy, which should take account of political and diplomatic realities as well as purely military problems. Under her system there was much discussion, but no central authority to act as arbiter between opposing points of view and, if necessary, to enforce its decisions. The result was a series of loosely co-ordinated actions, which had the appearance of unity, since they all tended in the same direction. But they were not the outcome of a policy properly so called, but rather the product of impulses, self-generating and uncontrolled—in the last resort, perhaps even uncontrollable.

(ii)
Konoye's Proposal

Against this background was played out the tragicomedy of Japan's negotiations with the United States. The full story does not belong in the present Volume, since Great Britain was not a partner in these discussions; but she was so deeply affected by their outcome that some sketch must be given. As we saw above,[1] Japan's original offer was almost derisory. She invited the United States to procure her access to the raw materials of the south which she required; to advise China to make peace and withdraw support from her if she refused; and to refrain, and advise her associates to refrain, from any increase in existing military establishments in the Far East. In return, Japan promised to respect the neutrality of the Philippines; not to use Indo-China as a base for further operations in the south; and to withdraw her troops from that country, in which she was to retain special rights, as soon as a satisfactory peace had been signed with China. Considered as a reaction to the embargo, the severest form of pressure short of war which could be applied to Japan, this was wholly unpromising. But there were two faint gleams of hope. The first was the pause in Japanese operations already referred to; the second the fact that Prince Konoye, the Japanese Prime Minister, had recently reformed his Cabinet. The egregious M. Matsuoka, hitherto Foreign Minister and the leading advocate of the German alliance, had been dropped and his place taken by Admiral Toyoda, a reputed Liberal.[2]

---

[1] See page 131.
[2] Langer and Gleason, pp. 631–41.

This was the position at the time of the Atlantic Meeting; but a further development followed soon afterwards. Immediately on his return to Washington the President sent for Admiral Nomura, the Japanese Ambassador, and delivered his promised 'warning', though in a much modified form. The main business of the meeting, however, was to discuss the resumption of negotiations; and the Ambassador took the opportunity to bring forward a new proposal. This was for a personal meeting between Prince Konoye and the President at some convenient point in the Pacific, at which the whole range of outstanding problems could be reviewed.[1] The idea of a meeting was not new in itself; it had been mooted once or twice before in earlier discussions. But it had hitherto been intended only as a ceremonial gesture, a suitable finale to negotiations already successfully concluded through the diplomatic channel. What was now proposed was a working session on the same lines as the Atlantic Meeting, at which the President and Prince Konoye should themselves be the principal negotiators.

The idea was well calculated to appeal to the President. It offered scope for the type of personal intervention which he most enjoyed; it was consistent with his policy of gaining time; and there was always the possibility, if the offer were sincerely meant, that a much needed settlement might result. His immediate response was therefore cordial. He told the Ambassador that he welcomed the invitation and went so far, though without finally committing himself, as to suggest that the middle of October might be the most convenient time and Juneau in Alaska a suitable place. Immediately after the meeting, Mr. Cordell Hull, who had been present, began to raise objections. He represented that what are now called 'meetings at the summit' were too often futile and even dangerous unless the main points of controversy had already been settled, or brought within sight of settlement, by ordinary negotiation. The Japanese were particularly adept at drafting broad and speciously worded agreements, which could later be turned to their own advantage. This was the method that Prince Konoye would certainly try to use at a personal meeting; and in such a setting it would be almost equally risky to accept or reject whatever fair-sounding formula he might propose.[2]

Mr. Hull had many reasons for taking this firm stand. He had resented his complete exclusion from the recent Atlantic Meeting and can scarcely have wished to see affairs in the Pacific, with which he had particularly concerned himself, handled in the same way. He knew that the President was a dashing rather than a sound negotiator, better fitted by temperament to deal with those who shared some-

---

[1] Langer and Gleason, pp. 693–8.

[2] Cordell Hull, *Memoirs* (1948), pp. 1023–7.

thing of his own outlook, than with determined opponents whose springs of action he found it difficult to grasp. His optimistic bonhomie, so often effective at home, might trap him abroad into an unwise agreement, of which the spirit would be disregarded, though the letter might be honoured. Mr. Hull also had reasons, which appeared to be sound, for doubting the sincerity of Prince Konoye's offer. Some months before, American cryptographers had succeeded in breaking the Japanese diplomatic cipher, with the result that wireless messages to and from Tokyo were now being regularly intercepted and read. There was nothing in these deciphers to suggest a change in Japanese policy.[1] On the contrary, their tone was uniformly bellicose and seemed to give the lie to all the Ambassador's fair words.[2]

With these arguments the Secretary had little difficulty in persuading Mr. Roosevelt that he ought not, after all, to meet Konoye, until the existing negotiations had made substantial progress. A week later, when the invitation was repeated through the United States' Ambassador in Tokyo, a reply was sent in these terms. Finally, on 28th August, Mr. Roosevelt received a personal message from Prince Konoye, again urging that they should meet and endeavour to reach an agreement in principle. Formal negotiations about matters of detail could follow later through the diplomatic channel. Konoye added that the situation was fast deteriorating and, unless something were done, might soon pass out of control altogether. After some days' delay, Roosevelt replied that he understood Konoye's difficulties and agreed with his estimate of the situation, but remained convinced that a personal meeting would be of no value, unless a basis of agreement had already been laid by diplomatic methods.[3]

This attitude was understandable; but it is an open question how far it was wise. There was another side to the story, which must be considered in relation to the peculiarities of the Japanese constitution. At the time of his invitation to Roosevelt, Konoye's position was extremely delicate. Though a cautious and even timid man by temperament, he had allowed himself to figure in the past as a leading and aggressive nationalist. He had been Prime Minister in 1937 at the time of the attack on China and again in 1940, when the Tripartite Pact was signed. But by the summer of 1941 his views had been considerably modified. He had realized that a complete change of tactics was necessary and even overdue. Japan had gained much from the

---

[1] Intercepted messages are an attractive but dangerous source of diplomatic information, since it is often impossible to tell whether the views expressed are those of the Government concerned, of one department of that Government or even of an individual. Thus the views of the Japanese Foreign Office or of Service attachés, as revealed in American deciphers, were not necessarily a true guide to the policy of the Cabinet or the Prime Minister.

[2] Hull, pp. 975–6 and 1012–1.

[3] Hull, pp. 1016–29; Langer and Gleason, pp. 698–709.

German alliance; but she could not afford to continue a policy which was bound to bring her into open collision with the United States. The time had come to draw back and patiently await the next opportunity. But it was one thing to entertain these views, another to enforce them. When it came to implementing his policy, Konoye found himself the prisoner alike of his constitutional status and of his own reputation.

To understand the position more exactly, we must go back to the end of June, when news of the German attack on Russia first reached Japan. Prince Konoye, whose change of heart was already beginning, supported the argument that the attack was a breach (at least in spirit) of the Tripartite Pact, which would justify Japan in making a radical change of policy. M. Matsuoka took an opposite view. He professed to regard the attack as a happy surprise, since it afforded Japan a long-awaited opportunity to settle accounts with her old opponent Russia. He urged that plans for an advance in the south should be suspended in favour of an immediate attack on Vladivstok, which should develop, as soon as forces could be concentrated, into a general offensive against Russian positions in the Far East. But this proposal found little favour even with the Army leaders, Matsuoka's strongest supporters. They were well aware that Japanese forces on the mainland were no match for the Red Army, and that an attack in that quarter, even if the military odds had been better, would yield none of the economic advantages to be expected from a campaign in the south. Nevertheless, Matsuoka, a vigorous and persuasive personality, was able to find enough support to ensure that debates in the Liaison Conference were bitter and prolonged. The final result was a compromise. On 2nd July it was agreed: (i) that Japan, while remaining faithful to the Tripartite Pact, should not at present intervene in the Russo-German war; (ii) that she should, nevertheless, reinforce her army in Manchuria and make preparations to pass to the offensive at some future date; (iii) that she should press on at the same time with her advance in the south, and in particular with the occupation of Indo-China, accepting the risk of war with Great Britain and the United States which that would entail; and finally (iv) that she would make every possible diplomatic effort to avoid war with the United States.[1]

This was less a policy than a desperate attempt to accommodate all possible points of view within the scope of a single document. But it was of some value to Konoye. It paved the way for the elimination of Matsuoka, who had now doubly lost face, both by his failure to predict the German attack on Russia and by the rejection of his policy after the event. It also embodied the principle of negotiation, in

---

[1] Japanese Monograph No. 147; Langer and Gleason, pp. 625–31.

however tenuous a form, in a document which the Army had signed. A few weeks later came the economic embargo, which reopened the debate in a new and sharper form. In some respects the situation was to Konoye's advantage, for he could now count on powerful support from the Navy. Admiral Nagano, the Chief of the Naval Staff, was deeply concerned about the state of the country's oil stocks. At the end of July, when the embargo brought this issue to a head, he sought an audience with the Emperor in order to impress on him the need for an early settlement with America. Failing that, the pressure of the embargo would force Japan into a war in which the Navy could not guarantee a victory. He is said to have added that, if a settlement could only be bought at the price of abandoning the Tripartite Pact, that sacrifice ought to be made.[1]

The Japanese Army, however, though now half-committed to the principle of negotiation, was still unwilling to accept the realities of the situation. They persisted in regarding diplomacy as no more than a cheap and ready method of obtaining the same results as they had previously hoped to obtain by war. They therefore laid down two absolute conditions: Japan should not abandon the Tripartite Pact; nor should she accept any terms, which would deprive her of the fruits of her long campaign in China or seriously limit her freedom of action in the south. Subject to this, they were willing that negotiations should take place, if the Prime Minister would make himself personally responsible for their success. Such was the origin of the absurd proposals put forward to the United States at the beginning of August. They represented the utmost concession that Prince Konoye could wring from the Liaison Conference; but no one was better aware than he that they provided no basis whatever for serious negotiation. He therefore advanced, and with great difficulty persuaded the Liaison Conference to accept, his further proposal for a personal meeting between himself and President Roosevelt.[2]

Since this meeting never took place, Prince Konoye's precise intentions must always remain open to speculation. But there seems to be no reason to distrust the account of them given in his Memoirs. His plan, according to this version, was to reach a private settlement with Roosevelt on whatever were the best terms obtainable and then, returning immediately to Japan, to lay the results before the Emperor for his ratification before his colleagues had time to intervene. He professed to believe that, as soon as the terms of the settlement were known, he would himself be assassinated;[3] but by then it would

---

[1] Kirby, Vol. I, Chap. 4; Japanese Monograph, No. 147; Langer and Gleason, pp. 654–62.

[2] Konoye Memoirs, pp. 339–40.

[3] This was not an idle fear; at that time even so respected a statesman as the Marquis Kido, the Emperor's chief political adviser, found it prudent to provide himself with a bodyguard.

be too late. Not even the Army would dare to upset an agreement to which the Emperor himself was a party.

Those who doubt Prince Konoye's sincerity may object that this story, told after the event, begs the only important question: what terms did he intend to offer the President? Would they have formed the basis of a genuine settlement; and if so, could they subsequently have been enforced? No one can answer these questions with any certainty; but it will at least be clear, from what has been said above, that without some such device as Konoye proposed, the chances of reaching a settlement were remote indeed. So long as negotiations were conducted through the ordinary channels and were open to comment and obstruction by the Services, and especially by the Army, at every stage, nothing better than a deadlock could be expected; and nothing better was obtained.

The conversations in Washington dragged on for more than two months. Admiral Nomura had endless circular discussions with Mr. Hull and many equally unproductive interviews with President Roosevelt. But since he was unable to offer any concessions beyond the trivialities already advanced, there was no point at which a settlement was even in sight. The two conditions imposed by the Army were an absolute barrier. By September, after more than a month of this futility, Prince Konoye's position at home was seriously undermined. He had suffered a grave and open rebuff when his invitation to Roosevelt had not been accepted; and he was now beginning to lose the indispensable support of the Navy. Admiral Nagano's primary concern was still with the oil stocks; but the inference which he drew from their condition was changing. As the negotiations dragged on without result, the stocks sank; and he was obliged to point out that they would soon reach a level at which Japan, no longer able to fight, would have forfeited her freedom of action. He therefore began, though reluctantly, to associate himself with the demand for a time-limit, which the Army was now insistently pressing. It was clear that Konoye's policy, or his attempt to frame a policy, had failed. After some further weeks of vain discussion he tendered his resignation and was succeeded on 17th October by General Tojo, the late War Minister.[1]

---

[1] Kirby, Vol. I, Chap. 4.

(iii)

Modus Vivendi

At the end of September the American Ambassador in Tokyo had reported that, if Konoye fell, he would be succeeded by 'a military dictatorship which will lack either the disposition or the temperament to avoid colliding head-on with the United States'.[1] This was the common opinion; but later information suggested certain qualifications. There was reason to believe that the Emperor had insisted, when he accepted Konoye's resignation, that the new Cabinet should continue the negotiations. There was also evidence that Tojo had been selected as Prime Minister, less as a representative of the Army's point of view, than in the hope that he would be able to restrain his military colleagues.[2] By the middle or end of October, therefore, though the situation had clearly worsened, no absolute disaster had occurred. The door of negotiation was still ajar.

At about this point pressure was brought to bear on the United States from various quarters, internal and external, to modify the firm but negative policy which she had so far followed. It was suggested that President Roosevelt might address a personal message to the Emperor, containing a proposal for lifting the embargo in return for Japanese good behaviour; or, alternatively, that he should convene a meeting—much on the lines of the rejected Konoye meeting—between himself, Tojo and Generalissimo Chiang Kai-shek.[3] On 3rd November the Ambassador in Tokyo sent a long cable to Washington, expressing the view that the policy of sanctions, which he had hitherto advocated, had now failed and was in fact pushing Japan towards war. He argued that negotiations should continue and criticized the State Department for their rigid and formalistic attitude. Too much time, he felt, had been wasted on barren 'statements of principle' and some new and more realistic approach should be found.[4]

Two days later President Roosevelt received a telegram from Mr. Churchill. It brought forward again the proposal for a general warning, for which the Prime Minister had struggled so hard at the Atlantic Meeting. Mr. Churchill's immediate context was the Japanese threat to Yunnan and the Burma Road, which then seemed to be developing; but his suggestions were clearly intended to have a broader reference.

---

[1] Grew Dispatch: *Foreign Relations of the United States, Japan II*, p. 645.

[2] Konoye Memoirs, pp. 395–6; Langer and Gleason, pp. 728–9.

[3] *Pearl Harbor Attack*, II, 530; IV, 1700; XV, 1727.

[4] *Pearl Harbor Attack*, XIV, 1045–57.

'What we need now [he wrote] is a deterrent of the most general
and formidable character. The Japanese have as yet taken no
final decision and the Emperor appears to be exercising restraint.
When we talked about this at Placentia you spoke of gaining time,
and this policy has been brilliantly successful so far. But our joint
embargo is steadily forcing the Japanese to decisions for peace or
war.'

On the same day, the Joint Board circulated a paper on the Far
Eastern situation. They pointed out that the U.S. Pacific Fleet was at
present inferior to the Japanese fleet and could not undertake a
major offensive unless all units were withdrawn from the Atlantic—a
course which they regarded as dangerous. On the other hand,
American air and naval strength in the Philippines was gradually
increasing. By the middle of December it would have become a
positive threat to any Japanese movement south of Formosa; and by
March 1942, a decisive deterrent. There was everything to gain,
therefore, by putting off the evil day as long as possible. A war
against Japan would, in any case, be defensive in the early stages;
and the Joint Board advised that it should not be undertaken unless
the interests of the United States were directly threatened by (i) a
Japanese attack on American, British or Dutch possessions; (ii) a
Japanese movement into Siam west of 100° East or south of 10°
North; or (iii) an attack on Portuguese or French territory in Timor
or New Caledonia.[1]

These proposals were not necessarily incompatible either with Mr.
Churchill's warning or with the other suggestions for a new diplomatic approach to Japan. But their main emphasis was on the need
to gain time; and it may well have been this that finally decided the
President not to change his tactics but to allow the situation to
develop as before. This decision was applauded by Mr. Hull, who
appears to have been seized at about this time by a brief and un-
warranted spasm of optimism. Mr. Stimson, the Secretary of War,
reported him as saying that he had great faith in the effect of the
Emperor's intervention and believed that he would be willing to
accept 'such cardinal points of American policy . . . as the evacuation
of China'. If so, added Mr. Hull, 'Why, we shall be in a wonderful
position'.[2]

This exuberance apart, the President's negative policy may well
have seemed the part of wisdom. So far, by doing nothing or almost
nothing, he had kept the negotiations with Japan alive and had
staved off the crisis for nearly three months. Why should the same

[1] It is interesting to note how closely these conditions resemble the definition of a
Japanese Act of Aggression given in the A.D.A. Agreement of February 1941, but then
rejected by the United States. (See Kirby: Vol. I, Chap. 3).

[2] *Stimson's Diary* (M S.), 28th October, 1941.

technique not continue to work for a little longer? Indeed, one could argue that in such a delicate situation almost any precipitate action —any action at all—might easily be fatal. Since the new Japanese Cabinet was apparently committed in principle to continuing the negotiations, the safest course was to do nothing and allow them to make the first move. But to abandon the initiative is often as dangerous in diplomacy as it is in war; and so it proved in this case. If any possibility still existed of reaching a peaceful settlement with Japan, the road to it was certainly not through inaction.

General Tojo, it is true, had received instructions from the Emperor to continue the negotiations; but the Imperial mandate, following the usual custom, was far from explicit. Though it directed the Cabinet to re-examine the minimum terms laid down by the Imperial Conference on 6th September, it said nothing about what new terms might be regarded as acceptable. That was left to be decided by the usual process of inter-departmental bargaining. It was clear, after Konoye's experience, that any comprehensive settlement would certainly be vetoed by the Army; and Tojo therefore turned his mind to the possibilities of a short-term or stop-gap agreement. When he met the Liaison Conference at the beginning of November, he presented two plans. The first (Plan A) was a restatement of Japan's minimum terms for a final settlement, which did not differ greatly except in wording from previous statements of the same kind. The second (Plan B) was a proposal for an interim settlement, which was regarded, at least by Tojo and his Foreign Minister, as representing a large measure of concession on Japan's part:

'1. The Governments of Japan and the United States agree that neither will militarily invade any area in South-East Asia or the South Seas with the exception of French Indo-China.

2. The Governments of Japan and the United States will co-operate mutually in guaranteeing the obtention of the materials they need in Netherlands India.

3. The Governments of Japan and the United States will mutually return to the situation prior to the freezing of their respective assets and the Government of the United States will agree to furnish Japan with the petroleum she needs.

4. The Government of the United States will put no obstacle in the way of Japan in her efforts to make peace with China.

5. The Japanese Government agrees to withdraw her army, which is at present stationed in French Indo-China, whenever peace shall have been established between Japan and China or a just peace firmly established in the Pacific area.

6. The Japanese Government agrees that, if the principle of non-discriminatory treatment in trade is to be applied throughout the world, the same principle should also be applied to the entire Pacific area; in other words, in China as well.

7. The two Governments shall make world-peace their common objective and shall co-operate at a suitable time for speedy realization of world-peace. However, in dealing with developments prior to the establishment of world-peace, the two Governments shall act in accordance with the viewpoint of protection and self-defence. Furthermore, in the event of the United States participation in the European war, Japan shall automatically carry out what she understands to be the obligations which befall to her as a party of the Three Power Agreement existing between Japan, Germany and Italy.'[1]

An addendum provided that the sixth and seventh clauses might be dropped, if necessary, and an extension added to the first clause, by which Japan assumed the further obligation to withdraw her troops from south to north Indo-China on the signing of the interim agreement.

After long discussion Plan A and Plan B were both accepted by the Liaison Conference and this decision endorsed by the Imperial Conference on 5th November. It was agreed that they should be presented in Washington in succession, Plan B not being brought forward until it was clear that Plan A had been decisively rejected. Similarly, the proposed modifications to Plan B were not to be mentioned so long as there was any hope of the Plan's being acceptable without them. Even with these qualifications, General Tojo had a hard struggle to secure agreement. The Army continued to argue that further negotiations were useless, since America's only object was to gain time in which to complete her own military preparations. It would therefore be better to face the issue at once and not to waste more time in futile discussions, while Japan's own resources dwindled. In the end these arguments were overruled, but not before the Army had exacted the condition of a strict time-limit. Negotiations were to be allowed to continue for three weeks only. Thereafter, if no satisfactory settlement had been reached, military action would follow automatically at a date to be settled by the Chiefs of Staff.[2]

It is not easy to assess the general state of feeling in Tokyo at this point. The tone of the newspapers and of speeches in the Diet during its session between 15th and 18th November was entirely bellicose; and the records of discussions at the Liaison and Imperial Conferences, so far as they exist, give a scarcely better impression. But much of this noise and sabre-rattling was the result of a kind of public competition in patriotism engendered by the Army's obstinate attitude. As often happens in such cases, even those who in private most strongly urged a settlement, felt obliged to join the public

---

[1] American translation from *Pearl Harbor Attack*, XII, 96–7 and 126.

[2] Langer and Gleason, pp. 852–4.

chorus, lest their courage or national spirit should be impugned. Below this surface there was certainly no lack of realism. Early in November, for example, the Japanese Foreign Office circulated a memorandum, remarkable both for its caution and good sense. It was in essence a plea for delay. As the paper pointed out, there was no longer any question of seizing a fleeting opportunity; despite Germany's dazzling victories, the war in Europe was likely to be a long one. In these circumstances, Japan had much to gain by patience. If action were postponed until the spring, Russia would be further weakened and Great Britain preoccupied by a renewed threat of invasion. The United States, though in general stronger, would be more deeply committed in Europe and therefore less free to act in the Pacific. On her side, Japan might have lost ground economically, but would have had the opportunity to consolidate her hold on Indo-China and Siam, the two indispensable bases for an advance in the south.[1]

We must suppose that, if Mr. Cordell Hull had read this paper, he would not have regarded it as the 'evidence of Japan's peaceful intentions', for which he had so often asked. Nevertheless, it represented the voice of peace, so far as that was still audible in Japan, and indicated the only basis on which a temporary settlement might have been reached. A settlement based on broad statements of liberal principle, as enunciated by Mr. Hull, was clearly impossible, since these principles were neither understood nor accepted in Japan. But a settlement based strictly on expediency might have been achieved. The attempt would have had the support, not only of the Emperor and General Tojo, but of a substantial party of moderates, that is to say, of men who, without questioning Japan's need to expand sooner or later, were strongly impressed by the danger and inexpediency of trying to do so at the moment.

Against this, it may be argued that America did right to stand on principle because, in her dealings with Japan, she was resisting precisely the same forces of aggression as Great Britain had previously had to resist in Europe. That is true; but the two cases were not parallel. In Europe in 1939 a temporary settlement, which delayed the outbreak of war by three or four months, would have had no value. In the Far East in 1941 such a settlement might have been of the first importance. The Western Powers were slowly gathering their strength; and there was a strong probability that, if Japan could be induced to halt her attack, she would find herself obliged in the changed circumstances of the following year to abandon it altogether. As President Roosevelt had already seen, it was worth while to bid high for delay. This point was, of course, fully appreciated in

---

[1] *Tokyo War Crimes Document*, No. 1559A.

Japan by the war-party as well as by the moderates. Indeed, the Army's fear of the consequences of a temporary settlement was one of the main reasons for their rigid insistence on conditions which they knew to be unacceptable. But this very fact suggests that a contrasting flexibility on the American side might have had its advantages. Even some degree of appeasement—to use the popular word of the day—would not have come amiss, if it had secured the final object of avoiding war.

Such was the atmosphere in which the last phase of the negotiations opened. On 7th November Admiral Nomura presented Plan A to Mr. Hull. During the next week or ten days a number of conversations followed between the Ambassador, who was later joined by M. Kurusu as special envoy, Mr. Hull and the President. It does not appear that Plan A was ever formally rejected. Indeed, that was scarcely necessary, since it was no more than a restatement of claims which were already known to be unacceptable. But the substance of the discussions left no doubt that the plan was dead. This result can hardly have surprised either the Japanese envoys or their Government. But Admiral Nomura, himself an earnest solicitor for peace, must have felt close to despair, when he heard Mr. Hull add that in his view negotiations had not yet even begun. All the endless discussions which had taken place since August, were to be characterized only as 'exploratory conversations'; and negotiations proper could not start until, in the Secretary's often repeated phrase, the two Governments had reached agreement on basic principles. There was one limited sense in which this was true, as it must be true in any negotiation; but it was a hard saying at a time when both parties—the Japanese envoys from their instructions and Mr. Hull from intercepted messages—were aware of the existence of a rigid time-limit.[1]

By this time, however, the urgency of the situation had begun to assert itself in Washington. Since it was now improbable that any final settlement could be reached with Japan, the Administration had turned their minds, like General Tojo, to the possibilities of an interim or stop-gap agreement. There had been no lack of proposals about the form which this might take. A number of widely differing plans and suggestions had flowed in from the President, from Mr. Hull, from officials of the State Department, from the Treasury and even from private individuals. At the expense of much discussion these various schemes were brought into focus and reduced to a single and comparatively simple formula, known henceforward as the *Modus Vivendi*. The first definite draft of this document was produced on 22nd November.[2] Two days before that Admiral Nomura and M.

---

[1] Hull, Chap. 77, pp. 1056–65; *Pearl Harbor Attack*, XII, 119–25, 131–7, 141.

[2] Hull, pp. 1058, 1067–8.

Kurusu, having advised their Government of the failure of Plan A, had received instructions to put forward the modified version of Plan B. It thus happened that the two stop-gap proposals, advanced from either side, reached independent maturity at almost the same time. It will be convenient to set them down in their final form side by side:

Plan B	*Modus Vivendi*
1. The two Governments would undertake not to make any armed advance in South-East Asia or the Southern Pacific area, except in the part of Indo-China where Japanese troops were already stationed.	1. The two Governments would declare that they had no territorial designs in the Pacific and would undertake not to make any advance by force or threat of force across any international border in the Pacific area, unless attacked.
2. Japan would withdraw her troops from Indo-China either upon the restoration of peace with China or upon the establishment of an equitable peace in the Pacific area. Meanwhile, she would move her troops in South Indo-China to North Indo-China on the conclusion of the present interim agreement.	2. Japan would withdraw and not replace her armed forces in Southern Indo-China and would reduce her total forces in that country to the number of 25,000.
3. The two Governments would co-operate in securing commodities needed by them from the Netherlands East Indies.	3. The United States would receive all imports from Japan, provided that two-thirds in any one month were of raw silk. The United States would also export goods to Japan, including food, medical supplies, raw cotton and oil for civilian use.
4. The two Governments would undertake to restore their commercial relations to those existing before the freezing of assets. The United States Government would also supply Japan with a required quantity of oil.	4. The United States would approach the British, Dutch and Australian Governments with a view to similar economic concessions on their part.
5. The United States would undertake to refrain from action prejudicial to the restoration of general peace between Japan and China.	5. The United States would not view with disfavour the opening of peace negotiations between Japan and China nor the conclusion of an armistice during their course. If desired, the United States would provide facilities for these negotiations to take place in the Philippines.
	6. This agreement to remain in force for three months only, unless extended.[1]

A close reading of the two texts, at first sight so similar, discloses a number of more or less important differences. Could these have been

---

[1] Woodward, Vol. I., Chap. 24, Section II; *Foreign Relations of U.S., Japan II*, pp. 755–6.

resolved by negotiation in the short time remaining? Perhaps not. Admiral Nomura's instructions left no doubt that Plan B was Japan's last word. M. Tojo informed him that no further concessions were conceivable and that it was only with the greatest difficulty that he had persuaded the Government to extend the time-limit from 25th to 29th November.[1] We must also suppose that the *Modus Vivendi* was America's last word. Indeed, some members of the Administration may well have regarded it as going too far. Under these conditions, with both sides standing pat, even the smallest gap might well have proved unbridgeable. Yet it must be added that some at least of the differences might have been resolved with little or no yielding on either side. The Japanese, for example, might well have accepted the American version of clause (1) on the practical ground that they had decided against an attack on Russia and that their operations in China would not cross any international border. A similar adjustment should have been possible over Clause (2); and the gap between the two versions in the economic clauses (3) and (4) was more of a degree than principle.

But in fact the experiment of trying to reconcile the two drafts was never made. Mr. Hull seems to have regarded them from the outset as totally incompatible. Indeed, if we may judge from his Memoirs, the first sight of the Japanese Plan B caused him to explode in righteous indignation. To sign such a document would, he said, be tantamount to a complete surrender:

> 'The President and I could only conclude that agreeing to these proposals would mean condonement by the United States of Japan's aggressions, assent to future courses of conquest by Japan, abandonment of the most essential principles of our foreign policy, betrayal of China and Russia, and acceptance of the rôle of silent partner aiding and abetting Japan in her effort to create a Japanese hegemony over the Western Pacific and Eastern Asia.'[2]

This was surprisingly violent language from an active sponsor of the *Modus Vivendi*, which resembled Plan B at so many points. One might almost suppose that Mr. Hull had suffered a change of heart and was now opposed to the whole concept of an interim agreement. But this was not so. On 22nd November he communicated the latest Japanese proposals to the British and Chinese Ambassadors and the Dutch and Australian Ministers, and showed them a draft reply which incorporated the *Modus Vivendi*. He records that the reaction to this draft, to which he evidently attached great importance, was generally favourable.[3] Two days later, President Roosevelt sent a private message to

---

[1] *Pearl Harbor Attack*, XII, 163–5.
[2] Hull, p. 1070.
[3] Hull, pp. 1073–4.

Mr. Churchill, giving a slightly abbreviated text of both proposals and adding with regard to the second or American draft:

> 'This seems to be a fair proposition for the Japanese, but its acceptance or rejection is really a matter of internal Japanese politics. I am not very hopeful and we must all be prepared for real trouble, possibly soon.'

Up to this point, then, we can regard the terms of the *Modus Vivendi* as representing America's settled policy; but an abrupt change was already on its way. On 24th November—the same day on which the President telegraphed to Mr. Churchill—Mr. Hull received the representatives of the associated Powers again. He was disappointed to discover that only the Dutch Minister was able to express definite approval of the American plan. His colleagues had not yet received clear instructions from their respective Governments, though it appeared likely, from what the Chinese Ambassador had to say, that his Government would be unwilling to agree.[1] On the following day came news of the British reaction in the form of a reply from Mr. Churchill to the President's cable. The operative paragraph, partly inspired by a message the Prime Minister had meanwhile received from Generalissimo Chiang Kai-shek, ran as follows:

> 'Of course, it is for you to handle this business and we certainly do not want an additional war. There is only one point that disquiets us. What about Chiang Kai-shek? Is he not having a very thin diet? Our anxiety is about China. If they collapse, our joint difficulties would enormously increase. We are sure that the regard of the United States for China will govern your action. We feel that the Japanese are most unsure of themselves.'

This lack of enthusiasm was certainly disappointing; but it did not amount on analysis to much which could fairly be called opposition. The Dutch Government had approved the *Modus Vivendi*; and none of the other Governments concerned had positively rejected it except the Chinese. In these circumstances one might have expected Mr. Hull, if he really attached importance to his plan, to have persisted. But evidently the effect of his conversations on the 24th and of the Prime Minister's cable of the 25th was decisive. On the following morning he sought a further interview with the President and laid before him a written memorandum, which stated that 'in view of the opposition of the Chinese Government and either the half-hearted support or actual opposition of the British, Netherlands and the Australian Governments . . . and of the additional opposition that will naturally arise through utter lack of understanding of the vast importance and value otherwise of the *Modus Vivendi*', all proposals for an interim agreement with Japan should now be dropped. Instead the reply to

---

[1] Hull, pp. 1076–7.

the latest Japanese communication should set out America's plan for a final settlement in the following terms:

1. A Non-Aggression Pact to be signed between the United States, Japan, China, the United Kingdom, the Netherlands, the U.S.S.R. and Siam.

2. The integrity of Indo-China to be jointly guaranteed by the United States, Japan, China, the United Kingdom, the Netherlands and Siam.

3. *Japan to withdraw all her forces both from China and Indo-China.*

4. *The United States and Japan to recognize no other Government in China than that of Generalissimo Chiang Kai-shek.*

5. The United States and Japan to abandon their extra-territorial rights in China and to urge other Governments to do the same.

6. The United States and Japan to sign a trade agreement for the mutual reduction of tariff-barriers.

7. The existing economic embargo to be lifted.

8. Both Governments to contribute equally to a dollar-yen stabilization fund.

9. *The United States and Japan to agree that no Pact with any third Power should be so interpreted as to conflict with the main object of the present agreement; that is, the preservation of peace in the Pacific.*

10. Other Governments to be invited to conform to the principles underlying this agreement.[1]

President Roosevelt, who was always more dependent on Mr. Hull's advice in Far Eastern than in European matters, agreed at once; and the new proposals were handed to Admiral Nomura and M. Kurusu on the afternoon of 26th November. There was, of course, no chance of their finding acceptance in Tokyo. The three clauses, printed above in italic, were enough in themselves to ensure the immediate breakdown of negotiations. Nevertheless there was still a brief hesitation on the Japanese side. The Liaison Conference met on 27th November to consider the American reply but failed to reach a final decision. On the following day the Elder Statesmen were called into consultation and recorded by a small majority their opposition to a war with the United States or, at least, their grave misgivings about its outcome. On 29th November the Liaison Conference met again and, observing that no change was likely in America's attitude, decided that the only course was now to fight. Two days later this decision was ratified by the Imperial Conference.[2]

In the meanwhile the Japanese armed forces, keeping to the original deadline of 25th November, had already put their preparations in hand. The task-force destined for the Pearl Harbor attack

---

[1] Hull, pp. 1082–3; *Foreign Relations, U.S. Japan, II*, pp. 766–70.

[2] Langer and Gleason, pp. 906–10.

had left port; a considerable armament was assembling in southern Indo-China; and 8th December had been selected as the day of the attack. Admiral Nomura and M. Kurusu, however, received orders to remain in Washington, where they continued conversations with the President and Mr. Hull, which had now become totally meaningless, if not actively fraudulent.

CHAPTER XI

FAR EASTERN DEFENCE

(i)

Naval Problems

DEFENCE IN THE Far East was in essence a naval problem. No land-force, however large, could protect the whole
coastline of Malaya, the Dutch East Indies and the Philippines, so long as Japan held command of the sea and could attack
when and where she pleased. Nor would it be easy, in territory where
distances were great and communications poor, to eject a hostile force,
once it had gained a footing. Under conditions of naval inferiority the
Allies' only course would be to concentrate their defence round selected strong points, such as Singapore and Manila, and try to keep open
their lines of communication with these bases, until the time when
a counter offensive could be launched. But as soon as they could
challenge Japan's command of the sea, the whole situation would be
reversed. Japan would then begin to suffer, as much as her opponents
before, from the wide dispersal of her forces and the need to protect
long and vulnerable lines of sea-communication. The greater the
area of her initial penetrations, the more precarious her future position would be.

The primary question, therefore, was what naval force the Allies
could bring together. Within the term Allies it is appropriate to include the United States. Although her exact position was still undefined, it was generally believed that she would not be able to stand
clear. Granted that, the naval odds did not at first appear uneven.
The Japanese Fleet was understood to consist of ten capital ships, ten
aircraft and six seaplane carriers, 18 heavy and 18 light cruisers, 113
destroyers and 63 submarines.[1] By the end of 1941 the Allies expected
to be able to assemble a force at least equal in size, though less homo-
geneous, since it would be made up of the ships of three nations.

In the Far Eastern area itself there were already three fleets or
detached squadrons. First came the U.S. Asiatic Fleet under Admiral
Hart at Manila, which consisted of one heavy and one light cruiser,
13 destroyers and 29 submarines. Next there was the Dutch contingent of three light cruisers, six destroyers and 13 submarines at
Batavia. Thirdly, under Admiral Layton, the Commander-in-Chief,
China Station, were three light cruisers, five destroyers and eight

---

[1] Roskill, Vol. I, Chap. 26.

M.T.B., divided between Singapore and Hong Kong. These could be supported, if necessary, by a further six light cruisers (including one belonging to the Free French) and four destroyers from the Australia and New Zealand stations. Taken together, these forces were not inadequate for local defence, though they included an unduly high proportion of old or even semi-obsolete ships.

The Allies' main strength lay farther back. Its principal component —and the only one immediately capable of a fleet-action with Japan —was the U.S. Pacific Fleet at Pearl Harbor. This consisted of eight capital ships, three aircraft carriers, 12 heavy and nine light cruisers, 67 destroyers and 27 submarines. Farther back still, since it had only a potential existence, was the British Far Eastern Fleet. In August, 1941, at the time of the Atlantic Meeting, the Joint Planners had recommended that one battleship from the Mediterranean (*Barham* or *Valiant*) should go east by mid-September, to be followed at the end of the year by four of the old R-class battleships, which were then refitting. No cruisers or destroyers could be spared; but one aircraft-carrier (*Eagle*) might be sent later. This fleet would be based initially on Ceylon for the protection of shipping in the Indian Ocean, but would also form the nucleus of a larger fleet—seven capital ships, one aircraft carrier, ten cruisers and 24 destroyers—which it was hoped to form by March 1942, and which would then move forward to Singapore.

These plans were not in fact carried out, for reasons which are discussed below; and, though a fleet was sent east before the end of 1941, it consisted of only two capital ships and four destroyers. But even with this reduced British contribution, the Allies achieved an approximate equality with Japan in all respects except the important one of aircraft-carriers. The comparative figures for the end of the year were as follows:

	Allies	Japan
Capital Ships	11	10
Aircraft-Carriers	3	10
Heavy Cruisers	14	18
Light Cruisers	22	18
Destroyers	100	113
Submarines	69	63[1]

But naval strength cannot be measured in numbers of units alone; and this was especially true in the Pacific, where the Allies suffered from certain obvious disadvantages, which greatly reduced their efficiency.

---

[1] Roskill, Vol. I, Chap. 26 (Table).

The most important, because the least easily remedied, was the dearth of bases from which to operate. The Allies possessed only two harbours in the Far East, Singapore and Pearl Harbor, which were equipped to serve as main fleet bases. They were over 6,000 miles apart; and the former was 3,000, the latter 3,400 miles from Japan. Moreover, now that the Japanese were installed in Indo-China, Singapore was open to a landward attack through Siam and could no longer be counted as wholly secure, even if covered by the presence of a fleet. Such advanced bases as the Allies possessed were still more exposed. Hong Kong, 1,400 miles north of Singapore, was only an outpost, which was not expected to withstand a serious attack. Manila, rather nearer to Singapore but nearly 5,000 miles from Pearl Harbor, had greater potentialities as a base and was more secure. But it was not equipped to receive the main fleet and was, besides, well within range of air-attack from Japanese bases on Formosa. Under these conditions the problem of applying Allied sea-power in the Pacific was not easy to solve.

It was further complicated by the heterogeneous nature of the force and the absence of a single command or even a single plan. During the Anglo-American staff conversations in Washington in the spring of 1941 it had been agreed to divide the Pacific into three theatres: (1) the Pacific area proper, covering the whole ocean space from the American coast to longitude 140° East (above the equator) or 180° East (below the equator); (2) the Far East area, forming a square from 92° East to 140° East and from 30° North to (approximately) 13° South; and (3) the Australia and New Zealand area, an irregular rectangle extending from 80° East to 180° East and bounded on the north by the equator as far as longitude 140° East and thence by the southern limit of the Far East area. The first of these theatres, the Pacific area, was to be an exclusively American responsibility; but the status of the other two was left obscure, commanders being merely directed to make 'such arrangements for mutual support as may be practical and appropriate'.

This agreement left the U.S. Asiatic Fleet in an ambiguous position. Admiral Hart was recognized as belonging to a different theatre from his superior, Admiral Kimmel, at Pearl Harbor; but his relations with Admiral Layton at Singapore were imprecise. Though they were directed to support each other, there was no joint plan; and neither was to be under the command of the other. During the course of 1941 various attempts were made to rationalize this situation. It was proposed that, for naval purposes, the Far East, East Indian (or Indian Ocean) and Anzac areas should be considered as a single unit under the general name of the Eastern Theatre. Admiral Layton, assisted by a combined staff at Singapore, would assume the strategic control of the whole area. But this solution was rejected by the Americans; initially, on the ground that Admiral Hart would 'lose his identity' and might be required to operate in waters 'of no strategic significance' to the United States; and later, on the ground that British naval forces in the Far East were too weak to make co-operation worth while. Negotiations continued throughout the year; but by December they had produced no more than an agreement on the procedure by which a joint plan might later be evolved, if circumstances were favourable.

In the event, therefore, Allied naval forces in the Far East were left much to their own devices. Admiral Layton formed a joint plan with his Dutch opposite number, in which a tentative rôle was also allotted to Admiral Hart's ships, should they wish to participate. It was likewise assumed that, in the event of war, Admiral Kimmel would be conducting offensive operations in some part of the Pacific. But the nature of his plans had not been disclosed; nor was it known what relationship, if any, they would bear to such operations as might be planned or carried out in the Far East area. This mutual isolation greatly increased the importance, though it could not increase the size, of the British Far Eastern Fleet, which now appeared as our sole effective instrument of defence. It is therefore appropriate to turn back to August and consider what became of the Joint Planners' recommendations.

On 25th August, immediately after his return from the Atlantic Meeting, the Prime Minister began an exchange of minutes with the First Sea Lord on the subject of the Far Eastern Fleet. He proposed that we should form a small but powerful force of modern battleships (including at least one of the *King George V* class) in the triangle Aden—Simonstown—Singapore to act as a deterrent to Japanese aggression. 'We have only to remember,' he wrote, 'all the preoccupations which are caused us by the *Tirpitz*—the only capital ship left to Germany against our 15 or 16 battleships and battle-cruisers—to see what an effect would be produced on the Japanese Admiralty by the presence of a small but very powerful and fast force in Eastern waters.' He went on to say that he did not like the idea of sending the old R-class battleships to the Indian Ocean. They might be useful for convoy protection; but it seemed to him a false principle to form a fleet, which was numerically large and costly in manpower, but not equipped either in speed or armour to fight the modern ships of the Japanese Navy.

The First Sea Lord, on the other hand, preferred dispositions very similar to those already recommended by the Joint Planners. He proposed that the four R-class battleships (*Revenge, Royal Sovereign, Ramillies* and *Resolution*) should be sent to the Indian Ocean before the end of the year, primarily to act as convoy escorts. During December and the following January they should be reinforced by three more modern ships, the *Nelson*, the *Rodney* and the battle-cruiser *Renown*. The aircraft-carrier *Eagle* was not available as she was being held in home waters for Operation 'Pilgrim'; but the smaller *Hermes*[1] was already on the East Indies station. These ships would provide the nucleus of the Eastern Fleet proper, which could not be formed until the following spring, owing to the shortage of cruisers and destroyers. Meanwhile, their primary duty would be trade protection in the Indian Ocean:

> 'Until we can form a fleet in the Far East which is capable of meeting a Japanese force of the strength they are likely to send south, it is necessary to deter Japanese action in the Indian Ocean.
>
> By sending capital ships to escort our convoys in the Indian Ocean we hope to deter the Japanese from sending any of their battleships to this area.
>
> By sending a battle-cruiser and aircraft-carrier to the Indian Ocean we hope to deter the Japanese from sending their 8″ gun cruisers to this area.
>
> It is not considered that the substitution of one of the *King George V* class for one of the above would give sufficient added security to justify the disadvantages which her absence from the home area would involve, as her speed is insufficient to run down a Japanese 8″ gun cruiser.
>
> Depending on the situation at the time, and if war with Japan has not broken out, it may be found desirable to send *Nelson*, *Rodney*, *Renown* and the aircraft-carrier to Singapore in the first instance, as they would thus form a greater deterrent. If war eventuated they would have to retire to Trincomalee.'

It will be observed that, although Mr. Churchill and Admiral Pound both used the word 'deterrent', they did so in different senses. Mr. Churchill's aim was to deter Japan by a show of naval strength from entering the war; Admiral Pound's to deter Japan in the event of war from operating her ships in the Indian Ocean. It may well be considered that, in the circumstances of August, the former was the more proper objective. But the question remains whether the Prime Minister's dispositions would have achieved the effect that he had in mind. The analogy with the *Tirpitz* was striking but far from conclusive. The danger, which so preoccupied the Admiralty, was that the *Tirpitz* should break out into the Atlantic, where she could do immense damage to our ocean convoys, which were not normally protected by any ship capable of fighting her. But the case was different in the Far East. It was not a question of trade convoys, but of major expeditions from Japan against one or other of her known objectives in the south. On any footing these would be heavily escorted;

---

[1] But from November *Hermes*, an old ship, was in dock at Simonstown.

19

and it was not likely that the influence of one modern battleship, more or less, would cause Japan to alter her plans.

After the first exchange of minutes in August, nothing more was heard of the matter until 16th October, when the Foreign Secretary wrote to the Prime Minister:

'The fall of Prince Konoye's Government is an ominous sign. Though the complexion of the new Cabinet is not yet announced, we must expect the constitution of one more under the influence of extreme elements. The Russian defeats must inevitably be having their effect upon the Japanese appetite. There is nothing to show yet in which direction Japan will move, if in any. But it is no doubt true that the stronger the joint front that the A.B.C.D. Powers[1] can show, the greater the deterrent to Japanese action.

In this connexion you will recall that we discussed some little time ago the possibility of capital ship reinforcements to the Far East. The matter has now become more urgent, and I should be glad if we could discuss it at the Defence Committee meeting tomorrow afternoon.'

By this time the *Repulse*, taking the place of her sister ship *Renown*, had already reached the Indian Ocean. The question at issue was whether she should be joined (in accordance with the Admiralty's plan) by the *Rodney* and later the *Nelson*,[2] to be followed by the four R-class battleships, or (in accordance with the Prime Minister's plan) by a single *King George V* class battleship, the *Prince of Wales*. On this point the same argument as before was joined, though it was observable that both protagonists had slightly shifted their ground. The Prime Minister argued that an attack in force on Malaya was unlikely. What we had most to fear was operations by Japanese battleships or battle-cruisers against our trade routes. If this occurred, the R-class battleships would be useless as convoy escorts and the presence of a fast modern striking force essential. The First Sea Lord argued that, whereas a single modern battleship could not deter Japan from moving southward, she would be deterred by the presence at Singapore of a force (such as the *Nelson*, and *Rodney*, and the R-class battleships), which would oblige her to detach the greater part of her main fleet to cover the operation, thus exposing the home islands. This was very different from maintaining, as he had previously done, that such a force, though it might show itself at Singapore in peacetime, would have to withdraw to Trincomalee as soon as war broke out. Indeed it destroyed the whole basis of his earlier and perhaps sounder argument, that we could do nothing effective against Japan until we could form a properly balanced fleet, including

---

[1] America, Great Britain, China and the Dutch.

[2] *Nelson* was then under repair.

a number of cruisers and destroyers which would not be available until 1942.

Nevertheless, even in their altered form, the two lines of thought were irreconcilable. The Defence Committee was strongly influenced by the Prime Minister's argument, ably supported by Mr. Eden, that the political influence of one of our most modern ships would far outweigh that of a larger but older fleet; but it could find no complete answer to Admiral Pound's objections. The result was therefore a compromise. It was agreed that the *Prince of Wales* should be ordered forthwith to Cape Town. Her arrival there would be noticed in Japan and would, no doubt, produce some effect in itself. Subsequently, a further decision would be taken about her final destination. So far all is clear. What followed is more mysterious; and no light is thrown upon it either by the Cabinet or the C.O.S. papers. On 25th October the *Prince of Wales* left for Cape Town, wearing the flag of Admiral Sir Tom Phillips, lately the Vice-Chief of the Naval Staff and now the designated Commander-in-Chief, Far East. On 11th November, five days *before* his arrival at Cape Town, Admiral Phillips received orders from the Admiralty to proceed to Ceylon and thence, in company with *Repulse*, to Singapore.[1] These orders were presumably issued as the result of the further decision promised at the Defence Committee meeting. But it is strange that there should be no record of when or by whom this decision was taken.

In the circumstances one can only guess what were the reasons which finally decided the authorities to send the *Prince of Wales* forward. It is probable that they were connected with the discussions with the United States, already referred to, about naval co-operation in the Pacific; and that the dispatch of two powerful ships to Singapore was intended, in part, as an answer to the American objection that British naval forces were too weak to make a joint plan worth considering. Colour is given to this view by the fact that, as soon as Admiral Phillips reached Ceylon, he was ordered to leave his flagship and fly direct to Singapore and thence to Manila to open discussions with Admiral Hart. He arrived in Manila on 4th December and, in the course of talks extended over three days, was able to reach certain agreements. They need not be discussed in detail, since they were never formally ratified and were in any case overtaken by events. But their main outline is of interest.

It was agreed, subject to the consent of the other Governments concerned, that the available naval forces should be divided into three groups: (1) the British battle fleet at Singapore,[2] reinforced by a Dutch cruiser and by Dutch and American destroyers, was to act as a

---

[1] Roskill, Vol. I, Chap. 26.

[2] This was assumed to include two R-class battleships in addition to the *Prince of Wales* and *Repulse*.

striking force against Japanese movements in the China Sea, against the Dutch East Indies or 'through the Malay barrier'; (2) a mixed cruiser squadron (one British, one Dutch and two American cruisers with four American destroyers) was to operate in the triangle North Borneo—Soerabaya—Darwin, mainly for the purpose of protecting convoys; (3) the remaining British (or Dominion) cruisers and light cruisers, together with five armed merchant cruisers, were to be retained in the Indian Ocean or the Anzac area for trade protection. The two Admirals also agreed that it was of the greatest importance that their operations should be co-ordinated with those of the U.S. Pacific Fleet and asked to be informed of Admiral Kimmel's plans, which they understood to include an offensive movement against the Marshall and Caroline Islands. Finally, though they did not include this in their formal report, they agreed privately that Singapore was not a suitable base for the British battle fleet and that arrangements should be made within the next four months to enable it to move forward to Manila.[1]

(ii)
The Position in Malaya

We do not know why Admiral Phillips accepted the idea of moving his base; but the explanation may be that he already had doubts about the security of Singapore. This is not to say that he had even considered the possibility that Japan might actually capture the naval base. It was enough for him to know, as he certainly did, that Malaya was likely to be the scene of fighting at an early stage and that local land and air forces, especially the latter, were seriously below establishment. Under these conditions there could be many threats to the base which fell short of an actual siege. For example, the nearest enemy air bases were then in the Saigon area, about 800 miles from Singapore; but if Japan established advanced bases in southern Siam or northern Malaya, she could reduce the range by half and might be able to mount a scale of air-attack which would make Singapore untenable as a main base.

Whether or not these were the arguments that weighed Admiral with Phillips, there is no doubt that our position in Malaya was extremely precarious. For this state of affairs no one, in a sense, was to blame. It would certainly have been unwise, at a time when we were barely

---

[1] Roskill, Vol. I, Chap. 26.

holding our own in Europe, to have diverted any large force to meet purely hypothetical dangers in the Far East. Indeed, no such force existed. But whether the best use had been made, during the past year or eighteen months, of the limited number of troops and aircraft that were available, is another question. The first part of the story has already been told in the previous Volume.[1] It will be remembered that the essential decision taken in August, 1940, was to entrust the primary defence of Malaya to the Royal Air Force, for which purpose a frontline strength of 22 squadrons or 336 aircraft was to be provided. The rôle of the Army was to be confined to the close defence of base-installations, airfields and other vulnerable points; and it was estimated that, when the Royal Air Force reached its full strength, a garrison of six brigades would suffice. But since it might be some time before the total of 22 squadrons could be found, it was proposed to provide an enlarged garrison of ten brigades in the interim.

By the summer of the following year, when we may take up the story in detail, this policy was still unchanged. The new Far Eastern appreciation, which the Chiefs of Staff circulated at the Cabinet's request on 28th July, 1941, followed much the same lines as its predecessor. The general aim was stated in the opening paragraphs as follows:

> 'Our basic policy is to hold in co-operation with the Dutch a crescent from Lashio to Tonga, of which Singapore is the focus.
>
> In the absence of the Fleet, we shall initially have to depend primarily on air forces for mobile defence in this area, the land forces having a strategically static role in the local defence of our territories.
>
> In any case, the southward trend of Japanese policy and the resulting situation in Indo-China and Thailand has created an overland threat to Malaya against which even the arrival of the Fleet would only partially guard.'

The paper went on to discuss the progress of current negotiations with the Americans and the Dutch and to consider the possibilities of Operation 'Matador', to which we shall return presently. The general tone was mildly optimistic; but in an appendix the Chiefs of Staff added certain remarks about the forces actually available in the Far East, which gave their picture a more sombre and realistic colouring.

In fact, the policy of defence by air-power was already dead. By this date, a full year after the original decision, the Commander-in-Chief, Far East, Air Chief Marshal Brooke-Popham, had only 180 of the promised 336 aircraft and those mostly of obsolete or semi-obsolete types. There appeared to be little hope of his obtaining more; and meanwhile the threat to his command had been greatly

---

[1] Vol. II. Chap. XXI.

intensified by Japan's occupation of Indo-China. Under these conditions he was unable even to form a viable plan, let alone to promise success. His views were clearly expressed in a signal to the Chiefs of Staff, dated 20th August:

'The lessons of Norway, Crete and the Battle of Britain have doubtless been absorbed by the Japanese, who must appreciate the importance of land-based air support in combined operations. Their probable plan for the capture of Singapore is to establish landing-grounds progressively nearer before attempting an actual assault on the fortress. In Indo-China they now possess air-bases just within operating distance of northern Malaya, while southern Malaya is at present only liable to raids and diversionary attacks. . . . Their probable first course is therefore an attack on southern Thailand [Siam] from where most of Malaya and all shipping in North Malacca Strait would become liable to air-attack. Progressive steps would then aim at the capture of landing-grounds in Kedah and Kelantan and finally Johore. Our aerodromes close to the east coast provide tempting objectives for seaborne expeditions, covered by land-based air forces during the final approach and subsequent operations.

To implement this plan without a high degree of security of sea-communications would be hazardous. But unfortunately it is in our ability to attack shipping that we are so weak. Greatly as we should like to turn the tables on the enemy and give them a "Namsos", the R.A.F. has not at present the strength to do so . . . The naval situation is well known and the absence of a fleet was the reason for the Chiefs of Staff's decision to rely primarily upon air forces. The air situation has been fully set out by me . . . in cables . . . to the War Office and the Air Ministry. The Wirraway and Wildebeest squadrons are likely to suffer heavy casualties. We have no reserve air crews and few reserve aircraft except Buffaloes. This means bluntly that at present not only is our ability to attack shipping deplorably weak, but we have not the staying power to sustain even what we could now do. As our air effort dwindles (as it would, if war came now) so will the enemy's chances of landing increase. Long stretches of beach cannot be strongly defended everywhere, and fighting inland is certain to occur. In these conditions our troops might expect to receive little support from the air. Mere multiplication of bodies is not an efficient substitute [? corrective] for weakness in the air; but in such circumstances it is clearly advisable to be amply strong on the ground.

British Malaya, excluding all mountainous jungle, has a much larger area than, for example, Eire. From north to south is farther than from Edinburgh to London. Owing to lack of communications the country does not lend itself to a system of defence based on the rapid movement of central resources. This same restriction would apply to an even greater extent to an enemy trying to overrun the country, but would not apply if he merely intended to gain control of certain aerodrome areas on the north and east. This he is likely to try to do very rapidly; and therefore the defending troops in these areas, together with their local reserves, must be strong. . . .'

As this signal indicates, the Army in Malaya was not much stronger in relation to its task than the R.A.F. It is true that, by the summer of 1941, the garrison had been raised to its maximum intended strength of ten brigades, organized as three divisions and one independent brigade; but many deficiencies still remained. The force was extremely weak in artillery, including anti-aircraft artillery; and there were no tanks.[1] Moreover, the general situation had greatly changed. In accordance with the policy of relying on air-defence, there had been a continuous development of aerodromes and other establishments in northern and eastern Malaya. Their importance to the R.A.F. was obvious, since it was only from airfields as far forward as possible that cover could be extended over the area, stretching across the Gulf of Siam to southern Indo-China, from which the enemy's attack was expected. But, from the military point of view, they posed an awkward problem of defence. This was particularly true of the group of airfields on the east coast in the Kota Bharu area and at Kuantan. In the ordinary way, a commander could have afforded to ignore a great part of the apparently vulnerable east coast. It was largely undeveloped jungle and swamp and was separated from the west coast by a considerable mountain range. An enemy landing in this area could therefore be contained without difficulty, so long as positions were held on the two roads and one railway line, which connected Kuala Lipis with Kota Bharu and Kuantan. But the existence of aerodromes altered the whole problem. It was essential to defend them; and this could only be done by isolating two substantial bodies of troops, one at Kota Bharu, the other at Kuantan, where they were unsupported and out of relation with the rest of the defence.

There was an equally difficult problem in the north-west, where a tongue of Malayan territory projects northward along the Siamese frontier. A prudent Commander would have preferred to ignore this salient; but that was impossible, since it contained the important complex of aerodromes at Alor Star and Sungei Patani. Once more it was necessary to site the defence as far forward as possible. This in turn raised another problem. As early as October, 1940, it had been suggested that the best plan for the defence of northern Malaya might be to advance into Siam in a forestalling action, occupy the port and aerodrome of Singora and establish a new line across the neck of the

---

[1] Kirby, Vol. I, Chaps. 3 and 4.

Kra Isthmus. This plan ('Matador') had since been approved and elaborated by Air Chief Marshal Brooke-Popham, and was under active discussion with the Chiefs of Staff. It had a number of obvious advantages: a shorter and better defensive line; the denial to the enemy of an important base; and much improved lateral communication between the forces defending Kota Bharu and those on the west coast. But it implied a distinct change in the rôle of the Army which, instead of confining itself to local defence under the general cover of the R.A.F., would open the campaign with a quasi-offensive movement.[1]

By July 1941, it was also necessary to take account of Japan's move into southern Indo-China, which greatly increased both the probability of an attack and the speed and weight with which it would be delivered. In these altered circumstances it is not surprising that the new G.O.C., General Percival,[2] should have felt the need for a much enlarged force. His final estimate was that, assuming the strength of the R.A.F. to remain static, he would require a minimum of five divisions for the defence of Malaya. They would be disposed as follows: one division in the north-west (Perlis and Kedah); one division on the east coast (Kelantan, Trengganu and Pahang); one division in reserve for northern Malaya; one division in Johore; and one division in Singapore, which would also provide a reserve for southern Malaya. In addition, he would require a number of ancillary troops, including armoured, anti-tank and light A.A. regiments.

Such was the position in July/August. It was evident that existing plans for the defence of Malaya had broken down. The R.A.F., unless largely reinforced, was incapable of carrying out its intended function of halting an enemy advance overland or destroying a sea-borne expedition before it could establish a bridgehead. The Army had been forced to abandon its original role of internal security and the close defence of naval and air bases, in favour of a wider plan for the defence of the whole country. But this plan was beyond its present strength. Moreover, it was open to serious military objections, since it involved an uneconomic and tactically unsound dispersal of force in order to cover the forward aerodromes constructed under the air defence policy. Some, though not all, of these objections would be met, it is true, by the proposed Operation 'Matador'. But this operation, which had obvious political implications, had not yet been formally approved; nor was it clear, in any case, that it would be possible to carry it out, since it depended on our having sufficient warning of Japan's intentions to be able to forestall her at precisely the point which she was most likely to select for her attack.

These were very serious problems, but no proposals for action

---

[1] Kirby, Vol. I, Chaps, 4 and 10.
[2] He took up his command in May 1941.

followed from London. On the contrary, the trend of subsequent events suggests that no action was considered to be necessary, though the international situation was now fast deteriorating. On 12th August the Cabinet, having been informed by the Prime Minister of his discussions with President Roosevelt at Placentia, asked the Chiefs of Staff to consider what improvement could be made in our position in the Far East within the thirty days' respite, which the President hoped to gain. Various proposals were considered, including the diversion of a medium bomber squadron, an Indian Infantry Brigade, two A.A. regiments and a number of light tanks from the Middle East; but it was finally decided that no steps should be taken. In the meantime a triangular discussion about possible variations in 'Matador', and the circumstances in which it should be undertaken, continued between the Cabinet, the Chiefs of Staff and the Commander-in-Chief, Far East.

On the 14th September the Chief of the Air Staff circulated a memorandum to his colleagues about air-strength in Malaya. He pointed out that the existing programme had now fallen so much behindhand as to be actively misleading. Unless priorities were drastically changed, there was no possibility whatever that the target of 336 first-line aircraft would be reached by the end of the year; and only slow progress could be made towards it in 1942. He had made a tentative allotment of 590 aircraft to the Far East for that year; but the rate of reinforcement would depend on production figures, which could not yet be accurately forecast. It was not possible to give any firm promise. The Chiefs of Staff took note of this without comment and the Commander-in-Chief was informed accordingly.

Two days later the Joint Planners were invited to report on a tactical appreciation, which had in the meantime been received from the G.O.C. Malaya. In this paper General Percival set out his plan for the defence of the country and explained in detail why he required the reinforcement, enumerated above, of rather more than two divisions. The Planners' comments, later accepted by the Chiefs of Staff, illustrate the state of mind prevailing in London at this time:

'We are unable, without knowledge of local conditions, to comment in detail on the requirements put forward by General Officer Commanding Malaya. In view however of our present weakness at sea and in the air, we consider the proposed increase to be a reasonable target figure in present circumstances.

Nevertheless, the reinforcement of the garrison to this figure cannot be completed in the foreseeable future. We estimate that, before such a programme can be fulfilled, our air forces will have been materially increased and a garrison of this strength will no longer be required. Furthermore, we may have considerably increased our naval forces in the Indian Ocean. In our opinion, therefore, the target figure for land-forces in Malaya can only be estimated from time to time in the light of our air-strength in that theatre'.

In view of the Chief of the Air Staff's memorandum and the facts of the naval situation, this was equivalent to saying that no land reinforcement could be found for Malaya for at least another six or nine months. In one sense this was hardly surprising. In the summer of 1941 shipping was scarce; we were deeply committed to the support of Auchinleck's forthcoming offensive in the Middle East; the force for 'Pilgrim'[1] was still standing by; and we were doing our best to find troops and aircraft for some operation in support of the Russians. There was indeed little to spare for the Far East. But in a period of rising tension six or nine months was a long time to leave an important base—and traditionally the security of Singapore ranked next after that of the United Kingdom—with a garrison which was declared on all hands to be inadequate. But this position was accepted, apparently without argument. In December, when the Japanese attack began, the strength of the Air Force was still approximately the same—13 squadrons with 158 first-line aircraft—as it had been in August. The only reinforcements which the Army had received, beyond its ten brigades, were one reconnaissance regiment (with 15cwt. trucks in place of armoured cars), one anti-tank regiment and three field artillery regiments.[2]

No single or completely satisfactory explanation can be given. Earlier in the year—in January and again in April and May—Mr. Churchill had discountenanced proposals to reinforce the Far East on the ground that everything was needed on other fronts, such as the Middle East, which were already actively engaged. He had then instructed the Chiefs of Staff to proceed on the assumption that war with Japan was improbable and had undertaken to inform them of any change in this state of affairs. By August or September, when the main decisions about Malaya were taken, no new instructions had come from the Prime Minister; but events had given their warning for him. The Japanese occupation of Indo-China, the embargo, the unpromising start to the negotiations in Washington—all these marked the beginning of a new and dangerous phase. But there was still something to be said on the opposite side. As we noticed in the last chapter, the immediate agitations of early August died away fairly soon. Japan's expected attack on Siam did not materialize; the tempo of her war preparations in the south appeared to slacken; and her negotiations with the United States lingered on. It seemed

---

[1] The pre-emptive occupation of the Atlantic Islands.
[2] Kirby, Vol. I, Chap. 10.

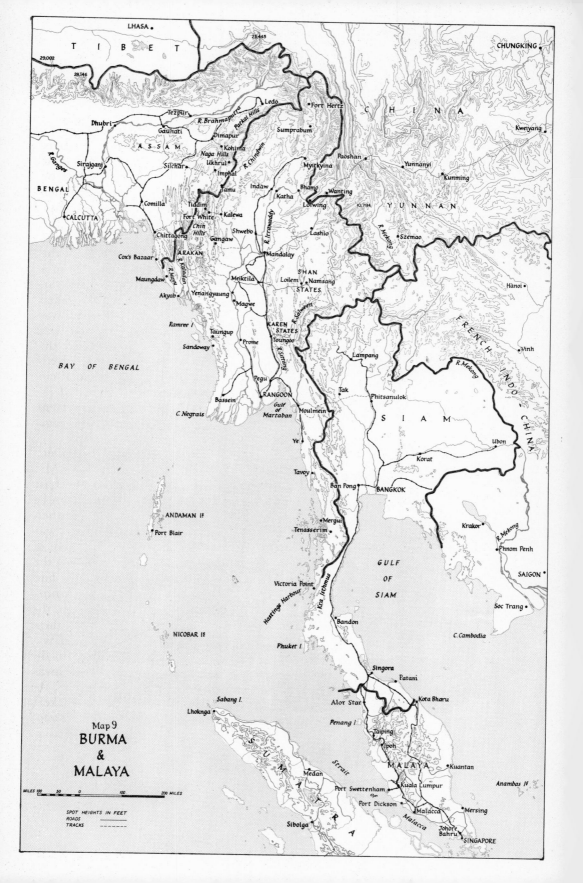

Map 9
BURMA
&
MALAYA

SPOT HEIGHTS IN FEET
ROADS
TRACKS

MILES 100   50   0   100   200 MILES

possible, at least it was arguable, that a pause would follow, extended perhaps over several months.

It must also be remembered that there was more than one opinion about Japan's probable course of action, if she did go to war. From the early part of July onwards Germany was urging her to attack Vladivostok rather than Singapore; and, though she rejected this plan, she did in fact reinforce her army in Manchuria. A movement of this kind could not escape notice. Reports of it presently reached London and Singapore, where they provided a factual justification for the belief—the all too welcome belief—that Japan's objective was in the north rather than in the south. We first hear of this on 16th August, when the Chiefs of Staff examined a Foreign Office paper on measures to be taken in the event of a Japanese attack on Russia. In the following month the Foreign Secretary raised the question again and a report was prepared by the Joint Planning Staff. Finally, on 1st October an unusually optimistic signal from the Commander-in-Chief, Far East, and the Commander-in-Chief, China Station, showed that the belief was still alive and had begun to exercise a certain influence on policy:

'It must now have become apparent to Japan that war with the United States, Dutch or ourselves probably means war with all three and possibly with Russia as well.

Japan is now concentrating her forces against the Russians and cannot suddenly change this into a concentration in the south, although she could still dispatch a sea-borne expedition from Japanese waters without our knowledge. Nevertheless we reiterate our view that the last thing that Japan wants at this juncture is a campaign in the south. . . .

Japan's more recent anxieties include; (a) the military alliance between Great Britain and Russia; (b) our improved situation in the Atlantic and Middle East; (c) the increasing anti-Axis attitude of the United States; (d) the virtual certainty of a military understanding between the British and Dutch in the Far East.

Taking into account: (a) the uncertainty whether or not Germany is going to bring Russia to terms before the winter; (b) even if Russia collapsed, the time that would elapse before the Japanese could disengage from the north; (c) the bad weather in the South China Sea area between November and January inclusive—it is highly improbable that Japan can be contemplating war in the south for some months. . . . '

This view of the situation was accepted in London, or at least was not contradicted when the Chiefs of Staff replied some few weeks later.[1] But in the meantime a new possibility had emerged and was

---

[1] An interim reply was sent on 9th October and a further one on 29th October.

under investigation. In the latter part of October Japanese troop concentrations were observed in the Canton area and in the Tong-King province of Indo-China. These were thought at first to portend a renewed offensive against Chinese positions in the Yunnan with the particular object of cutting the Burma Road and thus closing the last land-route by which the Chinese Goverment could draw supplies from the outside world. Such a move on Japan's part was probable enough and would not, in itself, have been an unhopeful sign. It would have meant that Japan was once more concentrating her energies on finishing the war in China and was therefore unlikely to be contemplating another major offensive in the south. But these hopes—if that term may be used of prospective operations against an ally—were shortlived. By the following month it was clear that the Japanese troops were moving south and taking up new positions more consistent with an early attack on Siam. But the evidence was not yet conclusive.

Early in November the J.I.C. submitted a further forecast of Japanese intentions. This paper began by pointing out that the negotiations between Japan and the United States, which were already in their fourth month, must now be supposed to be reaching their climax. In the near future Japan would have to settle the direction of her future policy and decide whether or not she was willing to accept the risk of war with ourselves and the United States. In the meantime she would concentrate on completing her operations in China, probably by an offensive in Yunnan such as her recent dispositions had suggested. If she then decided to allow the Washington conversations to fail, thus courting a new war, four choices would be open to her: she could attack Siam, Malaya, the Dutch East Indies or the Russian Maritime Provinces. Of these objectives the first and the last were regarded as the most probable. Covert infiltration into Siam had been in progress for some time; communications between Siam and Indo-China were being rapidly developed; and work was also in progress on the naval base at Camranh Bay and at least a dozen aerodromes in the south. In Manchuria preparations had been less extensive but were still too strongly marked to be ignored. Japanese forces there, though not yet strong enough for an offensive against Russia, had recently been increased from eleven to twenty-nine divisions; and this was difficult to explain purely as a defensive measure. The final conclusions of the J.I.C. were summarized as follows:

'(1) Japan will make a last effort to obtain a general agreement with the United States. If she fails, she will be faced with the necessity of deciding whether or not to take aggressive action involving risk of war with one or more major powers.

(2) Such action would be likely in the first instance to be

against Thailand, which Japan might think would involve the least risk of a major conflict. Occupation of bases in Thailand, including the Kra Isthmus, would be a sound strategic preliminary to subsequent operations against Malaya or the Netherlands East Indies. Recent military moves tend to support the opinion that Thailand is the next objective.

(3) Action against Russia is likely to be deferred until there is serious weakening of Russia's position in the Far East.

(4) In the absence of a general agreement with America operations against China will continue.

(5) In view of the latest evidence of diversion of forces southwards from northern Indo-China and Canton, we do not believe that the former concentrations in those areas imply an early attack on the Burma Road'.

It will be noticed that this paper, though markedly less optimistic than the October signal from the Commanders-in-Chief, was still reluctant to accept the conclusion that Japan intended anything more than a limited or preparatory offensive in the south. The idea of a direct attack on Malaya or the Dutch East Indies, still more on American possessions, was implicitly rejected. The reason is clear from the wording of the passage quoted. Even at that date few people were really prepared to believe that Japan would risk an open conflict with the United States, or, to speak more exactly, that she would dare to commit her main forces to an operation in the south, while the U.S. Pacific Fleet was still in being and able to act offensively against her. This supposition was, indeed, the basis of British policy in the Far East during this period; and it explains much that must otherwise appear complacent and over-confident in the attitude of the Cabinet and the Chiefs of Staff. They knew that the forces which they were sending to the Far East were inadequate; but they were unwilling to increase them to the detriment of other fronts, because they believed that our main defence (and the only deterrent that Japan would recognize) was to be found elsewhere—in American naval power.

(iii)
Duff Cooper's Report

We must now turn to another aspect of the situation. Experience in the Middle East had already shown the immense importance of political, economic and administrative problems in a theatre of war. Their solution could not be left to an already overburdened

Commander-in-Chief; nor could they be adequately dealt with on a piecemeal system, which involved constant reference to Ministers or departments in London. What was required was a single authority— a civil counterpart to the Commander-in-Chief—who could act as the Cabinet's agent in carrying out a comprehensive policy for the theatre as a whole. In the Middle East this function was now per- formed by the Minister of State; but no similar step towards unifica- tion had been taken in the Far East. There were several reasons for this. The area was not yet the scene of active operations; and there were important reasons—or what seemed to be so—for not interfering too much with the existing system. The Far East was a valuable source of raw materials; and it had been held that nothing should be done which might interfere with the free flow of rubber and tin from Malaya or oil from Burma. This ruling had even been maintained when there was a direct conflict, in the matter of raising and training a Volunteer Force in Malaya, between the Commander-in-Chief and the commercial interests concerned.

Nevertheless, during the summer of 1941 the need for a co-ordinating authority in the Far East became increasingly apparent. As early as June Sir Archibald Clark Kerr, then Ambassador in China, tele- graphed to the Foreign Office:

'Co-ordination at Singapore of naval, military and air activities and to some extent of propaganda and economic warfare has been provided for; but no such provision has been made for other civil activities. The problem is complicated as the Domin- ions, Colonies and India are all concerned as well as the Foreign Office, and Treasury and a number of other departments. At present co-ordination is affected in London, but with increasing difficulty of rapid communication detailed co-ordination from that centre as in peacetime is already becoming more difficult and may become impossible. Widely dispersed authorities within the area may then be forced to take decisions without guidance, which may or may not be in conformity with our interest in the area as a whole, or may run directly counter to action being taken elsewhere.

Largely as the result of this telegram, the Cabinet decided in July to send Mr. Duff Cooper, the Chancellor of the Duchy of Lancaster,[1] on a mission of inquiry to the Far East. His instructions were: 'to examine the present arrangements for consultation and communica- tion between the various British authorities in that area, military, administrative and political, and to report to the War Cabinet how these arrangements can be made more effective'. He left England at the beginning of August and arrived in the Far East a month later. During the next six weeks he was able to hold a series of consultations

---

[1] He had previously held office as Minister of Information.

at Singapore with the Governor, the naval and military authorities, with Sir Archibald Clark Kerr and others, and also to visit the Dutch East Indies, Burma and India.

By that time it was well on in October and the international situation was fast deteriorating. Mr. Duff Cooper therefore judged it best to send home an interim report at once, without waiting for the further visits to Australia, New Zealand and Hong Kong, with which he hoped to complete his mission. He had already seen enough to satisfy himself that our Far Eastern possessions were even less well-prepared for war in a political and administrative, than they were in a strictly military sense.

Mr. Duff Cooper's report, dated 29th October, opened with a broad survey of the changes which had taken place in the Far East over the past few decades. These were the result in the main of two complementary processes; the development of communications and the growth of nationalism or national consciousness. The former had gradually destroyed the happy isolation, both from each other and from the outside world, in which Asiatic countries had previously existed. The latter had changed, or was in course of changing, the whole political and economic pattern of the area. New centres of power were being created; new aspirations were in the air; and new policies were needed. Yet, as the report observed:

> 'Within this changed and ever-changing world of the Pacific the affairs of the British Empire were being conducted at the outbreak of war by machinery which has undergone no important change since the days of Queen Victoria. Four Government Departments were principally concerned. Two Ambassadors and one Minister reported to the Foreign Office on the affairs of Japan, China and Siam, while the same department was kept informed by Consuls-General of events passing in the Netherlands East Indies, in the Philippines and in French Indo-China. The Governors of the Straits Settlements and of Hong Kong reported to the Colonial Office. The Dominions Office was represented by High Commissioners in Australia and New Zealand, and the recent bestowal upon Burma of a Secretary of State of her own brought the India Office into the picture. Here, then, already existed a system under which four different types of official reported to and received orders from four different departments of State, and, save for the fact that the Ministers responsible for the departments met weekly in Cabinet, no effort was made to co-ordinate the activities of the officials or the policies of the departments concerned.'

This state of affairs, already sufficiently serious, had been much aggravated since the outbreak of war. The events of 1940, by cutting off Great Britain from the Continent, had greatly increased the difficulties of communication with the Far East. The result was that, at the very moment when Asian affairs were assuming a new and decisive importance, a wider gap than ever before had opened between the framers of policy in London and their executives in the Far East. At the same time, under the pressure of war, the number of separate and competing authorities in the area had multiplied. The Ministry of War Transport had a representative at Hong Kong and the Treasury a Financial Commissioner for the Far East at Shanghai; the Ministry of Information had established a Far Eastern bureau at Singapore and so, more recently, had the Ministry of Economic Warfare.

These new offices had not been created on any settled plan but piecemeal as new problems or emergencies arose; and there was often confusion and overlapping both among the new organizations and between them and older authorities. The work of the Far Eastern Information Bureau, for example, encroached on one side on that of M.E.W.'s local office, which had an interest in certain types of secret propaganda, and on the other on that of the Press Bureau[1] set up by the Commander-in-Chief, Far East. At the point where propaganda merged with foreign policy, the position was still more confused. It had come about by a series of accidents that diplomatic relations between the British authorities and Admiral Decoux, who governed Indo-China in the Vichy interest, were largely in the hands of the Commander-in-Chief, China Station. Admiral Layton was also in relations with the Free French Forces in the Pacific; and it was his policy to unite both these factions in a common resistance to Japan. No doubt there was much to be said for this; but it was not the policy of other Government Departments. On the contrary, the Ministry of Information, following directives from London, was campaigning actively against Admiral Decoux's administration and had thereby incurred the censure of Admiral Layton, who complained that his diplomatic manœuvres were being hampered.

These anomalies were, however, only symptoms of a more fundamental dislocation. The whole existing system of policy-making and administration in the Far East was in principle unworkable. That it was still working at all was due to the patience and co-operative spirit of individual officials, who were showing great readiness to yield to one another for the common good. But there was a limit to what private enterprise could do; and it was obvious, and universally admitted, that the system could not bear any further strains than had already been thrown upon it. Everyone agreed that as soon as active operations began, if not before, a radical reorganization would be necessary. It only remained to consider what form it should take.

---

[1] The Services Public Relations Bureau, locally known as ASPRO.

The only palliative measure so far carried out had been the formation earlier in the year of the Far Eastern Committee in London. But the existence of this body had rather complicated than eased the situation:

'Study of the minutes . . . reveals that in many cases where reference to London is clearly necessary, such reference is at present made from one quarter alone in the Far East, which necessitates further inquiries being made from London of other quarters in the Far East, and thus prolonged delay is incurred. If the various interested parties in the Far East had one superior official on the spot whom they could consult in the first instance, he having heard all the views expressed could present the problem in a digested form to London with all the facts and arguments and render it unnecessary for the authorities at home to make further inquiries.'

At first sight this seemed a strong argument for the immediate appointment of a Minister of State on the Middle Eastern model; but on further examination it was not clear that the two cases were entirely parallel. First, there was the important question of distance. A Minister in Singapore could not return to London so often or so easily as a Minister in Cairo. He would therefore find it difficult to take his place in Parliament and would also tend over a period to lose touch with his colleagues in the Cabinet. Certain other constitutional problems would also arise. In the Far East the Minister would have to deal with a great variety of authorities and officials, some of whom already stood in a special relationship with a Department at home. He could not, for example, intervene between a Governor and the Secretary of State to whom the latter was normally responsible. On the other hand, he could not be content to act merely as the servant or executive agent of individual Ministers in London, who were his colleagues and constitutionally his equals. Finally, there was the question of Commonwealth and international relations. In the Middle East there were few important Allies to be considered; and the interests of the Dominions were largely concentrated on the supply and maintenance of their military forces. But the situation in the Far East was very different. If the area became an active theatre of war, at least three Dominions—Canada, Australia and South Africa—would be directly and vitally concerned, as also would India and Burma. Moreover, the policy and operations of the Commonwealth would require to be co-ordinated with those of four principal Allies—the United States, Russia, China and the Netherlands. At present the arrangements for local co-operation, or even for the exchange of information, between these countries and ourselves were extremely defective:

20

'I found in the pursuit of my inquiries that complaints of lack of co-ordination between British authorities were far less common than complaints of a lack of co-operation between ourselves and our Allies. Complaints of this nature came to me from our own authorities and perhaps most frequently from such more or less detached spectators as American press-correspondents who, constantly travelling from one country to another, are struck by the lack of collaboration and even of common information. The Governor-General of the Netherlands East Indies—a highly competent official—expressed some surprise as well as considerable relief when I told him that Great Britain was anxious to avoid war with Japan. He told me that he had no previous warning of America's decision to freeze Japanese assets, although such a decision was of the greatest importance to the Netherlands East Indies, whose whole trade with Japan was conducted in American currency, and when he asked what information I had with regard to negotiations reported to be proceeding between the United States and Japan, I was bound to admit that I was in complete ignorance even as to whether such negotiations had ever been opened—an ignorance which he shared. In the same connexion H.M. Ambassador at Chungking recently drew the attention of His Majesty's Government to the lack of co-ordination in the help given to China by Great Britain and the United States.'

The solution to these problems, which Mr. Duff Cooper proposed, was the appointment of a Commissioner-General for the Far East. This official would make his headquarters at Singapore, where he would act as a local co-ordinator and, within certain limits, as the arbitrator or point of reference in all jurisdictional disputes or problems affecting more than one department. Since he would not himself be a Minister, his presence would not affect the normal chain of responsibility between Departments in London and their representatives in the Far East. On the other hand, he would be in a position to keep continuously before the Cabinet a connected picture of developments in the Far East as a whole and, where necessary, to refer problems to London in a digested form after consulting all the local interests concerned. He would thus become, not an originator of policy himself, but the prime source of the information and advice on which a general Far Eastern policy could be framed by the Cabinet. He would also serve as an executive agent, whether of the Cabinet as a whole or of individual Ministers, in all matters in which it was desirable that several departments should act together.

If the Far East became an active theatre, the Commissioner-General would add to his other functions the Chairmanship of the War Council at Singapore. He would not have any direct authority in military affairs; but it would be his business to keep the military authorities informed of the political and diplomatic situation and, so far as possible, to relieve the Commander-in-Chief of responsibility in this field. It would also be open to him to express opinions on military problems from time to time either to the War Cabinet or to the Service Ministers concerned. In all these respects his position would be similar to that of the Minister of State, who presided over meetings of the Middle East Defence Committee in Cairo. But it was probable that the War Council would be a slightly larger body, as it would be desirable to include representatives from Australia and perhaps from other Dominions and from India as well. Its exact composition could, however, safely be left to be decided later, in the light of the situation prevailing when operations began. Only one specification need be laid down beforehand: that the Council should be kept as small as was compatible with its prime function of co-ordination and central direction and should not be allowed to become an unwieldy body—a kind of local Parliament—which would rather obstruct business than forward it.

If only for this reason, it was clearly impossible that any Allied representatives should be included in the Council. The task of ensuring smooth co-operation in the theatre between ourselves, the United States, Russia, China and the Netherlands would therefore devolve to a great extent on the Commissioner-General personally. He would have to travel widely throughout the Pacific. This made it of particular importance that the right type of man should be selected: 'he must be a man who in his conferences with Ambassadors, Governors and Commanders-in-Chief can speak on terms of equality and who, when he visits India, will be received by the Viceroy and in Washington by the President'.

CHAPTER XII

THE JAPANESE ATTACK

(i)

Last-Minute Diplomacy

THE COLLAPSE OF the *Modus Vivendi* proposals in the last week of November left Washington in a curious mood. Though it seems to have been assumed that war with Japan was now inevitable, there was no uniform response to this emergency. On the 27th November the Navy Department warned the Commanders-in-Chief of the U.S. Atlantic, Pacific and Asiatic Fleets that, negotiations having broken down, an aggressive move by Japan, probably directed against the Philippines, Siam or Borneo, might be expected within the next few days.[1] But this warning was not followed by any action in the diplomatic field. Mr. Cordell Hull took no steps to communicate with the Allied governments; and President Roosevelt left Washington for a short holiday at Warm Springs.

It was therefore with some surprise that the Cabinet, on 28th November, learnt through the Admiralty of the warning given to American commanders on the previous day. Lord Halifax was at once instructed to discover whether these orders reflected the opinion of the U.S. Government as a whole. He saw Mr. Sumner Welles on the same day but learnt little to the purpose. He was shown the record of the President's last interview with the Japanese envoys and noted that it had been in very general terms, which might or might not evoke a further response from Japan. He was also told that, although the State Department shared the Navy Department's alarm, Mr. Welles did not himself think that Japan would do more than reinforce her troops in Indo-China, while awaiting the reactions of Great Britain and the United States. Lord Halifax then asked what the United States would do, if Japan made her next move against Siam alone without any direct attack on American, British or Dutch territory? Mr. Welles replied that no decision had yet been reached; the question would have to await the President's return. Another interview on the following day, this time with Mr. Hull, elicited no more.[2]

Meanwhile the need to co-ordinate British and American policy

---

[1] S. E. Morison, *History of Naval Operations in World War II* (1949), Vol. III, p. 77.

[2] Woodward, pp. 184–5.

in the Far East was becoming urgent. Among other things, an immediate decision was required about Operation 'Matador'. The Commander-in-Chief, Far East, had so far been told not to undertake this operation without a further ruling from London, which would be given within thirty-six hours of his reporting a Japanese movement against Siam. On 27th November Sir Robert Brooke-Popham objected that this restriction was absurd. As the Kra Isthmus was only thirty-three hours' sailing from Saigon, the proposed delay would make it impossible to forestall Japan, though to do so was the sole purpose of the operation. He requested permission to launch 'Matador' as soon as reconnaissance showed that an escorted Japanese convoy was approaching the Siamese coast. To this the Chiefs of Staff could only reply that American concurrence must first be sought. Without it—that is, if America would not accept a Japanese attack on Siam as a *casus belli*—we should run the risk of involving ourselves in war with Japan single-handed.

Not less important was the question of what steps, if any, could still be taken to restrain Japan. On 30th November Mr. Churchill sent a personal telegram to President Roosevelt, repeating a familiar argument. 'One important method,' he wrote, 'remains unused in averting a war between Japan and our two countries, namely a plain declaration, secret or public as may be thought best, that any further act of aggression by Japan would lead immediately to the gravest consequences'. Later telegrams from the Foreign Office to Lord Halifax elaborated this proposal, and made it clear that what the Prime Minister had in mind was a joint warning by the United States, Great Britain and Holland that, if Japan used Indo-China as a base for further operations, whether against Siam, Malaya, the Dutch East Indies or the Burma Road, she would do so at her peril. This was closely connected with the problem of 'Matador'. Our plan, if assured of American support, was to occupy the Kra Isthmus as soon as we received information that a Japanese attack on any part of Siam was impending. We had explored the possibility of an arrangement with the Siamese Government by which this movement would be made at their invitation; but they were unlikely to agree unless we could promise them effective support north of the Kra Isthmus which we could not do at present. But the proposed warning might alter the position. The Siamese Prime Minister had already expressed the view that it was the only thing which could save his country. If he were satisfied that the warning had been given, or was being given, he might be willing to concert plans for the defence of Siam as a whole.[1]

The President returned to Washington on the morning of 1st

---

[1] Woodward, p. 187.

December. During the next five days he had a series of interviews with Lord Halifax, at which these and related problems were discussed. The results on the whole were satisfactory. Mr. Roosevelt gave an undertaking that the United States would support, if necessary by force, whatever action Britain found it necessary to take in Siam. He also accepted the principle of a formal warning to Japan to be delivered by the Three Powers. But the diplomatic programme finally agreed on was surprisingly leisurely. On 2nd December the President addressed a message to Japan, asking for an explanation of the reinforcements, which were now flowing steadily into Indo-China. He proposed, if the reply were unsatisfactory, to follow this in a few days' time by a personal message to the Emperor, making it clear that Japan's present course must inevitably lead to war. He was anxious to wait for the Emperor's answer—of which he still had some hopes—before proceeding to the final step of a joint warning by the Three Powers. Moreover, he wished this warning to be delivered in two stages: first a Note from the United States and then, after an interval, simultaneous Notes from Great Britain and Holland. Only in this way, the President considered, could he satisfy the American public that his action had been taken from purely nationalistic motives and not in support of America's friends or potential allies.[1]

(ii)
The Japanese Plan

While these talks were proceeding, the Japanese had not been idle. Even before the Imperial Conference of 1st December extensive military preparations had been put in hand. The Japanese were well aware that the war, into which they were about to plunge, could not lead to victory in the accepted sense. Though she might win local engagements and even major battles, especially at the beginning of the war, Japan could not hope to defeat either the United States or Great Britain, because their home-bases and the main sources of their strength lay beyond her reach. It was not, however, Japan's object to defeat them, but only to prevent them from defeating her, as they were already doing, slowly but surely, by the operation of the blockade and the trade embargo. For this purpose Japan's first requirement was to seize the rich southern area, with its immense resources

---

[1] Woodward, pp. 187–8.

of oil, rubber, food and metal, which would make her proof against further economic pressure. If, thanks to the war in Europe, this operation could be carried out rapidly, and with little loss, it would then be possible—or so the Japanese planners calculated—to organize a defensive ring, enclosing the whole captured area, against which Great Britain and the United States would break their teeth in vain.[1]

This reasoning was not necessarily unsound. Japan would enjoy all the advantages of a central position and relatively short lines of communication, whereas her enemies would have to operate from distant bases in India, Australia or Hawaii, none of them less than 3,000 miles from the final objective. So long as the war in Europe continued, they would not be able to bring more than a fraction of their power to bear in the Pacific. Moreover, the war in Europe might end to their disadvantage, or at least under conditions which would greatly reduce their strength and provoke a mood of war-weariness in their people. In these circumstances would the Western Powers be willing to pay the price of defeating Japan? It was reasonable to hope that they would not, especially if their early attempts to break through the defensive ring were heavily repulsed, as Japanese strategists were confident that they could be.

Japan had ample forces for the rapid occupation of the southern area, which formed the first part of her plan; but she was not able to use them with complete freedom. Of the fifty-one divisions of which she disposed, twenty-one were still absorbed by the war in China; and, despite Germany's attack on Russia and the impossibility of serious operations in the north during the winter, a further force of thirteen divisions was judged to be necessary to observe the Red Army on the Manchurian front. When the needs of home-defence had been satisfied, this left only eleven divisions immediately available for operations in the south. The Army Air Force was distributed on a similar plan. Out of a total of five Air Divisions (with an approximate strength of 1,500 first-line aircraft), three were retained in Japan or on the mainland, leaving only two (approximately 700 aircraft) for the support of the southern operations. These were, however, to be reinforced by a land-based Air Fleet (450 aircraft) of the Japanese Naval Air Forces.[2]

This was not a large force with which to attempt the conquest of such an extensive area. Moreover, as speed was of the first importance, the Japanese planners rightly insisted that a local superiority of at

---

[1] Kirby, Vol. I, Chap. 5.

[2] Japan had two distinct air forces: the A.A.F. which was primarily responsible for the close support of ground-forces; and the N.A.F., responsible for the support of surface fleets, sea-reconnaissance, coastal defence and convoy protection. The first-line strength of the latter at the outbreak of war was rather over 1,000 aircraft, of which half were carrier-borne. Kirby, Vol. I, Table I.

least two to one would be necessary at each point of attack. This meant that the campaign would have to be carried out in carefully controlled phases, which would enable the same forces to be used over again in successive operations. The final plan, arrived at after much discussion between the Services, was as follows:

Phase One would open with simultaneous attacks on the three principal Allied bases in the area. (1) An attack on Hong Kong by one reinforced Division from 23rd Army in South China. (2) An attack from Formosa on the Philippines by 14th Army of two-and-a-half Divisions and one Air Division. This attack would be supported by an independent operation under naval control for the capture of the American staging-posts at Guam and Wake Island, in order to sever communications between the Philippines and Hawaii. (3) An attack on Malaya involving two Armies: 15th Army of two Divisions, with the task of occupying Siam (including the Kra Isthmus) and then advancing into Southern Burma so as to cut the reinforcement-route between India and Malaya; and 25th Army of four Divisions (including the Imperial Guards Division) and one Air Division, with the task of securing a bridgehead in northern Malaya, and then advancing south on Singapore.[1]

Phase Two would open approximately seven weeks later, by which time it was assumed that the occupation of Hong Kong and the Philippines would be complete. Elements of 14th and 23rd Armies, together with one fresh Division, would then be re-formed into 16th Army and would advance southward from the Philippines in order to seize key-points in Borneo, the Celebes, Amboina and Timor with southern Sumatra as the ultimate objective. While these operations were in progress, the naval task-force, which had previously captured Guam and Wake Island, would be directed against new objectives in New Guinea and the Bismarck Archipelago.

Phase Three would open after a further interval of approximately seven weeks. It was assumed that by then 25th Army would have completed the conquest of Malaya and the capture of Singapore, and 16th Army its Phase Two tasks. The stage would then be set for a combined operation from east and west by both these Armies against Java and Sumatra.

Phase Four. As soon as the occupation of the Dutch East Indies was complete, 15th Army would be reinforced and would enlarge its operations in Burma with the object of gaining control of the whole country. At the same time other forces would be directed against the Andaman and Nicobar Islands in the Bay of Bengal. These final conquests would complete Japan's defensive perimeter (as originally

---

[1] 14th, 15th and 25th Armies (and later 16th Army) came under the strategic control of Southern Army Group at Saigon.

planned), which would now extend from the Kurile Islands, north of Japan, through Wake Island, the Marshall and Gilbert Islands, the Bismarck Archipelago, New Guinea, Timor, Java, Sumatra, and the islands in the Bay of Bengal, to the frontier between India and Burma.[1]

This plan was subject to one, all-important condition: it could only be carried out, if Japan enjoyed complete command of the sea throughout the area of operations. In a strictly local sense this was not difficult to provide. For the close support of her southern operations, Japan was able to allot a task force consisting of two battleships, two light fleet carriers, eleven heavy and seven light cruisers, fifty-two destroyers and some sixteen submarines.[2] This was enough to deal with any opposition likely to be encountered from the U.S. Asiatic Fleet, the Dutch naval forces or the British Far Eastern Fleet as then constituted. But these were only the Allies' advanced forces. Behind them lay the U.S. Pacific Fleet; and it was this which constituted the real menace to Japan. Its strength was roughly equal (or even slightly superior) to that of the Japanese main fleet, once the forces required for the south and other detached operations had been subtracted.[3] It could be used to support the defence of the Philippines, to operate at large against Japanese communications or even to threaten the home islands; and in any of these cases a general fleet action might result, which Japan could not be certain of winning. Indeed, even without a general action and merely by remaining in being, it could exercise a potent and potentially disastrous influence on all Japanese operations. The success of the whole campaign depended, therefore, on Japan's ability to destroy the Pacific Fleet at the outset, or at least to cripple it so severely that it could not intervene during the vital three or four months, which were needed to complete the southern operations and establish the defensive perimeter.

The Japanese Naval Staff agreed that there was only one place, and only one time, at which they could be certain of meeting the Pacific Fleet on favourable terms: that was in its home port of Pearl Harbor at (or even immediately before) the outbreak of war. Accordingly, their plan provided for a powerful striking-force, consisting of the 1st, 2nd and 5th Carrier Squadrons, escorted by two battleships, two heavy cruisers and a destroyer-flotilla, to assemble at an unfrequented anchorage in the Kurile Islands. Ten days before the day set for the opening of hostilities, this force would sail on a voyage of rather more than 3,000 miles, well away from the shipping

---

[1] Kirby, Vol. 1, Chap. 5.

[2] See pp. 267-8 above.

[3] Kirby, Vol. I, App. 5.

lanes and the normal beat of American reconnaissance aircraft, which would bring it on the morning of D-day to a point 200 miles north of Pearl Harbor. From there some 350 aircraft—bombers, dive-bombers, torpedo-bombers and escorting fighters—would be flown off to the attack.[1]

To call this plan bold is an understatement. The risks of detection during the long approach were high; and the dangers of the subsequent withdrawal, unless the operation had been completely successful, were scarcely less. Bad weather at any stage might wreck the whole plan. No strike by carrier-borne aircraft on a comparable scale had ever been attempted before; and the outcome, even under the most favourable conditions, could not be predicted with any certainty. The earlier and much smaller British operation against the Italian fleet at Taranto offered a hopeful precedent; but later experience with much larger forces of land-based aircraft had shown how difficult it was to obtain decisive results against a well defended target. And if the chances of success were problematic, the penalties of failure were enormous. If the operation miscarried, Japan stood to lose some of the most powerful units of her fleet and two-thirds of her whole carrier-borne air force. Moreover, the offensive in the south would already have opened before the results of the Pearl Harbor attack could be known. In the event of failure, Japan might find herself committed to war with the strength of her own fleet seriously reduced, while that of the U.S. Pacific Fleet was unimpaired. If so, her early defeat was certain.

(iii)

Pearl Harbor and the Philippines

Japan's answer to the President's inquiry about her troops in Indo-China was received in Washington on 6th December. It was unsatisfactory and offered no explanation beyond a vague reference to a Chinese underground movement, against which it was necessary to take precautions. Mr. Roosevelt therefore proposed to send his message to the Emperor at once so that it should be delivered in Tokyo on the morning of 7th December (local time).[2] If he did not receive a

---

[1] Morison, Vol. III, Chap. 5.

[2] These vexatious differences in time and date can be expressed in the following table:

Pearl Harbor	Washington	London	Singapore	Tokyo
1.30 p.m.	7 p.m.	Midnight← →7.30 a.m.		9 a.m.

suitable answer within forty-eight hours—that is, by the evening of 8th December (Washington time)—he would send a formal warning on the following day. In accordance with the agreed programme, the parallel British and Dutch warnings would follow twenty-four hours later, that is on the morning of 10th December by Washington time.[1]

But it was already too late for these manœuvres. On 7th December the Japanese envoys in Washington received the text of a further Note, which they were instructed to deliver before 1.25 p.m. on that day. It was a long and disjointed composition, reviewing the past course of the negotiations, laying the blame for their failure on the 'Imperialistic' attitude of the British and American Governments, and ending with a sentence which might charitably be regarded as a declaration of war:

> 'The Japanese Government regrets to have to notify hereby the American Government that, in view of the attitude of the American Government, it cannot but consider that it is impossible to reach an agreement through further negotiations.'

Owing to some delay in de-coding, this communication was not handed to the State Department until a quarter past two in the afternoon. By then the Japanese attack on Pearl Harbor, timed to begin at 3.25 a.m. on 8th December (by Japanese time) or 7.55 a.m. on 7th December (by Hawaiian time), had already been in progress for three-quarters of an hour.[2]

The 7th December was a Sunday and dawn found the Pacific Fleet following the normal routine of that day. There was a total of ninety-four ships in harbour, including eight battleships, eight cruisers and twenty-nine destroyers, all lying peacefully at their accustomed moorings. Of the remainder of the Fleet, two aircraft carriers (*Lexington* and *Enterprise*), thirteen cruisers and twenty-four destroyers were by a most fortunate chance at sea on manœuvres; one aircraft-carrier (*Saratoga*) and one battleship (*Colorado*) were on the west coast of America. Despite the warning which the Commander-in-Chief had received only ten days before, it does not appear that any special precautions had been taken, apart from certain police-measures against sabotage. Rather more than a third of the officers of the Fleet were ashore, enjoying their week-end leave. The ships' main and secondary armaments were unmanned, as were three out of four of their anti-aircraft guns. On shore Air Force pilots were at four hours' notice. There had been little attempt at dispersal on the flying-fields; and aircraft were mostly parked in the open in orderly ranks, wing-tip to wing-tip, inviting destruction.

When the first wave of Japanese bombers appeared over Oahu

---

[1] Woodward, p. 188.

[2] Kirby, Vol. I, Chap. 5, Table of Comparative Times.

Island at 7.55 a.m., the defence was taken completely by surprise. Some thirty or thirty-five minutes elapsed before the first American fighter took the air; and in that interval between a half and two-thirds of the total force available had been destroyed or seriously damaged on the ground. The Japanese dive-bombers and torpedo-bombers were therefore able to press home their attack on the Fleet almost without air-opposition. Their success was remarkable. An hour and a half later, when the last wave of bombers withdrew, the Pacific Fleet had temporarily ceased to exist. Of the eight battle-ships in harbour, four had been sunk outright and only two (*Pennsylvania* and *Maryland*) had escaped serious damage. Three cruisers, three destroyers and a number of small craft had also been sunk and 219 aircraft destroyed or damaged on the ground or in the air. Total casualties, including civilians, were returned at 2,403 killed and 1,178 wounded. Japanese losses in the actual attack were only twenty-nine aircraft.[1] It was a victory comparable with the Battle of the Nile.[2]

Nevertheless, as they were presently to discover, the Japanese had fallen just short of complete success. Though they had destroyed the American battle fleet as it was, they had left intact or repairable the considerable force of three battleships (*Pennsylvania, Maryland* and *Colorado*), three aircraft-carriers (*Lexington, Enterprise* and *Saratoga*), twelve heavy and six light cruisers. Moreover, Pearl Harbor itself remained usable as a fleet base, very little damage having been done to shore installations. It has since been argued that, had the Japanese ignored the Fleet and concentrated instead on wrecking the work-shops, dry dock, oil storage and other base installations at Pearl Harbor, they would have imposed a far longer delay on the American counter-attack. That may well be so, though whether carrier-borne aircraft, primarily designed for attacks on shipping, would have been equally effective in another rôle is open to question.

The Japanese had originally intended that the attack on Pearl Harbor should be followed immediately by heavy air-raids on the Philippines; but this proved impossible. On the morning of 7th/8th December the airfields on Formosa, from which the main strike was to be made, were blanketed by thick fog. It was not until one in the afternoon, some hours after General MacArthur's headquarters had received news of the Pearl Harbor attack, that the first enemy bombers appeared over the airfields at Manila. The Japanese, having lost the advantage of surprise, were expecting heavy opposition and were astonished to find instead that the American aircraft had not even been dispersed, but were lying on the airfields as closely

---

[1] It is probable that a number more were lost while attempting to regain their carriers.

[2] Morison, Vol. III, Chap. 5; Watson, pp. 515–6.

packed as at Oahu. The success of this first attack was proportionately great. By the afternoon of 8th December General MacArthur
had lost half his heavy bomber force and upwards of a third of his
fighters. Thereafter the American airforce was able to make little
effective resistance; and control of the air over the Philippines passed
completely to Japan.[1]

After a lull on the following day, the Japanese resumed their
bombardment on 10th December, this time directing the attack
particularly on the naval base at Cavite in Manila Bay, which was
left wrecked and in flames. Some days before, in response to the
warning-orders of 29th November, the greater part of the Asiatic
Fleet had withdrawn to the south, though some submarines and light
craft remained at Manila. After the attack Admiral Hart withdrew
these units and was obliged to report that the naval base was no
longer tenable. The way was thus clear for the next phase in the
Japanese plan. Landings were made at two points in northern
Luzon on 10th December and a third landing at Legaspi in the south-
east two days later. These were preliminary operations with the
object of seizing positions for forward air-strips. The main attack
followed between 22nd and 24th December, when the Japanese
48th Division landed in the Lingayen Gulf on the west coast of
Luzon and the 16th Division at Lamon Bay on the east coast. Both
forces advanced on Manila, which, threatened from two directions
simultaneously, now became untenable.[2]

Without air-support, and with partly-trained and under-equipped
troops of the Philippine Army forming more than half his force,
General MacArthur could not hope to do more than fight a delaying
action. Plans for such a contingency had already been made. They
provided for a gradual withdrawal into the mountains and jungles
of the Bataan Peninsula, which forms the northern arm of Manila
Bay. This was a position of great natural strength, further protected
by the island fortress of Corregidor in the Bay itself. The intention
was to hold the bridgehead at Bataan until such time as reinforcements arrived and then launch a general counter-attack across central
Luzon. But the basis of this plan had already been destroyed at
Pearl Harbor; in the absence of an effective Pacific Fleet, no relief
expedition was possible. Consequently, the continued resistance of
the American forces, first under General MacArthur and then under
General Wainwright, though prolonged for another four or five
months,[3] could have only a moral significance. In practical terms,

---

[1] Louis Morton, *The Fall of the Philippines* (1953), pp. 80–8.

[2] Morton, pp. 93–4, Chaps. 6 and 8.

[3] The forces in the Bataan Peninsula surrendered on 9th April, 1942, and those in
Corregidor on 6th May.

the Japanese were already masters of the Philippines by 3rd January, when Manila fell. By that time a strong detachment from the Japanese base at Palau had also occupied Davao, the capital of the southern island; and the build-up for further operations against Borneo and Sumatra was already in progress.[1]

Japan's other operations on her eastern flank proceeded equally smoothly. On 8th December units of the 24th Air Flotilla, based on Truk in the Caroline Islands, bombarded the American outpost at Guam. Two days later the island was occupied by a naval landing-force. The next objective was Wake Island; but there the small Marine garrison set up a spirited resistance and was able to repulse the first attack on 11th December with considerable loss. Within the next ten days, however, heavy reinforcements were brought forward, including two cruisers and two aircraft-carriers from the striking-force, which was now returning to base from the Pearl Harbor operation. On 23rd December a further attack, made in over-whelming strength, carried the island. The Japanese forces engaged—that is, part of the 4th Fleet, the 24th Air Flotilla and certain attached troops—were then free to begin the next stage of their offensive against New Guinea and the Bismarck Archipelago.[2]

(iv)

Malaya

On 5th December, following Lord Halifax's conversation with President Roosevelt, the Chiefs of Staff authorized the Commander-in-Chief, Far East, to undertake 'Matador' as soon as he had reliable information, either that the Japanese were about to seize the Kra Isthmus, or that they had already occupied some other part of Siam. But by this time a further complication had clouded the issue. On 2nd December the Commander-in-Chief had received reports through London to the effect that certain members of the Siamese Cabinet were now urging Japan to make her first attack on Kota Bharu, that is, on Malayan territory only. It was anticipated that we should react to this by occupying the whole or part of the Kra Isthmus, thus putting ourselves (from Siam's point of view) in the position of aggressors. Siam would then retaliate by joining Japan in a declaration of war.

It is probable that this story was put about deliberately by Japan

---

[1] Morton, Chaps. 10 and 11.

[2] Morison, Vol. III, Chaps. 8 and 12.

as part of a scheme of tactical deception. Its provenance may not have been obvious at the time; but even so, it is difficult to see why it should have been treated with any respect. The earlier restrictions on 'Matador' had been intended to guard against two risks: the risk of precipitating a Japanese occupation of Siam under conditions in which we might appear to have been the aggressors; and the consequential risk of our becoming involved in war with Japan without American support. But if the first attack fell on Kota Bharu, we should at once be at war with Japan, whether we liked it or not. Moreover, it was certain that Japan's next step would be to occupy Siam, so as to secure a base for further operations against northern Malaya. In that event it would be, or would become, a question of purely minor and academic interest whether British or Japanse troops had crossed the frontier of Siam first.

Nevertheless, Sir Robert Brooke-Popham evidently attached a certain importance to these reports and, on 4th December, asked the Chiefs of Staff for specific authority to undertake 'Matador' in the circumstances described—that is to say, an attack on Kota Bharu not immediately accompanied by an operation on any part of Siam. The general authority which he had received on the 5th did not precisely cover this point, though he might have argued that a Japanese attack on Kota Bharu was bound to be followed by a movement against Siam, which would certainly include the Kra Isthmus. On this basis the authority already given was sufficient. But Sir Robert, on whom the need for caution had been so strongly impressed, still remained doubtful. He did not receive a final answer to his inquiry until the morning of 8th December, when he was authorized to proceed at once with 'Matador', if the Japanese landed at Kota Bharu. It thus happened that for three important days from the 5th to the 8th the Commander-in-Chief was uncertain how far he was free to act, and had his eyes fixed on the east coast rather than the Kra Isthmus. This was, no doubt, what the Japanese had intended.

On the morning of 6th December news reached Singapore that Japanese convoys had sailed from Saigon and from Camranh Bay and that Siamese frontier-guards were erecting road-blocks on their side of the Siam-Malay frontier. At a little after noon air-reconnaissance reported two (or possibly three) Japanese convoys about eighty miles south-east of Cambodia Point. The first, of three merchant ships escorted by a cruiser, was steering north-west; the second and larger, of twenty-two ships with an escort of cruisers and destroyers, was steering due west. Visibility was extremely bad, as it was already the season of the north-east monsoon with low cloud and frequent rainstorms. All efforts to regain contact with the two convoys after the first sighting were unsuccessful. At this stage, therefore, everything was guess-work. There could be no absolute certainty that the Japanese were engaged on anything more than manœuvres; nor, if they were, could the point of attack be forecast. It might be Siam or Malaya or even some point in the Dutch East Indies. In view of this, G.H.Q., Far East, took no action beyond ordering a general alert throughout the command.[1]

On the following day air-reconnaissance was intensified but produced little or no result until late in the afternoon. At about 5.30 p.m. a merchantman and a cruiser, presumably part of the convoy sighted on the 6th, were reported rather over 100 miles north of Kota Bharu on a course for Singora. An hour later there was a tentative report of four Japanese warships, believed to be destroyers, about 60 miles north of Patani on a southerly course parallel with the coast. With this information, scanty though it was, the picture began to clarify, but a wide choice of possibilities still lay open. If the ships sighted that afternoon were part of the original convoy (or convoys) and were bound for Singora and Patani, then 'Matador' was already useless, since the Japanese would reach their objective by sea before the 11th Division in Kedah could do so by land. On the other hand, in view of the reports received on the 2nd, it was possible that the Japanese objective was Kota Bharu. In that case there might still be time for 'Matador'; but it was doubtful, since he had not yet received an answer to his inquiry, whether the Commander-in-Chief had authority to order it. Finally, there was a chance—though a remote one, if the size of the convoy sighted on the 6th had been correctly reported—that the Japanese only intended a demonstration with the object of enticing us into a violation of the Siamese frontier, which they could then use as a pretext for the quasi-peaceful occupation of that country. If so, a premature launching of 'Matador' would be unfortunate.

Faced with these perplexities, the Commander-in-Chief decided to wait. General Heath, commanding III Corps in northern Malaya, was told that 'Matador' might be required on the following morning, but was warned to make no move until the results of an air-reconnaissance over Singora at first light were known. Thus all plans hung in suspense for the moment.

Shortly after midnight news came from 8th Brigade at Kota Bharu that three Japanese transports with escorting warships were anchored off the beaches and that landings were already in progress.[2] G.H.Q., Far East, still influenced, perhaps, by the theory that Japan intended to avoid Siamese territory in the opening phase, evidently mistook this for the main attack. Definitive orders to the 11th Division were still withheld; and arrangements were made to commit the

---

[1] For operations in Malaya see Kirby, Vol. I, Chaps. 11 and 12.
[2] The exact time of the first Japanese landing at Kota Bharu is disputed; but it appears to have taken place about half an hour *before* the attack on Pearl Harbor.

21

whole available strength of the R.A.F. to attacks on Japanese shipping off Kota Bharu from dawn onwards. This was a hasty and unfortunate decision. The early attacks, carried out that night by No. 1 Squadron from Kota Bharu, were not without success; one of the transports was sunk and heavy casualties inflicted on the enemy. But before dawn the Japanese had established their beach-heads and all shipping had withdrawn except for a few landing-craft. The later strikes, which involved eight out of the thirteen squadrons then stationed in Malaya, therefore fell upon the empty air.

Meanwhile, the main Japanese landings were proceeding un-hindered at Singora and Patani, the very points at which they had always been expected.

Sixteen transports, carrying the first flight of the Japanese 5th Division, arrived off these ports shortly after 2 a.m. on 8th December and the disembarkation began almost immediately. No more than token opposition was offered by the local Siamese forces. At about the same time a further series of landings was made elsewhere in Siam : by elements of the 55th Division at the neck of the Kra Isth-mus, and by a detachment of the Imperial Guards at Bangkok. Strong Japanese forces also moved overland across the Indo-Chinese frontier. Advanced parties of the 3rd Air Division accom-panied the forward troops to take over Siamese aerodromes and pre-pare additional air-strips. By the afternoon of 8th December the Japanese were in a position to operate 100–150 aircraft from southern Siam.

At 8.30 on the morning of the 8th December, Sir Robert Brooke-Popham received an answer to his inquiry of the 4th, which author-ized him to carry out 'Matador' or any similar operation involving a violation of the Siamese frontier, if the Japanese had already attacked Malayan territory. Approximately an hour later he also received the results of the dawn reconnaissance over Singora, which he had ordered on the previous night. These left no doubt that it was now too late for 'Matador'; and he therefore instructed General Percival that the alternative defensive plan should be put into operation at once. These orders did not reach 11th Division until four hours later, that is at 1.30 p.m. It was then that the full weight of past hesita-tions began to make itself felt. In theory 11th Division should have been ready to carry out either plan, the offensive or the defensive, at a moment's notice; but in practice this was not so. For weeks past attention had been concentrated almost exclusively on 'Matador'; all the transport and supply arrangements of the Division had been geared to a rapid forward move; and the last-minute switch to an alternative plan involved considerable dislocation. Moreover, owing to the shortage of local labour, work on the defensive positions, which the Division was to take up, had not been completed. The recent heavy rains had left some of the positions waterlogged; and no attempt had been made to provide telephone or telegraph lines, all of which had to be laid by the Division on its arrival.

Another point deserves attention. The 11th Division had to guard two possible routes across the frontier: the main road and railway line from Singora to Alor Star; and a branch road, which ran from Patani through the frontier village of Kroh and joined the main road at Sungei Patani about forty miles south. The former offered a suitable defensive position at Jitra, ten miles north of Alor Star, where the road and railway diverge. But the only suitable position on the branch road was that known as the Ledge, some thirty miles on the farther side of the Siamese frontier. In other words, both plans, the defensive no less than the offensive, involved a violation of the Siamese frontier; and to this extent the prolonged arguments about 'Matador' and the particular hesitations of the past few days had both been futile. They had accomplished nothing except to hold back Krohcol, the detached force detailed to guard the branch road, and handicap it by eight or nine hours in its attempt to reach the Ledge position before the Japanese could do so. In the event this delay was fatal. When Krohcol came in sight of its objective at nightfall of 9th December, it found the Japanese already in occupation and was obliged to withdraw to an extemporized defensive position some five miles farther back.

While these movements were in progress on the ground, the Japanese opened their air-offensive against Malaya. It began with a raid on Singapore in the early hours of the 8th, which did little damage but revealed alarming weaknesses in the organization of the defence. It continued throughout the day with concentrated attacks on all the northern airfields (with the exception of Kuantan), first by long-range aircraft from southern Indo-China, and later by fighters and light bombers operating from air-strips at Singora and Patani. Losses were heavy, the more so because the earlier raids caught many squadrons on the ground, refuelling and rearming after the abortive strike at Kota Bharu. By the end of the day no less than sixty of the 110 aircraft in northern Malaya had been destroyed or seriously damaged. This was more than one-third of the total force available for the defence of the whole country. No Air Force could hope to recover from such a scale of loss in the first day's fighting. By the morning of 9th December the Japanese had established a complete air superiority over the battle area, which they were not to lose for the rest of the campaign.

The stage being thus set, the further disasters, which followed rapidly, were in a sense inevitable. We had been out-generalled, we had lost control of the air; and we were now to be out-fought on the ground. By the morning of 12th December, when the Japanese opened their main attack on the Jitra position, the 11th Division was already insecure. The abrupt change from an offensive to a defensive plan, the inexperience of the staff, the inadequacies of the position itself and the unexpected boldness and tactical skill of the enemy had all combined to lower morale and, to some extent, to disorganize the command. Moreover, Krohcol had already been forced back to a position on the Malayan side of the frontier, which it could not expect to hold for more than a day or two. At any moment, therefore, the Jitra position might be outflanked by an enemy move on Sungei Patani. That evening, after heavy fighting during the day, the divisional commander obtained permission to withdraw to Gurun, an alternative position thirty miles to the south, which had been reconnoitred though not otherwise prepared. By then his Division was seriously depleted. One brigade had been reduced to a quarter of its strength; and the two others had both suffered heavily in men, guns and transport. In these circumstances it was unlikely that any but the briefest stand could be made at Gurun.

Meanwhile, the Japanese had also made steady progress in the Kota Bharu sector. By the afternoon of 8th December they were firmly established on the beaches and had advanced far enough inland to threaten, or appear to threaten, Kota Bharu aerodrome, which was hurriedly and perhaps prematurely evacuated by the R.A.F. Further landings took place that night, and thereafter the enemy's advance was continuous. Machang and Gong Kedah, the two remaining aerodromes in the north-east, were abandoned on the 10th; and with their loss the further defence of Kelantan became pointless. On 12th December General Percival gave permission for a general withdrawal, first to the railhead at Kuala Krai, and thence to the area Kuala Lipis-Jerantut, which controlled the lateral communications between the east and west coasts. This movement was carried out successfully between the 15th and the 22nd and contact with the enemy temporarily broken.

In the meantime certain incidents had taken place farther down the east coast at Kuantan, which, though of minor importance in themselves, contributed directly to the last and gravest of the week's disasters: the loss of the *Prince of Wales* and the *Repulse*. It will be remembered that Kuantan aerodrome had escaped attack on the 8th, when the airfields in northern Malaya suffered so severely. The enemy made good this omission with a heavy raid on the following day, which destroyed seven aircraft on the ground. The remaining squadrons were then withdrawn, though the airfield remained in use as an advanced landing-ground. Later on the same day a reconnaissance aircraft reported an enemy merchant ship and ten barges moving south along the coast to Kuantan. The beach-defences were alerted and, shortly after dark, duly reported that the enemy were attempting to land. Further reports of the same kind came in during the night; and there was intermittent artillery fire. The impression was thus created at G.H.Q. that a third Japanese landing was taking place on a similar scale to that at Kota Bharu. But the morning light revealed no enemy, only a few small boats, riddled by gunfire, stranded on the beaches south of Kuantan. If the Japanese had intended anything at all, it had only been a feint or a reconnaissance. But the damage, as we shall see presently, had already been done.

For the moment, in order to complete the story of the land-operations, we must return briefly to the Kedah front. As had been expected, the Gurun position proved untenable. After some fighting on the 5th, what remained of the 11th Division withdrew to a new position south of the next important obstacle, the Muda River. This movement had the effect of uncovering Penang; and the garrison of that island was accordingly evacuated on the night of the 16th. A comprehensive denial scheme was put into operation at the same time; but unfortunately, for reasons which are not clear, the need to scuttle or remove all shipping was ignored. Some twenty-four motor-craft and a large number of junks and barges were left intact in the harbour. These later proved of inestimable value to the Japanese, whom they provided with the means to out-flank and infiltrate troops in the rear of any position, which we might subsequently take up on the west coast.

Thus, at the end of the first week of operations, the outlook was as bleak as it could be. The whole of Perlis and Kedah had been abandoned; and the evacuation of Kelantan was in progress We had lost a third of our Air Force and with it control of the air, which it was unlikely that we should be able to regain, since all the northern air-fields were now in enemy hands. Of the three divisions then in Malaya, one, the 11th Division, had been so heavily mauled that it had almost ceased to exist as a fighting formation; and one brigade of another division, the 9th, though still substantially intact, was suffering from the moral effect of an almost equally severe defeat. In addition to all this, we had met with the major disaster at sea, which still remains to be described.

(v)

Disaster at Sea

The arguments which decided the Government to send the *Prince of Wales* and the *Repulse* to Singapore were set out in the last chapter. It will be remembered that the primary intention had not been to form a fighting-force—for which purpose the two battleships were wholly inadequate—but to create a vague, potential menace, which would tend to deter Japan and to embarrass her naval calculations. But this quasi-political application of sea-power, perhaps legitimate in itself, had come too late. By the time the two ships reached the Far East, Japanese planning was already complete; and the day of reckoning was too near for a gesture of this kind to affect the issue.

Had it been known in London how close we stood to the brink of war, the two ships, if sent at all, would no doubt have been recalled at once. As it was, they were the subject of grave and growing apprehensions at the Admiralty. On 1st December, the day of their arrival, a signal was made to Admiral Phillips, proposing that the *Prince of Wales* and the *Repulse* should leave Singapore. Two days later a further signal, endorsed by the Prime Minister, suggested that he should try to get Admiral Hart's agreement to the transfer of some American destroyers to Singapore and should then take the two capital ships away to the east. Admiral Phillips and his staff were thinking on similar lines. On 3rd December he reported his intention to send *Repulse* and two destroyers on a visit to Port Darwin. They sailed two days later, but were recalled on the 7th, as soon as the first news was received that an escorted Japanese convoy was at sea.[1]

On the evening of the same day, 7th December, Admiral Phillips returned to Singapore from his discussions with Admiral Hart at Manila. Next morning, when he received the news of the Japanese landings at Singora and Kota Bhara, he had to face an exceptionally difficult decision. Prudence dictated that he should at once remove his two capital ships from an area where the dangers to which they were exposed were out of proportion to any good they could hope to achieve. On the other hand, it was inconceivable that the Navy should deny support to the Army and the Air Force or withdraw without contributing anything to the defence of Malaya. Admiral Phillips therefore decided to attempt a raid on the Japanese shipping off Singora, relying on surprise to off-set the weakness and unsuitability of his force. It was a bold decision; but it must be added that he was not then fully aware either of the strength of the Japanese

---

[1] Roskill, Vol. I, pp. 558–9.

naval air forces in southern Indo-China or of the weakness of the R.A.F. in northern Malaya.[1]

The *Prince of Wales*, the *Repulse*, and four destroyers sailed on the afternoon of 8th December. Shortly after midnight that night Admiral Phillips received a signal from his Chief of Staff, whom he had left at Singapore, warning him of the presence of powerful Japanese bomber forces in southern Indo-China. The message added that the northern front in Malaya appeared to be crumbling and that it would not be possible to provide the fighter-cover requested over Singora. One element essential to the safety of the operation had thus disappeared; but Admiral Phillips decided to carry on, provided that he was not sighted by Japanese aircraft on the following day. But this condition was not fulfilled either. On the afternoon or early evening of the 9th the *Prince of Wales* reported Japanese reconnaissance aircraft; and with this sighting the last hope of surprise disappeared. Shortly afterwards the whole squadron reversed course for Singapore.

Meanwhile the Japanese were taking elaborate precautions to protect themselves against any incursion by Admiral Phillips' ships. Vice-Admiral Kondo, commanding the Southern Force, with two battleships, two heavy cruisers and a number of destroyers, was in a position south-east of Point Cambodia; and twelve submarines were patrolling the area between Kota Bharu and Singapore. On the afternoon of the 9th one of the latter had sighted Admiral Phillip's squadron and reported its position and course. Admiral Kondo then ordered the 7th Cruiser Squadron, which had escorted the convoys to Malaya, to fly off its aircraft in an attempt to locate and shadow the British ships.[2] At the same time the 22nd Air Flotilla at Saigon was ordered to make a night attack with torpedo-bombers. The aircraft took off at dusk but owing to Admiral Phillips' change of course, had to return to base without finding their target.

At midnight on 9th December Admiral Phillips received a further signal, informing him of the supposed Japanese landing at Kuantan. This seemed to provide a possible alternative target for the squadron, since it was unlikely that the enemy, who had last seen his ships late that afternoon on a northerly course, would expect him as far south as Kuantan by daylight. Accordingly, he altered course again to close the coast. About an hour later the squadron was again sighted by a Japanese submarine and its position reported. The news reached Admiral Kondo just after he had turned his whole fleet on to a southerly course in the hope of intercepting the British ships during the day. But the report of their new position made this improbable.

---

[1] For the loss of the *Prince of Wales* and *Repulse*, see Roskill, Vol. I, pp. 363–70; Kirby, Vol. I, Chap. II.

[2] These were probably the aircraft seen by the *Prince of Wales* that evening.

He therefore altered course again to the northward and ordered the 22nd Air Flotilla to make a further strike at dawn. Twelve reconnaissance aircraft took off while it was still dark to search the area, and were followed by thirty-four high-level and fifty-one torpedo-bombers organized in a succession of flights.

The *Prince of Wales* and the *Repulse* raised Kuantan at about 8 a.m. on 10th December, but saw, of course, no sign of the enemy. One of the accompanying destroyers was sent into the harbour and returned with the news that everything was perfectly peaceful. Admiral Phillips, still supposing that there must have been something in the original report, then turned back to investigate a small ship and a number of junks and barges, which had been sighted in the distance shortly before the squadron reached Kuantan. He was so engaged when the blow fell. The Japanese bombers on their outward flight had run down the 105th Meridian almost to the latitude of Singapore without seeing any sign of their target. They were now homing disconsolate, when at about 10.20 a.m. one of the reconnaissance aircraft sighted the British ships and signalled their new position.

The first flight of high-level bombers attacked at 11 o'clock, followed rapidly by several flights of torpedo-bombers. An hour and a half later the *Repulse*, having been hit by five torpedoes, turned over and sank. The *Prince of Wales*, though severely hit at the beginning of the action and largely out of control, survived until 1.20 p.m., when she also capsized and sank. Of the two ships' total complement of 2,921 officers and men, 2,081 were picked up by the escorting destroyers; but neither Admiral Phillips nor Captain Leach of the *Prince of Wales* was among them. So ended, almost before it had begun, the career of the Far Eastern Fleet. It was a disaster which, though smaller in scale, was comparable in effect with the loss of the American battle fleet at Pearl Harbor two days before.

(vi)

Hong Kong

The defence of Hong Kong island necessarily involves the defence of part of the adjacent mainland, namely the Kowloon Peninsula and the tract of land, known as the Leased Territories,[1] which extends about seventeen miles north of Kowloon to the line of the Sham Chun river. This area is an integral part of the Crown Colony. The

---

[1] They are held on a ninety-nine years' lease, granted by the Chinese Government in 1898.

harbour, on which the whole life on Hong Kong depends, is in the sheltered strip of water between the north shore of the island and the Kowloon Peninsula; and the main commercial docks are on the mainland side. The island also depends on the mainland for rather more than half its water-supply. In 1941 this was a point of particular importance to the defence, both because of the size of the civil population—close to a million on the island itself—and because the rain-water reservoirs, on which the island's local supply depended, were vulnerable to air-attack or artillery-fire from the mainland. Finally—though this was of less importance than it might have been, since no air-defence had been provided—the only aerodrome in the Colony is at Kai Tak on the mainland.

As we have seen earlier, Hong Kong was always regarded as an outpost, ultimately indefensible, though not to be given up without a struggle. But this description is at least partly misleading. Hong Kong was not, and could not be, an outpost in the sense that the American positions on Guam and Wake Island were outposts—strong points held for a purely military purpose. Hong Kong, on the contrary, was one of the major international ports of the world, and owed its origin and development to a commercial impulse, or rather to the juncture of a commercial impulse with the old exclusive policy of the Chinese Government, which made it inevitable that the main *entrepot* of the South China trade should be in foreign hands. The Colony had attracted a large population, Chinese by origin but, as to the great majority, British subjects by birth. They could claim the right to be defended against the King's enemies; but they could not be asked to endure the ultimate rigours of a defence *à outrance*. Indeed, their presence made such a course practically impossible as well as morally objectionable. We were thus obliged to approach the defence of Hong Kong with a divided mind. On the one hand, we had a duty to defend the island as long as we were able; on the other, we knew that we could not press the defence beyond a certain point.

Until November 1941, the garrison of Hong Kong consisted, apart from the troops manning the fixed coastal defences and certain locally raised units, of only two British and two Indian Battalions. Requests for reinforcement had been refused on the ground that it was useless to lock up troops in a fortress, which there was no possibility of relieving. At the end of July, however, the retiring G.O.C., Major-General Grasett, himself a Canadian, had conceived the idea that the Canadian Government might be persuaded to make another two or three battalions available, and that, with these additional troops, a prepared position on the mainland could be held for a considerable length of time. After some debate this had been accepted; and in October the Canadian Government had dispatched to Hong Kong a Brigade headquarters, two infantry battalions and certain ancillary units. But these were not troops of the first class. They had previously been carrying out garrison duties in Newfoundland and the West Indies, and were available for further service in Hong Kong only because their training had not reached the standard required for the operational divisions, which Canada was then forming. They were sent on the understanding that the value of their presence in the Far East would be as much moral as military.[1]

On the morning of 8th December, when the Japanese attacked across the Sham Chun river, the new G.O.C. Hong Kong, Major-General Maltby, thus disposed of a total force (including local levies) of two weak Brigades.[2] It was necessary even in the opening phase of the battle to hold back one Brigade on the island, lest the Japanese should supplement their main attack by sea-borne landings, as they could readily have done. There remained only three battalions and four improvised troops of field-artillery to occupy the prepared position on the mainland. This ran through hilly country well-adapted to defence; but its total length was eleven miles; and, according to the estimate of the C-in-C, Far East, it could not have been adequately manned by a force of less than two divisions. It is therefore much to the credit of General Maltby's three battalions that they should have been able, without air-support and with a marked weakness in artillery, to hold the Japanese 38th Division for five days. General Maltby's plans had in fact provided for a longer delay of up to a week or ten days; and this might have been achieved but for the unexpected and unlucky loss of one of the main redoubts in the line by a night attack. Nevertheless, the performance of the Mainland Brigade compared very favourably with that of the 11th Division in the exactly contemporary operations at Jitra.

The evacuation of the mainland was followed by a two days' pause, during which the island was summoned to surrender and refused. On 15th December the Japanese opened an intensive air and artillery bombardment. This lasted for four days with no respite except that afforded by a second summons to surrender. Considerable damage was done to the fixed defences. On the night of the 18th the first Japanese landings took place, not without loss, on the northeast corner of the island. From this point onwards the final reduction of Hong Kong was only a question of time. A detailed account of the subsequent operations has been given elsewhere. Here it is only necessary to say that the defence was maintained for another week, that is, until the morning of Christmas Day. By that time the troops, outnumbered, under-equipped in relation to their enemy and with little experience of active service, had been fought to a standstill. The

---

[1] *Report of Canadian Expeditionary Force to Hong Kong* (Ottawa, 1942), paras. 50–61.

[2] For operations in Hong Kong see Kirby, Vol. I, Chaps. 8 and 9.

island was cut off from its mainland water-supply; the local reservoirs were damaged or in enemy hands; and a severe water famine was impending. Under those conditions the Governor, Sir Mark Young, and General Maltby felt justified in surrendering. Commonwealth losses were returned at 4,440, or more than one in three of those engaged; Japanese losses at 2,754. But there is reason to think that the Japanese casualties were understated and that there was, in fact, an approximate equality of loss. One may say that, in proportion, the Japanese paid as heavily for Hong Kong as for any of their gains in the first phase of their aggression.

CHAPTER XIII

THE OUTLINES OF STRATEGY

(i)

After Pearl Harbor

MR. CHURCHILL HAS described in his Memoirs how the news of Pearl Harbor first reached him. On the evening of Sunday, 7th December, he was at Chequers with two guests, the American Ambassador and Mr. Averell Harriman. After dinner, listening to the nine o'clock news, they heard it announced among a number of minor items that Japanese aircraft had attacked American shipping at Hawaii and British shipping in the Dutch East Indies. It was some moments before the full significance of this news reached their minds. As soon as it had done so, the Prime Minister put through a telephone call to President Roosevelt, who presently confirmed, though without entering into details, that the Pacific Fleet had indeed been attacked, and that the United States were now at war.[1]

On the following morning the Prime Minister addressed a letter to the King, seeking his permission to leave the country:

'I have formed the conviction that it is my duty to visit Washington without delay, provided that such a course is agreeable to President Roosevelt, as I have little doubt it will be. The whole plan of the Anglo-American defence and attack has to be concerted in the light of reality. We have also to be careful that our share of munitions and other aid which we are receiving from the United States does not suffer more than is, I fear, inevitable. The fact that Mr. Eden will be in Moscow while I am at Washington will make the settlement of large-scale problems between the three great Allies easier.'

As soon as leave had been given, a telegram was sent to Mr. Roosevelt. The President's reply, though tactfully worded, suggested that he was a little taken aback by so much promptness and would have preferred to postpone the meeting until the New Year. But Mr. Churchill, who had every reason to fear what decisions might be taken in Washington under the first impact of the crisis, was insistent; and it was finally agreed that conversations should begin on or about 20th December. Since Mr. Churchill proposed to travel by sea, the

---

[1] Churchill, Vol. III, pp. 537–8.

voyage being expected to take a week, this left only three or four days for the dispatch of a great deal of necessary business.

On the morning of 8th December a formal Declaration of War, drafted by Mr. Churchill in the Foreign Secretary's absence, was handed to the Japanese Ambassador.[1] It may be added, as a curious commentary on the relative speed of constitutional processes, that the corresponding American declaration of war on Germany did not follow until three days later. On the following day, 9th December, a telegram was sent to Mr. Duff Cooper in Singapore, instructing him to assume at once the powers of Resident Minister in the Far East. It will be remembered that his own report, which had only recently arrived in London, had recommended a rather different procedure. But this was no time for niceties. There was evidently much to be done; and the wide and loosely defined powers of a Minister of State were well suited to immediate action in an emergency :

> '3. When Captain Oliver Lyttelton was appointed Minister of State at Cairo it was laid down that this did not affect the exist-ing responsibilities of His Majesty's Representatives in the Middle East, or their official relationships with their respective depart-ments at home. The same will apply in the Far East. The success-ful establishment of this machinery depends largely on your handling of it in these early critical days.
>
> 4. With your knowledge of the various public departments and of Cabinet procedure, it should be possible for you to exer-cise a powerful, immediately concerting influence upon Far Eastern affairs.'

Later on the same day the Prime Minister presided at a staff meet-ing at the Admiralty, which considered the impact of the Japanese attack on the naval situation. One of the main subjects of discussion was the future of the *Prince of Wales* and the *Repulse*, now all too clearly in an exposed and dangerous situation. It was agreed that they ought to leave Singapore, either for Australia, as Admiral Phillips had already suggested, or perhaps to join the remnant of the Pacific Fleet at Hawaii. A final decision was deferred for the moment, no doubt in order that the Americans might be consulted; but although the meeting could not have known this, it was already too late. Before the discussion had even begun, the two ships had sailed from Singapore on their last voyage. News of their loss was received in London early the following morning.

When Mr. Churchill addressed the House of Commons on 11th December, he had therefore a heavy budget of ill news to open. At any stage of the war the loss of two capital ships, in an action in which the enemy suffered no damage, would have ranked as a major

---

[1] Churchill, Vol. III, p. 544.

disaster. Now it was only one item in a longer tale of catastrophe. Reports of the fighting in Malaya, Hong Kong and the Philippines were still confused and incomplete; but enough was known to make it clear that Japan had scored a striking initial success. Still worse, the crippling of the U.S. Pacific Fleet, the only force then capable of meeting the Japanese navy on equal terms, had destroyed the whole basis of Western strategy in the Pacific. Until a new fleet could be gathered, Japan would be able to select her objectives at will and to concentrate her force against each in turn, confident of meeting no more than local opposition. It was thus only reasonable to expect, as Mr. Churchill warned the House, that further disasters would follow. Nor was much comfort to be found on other battlefronts. In the Middle East the 'Crusader' offensive, on which such high hopes had been built, and for which so many sacrifices had been made, had still not achieved a decisive victory despite increasingly heavy fighting. In this sombre scene the only encouragement that the Prime Minister could offer the House was to reiterate his belief that the united strength of Russia, America and Great Britain must in the end subdue all comers. The House heard him, as he records, almost in silence and 'seemed to hold its judgement in suspense'.[1]

That evening another staff meeting assembled at Downing Street, this time to discuss the military aspects of the situation. Although the news from the Far East was bad, and only too likely to grow worse, the situation did not yet appear desperate. It was agreed that a major diversion of force from other theatres, even if it were possible, would be strategically unsound. Although we could not afford, in Mr. Churchill's phrase, to accept indefinite defeat from Japan, we were still bound to regard her as a secondary enemy by comparison with Germany. Indeed, her chief value to the Axis lay in her power to draw away to the Pacific the forces which were now building up in Europe and the Middle East. By the same argument it was in our interest to resist that pull as much as possible. For these reasons only a limited redistribution of force was planned. One division and four fighter squadrons, then *en route* to the Middle East, were diverted to India; and India was instructed to retain another division, previously under orders for Iraq. The Middle East was to send an immediate reinforcement of eighteen light bombers to Malaya by the air-route across India and Burma. Admiral Layton, who had resumed command in the Far East on the death of Admiral Phillips, was informed that the plan to form a battle fleet in the Indian Ocean by the spring of 1942 still stood, but that he could not expect any immediate reinforcement beyond the aircraft-carrier *Indomitable*, due at Cape Town on 1st January.

---

[1] Hansard (1941–2), Vol. 376, Cols. 1686–97; Churchill, Vol. III, pp. 552–3.

The general aim of these re-dispositions was explained in a telegram which the Prime Minister sent to General Wavell on the following day:

'You must now look East. Burma is placed under your command. You must resist the Japanese advance towards Burma and India and try to cut their communications down the Malay peninsula. We are diverting the 18th Division now rounding the Cape, to Bombay, together with four fighter squadrons of the R.A.F., now *en route* for the Caucasus and Caspian theatre. We are also sending you a special hamper of A/A and A/T guns, some of which are already *en route*. You should retain the 17th Indian Division for defence against the Japanese. Marry these forces as you think best and work them into the Eastern fighting front to the highest advantage.

It is proposed at a convenient moment in the near future by arrangement between you and Auchinleck to transfer Iraq and Persia to the Cairo Command. The Russian victories and Auchinleck's Libyan advance have for the time being relieved danger of German irruption into the Syrian-Iraq-Persian theatre. The danger may revive, but we have other more important dangers to meet.

I hope these new dispositions arising from the vast changes in the world situation of the last four days will commend themselves to you. I shall endeavour to feed you with armour, aircraft and British personnel to the utmost possible, having regard to the great strain we are under. Pray cable me your views and needs.'

Three days later Mr. Churchill left England on the first and perhaps the most important of his war-time visits to Washington. The principal members of his party were Lord Beaverbrook, then Minister of Supply; two of the Chiefs of Staff, Admiral Pound and Air-Marshal Portal; and Sir John Dill, who had recently been succeeded as C.I.G.S. by General Sir Alan Brooke.[1] The intention was that Sir John Dill should remain in Washington in some liaison capacity, either as Mr. Churchill's personal representative or as head of the British Military Mission.[2]

This choice of advisers shows how the Prime Minister expected the forthcoming talks to develop. First, there would be a number of urgent questions to settle in the field of supply. Now that America was a belligerent, all existing agreements and priorities would be dislocated; and the problem was to ensure that we did not lose more than a minimum of the aircraft, weapons and munitions on which we had been counting. This would merge into the larger question of how far and how quickly American war-production could be ex-

[1] Previously C-in-C, Home Forces.
[2] Churchill, Vol. III, pp. 555-6.

panded and how its output should be divided in future between America's own armed forces and those of her Allies. All that was primarily Lord Beaverbrook's task. But it could only be carried out within the framework of a general strategic agreement, a coherent plan for the future conduct of the war. To negotiate that—or rather, to propose an outline plan and secure America's acceptance—was a task for the Prime Minister himself, supported by the Chiefs of Staff.

It was generally expected that the initiative would rest throughout with the British delegation. It had appeared at the Atlantic Meeting that strategic planning in the United States was still in a primitive stage, which scarcely looked beyond the defence of the American continent. Although the American Chiefs of Staff had been ready to criticize, often justly, British conceptions of how the war might be won, they had not put forward any alternative strategy of their own. They had seemed to be content with the generalities of ABC–1, reinforced by a few text-book maxims. It was not likely that this situation had altered much during the intervening months. On the contrary, a growing preoccupation with events in the Pacific had probably driven wider problems into the background. In these circumstances, it was evidently important that Mr. Churchill and his party should arrive in Washington with their own ideas clearly formulated. Whatever plans they brought forward would provide the main basis of discussion at the Conference, and might well decide the future pattern of Allied strategy. With this in mind Mr. Churchill and the Chiefs of Staff devoted the greater part of the outward voyage to preparing a series of papers on grand strategy. These will be considered presently; but first something must be said about the parallel negotiations which the Foreign Secretary was about to open in Moscow.

(ii)

Eden in Moscow

Mr. Eden's meeting with the Soviet leaders had been arranged in November; and he was already on his way when the news of Pearl Harbor arrived. Its effect was to increase rather than diminish the importance of his mission. All the problems and difficulties, which had clouded our relations with Russia over the past few months, were now likely to be intensified. Supplies would be short; our military potential in Europe would be further reduced by the opening of a new front in the Pacific; and our collaboration with the United

22

States, always an object of suspicion to Russia, would become more intimate. It was essential to try to grasp this situation before it became unmanageable, though the chances of doing so effectively were not high.[1]

M. Stalin had proposed two general subjects or themes for discussion: 'war-aims and the post-war organization of peace' and 'mutual military assistance against Hitler in Europe'. Both bristled with thorny problems for the negotiator. On the first or diplomatic subject the Government had so far been careful to confine itself to generalities. The Atlantic Charter, for example, had contained broad statements of principle, such as everyone could accept, but few precise commitments. All controversial questions, whether they concerned the government of Germany, the frontiers of Europe or the organization of the international body which was to replace the League of Nations, had been held over for settlement by some future Peace Conference. This, broadly speaking, was also the policy of the United States; but there was little reason to suppose that it would appeal to the Russians. It was even doubtful how far they were really convinced that it was our policy. More probably, they believed or feared that we were already in active discussion with the Americans and that they would be faced, at the end of the war, by an attempt on the part of the two Western Powers to impose an already agreed settlement, in which Russian interests had been played down or ignored. In particular, the Foreign Secretary anticipated that M. Stalin would press hard for an immediate clear-cut agreement on Russia's frontiers. We should be asked to recognize the annexations which she had made between 1939 and 1941 in the Baltic States, Rumania, Poland and Finland. But on this point the Cabinet was unwilling to give way. These annexations, made while Russia was still allied to Germany, were wholly contrary to the spirit of the Atlantic Charter; and we had besides given a specific undertaking to the United States not to conclude territorial bargains in advance of the Peace Conference.

The military discussions promised equal difficulties. It will be remembered that the Prime Minister, in his telegram to Stalin of 21st November,[2] had indicated that the Foreign Secretary would be empowered to discuss 'the sending of troops not only into the Caucasus but into the fighting-line of your Army in the South'. At that time the proposal (not disclosed in detail to the Russians) had been to send two divisions, the 18th and the 50th, and either eight or ten R.A.F. squadrons. But since then much had changed. Timoshenko's counter-offensive north of Rostov had removed the immediate German threat to the Caucasus; and other Russian successes, on the

---

[1] Churchill, Vol. III, p. 553.
[2] See pp. 217-18 above.

Leningrad front and before Moscow, had confirmed the belief that the Red Army was no longer in such desperate straits. Meanwhile, Auchinleck had launched 'Crusader', which was proving a longer and more costly operation than had been expected. By the first week of December one brigade of the 50th Division had already been drawn into the battle; and it was probable that the remainder, and perhaps part of the 18th Division, would be required, if Auchinleck were to complete his victory and follow it by an advance on Tripoli.

When the Caucasus was discussed again, immediately before Eden left for Moscow, it was clear that the plan in its original form was dead. In view of the Prime Minister's telegram and the general state of our relations with Russia, it could not simply be withdrawn; but it was not easy to find an acceptable substitute. After prolonged debate in the Cabinet and the Defence Committee it was finally agreed, on the Prime Minister's proposal, to offer the R.A.F. contingent alone. Mr. Eden was authorized to say that, although no land-forces could be spared, we would transfer ten Air Force squadrons to the south Russian front as soon as current operations in Libya were over, provided that Turkey (to whom we had a prior obligation)[1] had not been attacked meanwhile. But even this limited and conditional promise could not withstand the impact of later events. On 10th December, while he was on his way to Moscow, the Foreign Secretary received the following telegram from Mr. Churchill:

'Since you left much has happened. United States have sustained a major disaster at Hawaii and have now only two battleships effective in Pacific against ten Japanese. They are recalling all their battleships from Atlantic and have laid embargo on all exports of munitions for the time being. This is for your information alone. Secondly, we are going to be heavily attacked in Malaya and throughout the Far East by Japanese forces enjoying command of the sea. Thirdly, Italy and Germany about to declare war on United States. German Navy has already been ordered to attack American ships and a tripartite declaration of implacable war against British Empire and United States is expected either 10th or 11th. Fourthly, magnificent Russian success Leningrad, on whole Moscow front, at Kursk and in south; German armies largely on defensive or in retreat, complaining of terrible winter conditions and ever-strengthening Russian counter-attacks. Fifthly, Auchinleck reports tide turned in Libya but much heavy fighting lies ahead on this our second front. Sixthly, urgent necessity to reinforce Malaya with aircraft from Middle East. In view of the above you should not, repeat not, offer ten squadrons at present time. Everything is in flux about United States supplies and I cannot tell where we are till I get there.'

---

[1] See page 184 above.

Armed with these instructions, which did not permit a very optimistic view to be taken of their mission, Mr. Eden and his party arrived in Moscow on 15th December. At first everything was smooth and cordial. M. Stalin gave a cheerful account of the situation on the Eastern Front. He said that the Red Army now had the Germans at a decided disadvantage, especially in the matter of winter equipment, and hoped to maintain the impetus of their counter-offensive throughout the winter. It was true that the Germans were reorganizing; but he did not expect their new formations to come forward for another two months, and was determined to exploit this interval to the full. Mr. Eden replied with an account of our operations in Libya. It was then time to speak of the Caucasus. Eden explained the difficulties, much aggravated by the Japanese attack, which would prevent us from sending either land or air forces, as we had hoped to do. Stalin took the news calmly, saying only that he fully understood; Russia had also had her difficult times. But it presently became clear that he had not, in fact, abandoned his hope of bringing British forces into action on the Eastern Front. During later conversations between General Nye,[1] who had accompanied Mr. Eden as his military adviser, and the Russian General Staff a new plan was advanced for a joint operation in the Far North in January or February. It was to take the form of a sea-borne assault on Petsamo, to be followed, if successful, by a further attack on Kirkenes. The force required was estimated at three divisions, 130 fighters and 70 bombers with appropriate naval support. The Russians undertook to supply the troops (with the exception of a small Norwegian contingent), half the aircraft and a proportion of the merchant shipping, leaving us to supply the balance, including the whole of the naval escort.

This was by no means an unattractive proposition. The forces required were those which we could most easily supply, and the area of operation one which we had previously suggested ourselves. It was also true that the capture of Petsamo and Kirkenes would be of direct value to us as well as to the Russians, since these were two of the principal bases from which the Germans operated against our northern convoys. But the reader will remember that an almost identical project had already been examined and rejected, partly because of the difficulty of providing sufficient air-cover, and partly (in the case of Petsamo) because we did not believe that a sea-borne assault would be successful, unless it were supported by an overland advance from Murmansk. This addition to the plan was, however, expressly rejected by the Russians on the ground that the terrain was too difficult. Nevertheless, it was not for us to turn the project down out of hand:

---

[1] Then V.C.I.G.S.

'It was finally agreed that the British Military Mission in Moscow, in collaboration with the representatives of the Soviet Staff, should produce an outline of the plan as soon as possible. The plan to be in sufficient detail only to enable the Chiefs of Staff to come to a decision as to whether we could, or could not, take part in the suggested operation. The plan would be telegraphed to London, and, if approved, detailed planning would start as soon as possible. The importance of this proposed operation has increased as conversations have continued and the Russian delegation have clearly wished us to give our definite agreement to their proposals before we leave Moscow. They tend to look upon this proposal as something really tangible and said they would regard our acceptance as tantamount to fulfilment of the Military Agreement. You will see [from an earlier telegram] that it is proposed that conversations should be resumed in the spring on the question of possible assistance in the Far East. For these reasons it is politically most desirable that we should agree to this operation unless, indeed, military objections are overwhelming. The Foreign Secretary hopes that no adverse decision will be sent to the Russians before his return to London.'

The final subject of military discussion was Japan. On the principal question involved—whether Russia was willing to join with her allies in declaring war—Stalin took a firm and reasonable stand. He said that he had been obliged to withdraw forces from the Far East in order to support the front in the West. He did not expect to be able to replace them in less than four months and during that time had no intention of declaring war on Japan or provoking her in any way. But when his Far Eastern forces were once more up to strength, as he hoped that they would be by the spring, he would be willing to discuss the subject again. By that time, perhaps, Japan would have taken the decision out of his hands, either by declaring war herself or by making some obviously hostile move. He was inclined to hope that this would happen, as it would otherwise be difficult to secure popular support for a war in the East, which would inevitably seem remote to the Russian people. Eden made no comment on this, except to throw out a hint that the way in which Russia could help us most would be by making part of her submarine fleet available. But this was brushed jovially aside. Submarines, said Stalin, were not difficult to build; the productive capacity of Great Britain and the United States would settle the problem in six months.

Meanwhile, the diplomatic conversations proper had also been going forward; at first with some success. At the opening meeting on 14th December the Russians had tabled the drafts of two treaties, one dealing with mutual military aid, the other with diplomatic collaboration during and after the war. The terms of the latter did not go far beyond what Mr. Eden could accept and even had some points in common with a Cabinet paper, which he had drafted before leaving London. Much work evidently remained to be done; but the task of reconciling our views with the Russians did not seem impossible. At this point, however, the expected difficulties began to declare themselves:

> 'M. Stalin then suggested we should also sign a secret protocol which would embody our joint views for a settlement of post-war frontiers. He outlined in detail his conception of such a settlement for Europe as a whole which was drastic and severe upon Germany. I told him that while there was much in his proposal with which I personally agreed, it was impossible for me to enter into a secret agreement. For this there was several reasons. Moreover, I was pledged to the United States Government not to do so. Our own discussions of a peace settlement had not advanced to this point and I should have to consult my colleagues on his detailed proposals. I said that I would take back a full account to London, where his proposals would be studied, and we could then take the matter up through diplomatic channels. M. Stalin agreed to this and also to my communicating his proposals to the United States Government. He would be glad if the United States Government would join in agreeing to his proposals, but if not, he hoped that our two Governments could agree on our essential war-aims. He emphasized that his desire was to establish that our war-aims were identical, as then our alliance would be stronger. If our war-aims were different, then there was no true alliance.'

Further discussion made it clear that what Stalin wanted was an immediate agreement on Russia's post-war frontiers, with particular reference to her claims on Finland, Rumania and the Baltic States. Most of his other proposals, including those relating to the treatment of Germany and the future frontiers of Poland, he was willing to leave open for future discussion; but on this point he was adamant. Rather than abandon, or even defer, Russia's claims, he would prefer to sign no agreement at all. When Eden protested that he had not come to discuss precise and detailed questions of this kind, but only to negotiate an agreement in general terms, Stalin proposed an alternative formula, by which the two countries should bind themselves to 'work for the reconstruction of Europe after the war with full regard to the interests of the U.S.S.R. in the restitution of its frontiers violated by the Hitlerite aggression'. But this amounted to precisely the same thing, since Russia had been in possession of all the disputed territories at the time of the German attack.

The Foreign Secretary had no choice but to refuse, even though that should mean leaving Moscow without the agreement which he had come to sign. At first it seemed that the result would, in fact, be an open breach; but in the end, after two days' further negotiation, he was able to secure a compromise. Without otherwise modifying his attitude, Stalin agreed to postpone discussion on the Anglo-Soviet Treaty until the spring; M. Molotov would then pay a return visit to London and the whole question would be reopened. Meanwhile, a broadly worded communiqué would be issued on the current talks, which would serve the purpose, at least in the public eye, of an interim agreement. A suitable text was drafted, of which the operative paragraphs ran as follows:

'The conversations, which took place in a friendly atmosphere, showed identity of views of both parties on all questions relating to the conduct of the War and especially with the regard to the necessity for the utter defeat of Hitlerite Germany and the adoption thereafter of measures to render completely impossible any repetition of German aggression in future. Exchange of views on the questions relating to post-war organization of peace and security provided much important and useful material which will facilitate a future elaboration of concrete proposals on this subject.

Both parties are convinced that the Moscow Conversations constitute a new important forward step towards closer collaboration with the U.S.S.R. and Great Britain.'

(iii)

Churchill's Plan

We must now return to the strategic discussions on board the *Duke of York*. The first papers to be considered are three written by Mr. Churchill in the form of minutes addressed to the Chiefs of Staff. They have already appeared, almost verbatim, in his Memoirs, but are of sufficient importance to be reprinted here in full:

THE ATLANTIC FRONT

1. Hitler's failure and losses in Russia are the prime facts in the war at this time. We cannot tell how great the disaster to the German Army and Nazi régime will be. This régime has hitherto lived upon easily and cheaply won successes. Instead of what was imagined to be a swift and easy victory, it has now to face the shock of a winter of slaughter and expenditure of fuel and equipment on the largest scale.

Neither Great Britain nor the United States have any part to play in this event, except to make sure that we send, without fail and punctually, the supplies we have promised. In this way alone shall we hold our influence over Stalin and be able to weave the mighty Russian effort into the general texture of the war.

2. In a lesser degree the impending victory of General Auchinleck in Cyrenaica is an injury to the German power. We may expect the total destruction of the enemy force in Libya to be apparent before the end of the year. This not only inflicts a heavy blow on the Germans and Italians, but it frees our force in the Nile Valley from the major threat of invasion from the west under which they have long dwelt. Naturally, General Auchinleck will press on as fast as possible with the operation called 'Acrobat', which should give him possession of Tripoli, and so bring his armoured vanguard to the French frontier at Tunis. He may be able to supply a forecast before we separate at Washington.

3. The German losses and defeat in Russia and their extirpation from Libya may of course impel them to a supreme effort in the spring to break the ring that is closing on them by a south-eastward thrust either to the Caucasus or to Anatolia, or both. However, we should not assume that necessarily they will have the war energy for this task. The Russian Armies, recuperated by the winter, will lie heavy upon them from Leningrad to the Crimea. They may easily be forced to evacuate the Crimea. There is no reason at this time to suppose that the Russian Navy will not command the Black Sea. Nor should it be assumed that the present life-strength of Germany is such as to make an attack upon Turkey and a march through Anatolia a business to be undertaken in present circumstances by the Nazi régime. The Turks have 50 divisions; their fighting quality and the physical obstacles of their country are well known. Although Turkey has played for safety throughout, the Russian command of the Black Sea and British successes in the Levant and along the North African shore, together with the proved weakness of the Italian Fleet, would justify every effort on our part to bring Turkey into line, and are certainly sufficient to encourage her to resist a German inroad. While it would be imprudent to regard the danger of a German south-west thrust against the Persia-Iraq-Syrian front as removed, it certainly seems much less likely than heretofore.

4. We ought therefore to try hard to win over French North Africa, and now is the moment to use every inducement and form of pressure at our disposal upon the Government of Vichy and French authorities in North Africa. The German setback in Russia, the British successes in Libya, the moral and military collapse of Italy, above all the declarations of war exchanged between Germany and the United States, must strongly affect the mind of France and the French Empire. Now is the time to offer to Vichy and to French North Africa a blessing or a cursing. A blessing will consist in a promise by the United States and Great Britain to re-establish France as a Great Power with her territories undiminished. It should carry with it an offer of active aid

by British and United States expeditionary forces, both from the Atlantic seaboard of Morocco and at convenient landing-points in Algeria and Tunis, as well as from General Auchinleck's forces advancing from the east. Ample supplies for the French and the loyal Moors should be made available. Vichy should be asked to send their fleet from Toulon to Oran and Bizerta and to bring France into the war again as a principal.

This would mean that Germany would take over the whole of France and rule it as occupied territory. It does not seem that the conditions in the occupied and the hitherto unoccupied zones are widely different. Whatever happens, European France will inevitably be subjected to a complete blockade. There is of course always the chance that the Germans, tied up in Russia, may not care to take over unoccupied France, even though French North Africa is at war with them.

5. If we can obtain even the connivance of Vichy to French North Africa coming over to our side we must be ready to send considerable forces as soon as possible. Apart from anything which General Auchinleck can bring in from the east should he be successful in Tripolitania, we hold ready in Britain (Operation 'Gymnast') about 55,000 men, comprising two divisions and an armoured unit, together with the shipping. These forces could enter French North Africa by invitation on the twenty-third day after the order to embark them was given. Leading elements and air forces from Malta could reach Bizerta at very short notice. It is desired that the United States should at the same time promise to bring in, via Casablanca and other African Atlantic ports, not less than 150,000 men during the next six months. It is essential that some American elements, say 25,000 men, should go at the earliest moment after French agreement, either Vichy or North African, had been obtained.

6. It is also asked that the United States will send the equivalent of three divisions and one armoured division into Northern Ireland. These divisions could, if necessary, complete their training in Northern Ireland. The presence of American forces there would become known to the enemy, and they could be led to magnify their actual members. The presence of United States troops in the British Isles would be a powerful additional deterrent against an attempt at invasion by Germany. It would enable us to nourish the campaign in North Africa by two more divisions and one complete armoured division. If forces of this order could be added to the French Army already in North Africa, with proper air-support, the Germans would have to make a very difficult and costly campaign across uncommanded waters to subdue North Africa. The North-West African theatre is one most favourable for Anglo-American operations, our approaches being direct and convenient across the Atlantic, while the enemy's passage of the Mediterranean would be severely obstructed, as is happening in the Libyan enterprise.

7. It may be mentioned here that we greatly desire American bomber squadrons to come into action from the British Isles against Germany. Our own bomber programme has fallen short of our hopes. It is formidable and is increasing, but its full development has been delayed. It must be remembered that we place great hopes of affecting German production and German morale by ever more severe and more accurate bombing of their cities and harbours, and that this, combined with their Russian defeats, may produce important effects on the will to fight of the German people, with consequential internal reactions upon the German government. The arrival in the United Kingdom of, say, twenty American bomber squadrons would emphasize and accelerate this process, and would be the most direct and effective reply to the declaration of war by Germany upon the United States. Arrangements will be made in Great Britain to increase this process and develop the Anglo-American bombing of Germany without any top limit from now on until the end of the war.

8. We must however reckon with a refusal by Vichy to act as we desire, and on the contrary they may rouse French North Africa to active resistance. They may help German troops to enter North Africa; the Germans may force their way or be granted passage through Spain; the French fleet at Toulon may pass under German control, and France and the French Empire may be made by Vichy to collaborate actively with Germany against us, although it is not likely that this would go through effectively. The overwhelming majority of the French are ranged with Great Britain, and now still more with the United States. It is by no means certain that Admiral Darlan can deliver the Toulon fleet over intact to Germany. It is most improbable that French soldiers and sailors would fight effectively against the United States and Great Britain. Nevertheless, we must not exclude the possibility of a half-hearted association of the defeatist elements in France and North Africa with Germany. In this case our task in North Africa will become much harder.

A campaign must be fought in 1942 to gain possession of, or conquer, the whole of the North African shore, including the Atlantic ports of Morocco. Dakar and other French West African ports must be captured before the end of the year. Whereas however entry into French North Africa is urgent to prevent German penetration, a period of eight or nine months' preparation may well be afforded for the mastering of Dakar and the West African establishments. Plans should be set on foot forthwith. If sufficient time and preparations are allowed and the proper apparatus provided, these latter operations present no insuperable difficulty.

9. Our relations with General de Gaulle and the Free French movement will require to be reviewed. Hitherto the United States have entered into no undertakings similar to those comprised in my correspondence with him. Through no particular fault of his own his movement has created new antagonisms in French minds.

Any action which the United States may now feel able to take in regard to him should have the effect, *inter alia*, of redefining our obligations to him and France so as to make these obligations more closely dependent upon the eventual effort by him and the French nation to rehabilitate themselves. If Vichy were to act as we desire about French North Africa, the United States and Great Britain must labour to bring about a reconciliation between the Free French (de Gaullists) and those other Frenchmen who will have taken up arms once more against Germany. If, on the other hand, Vichy persists in collaboration with Germany and we have to fight our way into French North and West Africa, then the de Gaullists' movement must be aided and used to the full.

10. We cannot tell what will happen in Spain. It seems probable that the Spaniards will not give the Germans a free passage through Spain to attack Gibraltar and invade North Africa. There may be infiltration, but the formal demand for the passage of any army would be resisted. If so the winter would be the worst time for the Germans to attempt to force their way through Spain. Moreover, Hitler, with nearly all Europe to hold down by armed force in the face of defeat and semi-starvation, may well be chary of taking over unoccupied France and involving himself in bitter guerrilla warfare with the morose, fierce, hungry people of the Iberian peninsula. Everything possible must be done by Britain and the United States to strengthen their will to resist. The present policy of limited supplies should be pursued.

The value of Gibraltar harbour and base to us is so great that no attempts should be made upon the Atlantic islands until either the peninsula is invaded or the Spaniards give passage to the Germans.

11. To sum up, the war in the West in 1942 comprises, as its main offensive effort, the occupation and control by Great Britain and the United States of the whole of the North and West African possessions of France, and the further control by Britain of the whole North African shore from Tunis to Egypt, thus giving, if the naval situation allows, free passage through the Mediterranean to the Levant and the Suez Canal. These great objectives can only be achieved if British and American naval and air superiority in the Atlantic is maintained, if supply-lines continue uninterrupted, and if the British Isles are effectively safeguarded against invasion.

NOTES ON THE PACIFIC

1. The Japanese have naval superiority, which enables them to transport troops to almost any desired point, possess themselves of it and establish it for an air-naval fuelling base. The Allies will not have for some time the power to fight a general fleet engagement. Their power of convoying troops depends upon the size of the seas, which reduces the chance of interception. We can arrive

by surprise from out of the wide seas at some place which we hold. Even without superior sea-power we may descend by surprise here and there. But we could not carry on a sustained operation across the seas. We must expect, therefore, to be deprived one by one of our possessions and strong points in the Pacific, and that the enemy will establish himself fairly easily in one after the other, mopping up the local garrisons.

2. In this interim period our duty is one of stubborn resistance at each point attacked, and to slip supplies and reinforcements through as opportunity offers, taking all necessary risks. If our forces resist stubbornly and we reinforce them as much as possible, the enemy will be forced to make ever larger overseas commitments far from home; his shipping resources will be strained and his communications will provide vulnerable targets upon which all available naval and air forces, United States, British and Dutch—especially submarines—should concentrate their effort. It is of the utmost importance that the enemy should not acquire large gains cheaply; that he should be compelled to nourish all his conquests and kept extended, and kept burning up his resources.

3. The resources of Japan are a wasting factor. The country has been long overstrained by its wasteful war in China. They were at maximum strength on the day of the Pearl Harbor attack. If it is true, as Stalin asserts, that they have, in addition to their own Air Force, 1,500 German aeroplanes (and he would have opportunities of knowing how they got there), they have now no means of replacing wastage other than by their small home production of 300/500 per month. Our policy should be to make them maintain the largest possible number of troops in their conquests overseas and to keep them as busy as possible so as to enforce well-filled lines of communications and a high rate of aircraft consumption. If we idle and leave them at ease they will be able to extend their conquests cheaply and easily, work with a minimum of overseas forces, make the largest gains and the smallest commitments, and thus inflict upon us an enormous amount of damage. It is therefore right and necessary to fight them at every point where we have a fair chance, so as to keep them burning and extended.

4. But we must steadily aim at regaining superiority at sea at the earliest moment. This can be gained in two ways; first, by the strengthening of our capital ships. The two new Japanese battleships built free from Treaty limitations must be considered a formidable factor, influencing the whole Pacific theatre. It is understood that two new American battleships will be fit for action by May. Of course, all undertakings in war must be subject to the action of the enemy, accidents and misfortune, but if our battleship strength should not be further reduced, nor any new unforeseen stress arise, we should hope to place the *Nelson* and the *Rodney* at the side of these two new American battleships, making four 16-inch gun modern vessels of major strength. Behind such a squadron the older reconstructed battleships of the United States

should be available in numbers sufficient to enable a fleet action, under favourable circumstances, to be contemplated at any time after the month of May. The recovery of our naval superiority in the Pacific, even if not brought to a trial of strength, would re-assure the whole western seaboard of the American continent and thus prevent a needless dissipation on a gigantic defensive effort of forces which have offensive parts to play. We must there-fore set before ourselves, as a main strategic object, the forming of a definitely superior battle fleet in the Pacific and we must aim at May as the date when this will be achieved.

5. Not only then, but in the interval, the warfare of aircraft carriers should be developed to the greatest possible extent. We are ourselves forming a squadron of three aircraft-carriers, suitably attended, to act in the waters between South Africa, India and Australia. The United States have already seven regular carriers compared to Japan's ten, but those of the United States are larger. To this force of regular warship carriers we must add a very large development of improvized carriers, both large and small. In this way alone can we increase our sea-power rapidly. Even if the car-riers can only fly a dozen machines, they may play their part in combination with other carriers. We ought to develop a floating air establishment sufficient to enable us to acquire and maintain for considerable periods local air superiority over shore-based aircraft and sufficient to cover the landing of troops in order to attack the enemy's new conquests. Unless or until this local air superiority is definitely acquired even a somewhat superior fleet on our side would fight at a serious disadvantage. We cannot get more battleships than those now in sight for the year 1942, but we can and must get more aircraft-carriers. It takes five years to build a battleship, but it is possible to improvise a carrier in six months. Here then is a field for invention and ingenuity similar to that which called forth the extraordinary fleets and flotillas which fought on the Mississipi in the Civil War. It must be accepted that the priority given to sea-borne aircraft of a suitable type will involve a retardation in the full-scale bombing offensive against Germany which we have contemplated as a major method of waging war. This, however, is a matter of time and of degree. We cannot in 1942 hope to reach the levels of bomb discharge in Ger-many which we had prescribed for that year, but we shall surpass them in 1943. Our joint programme may be late, but it will come along. And meanwhile the German cities and other targets will not disappear. While every effort must be made to speed up the rate of bomb discharges upon Germany until the great scales pre-scribed for 1943 and 1944 are reached, nevertheless we may be forced by other needs to face a retardation in our schedules. The more important will it be therefore that in this interval a force, be it only symbolic, of United States bombing squadrons should operate from the British Isles against the German cities and sea-ports.

6. Once the Allies have regained battle-fleet superiority in the Pacific and have created a sea-borne air-power sufficient to secure local supremacy for certain periods, it will be possible either to attack the Japanese in their overseas conquests by military expeditions or to attack them in their homeland. It may well be the latter will be found the better. We must imagine the Japanese Air Force as being steadily and rapidly reduced and having no adequate power of replenishment. The approach to the shores of Japan near enough for our sea-borne air-power to ravage their cities should be freed from its present prohibitive cost and danger. Nothing will more rapidly relieve the Japanese attacks in the East Indian theatre. Under the protection of the superior battle fleet and the sea-borne air-power aforesaid, it should be possible to acquire or regain various island bases, enabling a definite approach to be made to the homeland of Japan. The burning of Japanese cities by incendiary bombs will bring home in a most effective way to the people of Japan the dangers of the course to which they have committed themselves, and nothing is more likely to cramp the reinforcing of their overseas adventures.

7. The establishment of air bases in China or Russia from which attacks can be made upon the Japanese cities is in everyone's mind. It is most desirable that Russia should enter the war against Japan, thus enabling her own and Allied aircraft to bomb all the main cities in Japan from a convenient distance. This would also make available a force of about seventy Russian submarines to harass the Japanese lines of communication with their overseas commitments, especially at the point of departure from Japan. However, this is not a point upon which we can press the Russians unduly at the present time. They have withstood and are withstanding the giant assault of the German Army. They have achieved undreamed of success. If their resistance to the German Armies were to break down, or even if their pressure upon them were relaxed, all the problems of the Caucasus, Syria, Palestine and Persia would resume the menacing shape they have only lately lost, entailing immense diversions of force upon Great Britain, and offering no satisfactory assurance of success. The influence of the German losses and defeats against Russia upon the German people must be very depressing, and if this is prolonged it may provoke stresses within the German régime of the utmost hopeful consequence. M. Stalin has indicated that perhaps in the spring he may be able to act against Japan. If he does not feel able or willing to do so now, it would be a mistake to press him unduly. Russia has more than rowed her weight in the boat, and she alone must judge when to take on more burdens. The question of whether air bases in Russia could be acquired without entailing war between Japan and Russia is worth while studying. It would certainly not be in Japan's interest, any more than that of Russia, to open up this new front of war. It might mean that an attitude of non-belligerency might be adopted by Russia at a period before

she would be willing to come into the war. Such an attitude of non-belligerency might permit aircraft, based on China, to refuel in Siberia before and after bombing Japan.

8. The danger of the Japanese using their numerous cruisers to raid all shipping between Australia and the Middle East, and even to assail our convoys round the Cape, will require to be met by the provision of battleship escort. We propose to use the four 'R' Class battleships for this purpose if we need to. It is to be hoped that United States will also be ready to help in convoying work against cruiser attacks in the Pacific.

9. Lastly, there is the question of whether we should ask the United States to base her battle fleet on Singapore, or perhaps make such a movement conditional on our adding our two battleships from the Atlantic. I am in much doubt about this. When we see what happened to the *Prince of Wales* and the *Repulse* in these narrow waters, soon to be infested with aircraft based at many points, we cannot feel that they would offer an inviting prospect to the United States. It would be represented as a purely British conception. One is not sure of the work they could do when they got there, and whether they would not suffer unduly heavy losses. It would redouble the anxieties and waste of force upon the defences of the Pacific seaboard of America. It would put out of the way all chances of a sea-borne offensive against the homelands of Japan. It is inconceivable that the United States' authorities would agree to it at any time which can at present be foreseen.

10. We cannot tell what will happen in the Philippines, and whether or for how long United States troops will be able to defend themselves. The defence or recapture of the Philippines cannot be judged upon theoretical principles. Wars of the present scale are largely wars of attrition and a wise choice of a particular battlefield is not necessarily the only criterion. The Philippines will undoubtedly appear to the United States as an American battleground which they are in honour bound to fight for. The Japanese will have to expend war-power and aircraft in this conflict, and even if it does not proceed in the best chosen theatre the process of exhaustion and wearing down of the weaker country by the stronger is of very great advantage and relief to us in the Pacific sphere.

11. For these reasons it would not be wise to press the Americans to move their main fleet to Singapore.

12. Nor need we fear that this war in the Pacific will, after the first shock is over, absorb an unduly large proportion of United States' forces. The numbers of troops that we should wish them to use in Europe in 1942 will not be so large as to be prevented by their Pacific operations, limited as these must be. What will harm us is for a vast United States Army of 10 millions to be created which, for at least two years while it was training, would absorb all the available supplies and stand idle defending the American continent. The best way of preventing the creation of such a

situation and obtaining the proper use of the large forces and
ample supplies of munitions which will presently be forthcoming,
is to enable the Americans to regain their naval power in the
Pacific and not to discourage them from the precise secondary
overseas operations which they may perhaps contemplate.

THE CAMPAIGN OF 1943

1. If the operations outlined in Parts I and II should prosper
during 1942 the situation in 1943 might be as follows:

    (a) The United States and Great Britain would have recovered
        effective naval superiority in the Pacific, and all Japanese
        overseas commitments would be endangered both from the
        assailing of their communications and from British and
        American expeditions sent to recover places lost.

    (b) The British Isles would remain intact and more strongly pre-
        pared against invasion than they were before.

    (c) The whole West and North African shores from Dakar to the
        Suez Canal and the Levant to the Turkish frontier would be
        in Anglo-American hands.

Turkey, though not necessarily at war, would be definitely incorporated in the American-British-Russian front. Russian positions would be strongly established, and the supplies of British
and American material as promised would have in part compen-
sated for the loss of Russian munition-making capacity. It might
be that a footing would already have been established in Sicily
and Italy, with reactions inside Italy which might be highly
favourable.

2. But all this would fall short of bringing the war to an end.
The war cannot be ended by driving Japan back to her own
bounds and defeating her overseas forces. The war can only be
ended through the defeat in Europe of the German armies, or
through internal convulsions in Germany produced by the unfavourable course of the war, economic privations, and the Allied
bombing offensive. As the strength of the United States, Great
Britain and Russia develops and begins to be realized by the
Germans an internal collapse is always possible, but we must not
count on this. Our plans must proceed upon the assumption that
the resistance of the German Army and Air Force will continue at
its present level and that their U-boat warfare will be conducted
by increasingly numerous flotillas.

3. We have therefore to prepare for the liberation of the cap-
tive countries of Western and Southern Europe by the landing at
suitable points, successively or simultaneously, of British and
American armies strong enough to enable the conquered popula-
tions to revolt. By themselves they will never be able to revolt,
owing to the ruthless counter-measures that will be employed,
but if adequate and suitably equipped forces were landed in
several of the following countries, namely, Norway, Denmark,

Holland, Belgium, the French Channel coasts and the French Atlantic coasts, as well as in Italy and possibly the Balkans, the German garrisons would prove insufficient to cope both with the strength of the liberating forces and the fury of the revolting peoples. It is impossible for the Germans, while we retain the sea-power necessary to choose the place or places of attack, to have sufficient troops in each of these countries for effective resistance. In particular they cannot move their armour about laterally from north to south or west to east; either they must divide it between the various conquered countries—in which case it will become hopelessly dispersed—or they must hold it back in a central position in Germany, in which case it will not arrive until large and important lodgements have been made by us from overseas.

4. We must face here the usual clash between short-term and long-term projects. War is a constant struggle and must be waged from day to day. It is only with some difficulty and within limits that provision can be made for the future. Experience shows that forecasts are usually falsified and preparations always in arrear. Nevertheless, there must be a design and theme for bringing the war to a victorious end in a reasonable period. All the more is this necessary when under modern conditions no large-scale offensive operation can be launched without the preparation of elaborate technical apparatus.

5. We should therefore face now the problems not only of driving Japan back to her homelands and regaining undisputed mastery in the Pacific, but also of liberating conquered Europe by the landing during the summer of 1943 of United States and British armies on their shores. Plans should be prepared for the landing in all of the countries mentioned above. The actual choice of which three or four to pick should be deferred as long as possible, so as to profit by the turn of events and make sure of secrecy.

6. In principle, the landings should be made by armoured and mechanised forces capable of disembarking not at ports but on beaches, either by landing-craft or from ocean-going ships specially adapted. The potential front of attack is thus made so wide that the German forces holding down these different countries cannot be strong enough at all points. An amphibious outfit must be prepared to enable these large-scale disembarkations to be made swiftly and surely. The vanguards of the various British and American expeditions should be marshalled by the spring of 1943 in Iceland, the British Isles and, if possible, in French Morocco and Egypt. The main body would come direct across the Ocean.

7. It need not be assumed that great numbers of men are required. If the incursion of the armoured formations is successful, the uprising of the local population, for whom weapons must be brought will supply the corpus of the liberating offensive. Forty armoured divisions at 15,000 men apiece or their equivalent in

23

tank brigades, of which Great Britain would try to produce nearly half, would amount to 600,000 men. Behind the armour another million men of all arms would suffice to wrest enormous territories from Hitler's domination. But these campaigns, once started, will require nourishing on a lavish scale. Our industries and training establishments should by the end of 1942 be running on a sufficient scale.

8. Apart from the command of the sea, without which nothing is possible, the essential of all these operations is superior air-power, and for landing purposes a large development of carrier-borne aircraft will be necessary. This however is needed anyhow for the war in 1942. In order to wear down the enemy and hamper his counter-preparations, the bombing offensive of Germany from England and of Italy from Malta, and if possible from Tripoli and Tunis, must reach the highest possible scale of intensity. Considering that the British first-line air strength is already slightly superior to that of Germany, that the Russian Air Force has already established a superiority on a large part of the Russian front and may be considered to be three-fifths the first-line strength of Germany, and that the United States resources and future development are additional, there is no reason why a decisive mastery of the air should not be established even before the summer of 1943, and meanwhile heavy and continuous punishment be inflicted upon Germany. Having regard to the fact that the bombing offensive is necessarily a matter of degree and that the targets cannot be moved away, it would be right to assign priority to the fighter and torpedo-carrying aircraft required for the numerous carriers and improvised carriers which are available or must be brought into existence.

9. If we set these tasks before us now, being careful that they do not trench too much upon current necessities, we might hope, even if no German collapse occurs beforehand, to win the war at the end of 1943 or 1944. There might be advantage in declaring now our intention of sending armies of liberation to Europe in 1943. This would give hope to the subjugated peoples and prevent any truck between them and the German invaders. The setting and keeping in movement along our courses of the minds of so many scores of millions of men is in itself a potent atmospheric influence.

These three papers, which form in effect a single document, deserve the most careful attention. As the reader will see at once, they contain the first sketch of the offensive strategy in Europe, which the Allies were to carry out with complete success during the course of the next three years. Here at last was a solution—or the outline of a solution—to the central problem set out in the previous chapters. How could the Allies, granted the limitations imposed on them by their shortage of manpower and shipping, hope to attack a superior German army entrenched in a central position in Europe? There was, indeed, little that was novel or spectacular in the plan proposed; it was a simple application of familiar principles of warfare. Where the Prime Minister's strength lay was in his ability to discern these principles clearly, and apply them correctly, on the vastly extended scale of modern operations. That was what General Ismay meant, when he said of Mr. Churchill that 'in his grasp of the broad sweep of strategy—"the overall strategic concept" as our American friends called it—he stood head and shoulders above his professional advisers'.[1]

Reduced to its simplest terms, Mr. Churchill's plan called for two consecutive operations: first, the clearing of the North African coast, which was to be the Allies' main offensive effort in 1942; secondly, the invasion of Europe from the West, which was timed for 1943 but did not actually take place until the following year. The essence of the plan was in the relationship between these two, widely separated operations. The first was intended to prepare the way for the second; the occupation of North Africa to create the conditions, which would make it possible to attack across the Channel. The simplest way to understand this is to trespass a little on the future by examining what were, in fact, the strategic consequences of the North African operation, the move which Admiral Raeder had long feared and against which he had warned Hitler.

The first result was to enable the Allies to effect an important concentration. At the time when Mr. Churchill wrote his papers, the main strength of the British Army was divided between two commands: Home Forces retained 36 divisions for the defence of the British Isles, while a Field Force of 25 divisions was building up in the Middle East. These two theatres were strategically independent and separated from each other (for practical purposes) by the long sea-route round the Cape, so that the limits within which one could be reinforced from the other were very narrow. Under these conditions a major attack on the mainland of Europe was impossible, since neither Home Forces nor the Middle East could be given the necessary offensive strength. We were rescued from this paralysis by the clearing of the North African coast, which brought our divided forces once more into strategic relation. It then became possible to reinforce one freely from the other, and to use the combined weight of both in operations against the Continent. By the same process we also received a welcome accession of strength in the form of 10 divisions, which the French National Committee was able to form in 1943 and early 1944, largely from North African cadres.

The second and more important result was to force a dispersal of effort on Germany. In the winter of 1941 the Mediterranean was a

---

[1] Memoirs of General Lord Ismay (1960), p. 163.

predominantly Italian theatre, where the German army's commitment did not amount to more than 10 divisions, of which the
majority were employed on garrison-duties in Greece and Yugoslavia. By the summer of 1943, with the Allies in control of the North
African coast, the position was very different. Germany had already
lost the force of between 10 and 11 divisions with which she had tried,
too late, to defend North Africa; and she now found that the whole
of southern Europe was exposed to attack. Before the end of the year
she was obliged to defend Italy against an Allied invasion and to
form a new front there, which presently absorbed 23 divisions. She
was also obliged to raise her garrisons in Greece and Yugoslavia,
where the Allies could now support extensive partisan-operations, to
the equivalent of some 20 divisions. We can say, therefore, that the
effect of the Allied operations of 1942 and 1943, which were carried
out by a Field Force of only 20–25 divisions, was to draw more than
40 additional German divisions to the Mediterranean, where nearly a
quarter of them were destroyed.

Meanwhile the threat from the West was increasing. During 1942
and 1943 Germany was not able to make any significant reduction in
the number of troops holding Norway, Denmark, the Low Countries
and France, since all these countries were exposed to Allied raids,
which might well have been supported by local risings in force.
Though there were frequent exchanges of troops, the total strength
of the garrison in the West remained constant at 40–45 divisions. By
the winter of 1943, when a major Allied operation was clearly imminent, substantial reinforcements were required. These could not
come from the Mediterranean, where Allied pressure was still at its
height, any more than it had previously been possible to feed the
Mediterranean from the West. In both cases, since no central
reserve existed, the additional troops could only be found at the
expense of the Eastern Front. The final position in June 1944, on the
eve of the Normandy landings, was as follows. In the West there were
now 77 divisions, of which 59 were in France and the Low Countries
and 18 distributed between Norway and Denmark. In the Mediterranean, excluding the south of France, there were approximately 50
divisions, more or less evenly divided between Italy on the one hand
and Greece and Yugoslavia on the other.

Thus, even before the Allies' culminating operation was launched,
three important results had been obtained:

(1) Germany had been forced to increase the number of troops
facing the Western Allies, or tied down as the result of their operations, from some 55 divisions in 1941 to 127 divisions in 1944.
This was a high service to the Red Army, on whose front the
weight of these additional divisions would otherwise have rested.

(2) What may be called Germany's Western Force had been

divided between two theatres, Western Europe and the Mediterranean, in such a way that no decisive resistance could be offered to the Allies on either front.

(3) Both in Western Europe and in the Mediterranean the Allies were able to exert a dispersed threat, extending over several countries, so that their main thrust—in Northern France in one case, in Italy in the other—could only be met by a proportion of the German troops in the theatre.

If the reader will turn back to Mr. Churchill's papers in the light of these facts, he will see how justly they estimated the various elements in this developing situation, even though the plan proposed was only in the form of a sketch, which would undergo many modifications before it was finally put into action. He may also reflect that the strategic situation would have been very different, if no prior operations had taken place in the Mediterranean, so that the Allies had possessed only one base, the British Isles, from which to launch their attack on Europe. In that case the Germans would have had little difficulty in assembling, if necessary, a force of 80 or 90 divisions in Western Europe in 1943 and up to 100 or 120 divisions in 1944. Since the weight of the Allied attack across the Channel was limited in the first phase, as later Volumes will show, less by considerations of manpower than by problems of transport and supply, this increase in enemy strength might well have been decisive. It would certainly have been enough to ensure that the operation, whenever it took place, did not obtain the rapid and spectacular results which were in fact achieved in 1944.

(v)

Review by the Chiefs of Staff

The Chiefs of Staff[1] also spent a great part of the outward voyage in discussing strategy both by themselves and with the Prime Minister. Their immediate object was to produce a paper on what they called 'the fundamental bases of joint strategy', which could be presented to their American colleagues at the beginning of the Conference, and which would provide a starting-point for subsequent discussions on troop-dispositions, supply-programmes, etc. With this in mind they

---

[1] In this and the two following chapters it will be convenient to speak of those who went to Washington—the C.N.S., the C.A.S. and Sir John Dill—as the 'Chiefs of Staff', and those who remained in London—the new C.I.G.S., the V.C.N.S. and the V.C.A.S.—as the 'C.O.S. Committee'.

had instructed the Directors of Plans to produce a short survey of the current military position. This document, which gave the Chiefs of Staff the material for their own discussions, provides an interesting contrast with Mr. Churchill's three papers. Whereas the Prime Minister's object was to draw the bold outlines of an offensive strategy for the next two years, the Planners were primarily concerned with the immediate defensive needs of the various theatres of war in the light of actual and prospective enemy moves. In effect, therefore, though not by intention, their paper was a reasoned catalogue of the difficulties, as they appeared in December 1941, of carrying out such a policy as Mr. Churchill described.

The Planners began by remarking that a German attempt to invade the British Isles in the spring, though apparently a desperate undertaking, could not be entirely ruled out. We should have to provide at least 'that minimum of protection which is necessary against large-scale destructive raids, particularly by airborne forces, as well as to ensure the best possible immunity for our shipping and industries both by day and by night'. It would thus be unwise, if not impossible, to divert any large land or air forces from Great Britain to other theatres. The same applied even more strongly to naval forces. Our naval commitments had recently been much increased, partly by the extension of the war to the Far East, and partly by the need to protect our sea-communications with Russia. At the same time the United States had been obliged to withdraw their ships from the Atlantic, where, despite our continued air-attack, the threat of a break-out by the German battle-cruisers from Brest still remained. 'Should these ships again become operative, or should Germany gain control of the heavy units of the French Fleet, we may well not be able to build up an Eastern Fleet of sufficient strength to support the Malay Barrier or to relieve Singapore.' Nor were the German battle-cruisers the only danger in the Atlantic. It was true that in recent months our losses from U-boats had declined; but the evidence was that this was due rather to the success of our evasive routeing than to any actual improvement in the defence. Meanwhile, both the numbers of German submarines at sea and the range of their activities were constantly increasing.

It was also necessary to take account of three possible moves by the Axis, any one of which would seriously affect our position at sea. The first was a German move into Spain, with or without the connivance of the Spanish Government, which would almost certainly result in Gibraltar's becoming untenable. Plans for the occupation of the Canary Islands in such an eventuality had already been made and a skeleton force was standing by at Freetown. But under present conditions it would not be easy to mount the operation at short notice or to find the full naval escort required, which would have to include two aircraft-carriers. We had also held staff-conversations with the Portuguese about the transfer of their Government to the Azores in the event of a German invasion, and the subsequent defence of the islands. The results had been satisfactory so far as they went; but apart from any such contingent arrangement, we had an immediate need, which was becoming daily more pressing, to use the Azores as a refuelling base for our Atlantic escorts. No agreement had yet been reached on this point. The second danger was that Germany, by arrangement with the Vichy Government, would establish submarine bases at the two West African ports of Casablanca and Dakar. If so, our sea-communications in the South Atlantic would be seriously menaced. We should be obliged to institute trade convoys, though this could only be done by withdrawing escorts from the already too lightly protected routes in the North Atlantic. There would also be a direct threat to Freetown, which was both an important source of iron-ore and the terminal of the air reinforcement route across Africa.

The third danger was in the Indian Ocean. On any footing we should now have to expect a certain threat from Japanese submarines and raiders to develop in this area. In view of the shortage of escorts we could offer little protection to our trade beyond evasive routeing and, perhaps, a slender anti-submarine escort for the more important convoys. This situation might become very serious, if, as unconfirmed reports had recently suggested, the Vichy Government were to give either Germany or Japan facilities to base U-boats in Madagascar. Plans to forestall such a move by seizing the naval base at Diego Suarez were under consideration; and it might be necessary to carry out this operation in order to cover our sea communications with Suez, the Persian Gulf and India.

The paper then turned to the Middle East, its observations opening with a cautious and even lukewarm reference to 'Crusader'. It was noted that current operations in Libya 'should greatly improve the position on our Western flank. At best it might be possible with America's aid to bring over all French North Africa to our side and to go a long way towards eliminating the active partnership of Italy. At the worst we should compel the enemy to further extension in occupying French North Africa and perhaps the Iberian peninsula as well.' In view of the earlier references to Gibraltar, Casablanca and Dakar and the grave consequences which would follow from their falling under enemy control, the last of these sentences may appear rather coolly worded. But the fact was that, in the eyes of the Planners, the Western flank in the Middle East was of less immediate importance than the Northern. They admitted that recent Russian successes in the Rostov area and elsewhere had given us a short respite in the north; but they were convinced that German plans for an attack—a far more serious attack than could ever be mounted from the West—had not been abandoned:

'Ample evidence is . . . accumulating that the Germans intend to bring heavy pressure to bear in the South-East, possibly even before the Spring. We must therefore prepare for a renewed enemy assault on the Caucasus, combined with heavy pressure on Turkey, who looks to us for assistance, particularly in air and mechanized forces. Our own forces at their present strength would not suffice to meet the full scale of this threat.

With the Japanese in control of the Netherlands East Indies oil and able to threaten the Indian Ocean, the retention of the Middle East has become of even greater moment than before. It covers the essential oil supplies of Iraq and Persia and denies German access to bases in the Indian Ocean. Its loss would cause the immediate collapse of Turkey and thus open the German road to the Caucasus; Russia's southern supply line through Persia would be closed.'

There remained the Far East. In that theatre, at present wholly dominated by the enemy, it was not possible to take more than limited and short-term views. The Planners summed up their opinions as follows:

'. . . In the present situation, our joint object during the next six months should be:
    To limit the advantages that Japan has gained by her recent successes and, in particular, to retain such points in the Far East as will prevent Japan from damaging the interests vital to the war effort of the Associated Powers, and as will enable them, at a later stage, to take the offensive and defeat Japan.
To achieve this object we must jointly hold:
In the Pacific: The American naval bases at Hawaii and Dutch Harbour.
In the East Indies: Singapore, Sumatra, Java and the chain of islands joining Java with Australia.
In the Indian Ocean: Rangoon and Ceylon.'

In order to do this, or our part of it, the first requirement was that we should build up a Far Eastern Fleet of sufficient strength to dispute with Japan the control of the South China Sea. But it was doubtful whether we could do this without withdrawing capital ships from the Mediterranean—a transfer which might have very serious consequences. While it was true that the blockade would not be directly impaired, 'the political effect on Turkey and Egypt will be incalculable. Such a withdrawal will also necessitate a strengthening of shore-based Air Forces in Cyrenaica and will curtail future offensive operations against Italy.' Either theatre, in short, depended on the other. We could only reinforce the Far East at the expense of the Middle East, and both theatres were already in danger.

This sombre list of defensive commitments, actual or prospective, in the British Isles, the Middle East and the Far East, and at sea in the Atlantic, the Indian Ocean and the South China Seas, did not leave much margin for offensive operations, apart from those, such as the occupation of the Canary Islands or Madagascar, which were directly dependent on expected moves by the enemy. It is therefore scarcely surprising that the next section of the paper, under the heading 'Strategic Policy in the European Theatre', should have re-affirmed the old wait-and-see strategy of bombing, blockade and subversion. 'But,' added the Planners, 'to these three softening processes we wish now to add a fourth, namely, to wear down the German war machine by (d) giving all possible support to Russia'. They pointed out that one of the most significant changes in the general situation since the time of the Atlantic Meeting was to be found in Germany's failure to defeat the Red Army. It opened immense possibilities for the future. 'If the Russian armies can be sustained, the Allies possess for the first time a front on land from which to make a direct assault on the frontiers of Germany at the first sign of enemy disintegration. For these reasons we regard the continuation of Russian resistance as of primary importance to the Associated Powers in their strategy for the defeat of Germany'.

Having thus defined the basis of their strategy, the Directors of Plans sketched its future application in the following paragraph:

'We hope that the offensive against Germany will take the form of large-scale land operations on the Russian front, large-scale bombing operations supplemented by amphibious raids of increasing weight from the United Kingdom and a gradual tightening of the ring around Axis-controlled Europe by the occupation of strategic positions in the Atlantic Islands, North and West Africa, Tripoli and Turkey. Every opportunity will be taken to try and knock out Italy as an active partner in the war. These operations will be followed in the final phase by simultaneous land operations against Germany herself from the West by the British, from the South by the United States and from the East by the Russians.'

It will be noticed that the effect of the last sentence was to confine future American intervention in Europe to the Mediterranean theatre. This may seem surprising in the light of after-events, though it was consistent with the attempts which had already been made to interest the Americans in North Africa,[1] where their influence with the French authorities was supposed to stand higher than ours. But the real basis of the Planners' proposal was logistic, as appeared clearly from a later paragraph:

---

[1] e.g. at the Atlantic Meeting.

'Our study of the problem of the final assault on the Continent has brought out very clearly the limitations imposed on the size of the forces by the difficulties of providing special landing-craft in sufficient quantity. For example, even for the short cross-Channel passage from England to the Continent, we do not foresee such forces exceeding 17 divisions, half of which will be armoured. We should not, therefore, be able to use large American forces from England in the final stage. Similar limitations would no doubt operate in any offensive against Europe from the Mediterranean basin carried out by American forces.'

The Planners' paper was discussed by the Chiefs of Staff on 17th December. They also had before them the first two of the Prime Minister's papers, that is to say, those relating to the Far East and to operations in Europe in 1942. A full debate followed, which was continued at a second meeting held that night; but unfortunately, there is no record of what passed. We know only that some draft notes were assembled to provide the basis for a further discussion on the following day, at which the Prime Minister and Lord Beaverbrook were also present. From the minutes of this meeting it may be inferred that the C.O.S. notes, in their original form, followed the line of the Directors of Plans rather than the Prime Minister and laid greater stress on immediate defensive needs than on future offensive operations. Mr. Churchill, at any rate, took the opportunity of reading to the meeting the draft of his third paper dealing with the position in 1943. He added that he thought it important 'to put before the peoples of both the British Empire and the United States the mass invasion of the Continent of Europe as the goal' for that year. It was agreed that the C.O.S. should extend their paper to include this point and also to stress the value of an early move of American army formations and bomber squadrons to the United Kingdom, even though the latter might involve some sacrifice in the supply of American aircraft to the R.A.F.

On 19th December a third and final meeting took place. The Prime Minister opened the discussion by saying that a stage had now been reached, when a list should be drawn up of the main points to be put forward to the Americans. In his opinion they were the following:

'(a) A concerted effort should be made by the United States and Great Britain to re-establish our naval position in the Pacific as soon as possible and to restore those of our possessions in the Far East which may meanwhile fall into enemy hands.

(b) The dispatch of a United States force to Northern Ireland (of the order of three divisions and one armoured division) to enable us to release trained British troops from the United Kingdom for overseas theatres.

(c) The bombing of Germany by United States squadrons based

on the United Kingdom. Initially this force might consist of six bomber squadrons.

(d) United States to take the lead in occupying North Africa by preparing an expeditionary force of, say, 25,000 men, to be augmented by a force totalling up to 150,000 men during the next six months.

(e) The United States to leave the largest number of destroyers possible in the Atlantic.

(f) United States to help in building improvised aircraft-carriers.

(g) The highest priority to be conceded by Great Britain to the aircraft required for equipping carriers.'

After what was described as 'considerable discussion' this sequence of proposals was agreed, subject to important reservations by Admiral Pound on the first point. He stressed the fact that combined operations, especially when undertaken in face of enemy shore-based aircraft, were notoriously costly. Before attempting to go over to the offensive in the Pacific, we should therefore assure ourselves of a substantial superiority in capital ships. This could not be attained for many months. Meanwhile we should be content with operations designed to wear down Japanese naval strength, taking as our immediate aim the re-establishment of an Anglo-American fleet at Singapore.

It was against this background of discussion that the C.O.S. produced the final version of their strategic paper, which is printed below. It will be noted that there was no longer any suggestion that the Americans should confine their operations to the Mediterranean, and that greater prominence was now given to Mr. Churchill's offensive plans for 1942 and 1943. If the paper, nevertheless, seems a rather colourless document, it must be remembered that its sole purpose was to secure the agreement of the American Chiefs of Staff to a minimum number of essential points, of which incomparably the most important was that stated in the first three paragraphs:

'I—GRAND STRATEGY

1. At the A-B Staff conversations in February 1941, it was agreed that Germany was the predominant member of the Axis Powers, and consequently the Atlantic and European area was considered to be the decisive theatre.

2. Much has happened since February last, but, notwithstanding the entry of Japan into the war, our view remains that Germany is still the prime enemy and her defeat is the key to victory. Once Germany is defeated, the collapse of Italy and Japan must speedily follow.

3. In our considered opinion, therefore, it should be a cardinal principle of A-B strategy that only the minimum of force necessary for the safeguarding of vital interests in other theatres should be diverted from operations against Germany.

II—ESSENTIAL FEATURES OF OUR STRATEGY

4. The essential features of the above grand strategy are as follows. Each will be examined in greater detail later in this paper:

(a) The realization of the victory programme of armaments, which first and foremost requires the security of the main areas of war industry.

(b) The maintenance of essential communications.

(c) Closing and tightening the ring round Germany.

(d) Wearing down and undermining German resistance by air bombardment, blockade, subversive activities and propaganda.

(e) The continuous development of offensive action against Germany.

(f) Maintaining only such positions in the Eastern theatre as will safeguard vital interests while we are concentrating on the defeat of Germany.

III—STEPS TO BE TAKEN IN 1942 TO PUT INTO EFFECT THE ABOVE GENERAL POLICY

The Security of Areas of War Production

5. In so far as these are liable to attack, the main areas of war industry are situated in:

(a) The United Kingdom.

(b) The West coast of North America.

(c) Russia.

6. The United Kingdom. To safeguard the United Kingdom it will be necessary to maintain at all times the minimum forces required to defeat invasion. We are prepared to answer any questions which the United States Chiefs of Staff wish to put to us about the defence of the United Kingdom.

7. The United States. The main centres of production on or near the West coast of North America must be protected from Japanese sea-borne attack. This will be facilitated by holding Hawaii and Dutch Harbour. We consider that a Japanese invasion of the United States on a large scale can be ruled out of account, whether Hawaii or Dutch Harbour are held or not.

8. The probable scale of attack and the general nature of the forces required for the defence of the west coast of America are, of course, matters for the United States Chiefs of Staff to assess. We are prepared to give our views if required.

9. Russia. It will be essential to afford the Russians such assistance as will enable them to maintain their hold on Leningrad, Moscow and the oilfields of the Caucasus.

Maintenance of Communications

10. The main routes which must be secured are:

(a) From U.S.A. to United Kingdom.

(b) From U.S.A. and the United Kingdom to North Russia.

(c) The various routes from the United Kingdom and U.S.A. to Freetown, South America and the Cape.

(d) The routes in the Indian Ocean to the Red Sea and Persian Gulf, to India and Burma, to the East Indies and to Australasia.

(e) The route through the Panama Canal, and United States coastal traffic.

(f) The route through the Panama Canal to Hawaii and Australasia.

In addition to the above routes we shall do everything possible to open up and secure the Mediterranean route.

11. The Security of these routes involves:

(i) Well-balanced A-B naval and air dispositions. We are ready to discuss joint dispositions with the American Chiefs of Staff.

(ii) Holding and capturing essential bases. The main bases which are, or may be required, apart from the terminal points to the various routes are:

Iceland.	Dakar.
Gibraltar or the Canaries.	Madagascar.
The Azores.	Ceylon.
Freetown.	Hawaii.

Closing and Tightening the Ring round Germany

12. This ring may be defined as a line running roughly as follows:

Archangel—Black Sea—Anatolia—the Northern Seaboard of the Mediterranean—the Western Seaboard of Europe.

The main object will be to strengthen this ring, and close the gaps in it, by sustaining the Russian front, by arming and supporting Turkey, by increasing our strength in the Middle East, and by gaining possession of the whole North African coast.

13. If this ring can be closed the blockade of Germany and Italy will be complete, and German eruptions, e.g. towards the Persian Gulf, or to the Atlantic seaboard of Africa will be prevented. Furthermore the seizing of the North African coast may open the Mediterranean to convoys, thus enormously shortening the route to the Middle East and saving considerable tonnage now employed in the long haul round the Cape.

The Undermining and Wearing-down of the German Resistance

14. In 1942 the main methods of wearing down Germany's resistance will be:

(a) Ever-increasing air bombardment by British and American forces based in the United Kingdom.

(b) Assistance to Russia's offensive by all means in our power.

(c) The blockade.

(d) The maintenance of the spirit of revolt in the occupied countries and the organization of subversive movements.

Development of Land Offensive on the Continent

15. It does not seem likely that in 1942 any large-scale land offensive against Germany, except on the Russian front, will be possible. We must, however, be ready to take advantage of any

opening that may result from the wearing-down process referred to in paragraph 14 to conduct limited land offensives in North-Western Europe or across the Mediterranean.

16. In 1943 the way may be clear for a return to the Continent, either across the Mediterranean or from Turkey into the Balkans, or by simultaneous landings in several of the occupied countries of North-Western Europe. Such operations will be the prelude to the final assault on Germany itself, and the scope of the victory programme should be such as to provide means by which they can be carried out.

The Safeguarding of the Vital Interests in the Eastern Theatre

17. First of all, the security of Australia, New Zealand and India must be maintained and Chinese resistance supported. Secondly, points of vantage from which an offensive against Japan can eventually be developed must be secured. Our immediate object must therefore be to hold :

(a) Hawaii and Dutch Harbour.

(b) Singapore, the East Indies Barrier and the Philippines.

(c) Rangoon and the route to China.

The minimum forces required to hold the above will have to be a matter for mutual discussion.'

CHAPTER XIV

THE WASHINGTON CONFERENCE (i)

(i)

American Strategy

THE AMERICAN POSITION on the eve of the Washington Conference is less easy to define than the British. We may take as a starting-point a signal which Mr. Churchill received from Lord Halifax while the *Duke of York* was still at sea. This passed on a private message or warning from Mr. Harry Hopkins to the effect that the British delegation would be unwise to bring forward too many cut-and-dried plans at the forthcoming Conference. The American Chiefs of Staff, said Mr. Hopkins, were preoccupied with the immediate crisis in the Pacific and had not yet given their minds to wider problems of strategy. In these circumstances to put detailed proposals before them would be, in his opinion, to invite a merely negative response. It does not appear that this warning was taken very seriously or that it caused any change in British plans; but there is no doubt that it was well founded. The American Chiefs of Staff were indeed reluctant to discuss strategy except in the most general terms, though their reasons for holding back were more complex than Hopkins's message suggested.

It was, of course, true that they were preoccupied with the Pacific. Since the Conference was to open within a fortnight of the disaster at Pearl Harbor, nothing else could be expected. It was also true that at this stage in the war grand strategy meant primarily strategy in the European theatre. The situation in the Far East was such as to make long-term planning almost impossible: nothing was conceivable for the moment beyond the resolute defence of such bases as the Allies still retained. But it was far otherwise in Europe, where the Western Powers were already stronger than they had been at any time since the Battle of France. It was becoming possible to plan for the future with some confidence; and it was urgently necessary to do so, if the golden opportunity of Russia's unexpectedly vigorous resistance was not to be lost. Both the British strategic papers—Mr. Churchill's especially—therefore put their main emphasis on European problems and on operations which could be carried out within the next few months. But it was precisely on this subject—the transition to the offensive against Germany—that the American Chiefs of Staff were least ready to reach a decision.

During the greater part of 1941 their energies had been concentrated on the logistic problem, in itself large enough, of rearming the United States while at the same time maintaining a flow of supplies to Great Britain, the U.S.S.R., China and other countries. They had had little time to study future plans of campaign. Moreover, they had had no realistic basis on which to do so, since they had not known, until the very moment of the Japanese attack, when or under what conditions the United States would enter the war. Consequently, they were not in a position to make detailed proposals in the field of grand strategy or to circulate papers comparable with those which had been prepared by Mr. Churchill and the British Chiefs of Staff. But that did not mean that they were willing to accept their ally's plans without qualification, or that they lacked strong views of their own about how the war should be fought.

There had already been indications at the time of the Atlantic Meeting that on certain points the American Chiefs of Staff differed sharply from their British colleagues. It is easy to exaggerate the extent of these differences; and it may well be that they were more clearly visible from the American than from the British point of view. The American official historian, for example, goes so far as to say that the comments made on British strategy at and after the Atlantic Meeting 'had warned the British of certain strong views held in Washington, and had provided unmistakable evidence that the United States was likely to be the controlling partner in any coming alliance'.[1] This view of the case would probably have surprised the British Chiefs of Staff of the day, who had not been aware of such a definite clash of opinion and who would themselves have endorsed much that their American colleagues had said. Nevertheless, it was true that the two countries did not see strategic problems in the same light. There were inevitable differences of emphasis and approach, even in a sense of principle, which arose naturally from corresponding differences in national temperament and policy.

It may be remarked first, that those who live in the United States tend to take, if only for demographic reasons, a rather rigid or black-and-white view of the art of war. The resources of their country are very large; they have rarely had to count the cost; and it is natural to them to find the solution to every problem in an overwhelming application of strength—the crash programme, the head-on collision, the quick victory. The more supple type of strategy, which seeks to gain its ends by the skilful employment of limited means, is not only unfamiliar but even in some degree suspect. Since it relies on manœuvre rather than frontal attack, it appears as a kind of pusillanimity, a flinching away from the essentials of the problem. This had

---

[1] Watson, p. 409.

been the basis of the American comments on the strategic paper circulated at Placentia. It had been criticized because it seemed to provide only for operations on the circumference and not for the single massive thrust at the centre, which was held to be the foundation of all sound strategy.

This American preference for the simple and direct was reinforced by considerations of national policy. The United States did not wish to enter the Second World War on the same terms (militarily speaking) as she had entered the First; that is to say, as a belated participant in plans already formed and largely carried out by others. It was felt that her status as a Great Power, if not the controlling partner in the alliance, both authorized and required her to play a much larger and more distinctive part. This suggested that, if she were forced to enter the war—as in fact she had been—before the build-up of her own forces was complete, it would not be wise to involve herself too deeply in existing Allied plans. These would tend to allot her a rôle proportionate to her actual rather than her potential strength, and would thus lead to the 'piecemeal and indecisive commitment of forces' so much deplored by the Joint Board. It might be better to stand aloof, so far as that was possible, until the forces of the United States had grown strong enough to be used in a final, knock-out campaign.

These arguments had a particular application in the European theatre. By the time of the Washington Conference there was already a strong body of opinion in the War Department, which held that the war in Europe could only be won by a head-on collision with the German army; that is to say, by a direct assault, however costly, on German positions in north-western Europe. All other operations, whether in the Mediterranean or elsewhere, were regarded not only as subsidiary but as undesirable diversions from this one main objective. Such a policy was in accordance with the principles described above; but its practical expression had so far been confined to departmental memoranda below the level of the Chiefs of Staff. Moreover, it was generally conceded, even by the most ardent proponents of the collision-strategy, that no such plan was feasible at the moment. It would have to wait for at least a year or eighteen months, until the Victory Programme had been realized and the immediate pressure in the Far East had slackened.

Meanwhile, the American position was necessarily undefined and even ambiguous. The historian of the War Department sums it up very accurately as follows:

'The American planners had remained non-committal. They did not go so far as to propose that the United States should either accept or reject the British concept of the transition from the defensive to the offensive against Germany. Before the 7th December the nearest they had come to stating a principle to govern decisions during the transitional period was to emphasize the need for economy of effort in "subsidiary" theaters. They classified as subsidiary theaters not only the Far East but also Africa, the Middle East, the Iberian Peninsula and the Scandinavian peninsula, in accordance with their premise that the plains of northwest Europe constituted the main theater, where we must come to grips with the enemy ground-forces. At the time of the Arcadia Conference the Army planning-staff again stated the idea of a great final offensive with the main effort in Western Europe, which should be made in conjunction with the strongest possible Russian offensive on the Eastern Front and secondary offensives wherever feasible. The Staff was convinced that this must be the final step, seeing no other area in which it would be feasible from a logistics viewpoint to transport and maintain forces required for an operation of such magnitude. The Army planners were disposed to consider all other operations as strictly holding operations, and to regard with disfavour any proposal to establish and maintain in a subsidiary theater the favourable ratio of Allied to enemy forces that would be necessary in order to take the offensive there.

It appeared to the Army Staff that the United States and Great Britain would in any event be compelled to act in accord with this view of strategy for several months to come. Thus from the American point of view there was no reason for dwelling on the principle for the time being. . . .'[1]

This attitude of reserve was understandable in the circumstances; but it was also unfortunate. It meant that the strategic discussions at Washington were unduly one-sided, since they proceeded on the basis of papers written from the British point of view only. The agreements reached thus tended to be more formal than real; they were not the product of a full debate such as would have enabled either side to explore the principles on which the other wished to act. The results of this omission were to be severely felt during the following year, which was a period of prolonged and heated controversy about strategic problems, especially those relating to Europe. It is possible that much of this later argument might have been avoided, or at least mitigated, if the differences between British and American conceptions of strategy had been more fully investigated during the Conference. It might then have been found that, although two contrasting schools of thought existed, their final conclusions were not necessarily incompatible. But in the absence of a full discussion, a confrontation of rival plans, there was a natural tendency for opinion to polarize and the gap between the two points of view to appear wider than it actually was.

---

[1] Maurice Matloff and E. M. Snell, *Strategic Planning for Coalition Warfare* (1953), Vol. I, pp. 101–2.

(ii)

W. W. 1

Mr. Churchill and his party arrived in Washington on the evening of 22nd December and plunged at once into business. The first important meeting took place that night between the Prime Minister, Lord Beaverbrook and Lord Halifax on one side, and the President, Mr. Cordell Hull, Mr. Sumner Welles and Mr. Hopkins on the other. The three papers, which Mr. Churchill had written on the outward voyage, were not yet ready for distribution; but their substance, and especially Mr. Churchill's plans for a limited offensive in Europe in 1942, provided the main theme for discussion. It is clear from his subsequent report to the Cabinet that the Prime Minister did not find his audience unsympathetic:

'There was general agreement that if Hitler was held in Russia he must try something else, and that the most probable line was Spain and Portugal en route to North Africa. Our success in Libya and the prospect of joining hands with French North African territory was another reason to make Hitler want, if he could, to get hold of Morocco as quickly as possible. At the same time, reports did not seem to suggest [that the] threat was imminent, perhaps because Hitler had enough on hand at the moment.

'There was general agreement that it was vital to forestall the Germans in North-West Africa and the Atlantic Islands. In addition to all the other reasons, the two French battleships, *Jean Bart* and *Richelieu*, were a real prize for whoever got them. Accordingly, the discussion was not whether but how.

Various suggestions were made:

(a) The United States Government might speak in very serious and resolute terms to Vichy, saying that this was the final chance to reconsider their positions and come out on the side that was pledged to restoration of France. As a symbol of this Pétain might be invited to send Weygand to represent him at an official conference in Washington.

(b) An approach might be made to Weygand in the light of a North African situation fundamentally changed by British advance and by United States entering into war, and their willingness to send a force to North Africa.

It was suggested, on the other hand, that the effect of such procedure might be to extract smooth promises from Pétain and Weygand, the Germans meanwhile being advised of our intentions, and that, accordingly, if these approaches were to be made, it would be desirable to have all plans made for going into North Africa, with or without invitation. I emphasized immense psychological effect likely to be produced both in France and among French troops in North Africa by association of United States with the undertaking. Mr. Hull suggested that it might well be that a leader would emerge in North Africa as events developed.

The President said that he was anxious that American land-forces should give their support as quickly as possible wherever they will be most helpful, and favoured the idea of a plan to move into North Africa being prepared for either event, i.e. with or without invitation.

It was agreed to remit the study of the project to Staffs on assumption that it was vital to forestall the Germans in that area and that the Libyan campaign had, as it was expected to do, achieved complete success. It was recognized that the question of shipping was plainly a most important factor . . .

In the course of conversation the President mentioned that he would propose at forthcoming Conference that United States should relieve our troops in Northern Ireland, and spoke of send-ing three or four divisions there. I warmly welcomed this, and said I hoped that one of the divisions would be an armoured division. It was not thought that this need conflict with prepara-tions for a United States force for North Africa.'

This appeared very promising; but when the first plenary session of the Conference assembled on the following day, it became clear that certain qualifications would have to be made. The President opened the proceedings by saying that he proposed to take as his theme for discussion a memorandum, recently received from Mr. Stimson, which dealt with the main problems of the war on a geo-graphical basis. First came the security of the British Isles and of their sea-communications with the United States. He felt that certain questions raised by Mr. Stimson about the British system of defence ought to be carefully examined; but he was not himself in favour of sending American troops to either England or Scotland. On the other hand, bomber squadrons might well be sent to England and the United States might also take over the defence of Northern Ire-land, thus freeing British troops for employment elsewhere. He was also of the opinion that the United States should supply the garrison for Iceland. No clear conclusion had yet been reached about the Atlantic Islands; but he inclined to the view that the Cape Verde Islands, which occupied such an important strategic position in the South Atlantic, were of greater significance to the United States than the Azores.

The President then turned to the Middle East and North Africa. He paid tribute to current British successes in Libya, but added that he did not think this a suitable theatre in which to engage American troops, though he was willing that the United States should assume responsibility for the important air-route from Brazil to West Africa and thence across the continent to Khartoum. This led to the question of the potential enemy threat to French North and West Africa. Everyone agreed that it was essential to forestall Germany in this area; but the problem was to know how to do so. There was always the risk of pushing the Vichy Government into the German camp or of putting them in a position in which they might be tempted to hand over the French Fleet. His own opinion was that the United States should certainly prepare forces for use in North Africa; but it was necessary to realize that shortage of shipping would limit the number of projects, which could be carried out simultaneously.

There remained the south-west Pacific. This was a very serious problem, which involved not only the United States and Great Britain, but also China and the Netherlands. He attached the very greatest importance to the holding of Singapore, which he hoped to see reinforced, not only from India and the Middle East, but also, if necessary, from Great Britain. The United States on their side would do their utmost to hold the Philippines and, if that proved impossible, would continue the struggle in the Dutch East Indies. With that in mind they were already planning to establish a safe base in Australia from which land and air reinforcements could be pushed north-wards. The Army Air Corps was also studying a plan for setting up an air-base on Chinese territory from which to attack the Japanese homeland. We could not count on any immediate help from Russia in the Far Eastern theatre, unless Japan were voluntarily to attack; but he understood that M. Stalin might find it possible to make some move in the following spring.

Mr. Roosevelt then summed up the strategic problem before the Conference by saying that it seemed to him essentially a question of the maintenance of communications in the widest sense, and in particular of communications (a) across the Atlantic (b) by sea and air with the Near and Far East and (c) across the Pacific with Australia, the Dutch East Indies and Singapore. He added that there were also other important matters to discuss, notably arms-pro-duction. He was very anxious to reach agreement on a new pro-gramme to cover the needs of 1943 and 1944; and this was a matter of some urgency, since it would affect the Budget statement which he was due to make on 5th January. He hoped that Lord Beaverbrook would meet Mr. Knudsen and the others chiefly concerned within the next few days and would go into this extremely important sub-ject with them.

This opening statement must have been something of a disappoint-ment to Mr. Churchill. It showed a definite slackening of the Presi-dent's enthusiasm of the night before and a reversion, especially in the summing-up, to a merely negative and defensive attitude. No doubt the President had been consulting his Staff and had been reminded by them of the narrow limits which would be imposed on American action in any theatre during the next few months. In his reply the Prime Minister, while accepting this position, did his best to turn the attention of the Conference to the future and to the need to form some positive, offensive plan. He warmly welcomed the President's proposals about Iceland and Northern Ireland. If three infantry and one armoured divisions could be provided, an equivalent number of British formations would be released to serve in India and Malaya or to relieve the Australian troops at present in the Middle East. Since it was unlikely that they would see immediate action, the American divisions need not be fully trained or equipped, but could complete their training on their new station.

Mr. Churchill then turned to the Middle East. He agreed that this theatre, though of vital importance to the Allies, was not suitable for the employment of American troops; and he asked for no help there except in supplies and the development of bases. But he reminded the Conference that current operations in Libya might very soon precipitate a crisis in North Africa. The arrival of British troops on the Tunisian frontier might well cause French opinion to move in our favour; it might also compel Germany to make fresh demands on France, which the French authorities—or at any rate those in North Africa—would feel ready to resist. In either case an opportunity would be presented by which we must not fail to profit. A force for North Africa was already standing by in England; if a similar American force could be prepared, ready to land on the Moroccan coast at the same time, we should be well placed to control the situation. It seemed to him that this was an urgent problem and one in which the United States might well take the lead, since their influence with the Vichy Government was no doubt greater than ours.

On the Pacific theatre Mr. Churchill had little to say, perhaps because the President had also said little. He referred briefly to the reinforcements which were reaching General Wavell, to the loss of the *Prince of Wales* and the *Repulse* and to plans for forming a British Far Eastern Fleet of three carriers and three R-class battleships, to operate initially in the Indian Ocean and as far east as Darwin. He then pressed strongly for further information about American plans. What was the present position in the Philippines? What were the plans for the future defence of Hawaii? Was any danger apprehended to the Western American seaboard? His own opinion was that there was no risk of a major attack, though minor incidents might occur. He added that he was anxious that Great Britain should not be a drain on the United States in her moment of anxiety. We should do our utmost, for example, to relieve the American navy of responsibility in the Atlantic, so as to release more ships for the Pacific. But it was necessary to remember that, though the rate of sinkings had fallen remarkably during the last four months, there were now more enemy submarines and aircraft at work than ever before.

Finally, Mr. Churchill reminded the Conference that the British Chiefs of Staff had drafted a paper on grand strategy and the general conduct of the war. He felt that the time had come when this paper, together with other matters arising from the present meeting, should be jointly discussed by the Chiefs of Staff.

This concluded the main business of the meeting. There was some further discussion about the supply of items of British equipment, notably anti-aircraft guns, to the American forces destined for Northern Ireland; questions were raised about the probable timing of a North African operation in relation to other troop movements; and Admiral Stark gave particulars of the expected rate of delivery of various types of American warship, emphasizing that the majority of newly-commissioned destroyers would be put into service in the Atlantic. But there was nothing in the nature of a debate. Though it was possible to detect a certain difference of emphasis between the President's remarks and the Prime Minister's, both had been careful to avoid controversial issues and to confine themselves, so far as possible, to those immediate military measures about which there could be little dispute.

The next stage was the detailed examination of these measures by the British and American Chiefs of Staff sitting together, and by their respective planning staffs. It will be convenient, by a slight anticipation, to refer to this body of military advisers as the Combined Chiefs of Staff[1] and to treat them from now onwards as if they already were the standing-committee, which in fact they became during the course of the Conference. But before we consider their reaction to specific moves such as the transfer of American troops to Iceland and Northern Ireland or the proposed North African operation, we must follow the fortunes of the British paper on grand strategy.

This came before the Combined Chiefs of Staff on three occasions, the 24th, the 27th and the 31st December; but it cannot be said that any exhaustive discussion took place. The only significant exchange was at the first meeting, when Admiral Stark asked whether the British had formed any idea of the actual size of the force, which the United States would have to send to Europe? Sir John Dill replied that their preliminary studies suggested that 15–17 divisions (including armoured divisions) was the largest force which could be landed or maintained on the Continent, if the operation took place in 1942 or early 1943. Later it might be possible to raise the total to approximately 40 divisions. Admiral Turner added that the American Navy

---

[1] It was agreed in Washington to reserve the word 'combined' for Anglo-American organs and enterprises, and the word 'joint' for those involving more than one service.

had arrived independently at the figure of 45 divisions as 'the maximum force which could be built up overseas with the shipping likely to be available'. General Marshall and the other army officers present made no comment.

The importance of these figures, thus casually introduced into the discussion, is obvious. As we have seen already, American objections to British strategy, so far as they had been formulated, were based on the theory that the Allies should concentrate all their resources in a single massive thrust on Berlin, and that all other operations, which did not contribute directly to this end, were merely wasteful and diversionary. But it was evidently useless to argue in these terms, if the maximum force available was to be of the order of only 40–50 divisions. So long as this limitation remained, there was no alternative to a step-by-step policy such as the British Chiefs of Staff proposed. No doubt their American colleagues, especially on the Army side, hoped and believed that the limitation would not remain; that a reduction in the rate of sinkings and a great increase in ship production would in time transform the situation and enable Allied strategy to be drastically remodelled. But they were not in a position to advance such an argument at the moment.

The British paper therefore had an easy, almost too easy, passage. Most of the amendments proposed were minor and verbal. Paragraph ten, dealing with communications, was rewritten and expanded so as to include a detailed statement (along the lines of Mr. Stimson's paper) of the main sea and air routes involved; the statement that a Japanese invasion of the United States could be 'ruled out of account' was slightly modified; and the adverb 'speedily' was dropped from the sentence in paragraph two, which stated that the collapse of Japan must inevitably follow on Germany's defeat. Some of the other changes were of slightly greater significance. Thus the sentence in paragraph four, which defined our current objectives in the Far East as 'maintaining only such positions as will safeguard vital interests', was modified by the addition of the words 'and deny to Japan access to raw materials vital to her continuous war-effort'. Similarly, in paragraph sixteen the specific reference to limited offensives 'across the Mediterranean' in 1942 was dropped, as also was the reference in the next paragraph to 'simultaneous landings in several of the occupied countries' in 1943. But these changes, though their general effect was to reserve the American position on certain contentious points, did not affect the main argument of the paper, as will be seen from the full text of the final version, which is printed at Appendix I.

Since this paper, known henceforward as W.W.1, thus became the first formal expression of an agreed Allied strategy, it is of some importance to list the various points on which it did—and equally those on which it did not—commit its two signatories. In the first place, it reaffirmed the principle of 'Germany first', which had been agreed in earlier conversations. 'Much has happened since February last, but, notwithstanding the entry of Japan into the war, our view remains that Germany is the prime enemy and her defeat is the key to victory.' But the paper did not attempt to define how this principle was to be carried into practice. The last paragraph listed certain areas which it was desirable to hold in the Pacific—Hawaii and Alaska, Singapore, the Dutch East Indies and the Philippines, Burma and the overland route to China, the Russian maritime provinces; but it was content to add that 'the minimum forces required to hold the above will have to be a matter of mutual discussion'. Similarly, the paragraph on the maintenance of essential communications, which included a reference to the need to reopen the Mediterranean, led only to the non-committal statement that 'the security of these routes involves (a) well balanced American-British naval and air dispositions and (b) holding and capturing essential sea and air bases'.

With regard to future operations in Europe the paper was only slightly more specific. It was agreed that the process of defeating Germany could be divided into four, overlapping phases. In the first the object would be to complete the encirclement of Germany by holding and strengthening a line running from Archangel to the Black Sea and thence along the northern coast of the Mediterranean and the western coast of Europe. Simultaneously with this, every effort was to be made to reduce Germany's power by supporting Russian operations in the Eastern Front, intensifying the air-offensive, maintaining the blockade and organizing subversive movements in the occupied countries. These operations, it was hoped, would open the way to a return to the Continent in 1943 'across the Mediterranean, from Turkey into the Balkans, or by landings in Western Europe'. But these attacks, the scope of which was not defined, were to be only 'the prelude to the final assault on Germany itself'. No date was assigned to this culminating operation; nor was anything said of the method to be employed.

To say this is not to criticize the paper or to ignore the important measure of agreement, which it embodied. It would not have been easy for anyone at this stage in the proceedings to have produced a complete and acceptable blue-print for the future conduct of the war. Nor would it have been wise (even without Mr. Hopkins's warning) for the British Chiefs of Staff to have tried to anticipate decisions which could only be taken after joint discussion at the Conference. Nevertheless, it is important to emphasize how wide a gap remained between the strategic principles outlined in W.W.1, and their practical application in the field in the form of an agreed plan of campaign. A form of words had been found to which both parties could assent; but that did not necessarily mean that they had yet discovered a common strategy.

(iii)

'Gymnast'

This point was well illustrated, when the Combined Chiefs of Staff came to discuss the various military projects in the Atlantic area, which had been proposed at the first meeting. These projects flowed naturally from the decision to regard Germany as the prime enemy; they were the expression of that decision in action. But the more closely they were examined, the more difficult it seemed to be to carry them out. Resources, especially of shipping, were found to be even more limited than had been expected; there was not complete unanimity about what ought to be done; and meanwhile the situation in the Far East was growing daily more desperate. There was thus a constant tendency to postpone and water down all proposals for military action in Europe, and to feed the resources thus husbanded to the Pacific, even though this meant a complete reversal in practice of the main strategic decision so far reached by the Conference. In the circumstances of the case this was inevitable; and no one will suggest that the Pacific theatre received more than it needed, or even so much. But the danger remained that this temporary reversal of policy might become permanent, if the eastern movement were not balanced by a clear-cut decision, accepted by both sides, about future action in Europe. But this was precisely what did not emerge.

The largest of the Atlantic and European projects, which was thus the key to all the others, was the proposed expedition to North Africa, for which the British code-name 'Gymnast' was adopted. It was, as we have seen, the basis of the Prime Minister's whole strategy for the next two years. It also commended itself, though perhaps less strongly, to President Roosevelt; but the latter's military advisers were far from enthusiastic. A paper circulated in the War Department went so far as to denounce the whole British argument as 'persuasive rather than rational' and 'motivated more largely by political than by sound strategic purposes'; and concluded that 'our acceptance of a commitment in North West Africa at this time would prove to be a mistake of the first magnitude'.[1] Whether General

---

[1] Matloff and Snell, Vol. I, pp. 104–5.

Marshall himself would have gone so far is uncertain; but there is little doubt that this was the common opinion of his staff. Nor was it entirely without foundation.

In the form in which it was presented at Washington, the North African operation had many hazards. The first was the uncertainty of the political situation. When planning for 'Gymnast' had first started in the previous October, the French Delegate General in North Africa had been General Weygand. He was a man of impressive personality, who was known to be, if not pro-Allied, at least strongly anti-German. It had not been entirely unreasonable to suppose that, if faced with the choice between an Allied and a German occupation, he would have preferred the former and would have found the means to make his choice effective. But since then General Weygand had been dismissed; and Marshal Pétain had entered into further negotiations with the Germans, of which the nature and results were still uncertain. It was true that he had subsequently renewed his assurances to the American Ambassador, Admiral Leahy, that he would never allow either the French fleet or French bases in North Africa to fall into German hands. But, even assuming his complete sincerity, how long could he maintain this position? He was clearly under heavy pressure; and there were even rumours that the Germans intended to replace him by Admiral Darlan, from whom the Allies could expect no sympathy at all.

Such was the position when the Chiefs of Staff instructed the Joint Planning Committee[1] to examine 'Gymnast'. It seemed likely that a crisis might break in North Africa at any moment; but it was impossible to forecast what form it would take. As the 8th Army continued to advance towards Tripoli, German pressure on the French to yield bases in North Africa would certainly increase. Marshal Pétain (or his successor) might yield or might try to resist. In either event a reaction favourable to the Allies might occur, though it was doubtful whether anyone, in the absence of General Weygand, would be able to command the undivided allegiance of the French North African forces. At best the opportunity offered would be a fleeting one; and it was to be expected that the Germans, if forestalled in North Africa, would immediately try to regain the territory, probably by a movement through Spain.

For planning purposes the Committee were instructed to make three assumptions:

(i) that we should receive an actual invitation to enter French North Africa, or at least an assurance that there would be no more than token resistance;

---

[1] An Anglo-American Committee formed during the Conference, which was the forerunner of the Combined Staff Planners.

(ii) that the Germans would not already be established in any part of the area in such strength as to be able to oppose our occupation of French Morocco; and

(iii) that, in the face of Spanish non-co-operation or even actual resistance, it would take the Germans a maximum of three months to establish bases in southern Spain, from which to mount a heavy attack.

But these assumptions, dubious in themselves, did not provide a satisfactory basis for planning a military operation; and the Committee soon found themselves unable to agree on the size of the force required. Everything depended on uncertain factors: the political and military situation at the time; the degree of co-operation to be expected from the French and the fighting value of their troops; the speed of the German reaction; and the size of the area which would have to be brought under direct Allied control. The British were inclined to believe that a *coup-de-main*, such as their original plans had provided for, would still be possible. The Americans took the more gloomy view that, if the whole of French North Africa were to be occupied, a force of not less than 300,000 men would ultimately be required.

An unsatisfactory compromise was finally reached on the basis of employing six divisions (three British and three American) and 348 aircraft (largely American) over the first three months. What might happen thereafter was left in the air. It was agreed that part of the British component, consisting of one armoured and one infantry brigade and three fighter squadrons, should land at Algiers in order to support the French in Tunisia against a possible German threat from Italy. Simultaneously, an American assault division, the spearhead of the main body, would land at Casablanca, which would become the base port for the whole expedition. Subsequently, the American forces, supported by the remainder of the British component, would move northwards to occupy the whole of French Morocco and establish positions from which they could, if necessary, enter Spanish Morocco by invitation. Finally, the two components, the Algiers force and the Casablanca force, would link up and control would be extended over the whole of French North Africa with the object of creating a base for future operations across the Mediterranean. But the rate of build-up would be very slow. It was agreed that the main base would have to be an Atlantic port, in view of the heavy scale of submarine and air attack to be expected inside the Mediterranean. But the capacity of Casablanca, the only suitable port, was limited and part would have to be reserved for necessary supplies for the French. It would therefore be at least three months before the whole force of six divisions with ancillary troops and aircraft could be put ashore.

It was evident that this plan fell between two stools. It was neither a *coup-de-main*, of which the essence is speed, on the one hand, nor a massive operation of war on the other. Moreover, it had already become clear during the course of planning that it could only be carried out, if all other major operations in the Atlantic area were halted, including the movement of American troops to Iceland and the British Isles. But these movements were an integral part of the plan. The Americans proposed to use their Marine Division for the initial landing at Casablanca, but were unable to do so until they had retrieved the 4,259 marines, who then formed part of the Iceland garrison. Similarly on the British side; though we were prepared to take the risk if necessary, it would clearly be unwise to move a force of three divisions and an air-component out of the United Kingdom, unless there were an immediate prospect of its being replaced by an equivalent American force. But despite the Prime Minister's protests it appeared that shortage of shipping imposed an absolute ban.

It was at this point that General Marshall brought forward his first proposal. On 26th December he drew the attention of the Conference to the fact that the first movement of American troops for Europe was now preparing. The proposed convoy would carry about 20,000 men, 14,000 for Northern Ireland and 6,000 for Iceland. He proposed that the necessary shipping should be taken up on the basis that it could, if necessary, be switched to 'Gymnast' at six days' notice, provided that the necessary orders were given before the 13th January. Thereafter the shipping would be committed for a period of about three weeks. After further but vain discussion about the possibility of finding additional shipping elsewhere, this proposal was accepted on 1st January. Meanwhile the Planning Committee was instructed to re-examine 'Gymnast' with a view to reducing the time taken to disembark the force and also to report on what could in fact be done, if the operation had to be carried out at short notice, overriding all other priorities.

The results of this inquiry were not encouraging. On 7th January the British planners presented their conclusions to their own Chiefs of Staff. On the first point—that of reducing the time of disembarkation—they reported that little could be done. Inquiries were being made in London about the use, in addition to Casablanca, of minor Atlantic ports such as Rabat and Port Lyautey; but it was not likely that these would help much, as communications with the hinterland were poor. On the second point—that of what could be done if immediate action were ordered—the planners were scarcely more hopeful. On the British side there would be comparatively little difficulty, though an early decision would have to be taken about the air-component, which could only be found by withdrawing aircraft from Fighter Command, or by reducing our promised delivery of Hurricanes to Russia. With that reservation the whole force was ready. If detailed planning could be assumed to have started on 7th January, then D-1, the day when loading was ordered, would be 15th February. The decision to embark troops would have to be taken by D-9 and the decision to sail by D-16; the first two convoys would reach Algiers and Casablanca respectively by D-28. To carry out the whole operation would involve a reduction of 25,000 men in the planned movement of troops to the Middle East, the cancellation of operations 'Pilgrim' and 'Bonus',[1] and a loss of three divisions to Home Forces.

But it was very doubtful whether the Americans would be able to keep to this time-table. Their assault division would no doubt be ready; but there was reason to suspect that the same was not true of the Army-Air units and base-units, which would have to accompany it. It would not be safe to rely on their coming forward before 15th February at the earliest; and it was probable even so that the Americans would ask for British specialist units to assist them in running the port of Casablanca. There was also serious doubt about the Americans' ability to find the necessary cargo ships and naval escorts for their convoys. The planners concluded:

'The whole Joint Plan as it now stands, depends on the provision by the Americans of the shipping and naval escorts for their own convoys, and not until they have completed a thorough shipping and naval appreciation (on the lines of C.R. 44 and 45) will the position be clear. It will be impossible to draw up a firm Joint Plan for any definite date of readiness or to assess the effect of the operation on North Atlantic trade until this is done.'

It began to look as if 'Gymnast' was disappearing into the mists; and so in a sense it was. The urgency, which had so far informed the planning, was beginning to relax. By this date, 12th January, it was already clear that 'Crusader' had not been completely successful; and Mr. Churchill was obliged to inform the Conference that 'the arrival of General Auchinleck's armies on the Tunisian border could not be expected as early as at one time it was thought possible'. At the same time, and in part for the same reason, the political tension had also slackened. Either German pressure on Vichy had been reduced or Marshal Pétain was successfully resisting; in any case an immediate crisis no longer seemed probable. In these circumstances the Conference was not unwilling to receive General Marshall's second proposal, the result of a more thorough study of American shipping resources and the immediate needs of the Far East. He now proposed to reduce the initial movement of American troops to Europe from 20,000 to 6,600 (4,600 to North Ireland and

---

[1] The occupation of the Atlantic Islands and a proposed operation against Madagascar.

the remainder to Iceland). By using the ships thus released it would be possible to form a January convoy for the Far East, comprising 21,800 American troops, 393 aircraft and some 200,000 tons of supplies. He thought it of the highest importance to carry out this movement as soon as possible, though to do so would involve, not only a further postponement of 'Gymnast', but also a reduction by thirty per cent of American supplies to Russia over the next three months. After some discussion, in which Russia figured far more prominently than 'Gymnast', General Marshall's proposal was accepted.

The effect on the North African operations was apparently disastrous. The Planning Committee reported that the earliest possible date for D-1 had now receded to 25th May; and even this was more than doubtful:

> 'The 25th May date cannot be accepted without certain reservations since no allowance has been made for ship losses and possible increased demands for shipping arising from enemy operations, accelerated production and additional lend-lease commitments. Furthermore, it seems probable that these vessels may continue to be needed in the Pacific for further movements to Australia.'

It might be thought, therefore, that the North African operation had been finally crowded out of the programme. But Mr. Churchill remained optimistic. He still held tenaciously to the strategy which he had proposed, and believed that he would be able in the end to carry President Roosevelt with him. No more could be done at present; but he regarded the undertaking to send American troops to the British Isles, even though its execution would now be delayed, as an important step forward. As he noted afterwards in his Memoirs:

> 'Every American division which crossed the Atlantic gave us freedom to send one of our British divisions out of the country to the Middle East, or of course—and this was always in my mind—to North Africa. Though few, if any, saw it in this light, this was in fact the first step towards an Allied descent on Morocco, Algeria or Tunis, on which my heart was set. The President was quite conscious of this, and while we did not give precise form to the idea, I felt that our thoughts flowed in the same direction, although it was not yet necessary for either of us to discuss the particular method.'[1]

---

[1] Churchill, Vol. III, p. 606.

(iv)

Command in the Far East

We must now turn to the deteriorating position in the Far East. Such reinforcements as could be found had already been directed to the theatre, where they were due to arrive at various dates from the beginning of January onwards. The intervening weeks were an inevitable period of waiting, during which strategy was, so to speak, in suspense. Mr. Churchill summed up the position in a telegram which he sent to the Prime Minister of Australia on Christmas Day:

'On Japan coming into the war we diverted at once the 18th British Division, which was rounding the Cape in American transports, with the President's permission, to Bombay and Ceylon, and Mr. Roosevelt has now agreed that the leading brigade in the U.S. transport *Mount Vernon* should proceed direct to Singapore. We cancelled the move of the 17th Indian Division from India to Persia and this division is now going to Malaya. A week ago I wirelessed from the ship to London to suggest that you recall one Australian division from Palestine either into India to replace other troops sent forward or to go direct, if it can be managed, to Singapore. I have impressed upon the military authorities the importance of not using up the forces needed for the defence of Singapore and Johore approaches in attempting to defend the northern part of the Malay peninsula. They will fall back slowly, fighting delaying action and destroying communications.

The heavy naval losses which the United States and we have both sustained, give the Japanese the power of landing large reinforcements, but we do not share the view expressed in your telegram to Mr. Casey of 24th December that there is the danger of early reduction of Singapore fortress, which we are determined to defend with the utmost tenacity.

You have been told of the air-support which is already on the way. It would not be wise to loose our grip on Rommel and Libya by taking away forces from General Auchinleck against his judgement just when victory is within our grasp. We have instructed Commanders-in-Chief Middle East to concert a plan for sending fighters and tanks to Singapore immediately the situation in Libya permits.

I and the Chiefs of Staff are in close consultation with the President and his advisers, and we have made encouraging progress. Not only are they impressed with the importance of maintaining Singapore, but they are anxious to move a continuous flow of troops and aircraft through Australia for the defence of the Philippine Islands. Should the Philippines fall the President is agreeable to troops and aircraft being diverted to Singapore. He is also quite willing to send substantial U.S. forces to Australia, where Americans are anxious to establish important bases for the war against Japan. General Wavell has been placed in command of Burma as well as India, and instructed to feed reinforcements arriving in India to Malayan and Burmese fronts. He, like everyone else, recognizes the paramount importance of Singapore. General Pownall[1] has now arrived. He is a highly competent Army officer.

You may count on my doing everything possible to strengthen the whole front from Rangoon to Port Darwin. I am finding cooperation from our American allies. I shall wire more definitely in a day or two.'

Though it is hard to see what more could have been said in the circumstances, this telegram was far from satisfying the Australian Government. Two days later Mr. Curtin published an ill-advised article in the *Melbourne Herald* in which he appeared to repudiate the link with Great Britain and to confide all Australia's hopes for the future to the United States.[2] He also continued throughout the Washington Conference to bombard Mr. Churchill with importunate telegrams demanding further, and often impossible, action: as that an Anglo-American fleet should be formed forthwith which could bring the Japanese fleet to decisive action, or that Russia should be induced to declare war on Japan by the immediate acceptance of all her claims to the Baltic States. Yet, if the tone, and sometimes the content, of these communications left much to be desired, an important and genuine grievance lay behind them. As we saw in an earlier chapter, Australia had long been dissatisfied with her position in the directing councils of the war. There had been difficulties over General Blamey's status in the Middle East and demands, difficult to satisfy but not in themselves unreasonable, for direct Australian representation in the War Cabinet. Now, in the Far East, Australia found herself confronted by an even more dangerous situation, and one for which she had far greater cause to blame Allied leadership. An Australian expeditionary force, which included all her best troops, was in the Middle East; the naval power, on which she had so long relied for her protection, had been temporarily swept away; and Singapore, the land-base to which she had contributed and which she had been taught to regard as the key to her own safety, was under direct and imminent threat. Under these conditions a very sharp reaction by the Australian Government was not only inevitable but right.

---

[1] The new Commander-in-Chief, Far East.

[2] His actual words were: 'Australia looks to America, free from any pangs as to traditional links or kinship with the United Kingdom.'

25

Nor could it be denied that the whole structure of command in the Far East was gravely defective. Mr. Duff Cooper's report had drawn attention to the tangle of conflicting authorities which existed on the British side; and the series of conferences which had produced the A.D.A. and A.D.B. Agreements,[1] though they had imposed a certain conformity on British, Dutch and American planning, had also revealed serious gaps in the system of international liaison. To these problems was now added the further one of securing effective co-operation with China, whose main supply-route along the Burma Road was directly threatened by events in Malaya, and who was besides the only Allied Power capable, or reputedly capable, of an immediate counterstroke against Japan.

Such was the background against which General Marshall, on Christmas Day, brought forward a proposal which was to have far-reaching consequences, though not perhaps in precisely the field that he had intended. He remarked in the course of a discussion between the Chiefs of Staff that:

> 'He did not think any satisfactory results could be expected in the Far East unless there were complete unity of command over naval, land and air forces. Experience in the last war had shown the need for this and recent events brought it about under stress of circumstances in certain areas of United States strategic responsibility. He would personally be prepared to go to the limit to bring it about though he would never favour the placing of individual portions of United States forces under the Commander of a particular British Service. The national forces must be used as far as possible in homogeneous bodies under their own commanders, but there should be one supreme authority over everyone. Suitable limitations could be imposed to safeguard the interests of each nation.'

Little comment was made on this at the time; but on the following day President Roosevelt raised the question at a plenary session. He said that he was not satisfied that the best use was being made of available resources under the present system and inquired whether the Chiefs of Staff had examined the possibility of a unified command. Once more the response was meagre. Mr. Churchill said that, although he would willingly discuss the proposal with the President, his own feeling was against it. The distances involved in the Pacific were immense; each local commander had his instructions and knew his duty; and the main problem was the disposition of available reinforcements, which was a matter for governments rather than for a Commander-in-Chief. Admiral King, almost equally unenthusiastic, made certain reservations on behalf of the United States Navy. But General Marshall was not discouraged. He had already secured the

---

[1] See Vol. II, pp. 503–4.

support of the President and, what was equally important, of Mr. Harry Hopkins, whose mind was naturally attracted to simple and bold solutions of this type. With this help he did not despair of persuading both Admiral King and the Prime Minister.[1] The latter, indeed, was by no means fixed in his opposition. Although he was sceptical of the immediate military value of Marshall's plan, he had already recognized the need to come to some general agreement with the Americans about command—which almost inevitably meant some form of unified command—in the various theatres of war. As he explained to a staff-meeting that night:

'His mind was moving in the direction of trying to achieve an agreement with the Americans on the following lines:
(i) Germany is recognized to be the main enemy.
(ii) The general direction of operations in the Pacific theatre should be from Washington.
(iii) The general direction of operations in the Atlantic theatre should be from London.'

The acceptance of General Marshall's plan, despite its practical drawbacks, might prove to be a necessary step in this direction.

Nor were the Chiefs of Staff entirely without sympathy with the proposal. At a meeting on the following day Admiral Pound asked General Marshall for details of the naval aspects of his plan. It was precisely in this field that we had so far found the Americans most difficult. For technical and other reasons, liaison between Admiral Layton at Singapore and Admiral Hart at Manila had weakened since the outbreak of war; and the Americans' insistence on keeping an absolutely free hand over the disposal of their forces was making co-operation difficult. If the installation of a Supreme Commander would tie American resources to a fixed policy, which was not dependent on local exigencies and the temperament of local commander, then the plan was certainly worth accepting. But the draft directive which General Marshall produced did not entirely fulfil these hopes. Sir John Dill criticized it as too restrictive and as making it needlessly difficult for the Supreme Commander to exercise the personal control which was the sole purpose and function of his office. The C.A.S. added that the directive seemed unduly preoccupied with political questions, which were surely best settled by the Governments concerned either in London or in Washington. Nevertheless, it was clear that opinion on both sides, British and American, was now moving towards the idea of a unified command in the Far East, though many practical difficulties still needed to be cleared away.

---

[1] Sherwood, Vol. I, p. 470; Churchill, Vol. III, p. 597.

25*

That evening the Chiefs of Staff informed the Prime Minister that they were ready to accept General Marshall's plan in principle, subject to certain alterations in the present draft directive. They recommended that an American officer should be appointed, but were anxious to see safeguards inserted lest the United States should use the appointment to press for an unduly large allocation of Allied forces in the Far East. To the surprise and dismay of the Chiefs of Staff, the Prime Minister anounced that the Americans were urging that General Wavell should be offered the Supreme Command. To their objections the Prime Minister replied that he did not think the Americans were 'attempting to shift disaster onto our shoulders'. He was not anxious either to hand over responsibility for Singapore to the Americans, or to give the Australians any reason to say that the British had been unable to help them. He felt, however, that it would be sounder to confine the Supreme Command to land and air forces, forming a separate command for all naval forces under an American Admiral, who should be instructed to conform to General Wavell's plans. He did not see how the General could exercise command of the naval forces of more than one nation, unless they were brought together under a single Commander with whom he could deal.

At a further Staff Conference on 28th December the Prime Minister reported that he had come to an agreement on the Far Eastern Command, subject to the approval of the War Cabinet. He had put the arguments of the Chiefs of Staff to the President; but the latter had insisted that General Wavell was the only suitable appointment. The terms of the agreement were set out in the Prime Minister's telegram to the Lord Privy Seal:

'I have agreed with the President, subject to Cabinet approval, that we should accept his proposal most strongly endorsed by General Marshall.

(a) That unity of command shall be established in the south-western Pacific. Boundaries are not yet finally settled but presume they would include Malay Peninsula, including the Burmese Front, to the Philippines and southward to the necessary supply bases, principally Port Darwin, and supply lines in Northern Australia.

(b) That General Wavell should be appointed Commander-in-Chief, or if preferred Supreme Commander of all United States, British, British Empire and Dutch forces of the land, sea and air who may be assigned by the Governments concerned to that Theatre.

(c) General Wavell, whose Headquarters should in the first instance be established at Surabaya, would have an American officer as Deputy Commander-in-Chief. It seems probable that General Brett would be chosen.

(d) That the American, Australian and Dutch naval forces in the theatre should be placed under the command of an American Admiral, in accordance with the general principles set forth in paragraphs (a) and (b).

(e) It is intended that General Wavell should have a staff in the same sort of proportion as Foch's High Control Staff was to the great Staffs of the British and French armies in France. He would receive orders from an appropriate Joint Body who will be responsible to me as Minister of Defence and to the President of the United States, who is also Commander-in-Chief of all United States forces.

(f) The principal Commanders comprised in General Wavell's sphere will be Commander-in-Chief, Burma; Commander-in-Chief, Singapore and Malaya; Commander-in-Chief, Netherlands East Indies; Commander-in-Chief, Philippines and Commander-in-Chief of the Southern Communications via the South Pacific and North Australia.

(g) India, for whom an acting Commander-in-Chief will have to be appointed, and Australia, who will have their own Commander-in-Chief, will be outside General Wavell's sphere except as mentioned above, and are the two great bases through which men and material from Great Britain and the Middle East on the one hand and the United States on the other can be fed into the fighting zone.

(h) United States Navy will remain responsible for the whole of the Pacific Ocean east of the Philippines and Australasia, including the United States approaches of Australasia.

(i) A letter of instructions is being drafted for the Supreme Commander safeguarding the necessary residuary interests of the various governments involved and prescribing in major outline his task. This draft will reach you shortly.'

The War Cabinet's reply on the same day left the Prime Minister with a free hand but did not conceal a certain uneasiness on several points. Would not a unified command in one theatre tend to draw to itself resources from other theatres not so endowed? The Japanese theatre was a secondary one by comparison with the German and the principal need was strategic unity over all theatres. There was also the difficulty of associating naval forces with cut and dried geographic areas, the question of the inclusion of Burma, Australia and New Zealand in the new Command and finally the composition and function of the 'appropriate Joint Body'. Was it to be yet another storey in the pyramid of command and would not its interpolation impose the very delays upon action which a unified Command was intended to obviate?

It was with these points in mind that the British Chiefs of Staff raised the matter at the next meeting of the Combined Chiefs of Staff on 29th December. They took the view that the right course

372 THE WASHINGTON CONFERENCE (I)

was to use existing machinery rather than to interpose a new organization and suggested the Combined Chiefs of Staff as the standing body:

'1. It is assumed that the chief matters on which decisions would have to be given would be:

(a) the provision of reinforcements.

(b) a major change in policy.

(c) departure from the Supreme Commander's directive.

2. It is suggested that no special body should be set up because it would tend to clog the machine for the following reasons:

(a) It would be necessary to have Dutch, Australian and New Zealand representation on this body.

(b) Each representative in (a) would probably wish for time to consult his government before giving an opinion.

3. It is proposed therefore that existing machinery should be used in the following manner:

(a) The Supreme Commander would telegraph to the Chiefs of Staff Committee, both in London and in Washington his proposal, whatever it might be.

(b) The Chiefs of Staff Committee in London would immediately telegraph to the British Mission in Washington to say whether or not they would be telegraphing any opinions.

(c) On receipt of these opinions, the United States Chiefs of Staff and the Representatives in Washington of the British Chiefs of Staff would meet and consider the problem and would submit their recommendations to the President and by telegraph to the Prime Minister and Minister of Defence. The Prime Minister would then inform the President whether he was in agreement with their recommendations.

4. As the Dutch Government is in London, and as the principal representatives of the New Zealand and Australian Governments are also in London, it is proposed that the agreement of these Governments to any proposal should be obtained by the British Government and this would be included in the final telegram to Washington.

5. Agreement having been reached between London and Washington, the orders to the Supreme Commander would be despatched from Washington.'

This proposal encountered some opposition, first from Admiral King and later from Mr. Harry Hopkins, both of whom were anxious to include in the scheme a general advisory body, composed of military representatives from all the interested nations. But the practical disadvantages of such a plan were obvious and it did not survive discussion. A final version of the directive, which followed the British draft in all essentials and established the direct control of the Chiefs of Staff over the Supreme Commander, was approved by the President and the Prime Minister at the plenary session on 1st January.

But there were still the other partners in the alliance to be considered. The Australians had agreed to the establishment of a unified command on the assumption that they would be members of the 'appropriate Joint Body'; and the New Zealand Government, more courteously but no less firmly, pressed the same claim. For these reasons, the War Cabinet on 2nd January, while welcoming the proposed solution and the elimination of any intermediate or advisory body, suggested that Australia and New Zealand, instead of being brought in only at the final stage 'after questions have been considered, first in Washington and afterwards in the War Cabinet in London', should appoint representatives to sit with the British delegation in Washington, when matters affecting their countries were discussed. The Prime Minister replied that it was the intention that the Dominion representatives in London should be consulted at an early stage by the Chiefs of Staff and pointed out what confusion would arise if simultaneous representations were made both in London and in Washington. He added that it was in any case undesirable that members of the Commonwealth should argue between themselves in front of the American Chiefs of Staff.

Australia was, however, asking for more than representation in matters that concerned her own area; what she wanted was close and continuous association with the central direction of the war. The New Zealand Government, on the other hand, in a well reasoned telegram, merely asked for representation in matters affecting the defence of New Zealand. 'We have [the telegram ran] very little knowledge indeed of the intentions of the higher direction of the war, whatever be the authorities now responsible for it either in London or in Washington. Indeed so far as American intentions are concerned we have practically no knowledge at all. We feel that we must be informed. We feel that we must have an eye, an ear and a voice wherever decisions affecting New Zealand are to be made and we are by no means happy with the arrangements, so far as we know them, for the conduct of the war against Japan'. Protests were also made by the Netherlands Government who felt that their interests in the most important of their overseas possessions might well be disregarded or subordinated to those of their Allies. Nevertheless, when the Dutch Prime Minister proposed to visit Washington, President Roosevelt exerted himself to dissuade him. The reasons for this apparently brusque treatment are explained in a telegram from Brigadier Hollis to General Ismay:

'. . . Our co-operation with America is developing unexpectedly well and provided we have no early setbacks will be lasting and profitable.

(iii) They (the Americans) are not accustomed to process whereby views of two or three or more Governments have to be obtained and exchanges and adjustments made to meet them. They regard this as a time-wasting procedure but they have to study their public opinion which is a very potent factor but operates in different way to ours.

(v) Reason for trying to step down Dutch visit to Washington and reluctance to bring Dominions into joint collaboration here was that we are just holding our own with British-American discussions. Collaboration with third or more parties would at this stage cause confusion and we would slip back into chaos.'

Nevertheless it was clear, if only on practical grounds, that some provision would have to be made for those whom the new scheme excluded. The apprehensions of the Dutch were partly allayed by the explanations and apologies of the Prime Minister and the news that General Wavell was to establish his Headquarters in Java, where a number of Dutch officers would be attached directly to him. But this was scarcely sufficient in itself and did not meet the objections of either the Australian or the New Zealand Government. Accordingly, it was proposed to set up a further committee in London. It was to be known as the Far Eastern Council and would be composed, under the chairmanship of the Prime Minister, of the Lord Privy Seal, Mr. Duff Cooper and representatives from Australia, New Zealand and the Netherlands. In the nature of the case, such a committee could only be advisory in the broadest sense and would have no executive power; but it was hoped to provide it with certain facilities on the technical level by attaching liaison-officers, who would work in association with the Joint Planners.

CHAPTER XV

THE WASHINGTON CONFERENCE (II)

(i)

A.B.D.A.

THE DETAILS OF the directive to be sent to General Wavell continued to occupy the Conference for some time after the main outlines of the new Command had been agreed. Much of the discussion turned upon the question of boundaries. These were eventually settled as follows:

'The A.B.D.A. Area is bounded as follows:

On the North—By the boundary between India and Burma, thence eastward along the Chinese frontier and coastline to the latitude of 30° North, thence along the parallel of 30° North to the meridian of 140° east. [Note: Indo-China and Thailand are not included in this area.]

On the East—By the meridian of 140° East from 30° North to the equator, thence east to longitude 141° East, thence south to the boundary of Dutch New Guinea on the South coast, thence east along the southern New Guinea coast to the meridian of 143° East, thence south down this meridian to the coast of Australia.

On the South—By the Northern coast of Australia from the meridian of 143° East, westward to the meridian of 114° East, thence north-westward to latitude 15° south, longitude 93° East.

On the West—By the meridian of 92° East.

Before we consider the strategic significance of these boundaries, attention must be drawn to two points which were the subject of considerable dispute. First, against the inclinations of the British Chiefs of Staff and of General Wavell himself, the area did include Burma; secondly, it did not include any part of Australia or New Zealand with the exception of Port Darwin, which was later added at General Wavell's request. The arguments for excluding Burma were many and obvious. The country had only recently been transferred back to the Indian from the Far Eastern command; and a further change at such a critical moment was technically undesirable. Moreover, India was the natural main base for the support of operations in Burma, just as Burma was the natural forward zone for the defence of India's eastern frontier. Strategically the two countries belonged together; and it seemed madness to separate them for the benefit of a new and artificially created command. But against this there were important arguments, as much diplomatic as military, which derived from the special position of China.

As soon as the principle of the A.B.D.A. Command had been agreed, President Roosevelt had dispatched the following telegram to Marshal Chiang Kai-shek:

'1. In order to ensure immediate co-ordination and co-operation in our common effort against the enemy, there is being established a supreme commander for all British, Dutch and American forces in the South-West Pacific theatre.

2. The advisability of a similar command of activities of the Associated Powers in the Chinese theatre appears evident. This theatre we suggest should include such portions of Thailand and Indo-China as may become accessible to troops of the Associated Powers. In agreement with the representatives of the British and Dutch Governments, I desire to suggest that you should undertake to exercise such command over all forces of the Associated Powers which are now, or may in the future be operating in the Chinese theatre.

3. It is our thought that, in order to make such command effective, a joint planning staff should at once be organized consisting of representatives of the British, Dutch, American and Chinese Governments. If you consider it practicable, and Russia agrees, a Russian representative might be included. This staff should function under your supreme command.

4. The Commander of the South-West Pacific theatre and the Commander of the British forces in India would be directed to maintain the closest liaison with your headquarters and a mutual exchange of liaison-officers between the three headquarters would be desirable.

5. Such arrangements would enable your counsel and influence to be given effect in the formulation of the general strategy for the conduct of the war in all theatres. Your views in this matter will be greatly appreciated by me.'

No doubt the President and his advisers exaggerated the purely military results which were likely to follow from these arrangements. It was a common error of American policy, both then and later, to over-estimate the war-potential of Chiang Kai-shek's China. Nevertheless, to keep China's army in the field at all and to secure some co-ordination between her policy and that of the other Allies was worth a considerable effort in itself and implied some such system as the President outlined. But this bore directly on the position of Burma. Marshal Chiang Kai-shek would not have been likely to favour the new system of command in the Far East if it had excluded the Burma Road, by then almost the only route by which any quantity of supplies could reach him from the outside world. He had already protested that Lend-Lease material destined for China had been

diverted to British use at Rangoon and that his offer of Chinese reinforcements had been (or so he alleged) brusquely rejected by General
Wavell. To pacify him on both these points Allied operational
control of the area seemed indispensable. Moreover, his offer of
troops, whether or not it was practicable or even seriously intended,
raised another important point. The President's telegram had offered
him operational control in Thailand and Indo-China, the area in
which it was then hoped that a Chinese counter-stroke might
develop. This was logical enough; but, if Burma were excluded
from the A.B.D.A. Command, the Marshal, following the same line
of argument, might well claim it as part of the Chinese theatre, or at
least as an area in which his troops could operate independently.

For these reasons the Prime Minister and the Chiefs of Staff were
finally constrained to agree to Burma's inclusion in the new command. But there still remained the question of the Burma Road. In a
memorandum of 10th January, General Marshall proposed that this
should be taken entirely under American control and that the
United States should also appoint an officer to command any
American or Chinese air forces which might be operating in Burma
for the protection of the supply-route.[1] These exceptional demands
were resisted on the British side, partly because they involved a
divided command in the country and partly because they would
have left British troops dependent, or potentially dependent, on
American-controlled communications. In the end a compromise was
reached, which was not fully satisfactory to either party. It was
agreed that the United States should appoint an officer to act both as
President Roosevelt's personal representative with Marshal Chiang
Kai-shek and as commander of American forces in China. He
would also control all United States' aid to China and for this purpose would exercise a general supervision over the Burma Road. He
was, however, to act through the British authorities in respect of
those sections of the Road which ran through British territory.
Similarly, if any forces under his command, or put at his disposal by
the Chinese Government, were to operate in Burma, he would come
(for this purpose only) under the control of General Wavell. It was at
best an unhandy arrangement and one which later gave rise to many
difficulties; but it may be said to have provided a temporary and
theoretical solution to an admittedly difficult problem.

The second question—that of the southern and eastern boundaries
of the command—raised two separate issues. The Governments of
Australia and New Zealand expressed the fear, the former with
particular vehemence, that Japan might make a direct attack either

---

[1] The reference here was to General Chennault's 'International Air Force', a volunteer
organization which had been operating in support of China. On the outbreak of war with
Japan it was incorporated into the regular forces of the United States.

on one or other of the Dominions or on their island dependencies to the north-east. They therefore asked that the whole of this area should be brought within General Wavell's command. They also drew attention to the fact that a dangerous gap existed in the proposed arrangement of naval commands. Below the equator the Pacific Theatre extended only as far as 180° East, whereas the eastern boundary of the A.B.D.A. Command had been fixed at 141° East. This left the whole area of the Coral and Tasman Seas as a kind of no-man's land, in which Australian and New Zealand naval forces would have to act alone and unsupported. The first of these points was disposed of comparatively easily; and the opinion of the Joint Planning Staff seems to have been accepted without question:

'The inclusion of the whole of Australia, the Australian islands and New Zealand, and presumably Fiji, would enormously enlarge General Wavell's area and place too great a burden on him, particularly in the early stages, after his assumption of command. He would become responsible ultimately for the land defence of both Australia and New Zealand, even if he delegated responsibility to the local commanders in those areas.

It is difficult to see how he would be able to effectively influence land operations in the southern part of Australia or New Zealand. He is unlikely to be able to send any troops from the northern part of his area to south-east Australia or New Zealand. If he wished to reverse the process and draw troops out of Australia or New Zealand, he is likely to run into very difficult political issues. The inclusion of the land territories of the two sovereign countries of Australia and New Zealand would lead to demands on their part for full permanent representation in the control machinery, and this would be difficult to resist. The granting of these demands would complicate the machinery considerably.'

The second point was rather more complex. To some extent the opinions, especially of the Australian Government, seem to have rested on a misapprehension. As Admiral Pound pointed out, they appeared to think:

'that all available naval forces were going to be collected together and put into the A.B.D.A. area to make some kind of naval concentration, leaving everything outside the area unguarded. This was, of course, quite untrue. All that had happened was that the forces actually in that area were being put under the command of one Admiral. The American Navy would not only be bound to escort their convoys right to Australia, but would frequently have to pass a covering force down into the waters east of the mainland.'

But this was only a partial answer to the problem. It was also true, as the Australian representative, Mr. Casey, pointed out, that the

Americans had always been anxious to limit their naval commitments in the Pacific in the area south of the equator. The argument went back to the previous April, when they had refused either to enlarge what was then the Far East theatre or to agree to any arrangement by which their ships might be used for convoy protection in the Anzac or Indian Ocean areas. At that time their refusal had been offset to some extent by the expectation that the Pacific Fleet would pass immediately to the offensive at the outbreak of war. A threat of this kind in the central Pacific would have drawn the focus of naval conflict away from the south and the south-east, and thus have offered some general protection to these areas. But now the position was reversed. The Pacific Fleet was temporarily incapable of offensive action; and the Japanese advance was creeping nearer and nearer to the Anzac area. It was no wonder that Australia and New Zealand should feel dangerously exposed.

This time, however, the Americans were less intransigent. The principle of a single naval command in the south-west Pacific, which had previously been one of the main stumbling-blocks, had now been conceded by the creation of A.B.D.A. The circumstances of the case required that the United States should escort convoys across the whole width of the Pacific to Australia; and Admiral Pound had therefore relatively little difficulty in persuading Admiral King to accept formal responsibility for the Anzac area. This meant withdrawing certain units—a heavy cruiser[1] and two destroyers— from what remained of the Pacific Fleet; but in the circumstances the sacrifice was inevitable. At the same time General Marshall agreed that the U.S. Army should participate in the defence of the islands by providing forces for New Caledonia, a French possession which otherwise fell within the Australian strategic sphere, and Fiji, which was the responsibility of New Zealand.

These boundary questions were not in themselves of the first importance. If they have been dealt with at some length here, it is because they illustrate a prime characteristic of the A.B.D.A. Command—namely, its artificiality. The command had not been created to facilitate the carrying out of a strategic plan, but simply in the hope that such a plan would be evolved on the spot, once unified control had been achieved. It was, in fact, an illustration of the belief, widely held in America, that most military problems can be solved by appointing a capable theatre-commander with full powers. On this basis A.B.D.A. Command made sense; on any other it was nonsense and fully justified General Wavell's reported comment, when informed of his appointment, that he 'had heard of men being asked to hold the baby, but this was twins'. Indeed, the comparison

---

[1] The U.S.S. *Chicago*, which had been at sea at the time of Pearl Harbor. She joined the two Australian cruisers *Australia* and *Canberra* and the light cruiser *Hobart*.

was more exact than he may have intended, for the main and insoluble problem of the A.B.D.A. area was that it contained within itself the elements of two distinct and separate commands. To see this, it is only necessary to examine the strategic objects set out in General Wavell's directive:

'The basic strategic concept of the A.B.D.A. Governments for the conduct of the war in your Area is not only in the immediate future to maintain as many key-positions as possible, but to take the offensive at the earliest opportunity, and ultimately to conduct an all-out offensive against Japan. The first essential is to gain general air superiority at the earliest possible moment through the employment of concentrated air-power. The piecemeal employment of air forces should be minimized. Your operations should be so conducted as to further preparations for the offensive. The general strategic policy will therefore be:

(a) To hold the Malay Barrier, defined as the line Malay Peninsula, Sumatra, Java, North Australia, as the basic defensive position of the A.B.D.A. area, and to operate sea, land and air forces in as great depth as possible forward of the Barrier in order to oppose the Japanese advance southward.

(b) To hold Burma and Australia as essential supporting positions for the Area, and Burma as essential to the support of China and to the defence of India.

(c) To re-establish communication through the Dutch East Indies with Luzon and to support the Philippines Garrison.

(d) To maintain essential communications within the Area.'

Let us consider first the repeated use of the expression 'Malay Barrier'. The uninitiated, reading this phrase, might be pardoned for supposing that the Dutch East Indies formed a defensive position, a line of rocky outposts, which nature had interposed between the Japanese and their final objective. Nothing could have been less true: the Dutch East Indies were themselves the objective. It was precisely in order to obtain control of these rich and indefensible islands that the Japanese had launched their two converging attacks, one on Malaya, the other on the Philippines. To speak of the Dutch East Indies as being or forming part of a barrier 'to oppose the Japanese southward advance' was to confuse the outside with the inside, the shell with the kernel. A more realistic statement of the case would have been to say that there were two barriers—Singapore on one side and Manila on the other—which jointly protected the rich prize lying between them. But these two outposts, both already under imminent threat when A.B.D.A. Command was created, lay 1,400 miles apart. There was no conceivable way in which reinforcements could be shared between them or the defence of one be made to contribute to the defence of the other. Still less was there any way in which a command with its headquarters in Java could use 'concentrated air-power' to influence events in two separate actions, each more than 1,000 miles away. Yet once either Singapore or Manila had fallen, nothing except overwhelming naval superiority, which the Allies did not then possess, could prevent the Japanese from making important lodgements in the virtually unprotected area in between.

Whatever happened, A.B.D.A. Command was bound to dissolve, as it finally did, into two distinct theatres of war. If (to take the best case first) both Singapore and Manila held, and the Allies passed to the offensive in accordance with the first paragraph of the directive, two separate axes of advance would impose themselves. One, ultimately based on India, would follow the line Burma-Malaya-Indo-China; the other, ultimately based on Australia, the line Celebes-Borneo-Philippines. Alternatively, if one of these two bases fell, operations within the command would no longer form a connected whole. The defence of Burma, if Singapore fell, would become a separate problem from the defence of Sumatra; and the defence of the Celebes and New Guinea, if the Philippines fell, a separate problem from either. Or again, if both bases fell, so that the Japanese were able to carry out the pincer movement at which they were aiming, the position in the centre would become untenable; and the headquarters of the Command would have to draw back towards one or other of its natural bases—either towards India in one direction or towards Australia in the other. In short, the Command as constituted had no natural strategic unity. It was an immense area, far too large for mutually supporting operations to be possible, and served by two opposing lines of communication and supply, one from the east, the other from the west. With or without the action of the enemy, it was bound sooner or later to split into two.

(ii)

The Combined Chiefs of Staff

It was for reasons such as these that the new C.I.G.S., Sir Alan Brooke, privately dismissed the whole A.B.D.A. plan as 'wild and half-baked'. He included in this condemnation not only the command itself, but also the arrangements for international control in Washington. He complained in his diary that they catered only 'for one area of action, namely the western Pacific, one enemy Japan, and no central control'.[1] Nor was this only a hasty or impromptu

---

[1] Arthur Bryant, *The Turn of the Tide* (1957), p. 295.

judgement. At the end of February, when A.B.D.A. finally collapsed under the pressure of the Japanese advance, the C.I.G.S. noted again:

'It is now quite clear that we can at last dissolve the A.B.D.A. organization and run the war on a rational basis. So far there is very little that was settled in Washington that is surviving the test of time. Burma has gone back to India Command, A.B.D.A. and Anzac become one, Pacific Council goes west and, for the matter of that, so does the Combined Chiefs of Staff. And thank God for it! We shall now run the war with two main spheres of interest, the Americans running the Pacific up to Asia including Australia and New Zealand, and the British running the opposite way round the globe including the Middle East, India, Burma and Indian Ocean.'[1]

It will be noticed that the idea expressed in the last sentence of dividing the world into two spheres of strategic influence, British and American, was the one which the Prime Minister had been considering at the moment when negotiations over the A.B.D.A. Command began. There was obviously much to be said for it. It was simple and logical and corresponded more or less with the facts of the case. But, as Mr. Churchill perceived more quickly than the C.I.G.S., it would not do as it stood. Although it might be true in practice that British influence would tend to predominate in Europe and the Middle East and American influence in the Pacific, either party would certainly wish to participate directly in the strategic control of both theatres. The agreed policy of tackling Germany first made it inevitable that large American forces—to say nothing of American munitions and supplies—would be employed in Europe; and in the Far East, whatever the ultimate distribution of forces, we had important political and territorial interests, which we were bound to protect. It followed that no division into spheres of influence was possible, or could be accepted, unless some central body were also brought into being, through which both Allies could share in the day-to-day direction of the war in each theatre. What was needed, in short, was the 'appropriate Joint Body' specified in the original A.B.D.A. proposals; and it was in order to secure this, the one essential point, that Mr. Churchill had accepted the plan, despite serious misgivings about its military value.

The appropriate Joint Body finally designated, as we have seen, was the Combined Chiefs of Staff; that is to say, a standing committee composed of the U.S. and British Chiefs of Staff sitting together. From our point of view, one of the weaknesses, or at least inconveniences, of this system was that, since the committee sat in Wash-

---

[1] Bryant, pp. 315–6.

ington, the British Chiefs of Staff were normally present only by deputy. But this was inevitable. Washington was the natural place from which to direct the affairs of the A.B.D.A. area, the point of origin of the whole system; and, in more general terms, the choice reflected the growing importance of America in the Allied war-effort. But there was also another reason. 'We believe,' wrote the Joint Staff Mission, 'that this co-ordination can only take place in Washington, as we consider it unlikely that the U.S. Chiefs of Staff would delegate sufficient responsibility to their representatives in London.' This was certainly true and probably decisive in itself.

This point once settled, the proposed organization was admirably simple. The U.S. Chiefs of Staff undertook to meet members of the Joint Staff Mission, of which Sir John Dill now assumed the leadership, at weekly intervals, or more often if necessary. A common office was provided, together with a combined secretariat and a small planning staff. Beyond that there was no attempt at integration. Both sides continued to make use of, and to act through, their ordinary national staffs and agencies; and in general it was only during the periods of international conferences, when the Chiefs of Staff were sitting together in person, that the combined planning staff came into its own. The functions of the new body were officially defined as follows:

> 'The Combined Chiefs of Staff shall develop and submit recommendations as follows:
> (a) for the A.B.D.A. area specifically, as set forth in the directive . . . dated 5th January, 1942;
> (b) for other areas in which the United Nations may decide to act in concert, along the same general lines as in (a) above, modified as necessary to meet the particular circumstances.
> The Combined Chiefs of Staff shall:
> (a) determine and recommend the broad programme of requirements based on strategic policy;
> (b) submit general directives as to the policy governing the distribution of available weapons of war;
> (c) settle the broad lines of priority of overseas movements.'

Thus was born—and it was easily the most important outcome of the Washington Conference—the organization, which Sir Alan Brooke was later to recognize as 'the most efficient that had ever been evolved for co-ordinating and correlating the war strategy and effort of the Allies.'[1] Before we examine this second judgement, so strangely different from the first, something should be said of one important function, which the Combined Chiefs of Staff performed unseen, merely by the fact of their existence. They provided a meeting place between two different chains of professional responsibility;

---

[1] Bryant, p. 316.

an indispensable link between the British system and the American. It was a neat solution to a vexatious problem, which introduces itself into all attempts to achieve unity of command in time of war.

Each Government concerned is necessarily responsible to its own people for the use to which the nation's armed forces are put and for the success or failure of their operations. This responsibility cannot be evaded; and it follows that no Government can place its forces without reserve under a foreign Commander-in-Chief, whose actions it cannot control. It is always necessary to insert an escape-clause into the instructions of the national commander, which will allow him to disavow his superior's orders and appeal directly to his own Government. We have seen in an earlier chapter that this problem could give rise to serious difficulties even within the close circle of the Commonwealth, and in circumstances in which the ultimate primacy of one of the two Governments concerned was not in dispute. Between two major powers, such as Great Britain and the United States, who were making a roughly equal contribution to the war, the problem would have been seen in its most acute form. The Combined Chiefs of Staff system by-passed the whole difficulty. British troops serving under an American Supreme Commander did not escape from national control, since the Commander derived his authority from, and reported to, a joint body of which the British Chiefs of Staff were members. They in turn were responsible to the Prime Minister, in his capacity as Minister of Defence, and through him to the Cabinet and Parliament. Similarly, American troops serving under a British commander were still within the control of the U.S. Chiefs of Staff and through them of the President and Congress. The chain of responsibility thus remained intact and the necessary safeguards introduced themselves automatically.

With this preamble we can return to the even more important question of strategic control. It should be noted first that, in Sir Alan Brooke's words, the Combined Chiefs of Staff were the 'co-ordinators and correlators' not the originators of strategy. Their primary function, as the directive quoted above shows, was to elaborate in detail and to oversee the execution of a strategy *already agreed* by the Governments concerned. In certain circumstances—as, for example, during the early part of the First World War, when military opinion was dominant—this qualification might have been little more than a constitutional fiction; but that was not so in the present case. Both the President and the Prime Minister had strong views of their own on strategy; and the final control remained firmly in their hands. They were not the men to defer to professional opinion merely because it was professional; nor were the Chiefs of Staff tempted on their side to step outside the advisory role, which was properly theirs.

The setting up of the Combined Chiefs of Staff was thus only part

of a larger system of control. We may regard the periodic Conferences, at which Mr. Churchill and Mr. Roosevelt were sometimes
joined by the heads of other states, as the formal sessions of a loosely-
organized Allied War Council, which met for the purpose of deciding
grand strategy. In one sense it is even true to say that this Council
was in permanent session. Between its formal meetings, which took
place every five or six months, an elaborate system of personal communications, in which Mr. Churchill played a leading part,[1] enabled
all the partners in the alliance—including those who did not normally
attend the meetings—to be regularly informed and consulted. The
presence of a continuous element of decision and control at the
highest political level was thus ensured, in a degree which students of
earlier wars may sometimes find remarkable.

Within this framework the Combined Chiefs of Staff had two tasks
to perform. The first was purely advisory; the second, which increased in importance in the later stages of the war, when the main
strategic decisions had already been taken, was largely executive.
During the periods when international conferences were sitting, the
Combined Chiefs of Staff were able to meet in person. They reviewed
the war situation in the light of the continuous discussions which had
already taken place by deputy, and were usually able to make an
agreed recommendation to the President and the Prime Minister.
These proposals were then discussed at plenary sessions of the conference, at which the Chiefs of Staff were also present as advisers to
the heads of their respective Governments. It was at these meetings,
or at further private discussions between the two statesmen, that
the final decisions were taken. When all was agreed, the necessary
orders to field commanders were issued through the Combined
Chiefs of Staff. This was their second task and one which continued
and developed during the periods between the conferences. The
Combined Chiefs of Staff then acted as a kind of standing committee
for military affairs, which was able to keep the whole course of the
war under review, to transmit the necessary orders and to make day
to day adjustments and recommendations within the agreed strategy.
Thus, in Mr. Churchill's words, 'there was never a failure to reach
effective agreement for action, or to send clear instructions to commanders in every theatre. Every executive officer knew that the
orders he received bore with them the combined conceptions and
expert authority of both Governments.'[2]

We have only to look back at the immediate past to see by contrast how smoothly the system worked. In the First World War, for

---

[1] It may be noted as an example that, during the first eighteen months of his administration, 274 personal telegrams went to the Prime Ministers of the four Dominions—an
average of about one every ten days to each of them.

[2] Churchill, Vol. III, p. 609.

example, a Supreme Allied War Council with a permanent staff and secretariat only came into existence in the winter of 1917 under the shock of the Italian defeat at Caporetto. Its members included the Prime Minister and one other Minister from each of the major allies; but even with this weight of authority behind it, it proved almost wholly ineffective as an instrument of strategic control. 'Its principal usefulness,' says one historian, 'lay in the co-ordination of Allied transport of munitions and supplies. . . .'[1] Largely for this reason, it was not until the end of the following March, after a further series of disasters, that approximate unity of command was achieved on the Western Front. But Marshal Foch, the titular Generalissimo, was in fact little more than a co-ordinator. His instructions laid down that 'full tactical freedom should be left to the commanders of the national armies, and that each should have a right of appeal to his own Government if he considered that the orders given him endangered the security of his army'.[2] Within these narrow limits Marshal Foch had to work as best he could, assisted only by a small personal staff.

It is instructive to compare these limited and tardy arrangements, effective in only one theatre of war, with the rapid establishment and smooth functioning of a whole series of Allied commands between 1942 and 1945. But it would be a mistake to suppose that the Combined Chiefs of Staff system was one which could be applied, like an algebraical formula, to any given set of circumstances. No less than the cumbrous and imperfect system of 1914–18, it was a product of the times; and certain special conditions were required to make it work. The nature of the first is implicit in what has been said already. Without a firm political direction, which also implied a wide measure of agreement as to aims and methods between the two Governments concerned, the system would have been ineffective. It was, moreover, a system which catered for only two partners; and it was desirable, if not actually essential, that they should speak the same language and share, at least to some extent, a common tradition of thought and action. If the Combined Chiefs of Staff had become a large multi-lingual committee, dependent on interpreters and reflecting widely different habits of mind, its whole efficiency would have been destroyed. Instead of being a compact and unobtrusive instrument of action, it would inevitably have become a forum for debate and a focal point for national and professional rivalries. Lastly, we may notice that the system could only operate smoothly, so long as the two Powers concerned were making an approximately equal contribution to the war. With one or the other markedly predominant the delicate balance of the mechanism would have been

---

[1] C. R. M. F. Crutwell (1934), *A History of the Great War*, p. 500.

[2] Crutwell, p. 510 (Note).

upset; and the Combined Chiefs of Staff would have tended to become, not a free association of professional experts capable of expressing a collective opinion, but a kind of *Parlement* for registering the decisions of the major Power. Signs of such an imbalance were in fact visible in the closing stages of the war, when the strength of the United States was still growing, while that of Great Britain had passed its peak; but by then the machine was working smoothly and had acquired sufficient impetus to carry it forward until the final defeat of the enemy.

Nevertheless, we must say that the system came into being at an exceptionally favourable moment. At the beginning of 1942 Great Britain and the United States stood on an almost exact equality. It was already clear that America's manpower and productive capacity must in the end make her the predominant partner in the alliance; but it would be at least eighteen months or two years before her main strength could be deployed; and meanwhile the greater experience and more cohesive organization of Great Britain corrected the balance. Moreover, a certain grouping, very convenient in the circumstances, had already taken place among the other Allied nations. The four Dominions and the European governments in exile were accustomed to a system by which the major decisions of the war were taken in London on the initiative of the British Government; and it did not seem unnatural that Great Britain should also represent them in their dealings with the United States. On the other hand, America had long enjoyed close relations with China and (so far as they were concerned) the South American republics, who were thus drawn naturally into her orbit. The remaining partner in the alliance, Soviet Russia, was fighting a lonely and self-centred war on a distant front, in which she neither invited nor allowed a close collaboration with anyone. The way was thus open for an intimate association between the two Anglo-Saxon powers on terms which could only be shared indirectly with others. But this result, a natural product of the conditions of 1942, might not have been so easily achieved at a later date.

Lastly, it is proper to pay tribute to the character of the officers chiefly concerned. The Combined Chiefs of Staff Committee could only work effectively so long as all its members were at the same time ready collaborators with each other and faithful servants of their own Governments. The presence of even one man who followed, however moderately, the path of personal ambition, would have thrown the whole machine out of gear. In this respect a particular responsibility rested on Sir John Dill. It was essential—and never more so than during the early months of the alliance—that the British Chiefs of Staff should be represented in Washington by a man in whom they had absolute confidence and who was able to live in

26

equal sympathy with his American colleagues. To preserve this exact balance, neither pressing the British point of view so strongly as to hamper his relations with the Americans, nor absorbing theirs so completely as to become an inadequate spokesman for his own principals, was a task of the greatest difficulty. Before his early death in November 1944, Sir John Dill had performed a service for his country as great, perhaps, as that of any other soldier of his generation.

(iii)
American Production

We must now turn to the economic aspects of the Conference, which were no less important than the military. Once more there were two interlocking problems, the immediate and the long-term. The former, about which there was still much uncertainty at the time when Mr. Churchill and his party left England, concerned the distribution of American supplies over the next few months. On the day of Pearl Harbor the United States had halted all deliveries of war material to Lend-Lease countries, not excluding what was already on the dockside or even actually loaded. It is true that this embargo—justified perhaps by the suddenness and severity of the crisis—had not lasted long in its extreme form. Within a few days normal deliveries had been resumed except in certain categories such as small-arms ammunition, aircraft and aircraft engines. Our net losses had not been very great.[1] Nevertheless, the fact that this abrupt decision had been taken without any consultation whatever was in itself disturbing.

We were ready to agree that in the new circumstances some adjustment was necessary. Now that America was herself a belligerent, a far larger proportion of her output would be claimed by her own armed forces; and the agreements reached at the London Conference in September, which had regulated the supply of American material up to July 1942, would have to be revised accordingly. But there were certain classes of material to which we could not forego our claim without seriously impairing our own efficiency. Even here we might have to accept some reduction; but it was essential that such decisions should be taken jointly and in the light of an agreed Allied strategy.

During the course of the outward voyage Lord Beaverbrook cir-

---

[1] Duncan Hall and C. C. Wrigley, *Studies in Overseas Supplies* (1956), p. 171.

culated a paper on this aspect of the problem. It opened with a characteristically abrupt metaphor—'The United States,' he wrote, 'must be persuaded to believe that British industry is a three-legged stool . . . While we can balance on three legs, we cannot do so on two.' The legs or props in question were: first, the industrial plant of the United Kingdom; secondly, the raw materials of the Commonwealth; and thirdly, the share of American production (and in certain cases of American raw materials) which had so far enabled us to bridge the gap between our own output and our total requirements. Our immediate needs under this third heading were then set out by Lord Beaverbrook in four attached lists, covering the demands of (1) the War Office, (2) the Admiralty, (3) the Ministry of Supply and the Ministry of Aircraft Production acting together, and (4) the Ministries of Food, Shipping and Petroleum, together with a number of miscellaneous items. A fifth list, showing the requirements of the Air Ministry, was presented separately. Although every effort had been made to keep these lists to the bare minimum and to throw the emphasis on to raw materials and semi-manufactured goods rather than completed weapons of war, the result was still formidably comprehensive. It included tanks and tank components, tank transporters, heavy trucks; tank and anti-tank ammunition, 37-mm. guns for British built armoured cars, and most types of small-arms ammunition—all urgently needed for current operations in the Middle East; six auxiliary aircraft-carriers, Oerlikon guns and ammunition, torpedoes and torpedo components, small-boat engines; 6,000 Merlin aircraft engines and spares for other engines already delivered, plywoods and veneers used in aircraft production, aircraft and engine forgings; a wide range of machine-tools; 4 million tons of finished steel, 250,000 tons of alloy steel and drop-forgings, nickel alloys and various chemicals; 60,000 tons of copper and 99,000 of zinc; an increase in certain food imports so as to release agricultural labour for the Army; and an almost indefinite demand for newly built merchant shipping. Finally, there were some 8,000 aircraft, due to us under the London agreements during the period between September 1941 and June 1942, of which we still hoped to receive— and most urgently required—the largest possible number.

With certain exceptions such as shipping and aircraft, where a longer period was applicable, Lord Beaverbrook's lists were only intended to cover the immediate future; and he added a warning that supplementary lists would have to be presented in three months' time. His policy, in short, was to acknowledge the existence of a crisis by accepting a temporary reduction in American supplies with a good grace, but to make it clear at the same time that the reduction could only be temporary. After a very brief delay the flow would have to be resumed on a bigger scale. This implied a large and rapid increase in

American production—indeed, a revolution; and it was here that the immediate problem merged into the long-term.

It will be remembered that, throughout 1941, there had been steady pressure from statesmen and officials on both sides of the Atlantic for the full mobilization of American industry. This campaign had found its chief expression in the concept of a Victory Programme; that is to say, a combined programme of Anglo-American production, which should aim to provide all the principal weapons of war required to carry out an agreed strategy. But though the principle of such a programme was now widely accepted, the practical results had so far been disappointing. A fairly complete survey of present and future British needs, showing the extent to which they could be met from our own production, had been circulated at the London Conference in September. But no equivalent figures had then been available from the American side, either for her own needs or for those of the other Lend-Lease countries whom she was supporting. Little progress had therefore been made in the task of producing a combined programme. The Sub-Committee concerned had had to content itself with recommending that, when these additional figures were known, the resultant grand totals should be referred to the production authorities in the United States, who should be asked to express an opinion on their feasibility. The Committee had added that:

> 'the modifications necessary to relate the total programme to the realities of United States and British Empire industrial production . . . should be discussed between the United States and British Staffs in Washington on a strategical basis.'[1]

These further discussions had not in fact taken place, no doubt because American policy in the months before Pearl Harbor had been too uncertain to allow of such concrete planning. By December, however, the Office of Production Management had produced its own tentative plan for the years 1942 and 1943. This was based on a combination of the British survey of September, some figures for Russian requirements obtained at the Supply Conference in Moscow, and certain estimates—in some cases merely conjectural[2]—of America's own needs. It was not a Victory Programme in the original sense of that term, since it was not a product of joint discussion and lacked a strategic basis; but it marked a clear advance on previous plans both in scope and coherence. The American production experts estimated that, in order to carry it out, it would be

---

[1] Duncan Hall, p. 333.

[2] Two of the departments concerned, the Navy Department and the Maritime Commission, had refused to supply the O.P.M. with any figures at all, on the ground that they could not tell what their requirements would be, until the country was actually at war.

necessary to double the country's war production in the coming year; but they did not believe that such an expansion would be possible, unless the United States were actually at war. The officials of the British Supply Council, on the other hand, notably M. Jean Monnet, criticized the programme in an opposite sense, holding that it fell short by at least 50 per cent both of what was possible and what was necessary. In support of their argument they were able to point to the fact that, in December 1941, war production was only absorbing some 15 per cent of America's total industrial capacity.[1]

Such was the position at the time of Pearl Harbor. But this event, though it swept away the barrier of American neutrality, which had so far obstructed all production plans, could not revolutionize the situation overnight. On the contrary, it brought with it, as we have seen, a host of immediate problems in the field of supply, which necessarily took precedence over plans for the future. It was, therefore, on the earlier O.P.M. programme, only slightly modified, that President Roosevelt proposed to base the message to Congress, asking for new production targets, to which he had referred at the first session of the Conference. He had then invited Lord Beaverbrook's advice; what response he received is best told in the words of the economic historian:

'In a letter to the President of 27th December, and in a series of later meetings on supply, presided over by the President or the Vice-President, Lord Beaverbrook pressed the case for bringing American production up to the levels of Great Britain and Canada. He took as basis Monnet's document of 10th December. Its conclusion was that "United States production schedules at present indicated in 1942 should be capable of at least a fifty per cent increase". Lord Beaverbrook suggested that the United States should produce 45,000 tanks, 17,700 anti-tank guns, 24,000 fighter planes, as well as double their output of anti-aircraft guns. At a meeting on 29th December with the United States production chiefs, Mr. Donald Nelson, who was present, records that the Minister of Supply emphasized "over and over again the fact that we should set our sights high in planning for production of the necessary war *matériels*". Lord Beaverbrook had discussed the air programme with General Arnold and Mr. Lovett on the 27th. He presented the case made out on the British side (in a Note presented by the British Air Commission) for an "immense step up" in the scope of the joint air programme. If America built aircraft on the British scale, the Note argued, this would mean an output of combat aircraft of 6,300 a month. The heavy bomber target should be raised from 1,000 a month at the end of 1942 to 2,300 a month at the end of 1943. Both these targets were accepted by Hopkins in a talk with the head of the

---

[1] Duncan Hall, pp. 335 and 339.

British Air Commission on New Year's Day. The President was convinced and issued the necessary directions to the Departments. The Prime Minister cabled the results to London on 4th January with the comment "Max has been magnificent and Hopkins a godsend". In the *Grand Alliance*, writing of the President's production goals seven years later, he could record the verdict of history: "These remarkable figures were achieved or surpassed by the end of 1943." They were reached or passed for aircraft, doubled for ships, doubled or tripled for some calibres of guns; if for tanks they were not reached, they could have been if it had been necessary."[1]

We may regard Lord Beaverbrook's intervention as the climax of the campaign for increased production which had been waged throughout 1941; and the results were indeed remarkable. In his telegram to the War Cabinet Mr. Churchill set out the earlier American targets for some of the principal weapons of war side by side with the new targets, which President Roosevelt announced to Congress on 6th January:

War Material	Original U.S. Target for 1942	Victory Programme	
		for 1942	for 1943
Merchant shipping in deadweight tons	—	8,000,000	10,000,000
Operational aircraft	31,250	45,000	100,000
Tanks	29,550	45,000	75,000
Anti-aircraft guns	8,900	20,000	35,000
Anti-tank guns	11,700	14,900	Not fixed
Ground and Tank machine-guns	238,000	500,000	Not fixed

It will be clear from these figures that the main point had been gained. American war-production had at last been freed from its self-imposed restraints and launched on a course of expansion appropriate to the scale of events and the broad requirements of Allied strategy. In certain fields—and those not the least important—the effect of this sudden release of energy was immediate. The production of small-arms ammunition, for example, rose so steeply that Great Britain actually received more in the first five months of 1942 than she had been allotted under the September agreements. The same was true of other critical items on Lord Beaverbrook's emergency lists; increased production mitigated, or even actually averted, the anticipated short-term crisis. Though certain inevitable deficiencies remained, on balance we may be said to have gained rather than

---

[1] Duncan Hall, p. 342.

lost in the months immediately following Pearl Harbor. Such was the general picture; but there was one notable exception. American aircraft production, plagued by the same teething-troubles as had previously upset British programmes, shows no striking increase and even lagged slightly behind the September estimates. Moreover, it was precisely in this field that America's own immediate requirements were highest, since her Air Force expanded more rapidly than her Army. The result was a fall of almost exactly 50 per cent—a vast drop—in the promised deliveries of aircraft. Under the terms of the September agreement, which we had only accepted with great reluctance, we had been due to receive 8,234 aircraft of all types in the nine months between October 1941 and July 1942. In fact, we received only 4,031 and still fewer—less than half again—during the second six months of the year.[1]

(iv)
Joint Boards

In general the new Victory Programme was eminently satisfactory. It solved, or could be expected to solve in due course, many of the main problems of supply, which had so far troubled the Allies. On the other hand, there was much to criticize in the method by which this result had been achieved. Although detailed and methodical planning had played its part at the beginning, the final and operative decisions had been taken personally by the President in a single, sweeping gesture, which had evidently owed much to his sense of what was politically opportune. Moreover, the whole system of basing a programme on spectacular targets for certain selected weapons of war was open to question. What was really required was a complete and balanced programme, in which all requirements, large or small, would find their due place, even though this might mean a reduction in some of the major targets. In short, the programme as it stood lacked a clear strategic basis; it was the product of a stroke of policy rather than a plan of campaign.

One of the principal reasons for this was that the American system of planning and control was still very primitive. In September 1942, some nine months after the Washington conference, Captain Lyttelton, by then Minister of Production, was to describe it as follows:

---

[1] Hall and Wrigley, pp. 174–6.

'The Americans have never been accustomed, in consideration of military or quasi-military matters, to link harmoniously the civil and military interests. They have no War Cabinet and they have no Defence Committee at which requirements, both civil and military, can be scrutinized and programmes framed with due regard for the merits of the case. Nor have they any means by which the conflicting views of the several agencies can be harmonized and a common policy reached. The whole burden of grouping the extravagant demands of the War Department and of co-ordinating the action of the many agencies which have been created fall on one man—the President.'[1]

Such attempts as had so far been made to remedy or ameliorate this situation had not been successful. Immediately after Pearl Harbor, for example, the President had appointed a Strategical Board under the chairmanship of Harry Hopkins. This Board, of which the two other members were General Marshall and Admiral Stark, had been charged with the task of 'establishing programmes for the allocation of munitions to the United States and defence-aid countries, and of preparing a production programme to achieve sure and final victory'. Had it continued to exist, it would thus have become, not only the final arbiter in the matters of supply, but also a dominant influence on strategy. But in fact the experiment was a failure. It does not appear that the Board ever met; and, apart from certain activities of General Marshall's deputy, General Moore, in the field of Lend-Lease allocations, it performed none of the functions assigned to it.[2]

By the time the Washington Conference assembled the Board was already dead; but it was not yet clear what substitute, if any, was to be provided. Though it seems to have been generally assumed that Mr. Donald Nelson would soon succeed Mr. Knudsen as the principal authority in matters of war-production, the probable scope of his powers and the nature of his relations with the military were still uncertain.[3] In these circumstances the task of the British delegation was not an easy one. They had arrived in Washington with fairly clear-cut ideas about Anglo-American co-operation in the field of production and supply, and the sketch of an elaborate organization to carry these ideas into practice. But once more, as in the field of strategy, they found themselves a little ahead of the game. American ideas on the same subject were nothing like so fully developed; and

---

[1] Quoted in Duncan Hall, p. 379.

[2] R. M. Leighton and W. R. Coakley: *Global Logistics and Strategy, 1940–43* (1955), pp. 247–8.

[3] Mr. Nelson was in fact appointed Chairman of the War-Production Board, the successor of Mr. Knudsen's Office of Production Management, on the penultimate day of the Conference.

it was therefore a matter of some delicacy to put forward the British plan without giving the appearance, either of asking for the impossible, or of instructing the Americans how to conduct their own affairs.

The British proposals in their original form were set out in a memorandum by Sir John Dill on 31st December. On the same day the Joint Staff Mission also circulated a paper, which covered the same ground in slightly different terms. After some discussion these two papers were amalgamated into a memorandum, dated 7th January, which gave the considered views of the British Chiefs of Staff on future Anglo-American organization. The system proposed was in three tiers. At its head (on the British side) was Sir John Dill, who was to remain in Washington as the personal representative of the Minister of Defence; he would have access to the President and other high authorities and would also consult, as required, with the American Chiefs of Staff. On the next level there was to be an Anglo-American body, corresponding to what later became the Combined Chiefs of Staff, on which the members of the Joint Staff Mission would sit as representatives of the British Chiefs of Staff. This was to 'settle broad issues of priority as affecting production', for which purpose it would be assisted by a Permanent Planning Staff with appropriate technical officers. It was also to issue 'general directives laying down policy to govern the distribution of available weapons of war'. These directives were to be carried into effect by attached Allocation Officers, appointed on a service basis and forming an additional committee on the third level. Provision was also made for a Combined Intelligence and a Combined Shipping Committee, both working under the Combined Chiefs of Staff.

It will be noticed that this scheme of organization was incomplete in one important respect. It did not include any body specifically charged with the planning of war-production and the framing of future Victory Programmes. Dill's original paper had in fact provided for two such bodies—a Joint Supply Board, possibly under the chairmanship of Harry Hopkins, which 'was to deal with production, allocation of raw materials etc. on the highest level'; and a 'Joint Ministerial Defence Committee', which was to sit in Washington and exercise, apparently, some control over the Combined Chiefs of Staff. But it was evidently felt that neither of these proposals was practical, at any rate at the moment. The most that could be done was to put the allocation of finished war-material firmly in the hands of the Combined Chiefs of Staff and leave them to exert the influence on production plans, which this position would certainly imply. It was agreed that the present Victory Programme appeared to be out of balance in certain respects; but it would probably be best to wait until obvious inequalities or bottle-necks had declared themselves. The Combined Chiefs of Staff would then be able to review the position and recommend suitable priorities.

The second weakness in the system was that it would have placed a heavy administrative burden on the Combined Chiefs of Staff by making them responsible for all the detailed work of allocation as well as the broad decisions. For this reason the British Chiefs of Staff welcomed a new proposal brought forward on 13th January by the A.C.I.G.S., General Macready. The essence of this plan, which he had already discussed with his opposite number General Moore, was that British and American production should be regarded as a single pool, which should then be divided in bulk between two Allocation Committees, one in London and one in Washington, each serving a group of countries. The London Committee would deal with the British Commonwealth and the European governments in exile; the Washington Committee with the United States, China and Latin America. General Macready anticipated that both committees would have a joint membership, so that the whole system would be, so to speak, under Allied control and would not involve a division of the war into separate spheres of influence. There was obviously much to be said for this. It would relieve the Combined Chiefs of Staff of a great deal of work; and the creation of two main centres of allocation, each staffed by an Anglo-American committee, would go far to remove the danger that the American Services, in their eagerness to expand, would absorb an unduly large share of the weapons available.

On the same afternoon the British Chiefs of Staff discussed their proposals, now amended in the light of Macready's plan, with their American colleagues. In the hope of securing immediate agreement on what seemed to them the main point, they had prepared in advance a draft minute addressed to the President and the Prime Minister. It ran as follows:

> 'We, the Combined U.S.-British Chiefs of Staff, are agreed in principal that finished war material should be allocated in accordance with strategic needs. We accordingly submit that appropriate bodies should be set up under the authority of the Combined Chiefs of Staff in Washington, and of a corresponding body in London, for the purpose of giving effect to this principle.'

At first they were not able to make much progress. The Americans, when the full scheme was explained to them, objected to the position assigned to Sir John Dill on the reasonable ground that there ought not to be any military representation in Washington above the level of the Combined Chiefs of Staff. They also objected to the last sentence of the draft minute, since it seemed to imply that the London Committee would be independent of the Washington Committee and responsible to some new and unspecified body. It must be clearly understood, said General Marshall, that there could be only one Combined Chiefs of Staff, and that nothing but confusion would follow from trying to create duplicate bodies.

This was plainly true and the British Chiefs of Staff made no attempt to dispute it; but they found their colleagues very unwilling to pass on from criticism to positive action. It was explained that the American system for the control of supply and allocation, as also of Intelligence and shipping, was still under review. Until its shape had been finally decided, the American Chiefs of Staff hesitated to make any recommendations about Anglo-American organization or even to put their names to the draft minute. But on this last point they were strongly pressed by the British, who urged that an important point of principle was involved. In their view it was essential that all allocations of war material should be made on a strategic basis, and hence by or under the control of the Combined Chiefs of Staff. Did their American colleagues agree? If so, no time should be lost in making the position of both parties clear to the President and the Prime Minister. After some further discussion this point was conceded and the American Chiefs of Staff agreed to sign the minute, subject to a change in the last sentence to make it clear that both Allocation Committees would be under the control of the Combined Chiefs of Staff.

This concluded the military side of the negotiations. The results achieved may seem meagre by comparison with the elaborate scheme outlined in the original British paper; but in fact they had considerable importance. Simultaneously with the discussions between the Chiefs of Staff other negotiations were taking place at a different level. The starting point was a proposal, made early in the Conference by Mr. Hopkins, that a two-man Board, with one American and one British representative, should be appointed to advise on the allocation of war material. When Mr. Churchill discussed this plan with the British Chiefs of Staff on 12th January, he said that he was inclined to think that some such arrangement might be necessary, if only to ensure that we received a fair share from the American Services. The Chiefs of Staff replied that it was fundamental to their whole position that allocation should be under direct military control; but they agreed that it might well be desirable to have a court of appeal, and suggested that Mr. Hopkins and Sir John Dill might sit together in that capacity.

There the matter rested for the moment; but it soon became clear that Hopkins's idea was not dead. It presently developed, perhaps under the influence of Macready's proposals, into a more elaborate plan for twin Boards in Washington and London, the former under Mr. Hopkins and the latter under Lord Beaverbrook, which were to deal with the whole problem of allocations independently of the Combined Chiefs of Staff and under the direct authority of the President and the Prime Minister. It was at this point that the influence of the C.C.O.S. minute proved to be decisive. When President Roosevelt outlined the new plan to General Marshall on 14th January, he met with a steady refusal. Secure in the support of his professional colleagues, General Marshall insisted that the allocation of war material must be under military control; rather than accept any other position, he would prefer to resign. Unexpectedly, Mr. Hopkins, who was also present at the meeting, supported him, saying that he was perfectly willing that the Washington Board, if it ever came into existence, should act as a sub-committee of the Combined Chiefs of Staff. This was decisive, and the plan was re-framed accordingly.[1]

Later on the same afternoon the President discussed the amended plan with the Prime Minister and Lord Beaverbrook. Mr. Churchill was at first inclined to be sceptical. He had never been enthusiastic about leaving the final decision in matters of supply entirely to the military; he also remembered, perhaps, what his own Chiefs of Staff had said about the need for a court of appeal. In the end, however, he was persuaded to allow the new plan to be put into action as a temporary measure. On 20th January a joint statement was issued in the following terms:

'1. The entire munition resources of Great Britain and the United States will be deemed to be in a common pool, about which the fullest information will be interchanged.

2. Committees will be formed in Washington and London under the Combined Chiefs of Staff . . . These Committees will advise on all assignments, both in quantity and priority, whether to Great Britain and the United States or other of the United Nations in accordance with strategic needs.

3. In order that these Committees may be fully apprised of the policy of their respective Governments, the President will nominate a civil Chairman, who will preside over the Committee in Washington, and the Prime Minister of Great Britain will make a similar nomination in respect of the Committee in London. In each case the Committee will be assisted by a Secretariat. . . .'

A final clause provided that, in the event of disagreements, which were expected to be rare, the issue would be resolved by the President and the Prime Minister in consultation. The final solution thus contained elements of compromise. The Combined Chiefs of Staff obtained control of the allocation of all war material; but they exercised this power indirectly through two civilian Boards, from which an appeal lay to Mr. Churchill and Mr. Roosevelt personally. This was probably the best solution that circumstances allowed; and

---

[1] Leighton and Coakley, pp. 251–2; Sherwood, Vol. I, pp. 484 et seq.

in fact it continued in force with very little alteration until the end of the war, though inevitably, as time went on and the volume of American production grew, the influence of the Washington Board increased and that of the London Board declined. Further discussion led to the creation of two other Boards: a Combined Raw Materials Board under Mr. Batt of the American War-Production Board and Sir Clive Baillieu of the Ministry of Supply; and an Anglo-American Shipping Adjustment Board, on which Sir Arthur Salter sat with Admiral Land of the Maritime Commission. These were, however, purely civilian bodies, which were not brought within the ambit of the Combined Chiefs of Staff. Their setting up was, indeed, little more than a formal recognition of the informal working arrangements, which members of the British Supply Council had already developed with their American opposite numbers. But that was all that efficiency required; an attempt to impose a strictly symmetrical system would probably have done more to hinder cooperation than to promote it.[1]

Before the Washington Conference broke up, therefore, effect had been given to much of the British plan, though not always in the form originally proposed. What was still missing was the coping-stone of the whole structure: namely, an Anglo-American body, such as Dill's proposed Supply Board, which could undertake the planning of future Victory Programmes. The difficulties, largely on the American side, which stood in the way of this final achievement, have already been mentioned; and it was another six months before it became possible to take the next forward step, which also proved to be the last. In June 1942, a Combined Production and Resources Board was brought into being with Mr. Donald Nelson and Captain Oliver Lyttelton as its two members. This proved a useful instrument for the exchange of information and the correction of anomalies; but it was not able to make much progress with the main task of bringing Anglo-American war production within the scope of a single coherent plan. Continuing tensions within the American administration, strategic disputes and imprecisions, and the consequent difficulty of obtaining a clear picture of future military needs, all combined to produce a situation in which methodical planning had to give place to improvization and conjecture. The machinery of control was there; but it was found in practice that it could not master events; at the most, it could only keep pace with them.[2]

---

[1] Hall and Wrigley, Chap. V.

[2] Duncan Hall, Chap. IX, Section V.

(v)
United Nations Declaration

One final achievement of the Washington Conference must also be mentioned. This was the signing on 1st January, 1942, by a total of twenty-six nations of the declaration afterwards known as the United Nations Pact. It had little significance in terms of grand strategy; but it served, as Mr. Churchill put it, to show 'who we were and what we were fighting for'. The declaration was in the following terms:

'A Joint Declaration by the United States of America, the United Kingdom of Great Britain and Northern Ireland, the Union of Soviet Socialist Republics, China, Australia, Belgium, Canada, Costa Rica, Cuba, Czechoslovakia, the Dominican Republic, El Salvador, Greece, Guatemala, Haiti, Honduras, India, Luxemburg, the Netherlands, New Zealand, Nicaragua, Norway, Panama, Poland, South Africa, and Yugoslavia.

The Governments signatory hereto:

Having subscribed to a common programme of purposes and principles embodied in the Joint Declaration of the President of the United States of America and the Prime Minister of the United Kingdom of Great Britain and Northern Ireland, dated 14th August, 1941, known as the Atlantic Charter.

Being convinced that complete victory over their enemies is essential to defend life, liberty, independence, and religious freedom, and to preserve human rights and justice in their own lands as well as in other lands, and that they are now engaged in a common struggle against savage and brutal forces seeking to subjugate the world, DECLARE:

(1) Each Government pledges itself to employ its full resources, military or economic, against those members of the Tripartite Pact and its adherents with which such Government is at war;

(2) Each Government pledges itself to co-operate with the Governments signatory hereto, and not to make a separate armistice or peace with the enemies.

The foregoing declaration may be adhered to by other nations which are, or which may be, rendering material assistance and contributions in the struggle for victory over Hitlerism.'[1]

It will be noticed that the signatories of this declaration did not include the Free French, who had been fighting since the summer of 1940 with as much vigour as their means allowed, and who controlled territory in Africa and the Pacific which was of some strategic importance to the United Nations. This omission was the result of

---

[1] Cmd. 6388: Declaration of the United Nations, 1 January, 1942.

steady pressure by the State Department, which must remain among the curiosities of American diplomacy. Although larger issues were dimly discernible in the background, the immediate cause was insignificant. While the Conference was sitting, General de Gaulle, with the warm approval of the local inhabitants, had assumed control of two French islands in the North Atlantic, St. Pierre and Miquelon. This action, in general a matter for minor congratulation, ran counter to the policy of Mr. Cordell Hull, who had previously entered into agreements with the Vichy authorities for the preservation of the *status quo* in French possessions in the Western Hemisphere. For reasons which he has explained at some length in his Memoirs, the Secretary reacted violently, even to the point of suggesting that the 'so-called Free French' should be summarily ejected by the United States Navy. No such action followed; and the incident is only recorded here because it proved to be the first act in a long struggle between the State Department and the Free French movement, which was later to involve the Allies in many difficulties.[1]

---

[1] Hull, Vol. II, Pt. 6, Section 82.

EUROPE AND THE
MEDITERRANEAN
June 1941

MILES 100   0   100   200   300   400 MILES

Legend

Area under Allied control.

Area under Enemy control.

Area not brought under Allied
control until July 1941

Area under control of Vichy.

U.S.S.R.

Arct

Iceland

Eire

United Kingdom

North
Sea

Denmark

Nor

Swe

Holland

Belgium

Germany

Czechosl

Austria

Jug

France

Switzerland

Italy

Atlantic

Ocean

Portugal

Spain

Corsica

Sardinia

Gibraltar

M e d i t e r r a n

Sicily

Sp.

Malta

French
Morocco

Rio de Oro
(Sp)

Algeria

Tunisia

Libya